HUMAN RESOURCE MANAGEMENT IN PUBLIC SERVICE

SECOND EDITION

For Dira
　　　　—EMB

For Loretta
　　　　—JSB

For Colleen
　　　　—JPW

HUMAN RESOURCE MANAGEMENT IN PUBLIC SERVICE

Paradoxes, Processes, and Problems

SECOND EDITION

Evan M. Berman ■ James S. Bowman
Louisiana State University *Florida State University*

Jonathan P. West ■ Montgomery Van Wart
University of Miami, Florida *University of Central Florida*

SAGE Publications
Thousand Oaks ■ London ■ New Delhi

For information:

Sage Publications, Inc.
2455 Teller Road
Thousand Oaks, California 91320
E-mail: order@sagepub.com

Sage Publications Ltd.
1 Oliver's Yard
55 City Road
London EC1Y 1SP
United Kingdom

Sage Publications India Pvt. Ltd.
B-42, Panchsheel Enclave
Post Box 4109
New Delhi 110 017 India

Printed in the United States of America

Library of Congress Cataloging-in-Publication Data

Human resource management in public service: Paradoxes, processes, and problems /
Evan M. Berman . . . [et al.].— 2nd ed.
   p. cm.
Includes bibliographical references and index.
ISBN 1-4129-0421-8 (cloth)
  1. Civil service—Personnel management. I. Berman, Evan M.
JF1601.H86 2006
352.6—dc22   2004029458

This book is printed on acid-free paper.

05 06 07 08 10 9 8 7 6 5 4 3 2 1

Acquisitions Editor:	Al Bruckner
Editorial Assistant:	MaryAnn Vail
Copy Editor:	Robert Holm
Production Editor:	Diane S. Foster
Typesetter:	C&M Digitals (P) Ltd.
Proofreader:	Libby Larson
Indexer:	Will Ragsdale
Cover Designer:	Michelle Lee Kenny

CONTENTS

PREFACE

*H*uman *Resource Management in Public Service: Paradoxes, Processes, and Problems* introduces managers and aspiring managers to this personally relevant and professionally exciting
field. Not only do all people encounter human resource processes, but these issues are frequently
found in headline news reports. Execrable or exemplary, such cases make this an unusually
interesting field to study. Whether the topic is genetic testing in the recruitment and selection
function, pay reform initiatives in compensation, employee and management competencies in
training and development, novel ways to evaluate individuals in the appraisal process, or the
right to strike in labor-management relations, there is no shortage of controversy.

This second edition retains many essential qualities and purposes of the first while incorporating numerous revisions and refinements. Specifically, because employees and managers
alike regularly confront human resource problems, the book probes such issues from the viewpoint of each. It discusses these problems and explains how they arise and what can be done
about them. It continues to offer paradoxical perspectives about the inherent challenges as well
as the unique political and legal context of the public sector management within which they take
place. Further, this edition offers an updated and expanded treatment; new material on pay for
performance, staff bonuses, and workforce networking; additional sections on discipline and
networking; more skill-building exercises; and revised exercises and text boxes that discuss
recent developments. Our team, combining more than 100 years of academic and professional
experience (surely, we can't be *that* old!), has crafted a volume that

- assumes that readers are or will be generalist line managers,
- presents a comprehensive range of topics and issues,
- illustrates these discussions with a blend of examples from local, state, and federal
  jurisdictions, and
- encourages students not merely to peruse the material but to apply it.

As longtime members of the American Society of Public Administration and widely published in the field (see About the Authors), we know that what shapes an agency, commission,
department, or government enterprise is its people and how they are managed. That understanding motivated us to write the type of text described below.

The Introduction, after articulating the importance of human resource management, sets out
the book's provocative theme—that paradoxes pervade the field; it then shows how they can
be explored and addressed. The chapters that follow feature learning objectives, essential
knowledge and skills, pertinent editorial exhibits, key terms in bold, telling endnotes, and management exercises. The intent is to make the material user-friendly and accessible by highlighting dilemmas, challenging readers to resolve them, and enticing them to go beyond the
text to discover and confront others. The idea is not merely to stuff minds but to stretch them.

Part I, "Context and Challenges," showcases two topic areas. Chapter 1, "Public Service Heritage," takes an unusual approach: it examines the normative and ethical underpinnings of the field by discussing reform movements from past generations to the present day. Knowledge of what has gone before is helpful for understanding contemporary issues and avoiding past mistakes—which themselves were often reincarnations of earlier errors. Paradoxes abound. Today, for example, both the "thickening" of "top" government and the "hollowing" of "big" government (the increase in political appointees, the decrease of career public servants) are occurring at the same time. Because much of human resource management is framed by law, Chapter 2 introduces legal obligations that agencies and their employees must recognize—not merely to conform with the law but also to grasp its spirit. Thus what is legal may not be ethical, and vice versa—as law represents minimally acceptable behavior, but ethics inspires exemplary action.

With these foundations in place, attention turns to the core management functions in Part II, "Processes and Skills." Rife with ironies, these chapters are sequenced, reflecting the stages of employment from start to finish. Thus employees encounter recruitment and selection first, followed by being placed into the organization, compensated, trained, and evaluated. In the process, they face issues such as the following:

- The pseudoscience of employee selection
- The oftentimes unrecognized importance of position management—and why it may be absorbed into cyberspace
- The impossibility of knowing how much someone should be paid
- The important yet uncertain nature of "employee-friendly" policies, policies that can be quite unfriendly
- The challenges involved in creating training and development policies
- The contradictions of personnel appraisal

The critical approach found in these chapters—stalking, contesting, and seeking resolution to paradoxes—is a distinctive feature of this work.

Finally Part III, "Designing the Future," begins by exploring labor-management relations as the capstone of human resource management. That is, both the foundations of the field and its functions have been—and will be—affected by the relationship between public employers and their employees. The key conundrum: the framework undergirding this relationship actually undermines it—a fact that is largely unrecognized. The next chapter glimpses into the new century by focusing on productivity and quality—and the tensions they produce. The volume closes with conclusions and provocations about emergent technologies, human competencies, productivity, and the role of human resource management in developing them. A glossary and indexes will assist inquisitive readers in exploring the material and discovering new resources. In so doing, we hope that they will contact us with suggestions for further improvements in the book.

Welcome to human resource management in a text that is, paradoxically, both conventional and unconventional in its coverage of issues affecting the future of all readers in their careers.

—*Evan M. Berman*

—*James S. Bowman*

—*Jonathan P. West*

—*Montgomery Van Wart*

ACKNOWLEDGMENTS

The authors are pleased to recognize the many individuals who helped us in this work. We thank Al Bruckner at Sage for his encouragement and support and our colleagues in the American Society for Public Administration. We are also grateful to Barbara Moore and Christine Ulrich of the International City/County Management Association, as well as the Council of State Governments, the AFL-CIO, the International Personnel Management Association, the American Society for Public Administration, the Families and Work Institute, and the National Academy of Public Administration. In addition, the following provided helpful advice: Ms. Doris Jui, the University of Miami School of Business Administration librarian; Clint Davis, Iowa Department of Personnel; Polk County Department of Personnel; City of Des Moines Personnel Department; City of Ames Personnel Department; and Iowa State University Department of Human Resources. All of us have benefited from our students and graduate assistants, with special appreciation to Roma Perez, Frederick Baker, Gloria Paris, Kiril Dimov, Charles Crapse, Nathalia Gillot, Emily Joseph, Jacob Polakoff, Matthew Simmons, and Paul Suino. Finally, but not least, we thank the anonymous reviewers for their dedication to this project.

INTRODUCTION

If there are two courses of action, you should always pick the third.

—Proverb

There are two questions virtually everyone asks: "Why is managing people so hard?" and "Why do people dislike management so much?" The answers to both questions are about *paradoxes*—seemingly incompatible ideas and practices that have to be made to work well together in organizations. Working well means that they are, on the one hand, efficient and effective at achieving their intended purposes and, on the other, that they are the kinds of places where people would like to be. This book, written for current and future public managers, not personnel technicians, highlights paradoxes in human resource management and invites you to join the search to improve work life in organizations. Although human resource management may start with identifying workplace problems (the subject of scathing criticism over the past century and the "Dilbert" cartoons of today), the purpose is ultimately to find ways to make life better for employees and to enhance performance of public institutions as a whole.

In so doing, this text seeks to both "build in" (Latin: *instruere*) and "draw out" (*educare*). That is, most people benefit from an integrated, structured knowledge base, more so than disconnected facts and ideas. Yet learning is not simply instruction; it is also an unpredictable process of exploring and questioning, a process that draws out the best in the human mind. Accordingly, truly "own" this publication by annotating these pages with your ideas, disputes, satisfactions, discomforts, experiences, comparisons, applications, inventions, and paradoxes. Then interact with other readers in a live or virtual classroom to stretch your thinking about the management of work. The way to get the most out of the book is to get into it! Ask more of yourself than anyone can ever ask of you; that way you will always to be ready for anything. Nothing is as exhausting as underachieving. Become knowledgeable, for without knowledge progress is doomed, and be ready to contribute, as giving ensures growth.

MANAGING PEOPLE

What, then, is *human resource management?* If an organization can be defined as a group of people working toward a goal and management as the process of accomplishing these goals through other people, then the subject of this volume is the development of policies for effective utilization of human resources in an organization. Stated differently, all decisions affecting the relationship between the individual and the organization can be seen as dimensions of human resource management. Psychological and productivity goals are pivotal to this relationship. That is, the work performed must be meaningful to employees as well as to the institution. Not surprisingly, these two goals are interactive, reciprocal—and sometimes contradictory.

Human resource management, then, is a titanic force that shapes the conditions in which people find themselves. Its daily practice is an area that administrators are responsible for and can have a genuine impact on. Human resource management *matters*. Indeed, the most important job of an administrator is to help the organization use its most valuable asset—people—productively. From deciding how individuals will be recruited to how they are then compensated, trained, and evaluated, human resource administration has a significant, even definitive, effect on the careers of all employees. Legislative officials and chief executives may have authority to design new programs and approve budgets, but it is managers who hire, place, pay, develop, and appraise subordinates. They will spend more time on managing people than on anything else. Nothing is of more consequence; nothing is more difficult.

And it is not going to get easier. Not only have personnel specialists in many jurisdictions been "downsized," but they are experimenting with entirely new approaches to human resource management, including far-reaching civil service reform (e.g., the states of South Carolina, Georgia, and Florida, as well as selected federal agencies such as the Department of Homeland Security). Managers are being required to do more with less, despite the fact that human resource issues are becoming—as this text demonstrates—more numerous and complicated. Clearly, a supervisor who regards personnel concerns as a nuisance to be endured will be overwhelmed by additional responsibilities and the need to deal with them. As one wise official stated, "Put human resource management first because it is the most important." The unimpeachable fact is that a leader who does not take care of people will have no one to lead; fail to honor people, and they will fail to honor you. The tragedy: few are trained to manage employees.

THE PARADOX PUZZLE

An inexorable element of the world is that it evolves and becomes more complex, making management of organizations more difficult. Rapid and spastic change spawns confusing, contradictory paradoxes (from the Greek *para* "beyond" and *doxa* "belief"). Existing in a twilight zone between the rational and irrational, they are anomalous juxtapositions of incongruous, incredible contentions. Seeming absurdities, such riddles contradict oversimplications and over-rationalizations in conventional thinking. In so doing, they produce humility, vitality, and surprise; the beginning of wisdom is the realization of ignorance. These gnarly predicaments jolt the brain, alternately puzzling and inspiring people to wring further understanding by making the unknown known (Rescher, 2001). This creates a deeper comprehension of the principles behind the paradoxes, furnishes valuable insights, and provides unexpected solutions to thinking about people and institutions. As F. Scott Fitzgerald said, "The true test of a first-rate mind is the ability to hold two contradictory ideas at the same time."

Full of paradoxes, the management of human resources embodies clashes between apparent truths that sow confusion and tax the ability of administrators. Paradoxes lurk, and they mock both study and practice. Everyone agrees in principle that people are essential, for example, but often they are taken for granted in organizations. One key conundrum, as obvious as it is ignored, is the *paradox of democracy*. Citizens have many civil rights in the conduct of public affairs (e.g., freedom of speech, elections, assembly), but employees experience precious few such rights in organizations (e.g., subordinates seldom choose superiors). One part of American culture stresses individualism, diversity, equality, participation, and a suspicion of power, but another emphasizes conformity, uniformity, inequality, and submission to authority. Indeed, the unity of opposites revealed by paradoxes is at the heart of the human condition—birth and death, night and day, happiness and misery, good and evil.

People may value freedom very highly, but in the end they work in organizations that significantly reduce it. As Rousseau observed, "Man is born free, but everywhere he is in chains." Political democracy lies uneasily alongside economic authoritarianism. "We the people" mandates sovereignty over political and economic life; political power has been democratized to serve the many; but economic power nonetheless serves the few (Kelly, 2001). "We stress the advantages of the free enterprise system," Robert E. Wood, former chief executive of Sears is quoted as saying, "but in our individual organizations, we have created more or less a totalitarian system." Because capitalism and democracy are mutually exclusive concepts, the manner in which this contradiction is resolved greatly affects quality of life. Does the economy exist for society—or vice versa? In a time when freedom is endangered from within and without, it must be demanded.

A related fundamental riddle is the *paradox of needs*—individuals and organizations need one another, but human happiness and organizational rationality are as likely to conflict as they are to coincide. Many institutions today remain predicated on the machine model of yesteryear; indeed, the vast majority of them were born in the machine age of the industrial era. A top-down, command-and-control approach, revealed by the hierarchical organization chart, seeks to impose static predictability, demand efficiency, and expect self sacrifice—the hallmarks of bureaucratization. But human beings are, by definition, premised on not a mechanical model but an organic one—they are everything machines are not: dynamic, growing, spontaneous problem-solvers. Thus, not only do people surrender their democratic liberties, but they also give them up to work in organizations quite unlike themselves. Human flourishing is no mean task in such conditions.

The cardinal human resource management problem is this: "Do organizational processes and procedures help or hinder the resolution of these two grand, bittersweet paradoxes in democratic and work life?" To put it bluntly, what difference does it make if people function efficiently in a schizophrenic civic culture and in dysfunctional work organizations? Such issues cannot be left unaddressed by institutions whose stated purpose is to champion public, not private, interests—ultimately, government by, for, and of the people. Human resource management in democracy is simply too important to be left to those who would see it as a technical problem. Public administration has always been about governance, not merely management. Unmasking the false clarity found in taken-for-granted operational assumptions can bring about a broader view of the role of citizens in society and organizations.

"There is," then, "nothing like a paradox to take the scum off your mind" (Justice Holmes in Vaill, 1991, p. 83). Starting with a "clean slate" (Exhibit 0.1) is a vital position from which to reconcile points of view that often seem, and sometimes are, irreconcilable; in fact, dealing with contradictions defines much of a manager's job. Nonetheless, contemplating ironic, ambivalent, inconsistent, poisonous paradoxes is something few employees and managers relish; attempting to make sense out of what seems wholly illogical is generally avoided.

Yet it is precisely because paradoxes reveal the tensions in operating assumptions that exciting opportunities exist for investigation, discovery, insight, and innovation in managing organizations. Using paradoxes as a way to think about human resource administration is hardly a

---

✖ **EXHIBIT 0.1**   "Close enough for government work"—A Linguistic Hijacking

---

There is much to be said for forcing people to rethink the basic assumptions of how they run their operations by starting with a clean slate. We all "know," however, certain things that may not be true. Some are all too willing to chuckle after some imperfection is found and say, "Close enough for government work." The phrase originated with government contractors who were making uniforms for the military 150 years ago. Because government standards for uniforms were so high at that time, saying that something was "close enough" meant that it was genuinely first-rate quality. How far we've come! It's all too easy to let the "can't do" types in the office beat down our optimism and desire for change. Starting with a clean slate challenges assumptions about how work is done and how it might be changed.

SOURCE: Adapted from Linden (1994, p. 155).

---

panacea, however. What it will provide is an occasion for reflection on, and questioning of, perplexing organizational routines. The right queries can provoke interesting, different, and—sometimes—quite suitable answers. If nothing else, a deeper understanding of dilemmas will be achieved, which is, of course, the first step toward their resolution. Ways to embrace paradoxes include inquiring into the bases of clashing perspectives, identifying and appreciating the best of different viewpoints, and striving to create new viewpoints that incorporate a balance of divergent opinions. In other words, systematic, *dialectic* reasoning juxtaposes contradictory opposing ideas (theses and antitheses) and seeks to resolve them by creating new syntheses. Jazz, for instance, "beautifully expresses the dialectic between hope and despair," the tension between individual freedom and the greater good (Hertsgaard, 2002, p. 59). Leaving your "comfort zone" to engage in this mode of thinking should be as challenging as it is rewarding; change is inevitable, growth is optional. "You cannot solve the problem," Einstein once said, "with the same kind of thinking that created the problem."

Developing a capacity to thrive on paradoxes is important because they will only multiply in the years ahead with the emergence of the information superhighway, the virtual workplace, and a demographically diverse workforce. Make no mistake about it: any changes in how people are managed are unlikely to be effective without recognition of the paradoxes born in the 21st century. Know too the paradox that embodies all such paradoxes: as contradictions proliferate, the expectations to resolve them become increasingly intense. Online resources available to assist in this quest are shown in Exhibit 0.2

✖ **EXHIBIT 0.2**   Virtual Human Resource Applications and Resources

---

A problem is a chance to do your best.

—Duke Ellington

Many dimensions of human resource management have Web-based applications now, and there will be more during the third millennium. They include relevant laws and regulations, job postings, online

(Continued)

(Continued)

virtual recruitment centers (interactive voice response systems, computerized interviews, and background checks), job analysis software, benefit programs, performance assessment, virtual reality training, and expert systems in areas such as employee discipline.

The following are useful sites, with links to others, to consult in dealing with the paradoxes:

HR Live (www.hrlive.com)

HR Forum (www.hrforum.com)

Human Resources Professional's Gateway to the Internet (www.hrprosgateway.com/www/index2.html)

Human Resource Executive (www.workindex.com)

Human Resource Management Information (www.ihrim.org)

Institute of Industrial and Labor Relations (www.ilir.uiuc.edu)

International Personnel Management Association (www.ipma-hr.org)

National Association of State Personnel Executives (www.naspe.net)

National Public Employer Labor Relations Association (www.npelra.org)

Society for Human Resource Management (www.shrm.org)

United States Equal Employment Opportunity Commission (www.eeoc.gov)

United States Office of Personnel Management (www.opm.gov)

CHALLENGES AHEAD: CARPE DIEM

Reading is a commitment to the future, an odyssey characterized by the unexpected. To facilitate the journey, this text contains critical questions for you and your organization, be it a governmental agency, nonprofit organization, or educational institution. It reveals logical inconsistencies and conflicting assumptions in human resource management; in so doing, intriguing occasions arise to position problems in quite different ways. The charge is to recognize and use this fact—i.e., to manage conflicts for mutual benefit. *Human Resource Management in the Public Service: Paradoxes, Processes, and Problems* is a reality check on management and the workplace to enrich the organization's human capital (Davenport, 1999).

Louis Pasteur once said that chance favors the prepared mind. Because the trends discussed in this volume will change you whether you read it or not, an authentic opportunity now presents itself to "seize the day" and think creatively about managing people. To do this, use the text as a springboard and expand on the example of Leonardo da Vinci (Exhibit 0.3) by developing your own techniques of discovery. The analysis here will spark, but seldom settle, discussions about how to "do" human resource management. Revealing useful insights does not necessarily lead to easy answers. Reader learning, instead, will develop as much, we hope more, from personal reflection as from pedagogical suggestion. Indeed, we hope to change you from thinking as you normally do, but fall far short of telling you what to think. The book is peppered with precipitous, pernicious, perfidious paradoxes designed to propel you toward reflection on, and resolution of, work life puzzles. Complete escape from paradoxes, however, is unlikely, as pathways through them may, ironically, generate new problems. But they also create new opportunities and, together with the tools and strategies presented here, a chance to achieve democratic freedom in organizations and a matching of individual and institutional needs.

✂ EXHIBIT 0.3   Da Vinci's Parachute

"There is no use in trying," said Alice; "one can't believe impossible things."

"I dare say you haven't had much practice," said the Queen. "When I was your age, I always did it for half an hour a day. Why, sometimes I've believed as many as six impossible things before breakfast."

—Lewis Carroll, *Through the Looking Glass*

The example of Leonardo da Vinci—an accomplished painter, inventor, sculptor, engineer, architect, botanist, and physicist—has inspired people for hundreds of years to tap their creativity (Gelb, 1998). Thus, for instance, by studying the science of art, his masterpiece, the *Mona Lisa*, reveals how many different truths can be held, and enjoyed, simultaneously. Conversely, by studying the art of science, he invented a perfectly designed parachute—centuries before the airplane. To wit, as long as you are going to think anyway, you may as well think big!

In doing so, resist your first impulse, as jumping to conclusions stifles creativity. "I don't know," is often one of the wisest things that can be said as a prelude to contemplation. A mind is like da Vinci's parachute (it can only function when it is open), and paradoxes will never be adequately addressed without the creativity of a nimble mind. Ask yourself, for instance, "What would I attempt to do if I knew I could not fail." "If the obvious ways to deal with a problem did not exist, then what would I do?" Answers may not be immediate, specific actions but rather may evolve from a different perspective, a changed basis for choices, or an alternative way of thinking. As John Lennon once said, "Reality leaves a lot to the imagination."

The act of discovery, in short, consists not of finding new lands but in seeing with new eyes. (For instance, what color are apples? White, of course, once you get inside.) To nurture this capacity to think "outside the box," do at least one of the following every day:

- Take a 5-minute "imagination break."
- Look into a kaleidoscope.
- Pretend to be the secretary of a major government agency.
- Make odd friends.
- Develop a new hobby.
- Talk to someone from a different walk of life about a challenging problem.
- Use healthy snacks (chocolate, some claim, is not a vegetable) as imaginary "brain pills."
- Form a team and use the "25 in 10" brainstorming approach: aim for 25 ideas to solve a problem in 10 minutes.

It is no surprise, for instance, that Japanese workers are encouraged to learn flower arranging, practice the highly ritualized tea ceremony, and play team sports to appreciate the value of beauty, precision, and cooperation in producing goods and services.

REFERENCES

Davenport, T. O. (1999). *Human capital: What it is and why people invest in it.* San Francisco: Jossey-Bass.

Gelb, M. J. (1998). *How to think like Leonardo da Vinci.* New York: Delacorte.

Hertsgaard, M. (2002). *The eagle's shadow: Why America fascinates and infuriates the world.* New York: Farrar, Strauss, & Giroux.

Kelly, M. (2001). *The divine right of capital: Dethroning the corporate aristocracy.* San Francisco: Berrett-Koehler.

Linden, R. M. (1994). *Seamless government.* San Francisco: Jossey-Bass.

Rescher, N. (2001). *Paradoxes: Their roots, range, and resolution.* Chicago: Open Court.

Vaill, P. B. (1991). *Managing as a performing art.* San Francisco: Jossey-Bass.

Part I

CONTEXT AND CHALLENGES

1

THE PUBLIC SERVICE HERITAGE

Context, Continuity, and Change

When government has the right people, and the right system, and the right intentions,
many good things are possible. The trick is knowing which ones they are.

—Alan Ehrenhalt

After studying this chapter, you should be able to

- Understand the changing environment, key principles, and operating characteristics of public **human resource management** (HRM)
- Distinguish the various **tides of reform** that are part of the public service heritage
- Identify the paradoxes and contradictions in public service history
- Recognize how legacies from the past affect HRM in the present
- Assess the contributions of the Bush administration's reforms to effective management
- Show how values influence managers in addressing human resource issues
- Describe ethical judgments required in human resource management and use guiding questions to making such decisions

Concern about good government has deep roots in America. It has long been recognized that for government to be effective, good people must be hired, trained, and rewarded. There is also a well-established tradition that a properly designed system for managing people is critical to good government. Indeed, two schools of thought have emerged over time, one arguing that breakdown in government performance is an "incompetent people" problem and another arguing that it is an "evil system" problem (Ehrenhalt, 1998). Others have pointed to an "ethics" problem that demands attention if confidence in government is to be restored (West & Berman, 2004). As the above quotation suggests, good intentions and the ethical actions that ideally result from them are critical to create a high-performance workplace.

These three things in combination—good people, good systems, and good intentions—are the focus for this chapter. Good people are needed to manage government's most important resource—its employees. A few work in the human resource department, but the vast majority are line and staff managers. Their abilities are critical to the performance and achievement of public purpose. The system in which these people operate is also crucial to the achievement of results. Managing human resources has taken many forms over time and involves activities such as recruitment, compensation, classification, and training. The third component, intentions, refers to the tasks one proposes to accomplish and the values guiding the effort. Intentions of employees and managers, informed by individual and organizational values and ethics, guide their actions for good or ill. Admirable intentions are crucial to government performance, especially given today's emphasis on citizen service.

The discussion begins by identifying various important human resource management functions. This is done from the perspective of a municipal human resource official who faces "people management" problems that must be addressed cooperatively with line administrators. Managing people in government requires knowledge of the organizational context, key operating principles, the history of reform "tides" affecting the public service, and the institutional environment. Following a discussion of these topics, this chapter shifts attention to more contemporary developments: initiatives to introduce change by reforming government and the role of values and ethics in providing continuity to HRM. Throughout, there is no shortage of paradoxes.[1] Knowledge of the public sector heritage provides a foundation for more specialized chapters to follow.

A DAY IN THE LIFE OF MARIA HERNANDEZ

Maria Hernandez is the human resource director of a large southeastern city. She heads a department organized into five divisions—Examinations, Development and Training, Classification, Employee Relations, and Compensation/Benefits. Like most large city HR directors, Ms. Hernandez faces a thorny set of issues that pose challenges, threats, and opportunities to her and to city government. Her work life is complicated by a rapidly changing workforce, an increasingly cumbersome legal/regulatory environment, declining budgets, heightened citizen complaints, pressures for higher productivity, outsourcing, restive unions, and pending layoffs. In addition, she faces the frequent turnover of political leadership, the increasing impact of technology, and the visible and public way in which government decisions are made. Maria earned her MPA degree with a concentration in personnel management more than 20 years ago. She has been working for the city since that time, progressing up the ranks to HR director, a position she has held for the past 10 years.

Rising at 6:00 A.M., Maria is dressed and having morning coffee when she hears a local TV news brief reporting an increase in the area's unemployment rate. This development will increase the number of people seeking work with the city, and pending municipal layoffs will add to the unemployment problem. These upcoming layoffs are linked to the city's decision to contract with the private sector for services in the area of transportation and tree trimming/planting, and many of the city department heads have contacted her about the best way to deal with the people issues that arise from privatization. Several department heads are especially concerned about avoiding litigation that might arise from layoffs.

Hernandez also reads in the paper that the mayor is rejecting demands from the city's sanitation workers for salary hikes and changes in work rules. The unions, in turn, are reluctant to endorse the city manager's proposal for productivity improvements and further privatization efforts. Labor unrest among the city's sanitation workers could spill over and affect other unionized employees who are still at the bargaining table hammering out next year's agreement.

Maria is meeting later today with the city's negotiating team to get an update and to strategize in hopes of averting a strike. The department heads expect that she will help resolve this problem.

In addition, the newspaper contains a story in the local section detailing some of the facts involved in a lawsuit filed against a city supervisor who is charged with sexually harassing one of his employees. This is not the first time this particular supervisor has run into difficulties of this type, and Hernandez is concerned about the potential fallout from this case. Her office has been conducting sexual harassment training in most departments during the past year. Although this helps reduce the city's legal exposure, she must still be on top of potentially litigious situations: She has made it her policy to promptly investigate every rumor about possible sexual harassment.

Hernandez arrives at work by 7:30 A.M., having dropped her children at school and car-pooled to work with fellow city workers. The car pool conversation reveals concerns among dual-career couples who have youngsters and the need for on-site child care as well as more flexible working conditions. This is an issue Hernandez has tried to address by proposing a set of employee-friendly initiatives for consideration to the city manager. Action on this item has been slow and piecemeal, but many employees and a newly elected city councilperson have been pushing for it. Some managers have also told her that it would make the city more competitive in its recruitment.

Hernandez reviews her day's schedule (see Exhibit 1.1). Many of these topics can move the city forward and help its employees and managers to be more productive. Although her day is tightly structured around a series of meetings, she tries to set aside a block of time each day to consider the longer range initiatives she is pushing, including a new plan to implement performance measurement in key departments, incentive pay for selected workers, online access to human resource policies and procedures, and a cafeteria-style employee benefit plan. She also hopes to start a preretirement training program for all city employees over 55 and to broaden the description of job classes. Nevertheless, human resource issues are sometimes unpredictable, and she knows that she will be interrupted many times as managers and employees ask her opinion on ways to deal with them. When she leaves the office at 6:30 P.M., Maria

EXHIBIT 1.1 Maria Hernandez's Monday Schedule

8:00	Staff meeting with human resource professionals
9:00	Conduct employee orientation for new hires
10:00	Department heads—implementing new performance measurement program
11:30	Assistant city manager, budget officer, and department reps (discuss recruitment plan)
12:00	Lunch with legal counsel—review status of pending lawsuits and sexual harassment charge
1:45	Labor negotiating team—update on bargaining issues and impasses
2:30	Media briefing—tout elements of family-friendly policy initiative for city employees
4:00	University contractors—review design of training program regarding computer network
5:30	Administrative assistant—review plans for updating all job descriptions

picks up her children at the day care center. After dinner, she reviews two reports on subjects that will occupy her attention at work early the next morning.

Hernandez's day shows the broad range of issues that might be encountered by today's human resource director. These include coping firsthand with worker unrest, labor shortages, productivity and performance measurement, and errant employees. They also involve crafting employee-responsive policies, dealing with the insecurities of those employees vulnerable to layoffs, and feeling the pressures for greater efficiency. Managers must hire, promote, discipline, and fire employees. They have to respond to grievances, evaluate performance, recommend pay rates, approve job reclassifications, and motivate workers. The constitutional rights of employees must be respected, and managers must be careful not to run afoul of legal requirements (e.g., those dealing with affirmative action; sexual harassment; and age, gender, or handicap status).

These challenges suggest the range of activities that fall within the purview of human resource management—challenges that seek to increase the ways that people contribute to public organizations from the initial hiring through development, motivation, and maintenance of human resources. Strategic human resource management has evolved from what was previously called **personnel administration**. Whereas traditional personnel administration was concerned primarily with internal processes—recruitment, compensation, discipline—and the application of the rules and procedures of the civil service system, human resource management embraces a broader, more strategic, and "people-focused" definition of the management of human capital with an eye to the kind of workforce needed. This includes employee and organizational development, organizational design, performance management, reward systems and benefits, productivity improvement, staffing, employee-employer relations, and health and safety (Abramson & Gardner, 2002; Bernardin & Russell, 1998; Elliott, 1998; Sylvia, 1998). **Civil service** refers to the branches of public service, excluding legislative, judicial, or military: positions typically are filled based on competitive examinations, and a professional career public service exists with protection against political influence and patronage.

The next section reviews the changing work environment and the principles and operating characteristics of human resource management. The historical and institutional context is then examined to better understand the origins and impacts of administrative reforms affecting the public service. Next, recent efforts to reform government and improve its performance are explored. Finally, the role of values and ethics in government is highlighted, as are some ways to manage ethics.

A DYNAMIC ENVIRONMENT AND KEY PRINCIPLES

Work Environment

Managers today need to be mindful of several trends in the government environment. These trends are important because they provide the context in which decisions are made. The bulleted items below highlight significant developments for human resource management in the foreseeable future.

- *Changing workforce.* The workforce is smaller, grayer, and composed of more women and minorities than in previous years (Condrey, 2005). Paradoxically, there is a need for workers with higher-level skills, knowledge, and ability to meet the call for "learning organizations" (i.e., those that succeed in creating, accumulating, and transferring knowledge and adjusting its actions based on new knowledge). Today's employees also have different expectations and priorities than did their predecessors. For example, Generation X workers (those born between 1960 and 1980) are more likely to change careers and sectors often; demonstrate less loyalty to their employer; be comfortable with new technology; be more independent; be more comfortable working on multiple projects; and seek balance between their work and personal lives (Brackey, 2000; Gilles, 2000; Kirch, 2002).

- *Declining confidence in government.* In spite of a brief spike in 2001 after 9/11, opinion polls since the 1960s have shown a steady erosion in confidence and trust in government at all levels. In the early 1960s, six out of ten Americans claimed to trust the federal government most of the time. By 1994, only one in five made that claim, and since then trust has improved somewhat but remains well short of the levels of the early 1960s (Edwards, Wattenberg, & Lineberry, 2004). Although trust in state and local government is higher than for federal, declining confidence is evident at those levels as well. This can erode the morale of the public service and impede performance. Rebuilding trust is an important challenge facing the public sector at all levels.

- *Declining budgets.* A combination of tax limitation measures, budget cuts, and political pressures to curb future expenditures has occurred at all levels of government.

- *Downsizing/upsizing.* The size of the federal civilian workforce was cut by 351,000 (to 1.8 million) between 1993 and 2003; buyouts and early retirements were the preferred approach rather than disruptive layoffs. Staff in human resource offices have been especially hard hit by layoffs at all levels, with reductions at the federal level averaging more than 20% from 1992 to early 1999 (Hornestay, 1999). This has left line managers with additional, burdensome administrative tasks. The combination of federal downsizing, scandal, and the war on waste led Paul Light (1999, 2000) to warn of a looming brain-drain and to predict further decreases in government-centered public service with a corresponding increase in multisectored service. By contrast, the size of the state and local government workforce increased by 2,159,211 (to 15,602,141 full-time equivalents) from 1993 to 2002 (U.S. Bureau of the Census [U.S. Census], 1993, 2002). Despite this, many individual jurisdictions have experienced workforce reductions. These reductions are often linked to privatization, deregulation, budget/service cuts, and program terminations.

- *Demands for productivity.* Doing more with less leads to initiatives to improve performance without raising costs. A survey by the U.S. Merit System Protection Board of 9,700 managers and employees found that three of four supervisors assumed additional responsibilities, but only one in five detected any new flexibility in taking personnel actions (Hornestay, 1999). The federal Human Capital Survey reported that just 30% of employees believe awards programs offer an incentive to do their best (Office of Management and Budget [OMB], 2004).

- *Emerging virtual workplace/virtual government.* With the advent of new information technologies, some traditional 9-to-5 workplaces with fixed central office locations are being replaced in innovative organizations with more flexible arrangements (telecommuting, contract labor). This development alters relationships between employers and employees and raises questions about how human resource professionals give support to the variety of work arrangements in a virtual workplace (Jones, 1998; West & Berman, 2001). In addition, virtual workplaces alter the relationship between citizens and government. Numerous federal government initiatives begun in the mid-1990s enable citizen transactions to be conducted

---

✖ **EXHIBIT 1.2**   Key Web Sites of Government Agencies and Professional Associations

---

Government agencies

Bureau of Labor Statistics	stats.bls.gov
Federal Labor Relations Authority	www.flra.gov
Merit Systems Protection Board	www.mspb.gov
National Labor Relations Board	www.nlrb.gov
U.S. Office of Personnel Management	www.opm.gov

Professional associations

American Society for Public Administration	www.aspanet.org
Council of State Governments	www.cos.org/csg/default
Ethics Section, American Society for Public Administration	www.aspanet.org/ethics/index.html
International City/County Management Association	www.icma.org
National Academy of Public Administration	www.napawash.org
National Association of County Governments	www.naco.org

---

electronically. Indeed, the 1998 Government Paperwork Elimination Act (GPEA) states that federal agencies must allow people the option of submitting information or transacting electronically. These are just a few ways that new information technology can influence the public workplace (discussed further in Chapter 7); key Web sites of government agencies and professional associations are included in Exhibit 1.2.

- *Reforming/reengineering initiatives.* Alternative approaches to the delivery of goods and services are being proposed and implemented with increasing frequency (discussed later in this chapter).

- *Centralization/decentralization of human resource activities.* At federal, state, and local levels, there has been a reallocation of responsibilities from centralized staff agencies (e.g., **U.S. Office of Personnel Management**) to line agencies and managers. Administrators at the operational level now have greater flexibility and discretion in the acquisition, development, motivation, and maintenance of human resources.

These trends influence the way officials carry out their functions; each trend has important implications for human resource management (their relevance is considered in detail in this book).

HRM PRINCIPLES

Managers need to be mindful not only of the changing environment but also of several principles of human resource management. Seven tenets, in particular, should be in the forefront of managerial thinking and are further explored in this and subsequent chapters:

- *Many roles of public service.* Stakeholders expect civil servants to do many different things (ensure effective government performance, implement controversial social policies, respond to political imperatives). Often civil servants are called on to respond to conflicting pressures simultaneously, but managers need to provide leadership in reconciling competing demands (e.g., designing layoffs to balance the budget and simultaneously addressing other factors, such as adhering to the principle of seniority, complying with EEO/AA requirements, meeting performance standards, and maintaining ethical principles). The overriding priority has been and will continue to be organizational effectiveness.

- *Values matter.* **Neutral competence** of the public service has been stressed since the beginning of the **merit system** in the late 1800s, but "neutrality" (noninvolvement of employees in partisan political activities) should not suggest that values of the workforce are irrelevant; managers recruit and reward employees who are competent *and* who exhibit integrity, because ethics is consistent with higher performance and fewer legal troubles (Berman & West, 1998; Bowman, West, Berman, & Van Wart, 2004). In addition, public sector values are changing. Exhibit 1.3 compares traditional values with newer, competing values. Managers need to assess values in their jurisdictions and adjust their leadership styles as appropriate.

- *Understanding the rationale for a personnel system.* The public workforce is subject to different personnel systems (e.g., elected officials; appointed officials; federal, state, city, county, and special-purpose district employees). Each has its unique rationale and operating limitations. Effective managers understand their system's rationale and find ways to deal with its limitations.

- *Alternatives to civil service.* Public services historically have been delivered by civil service employees; however, alternative mechanisms have emerged (e.g., purchase of service agreements, privatization, franchise agreements, subsidy arrangements, vouchers, volunteers, self-help, regulatory and tax incentives). These arrangements affect managers by redefining relationships with service providers, altering control structures, and reshaping administrative roles (Klingner & Lynn, 1997).

- *Rule of law.* Personnel systems, processes, and rules are often based on legal requirements. The complexity of this environment is a fundamental difference between the public and private sectors, and it influences how human resources are managed. For example, legal requirements establish minimum standards of conduct and specify the missions of the public workforce. Law is important, and limiting liability is a legitimate managerial concern, but administrators need to be more than compliance officers. Merely conforming to legal strictures does not ensure high performance.

- *Performance.* Human resource management seeks optimal contributions to an organization by acquiring, developing, motivating, and retaining people. This requires an understanding of human relations and what motivates workers. Monetary incentives alone are insufficient motivators. Managers must be aware of the available tools and the ways to use them to ensure high performance.

- *Public accountability/access.* Another distinguishing feature of human resource management is that government decisions are subject to intense public visibility and scrutiny. This influences how work is done, how resources are managed, how decisions are made, and how systems are developed. Unlike the business sector where decisions usually are made in

✖ **EXHIBIT 1.3**   A Comparison of Traditional Public Sector Values With Those Competing for Emphasis

Traditional	New
Macrolevel values	
Monopoly	Competition
Regulation (organization for control)	Market incentives (organization around mission)
Reduction vs. growth	Continuous improvement
Adding programs	Changing programs
Values about structure	
Centralized	Decentralized
Supervisor as controller	Supervisor as helper
Nondemocratic	Participative
Individual work	Teamwork
Hierarchical organization	Flat organization
Simple jobs	Multidimensional jobs
Single service	Multiple versions of service
Values about work	
Expert focus (internally driven)	Customer focus (externally driven)
Focus on tradition (status quo)	Focus on innovation (change)
Problem analysis	Seeing possibilities
Measurement is feared	Measurement is an opportunity
Protective	Productive
Performance	Ability
Inspection and control	Prevention
Values about employees	
System indifference	Employee needs
Employee as expense	Employee as asset
Manager focus	Employee focus
Appraisal/sanction/ranking	Development/learning/recognition

SOURCE: Adapted from Montgomery Van Wart, "The First Step in the Reinvention Process: Assessment," *Public Administration Review, 55*, 1995, p. 431. Reprinted with permission of the American Society for Public Administration.

private (the Freedom of Information Act does not apply), public sector decisions typically require greater citizen access and input. Officials must remember that they are accountable to the populace, but they often face tension between their primary responsibility to all citizens and loyalty to their organizational superiors or their own consciences.

With this brief introduction to environmental considerations and operating principles, attention is turned to the past for some historical perspectives on key issues and reforms, as well as institutional arrangements that affect human resource management.

HISTORICAL AND INSTITUTIONAL CONTEXT

Tides of Reform

A useful framework for considering the history of reform efforts is provided by Paul Light in *The Tides of Reform* (1997). He identifies four reform philosophies, each of which has its own goals, implementation efforts, and outcomes: scientific management, war on waste, watchful eye, and liberation management. Although Light's analysis focuses on these four tides as they influence the overall performance of government, Light's framework is borrowed here to briefly examine the implications of these four philosophies for human resource management.

Scientific Management

The first tide is **scientific management**. Here the focus is on hierarchy, microdivision of labor, specialization, and well-defined chains of command. This philosophy, usually associated with Frederick Taylor, is manifest in the bureaucratic organizational form with its emphasis on structure, rules, and search for "the one best way." Technical experts in this environment apply the "scientific" principles of administration (e.g., unity of command, **POSD-CORB**—planning, organizing, staffing, directing, coordinating, reporting, and budgeting). The scientific management approach is evident in recommendations from two presidential commissions: the Brownlow Committee (1936–1937, changing the administrative management and government structure to improve efficiency) and the first Hoover Commission (1947–1949, reorganizing agencies around an integrated purpose and eliminating overlapping services). Herbert Hoover is a patron saint of scientific management, and the National Academy of Public Administration's Standing Panel on Executive Organization is a patron organization. Light also provides examples of defining legislation (1939 Reorganization Act establishing the Executive Office of the President), expressions (1990 Chief Financial Officers Act centralizing control over financial affairs), and contradictions (1994 **National Partnership for Reinventing Government** initiative for improving government performance). The latter is a contradiction because its employee empowerment initiatives weakened, rather than strengthened, top-level unified command.

Scientific management has implications for human resources. It emphasizes conformity and predictability of employees' contributions to the organization (machine model), and it sees human relationships as subject to management control. Hallmarks of scientific management such as job design (characterized by standard procedures, narrow span of control, and specific job descriptions instituted to improve efficiency) may actually impede achievement of quality performance in today's organizations where customization, innovation, autonomous work teams, and empowerment are required. Similarly, various HR actions mirroring scientific management differ from avant-garde practices. For example, training is changing from emphasis on functional, technical, job-related competencies to a broader range of skills, cross-functional training, and diagnostic, problem-solving capabilities. Performance measurement and evaluation has been shifting from individual goals and supervisory review to team goals and multiple reviewers (customer, peer, supervisory). Rewards have been moving from individually based merit increases to team/group-based rewards—both financial and nonfinancial. Nevertheless, current emphasis on productivity measurement, financial incentives, and efficiency reflects the continuing influence of scientific management.

War on Waste

The second reform tide is the **war on waste**, which emphasizes economy; auditors, investigators, and inspectors general are used to pursue this goal. Congressional hearings on welfare fraud are a defining moment in this tide, and the 1978 Inspector General Act is defining legislation. The 1992 Federal Housing Enterprises Financial Safety and Soundness Act is an expression of the war on waste with its provisions to fight internal corruption. The 1993 Hatch Act Reform Amendments are a contradiction to this tide because they relaxed (rather than tightened) limits on the political activities of federal employees. The patron saints for the war on waste are W. R. Grace, who headed President Reagan's task force (1982–1984) to determine how government could be operated for less; Jack Anderson, the crusading journalist who put the spotlight on government boondoggles; and Senator William Proxmire, who originated the "Golden Fleece Award." Citizens Against Government Waste is the patron organization for the fight to achieve economy in government.

The implications of the war on waste for HRM are plentiful. Preoccupation with waste leads to increases in internal controls, oversight and regulations, managerial directives, tight supervision, and concerns about accountability. It can result in a proliferation of detailed rules, processes, procedures, and multiple reviews that are so characteristic of government bureaucracy and that influence personnel management. Critics who detect waste and attribute it to maladministration of public resources or unneeded spending may focus on the deficiencies of employees. Fearful workers seek cover from criticism when they do things by the book. Managers concerned with controlling waste try to minimize idle time, avoid bottlenecks, install time clocks, audit travel vouchers and long distance phone records, inventory office supplies, and monitor attendance and punctuality. Use of temporary rather than permanent staff and service privatization may be ways to contain costs while maintaining performance standards. Clearly, contemporary human resource practices are linked to the war on waste heritage.

Watchful Eye

The third tide of reform, "the **watchful eye**," emphasizes fairness and openness. Whistleblowers, the media, interest groups, and the public need access to information to ensure that rights and the general interest are protected. Congress and the courts become the institutional champions seeking to ensure fairness. The need for the watchful eye and more open government became apparent after abuses of Watergate (the Woodward and Bernstein *Washington Post* investigation) and Vietnam (Pentagon Papers, Gulf of Tonkin). The 1947 Administrative Procedure Act is the defining statute for this reform tide, and the 1989 **Ethics Reform Act** is its most recent expression. The former was important because it established procedural standards regarding how government agencies must operate. Specific provisions of the 1989 Ethics Reform Act are efforts to curb lobbying influence and promote ethics in government. Two pieces of legislation are contradictions to the watchful-eye philosophy: the 1990 Administrative Dispute Resolution Act (authorizing federal agencies to use a wide range of ADR procedures to save money and avoid litigation) and the 1990 Negotiated Rulemaking Act (authorizing negotiated rulemaking by federal agencies to resolve disputes more quickly, more satisfactorily, and less expensively). Both of these consensus-seeking laws run counter to the adversarial processes of the Administrative Procedure Act. John Gardner and Common Cause as well as Ralph Nader and Public Citizen provide examples of the patron saints and organizations linked to the watchful eye.

Human resource implications from this philosophy can be identified as well. Concern about ethical conduct of employees leads to greater scrutiny in the hiring process to ensure integrity, as well as job-related competence, of new recruits. It also minimizes the illegitimate use of hiring criteria such as sex, race, age, and handicap status. Such concerns should minimize arbitrary decisions to fire employees. Creating an organizational culture of openness, transparency, careful record keeping, and compliance with full disclosure and sunshine requirements is consistent with the watchful-eye philosophy. Adoptions of minimum standards of conduct or codes of ethics along with ethics training are other examples. Union stewards are likely to cast their watchful eyes on negotiated contract violations and to blow the whistle when they occur. Professional employees will be alert to actions that conflict with ethics codes in a watchful environment. Managers should seek congruence between the standards espoused by the organization and the behavior of public workers. Calls for integrity at all levels of government reflect the contemporary influence of the watchful-eye mentality.

Liberation Management

The final tide of reform is called **liberation management**. Its goal is higher performance in government. Buzzwords like "evaluations," "outcomes," and "results" are associated with this tide. Achieving high-performance goals falls to frontline employees, teams, and evaluators. At the national level, the impetus for liberation management is generally the president. The most visible participant, however, was former Vice President Al Gore and his National Performance Review initiatives. The 1993 Government Performance and Results Act is the defining statute and expression of this philosophy, and its most recent contradictions are the 1989 **Whistleblower Protection Act** and the 1994 Independent Counsel Reauthorization (the latter expired in 1999). The latter two are contradictions because they promote vigilant monitoring to detect wrongdoing. Al Gore and Richard Nixon (because of his interest in reorganization) are identified as patron saints of this tide; the Alliance for Redesigning Government is the patron organization.

Liberation management also holds implications for managing people in government. Public administration trends toward employee empowerment, reengineering, work teams, continuous improvement, customer service, flattened hierarchies, and self-directed employees reflect the breakdown of the bureaucratic machine model and the move toward liberation. Belief in harmonious relations between employees and management increases the prospects for productive partnerships. Decentralization of personnel management expands authority and discretion of line agencies and gives managers freedom to achieve provable results. Before these strategies are implemented, it is necessary to determine the "readiness" of employees and units to assume new responsibilities, forge new relationships, and increase outputs. Line administrators can facilitate this state of readiness by identifying likely candidates for training and development and by tailoring incentives to the particular motivational needs of individual employees. Although the public sector will not "banish bureaucracy," greater flexibility is evident at all levels of government and is likely to increase in the future.

Tide Philosophies in Legislation

Two landmark pieces of legislation affecting federal HRM can be assessed using Light's framework: the 1883 **Pendleton Act** introducing the merit system to the federal government and the 1978 **Civil Service Reform Act** (CSRA) refining the merit system and modifying the institutions by which it operates. The Pendleton Act is "a signal moment in the march of scientific management, but it also involved a war on waste, a bit of watchful eye, and an ultimate hope for liberation management" (Light, 1997, p. 18). The CSRA of 1978 manifests each of the four tides:

> [A] Senior Executive Service (SES) to strengthen the presidential chain of command (scientific management), a cap on total federal employment to save money (war on waste), whistleblower protection to assure truth telling from the inside (watchful eye), and pay for performance to reward employees for doing something more than just show up for work (liberation management). (p. 71)

Understanding the tides of reform helps to appreciate the public service heritage by highlighting recurring themes that characterize such changes (Exhibit 1.4). Paradoxes are also apparent. Two of the reform tides—war on waste and watchful eye—are based on mistrust and cynicism regarding government; the two other tides—scientific management and liberation management—reflect trust and confidence in government. The paradox is that reform reflects both trust and distrust in government, and it may cause both as well. As the Pendleton Act and CSRA demonstrate, however, these conflicting impulses are embedded in these two landmark laws dealing with HRM (and many other statutes as well).

Institutional structures and procedures are important because managers must operate through them to achieve their objectives. These institutional arrangements have evolved over time, and understanding their purposes, functions, and limitations helps managers to think

⊠ EXHIBIT 1.4   Tides of Reform

Key Characteristics	Scientific Management	War on Waste	Watchful Eye	Liberation Management
Goal	Efficiency	Economy	Fairness	Higher performance
Key input(s)	Principles of administration	Generally accepted practices	Rights	Standards, evaluations
Key product(s)	Structure, rules	Findings (audits, investigations)	Information	Outcomes, results
Key participants	Experts	Inspectors general, the media	Whistleblowers, interest groups, the media, the public	Frontline employees, teams, evaluators
Institutional champion(s)	The presidency	Congress	Congress and the courts	The presidency
Defining moment(s)	Brownlow Committee, First Hoover Commission	Welfare fraud hearings	Vietnam, Watergate	Gore National Performance Review

Key Characteristics	Scientific Management	War on Waste	Watchful Eye	Liberation Management
Defining statute	1939 Reorganization Act	1978 Inspector General Act	1946 Administrative Procedure Act	1993 Government Performance and Results Act
Most recent expression	1990 Financial Officers Act	1992 Federal Housing Enterprises Financial Safety and Soundness Act	1989 Ethics Reform Act	1993 Government Performance and Results Act
Most recent contradiction(s)	1994 Reinventing Government Package	1993 Hatch Act Reform Amendments	1990 Administrative Dispute Resolution Act, 1990 Negotiated Rulemaking Act	1989 Whistle-blower Protection Act, 1994 Independent Counsel Reauthorization
Patron saint(s)	Herbert Hoover	W. R. Grace, Jack Anderson	John Gardner, Ralph Nader	Richard Nixon, Al Gore
Patron organization(s)	National Academy of Public Administration (Standing Panel on Executive Organization)	Citizens Against Government Waste	Common Cause, Public Citizen	Alliance for Redesigning Government

SOURCE: Adapted from P. C. Light, *The Tides of Reform*: *Making Government Work 1945–1995* (New Haven, CT: Yale University Press), pp. 21, 26, 32, and 37. © Copyright 1997 by Yale University Press. Reprinted with permission.

strategically about the threats and opportunities in their human resource environment and how to cope with them. The next section examines the goals and characteristics of these institutions.

Institutional Context

As noted above, the Pendleton Act of 1883 and the CSRA of 1978 established the institutional framework for federal HRM. The Pendleton Act created a bipartisan **Civil Service Commission** (CSC) as a protective buffer against the partisan pressures from the executive and legislative branches. It also served as a model for use by reformers seeking change in subnational governments. The merit system was established as a result of this act, but its coverage was initially limited to 1 in 10 federal workers. Competitive practical exams were introduced, and a neutral (nonpartisan), competent, career civil service with legally mandated tenure was expected to carry out the business of government. Entry into the civil service was permitted at any level in the hierarchy, unlike systems where new recruits were required to start at the entry level and work their way up.

The reform movement that led to the Pendleton Act was clear about what it was against but less clear about what it favored. This has led some observers to describe the reformers' efforts as essentially negative. They wanted to get rid of the **spoils system** (appointment based on political favor) and the evils (graft, corruption, waste, incompetence) associated with it. Separating politics from administration was key to accomplishing this objective. Using moralistic arguments, reformers campaigned against what was "bad" in the civil service (politics/spoils) and, to a lesser extent, for "good" (merit/administration) government and improved efficiency (see Chapter 4 for further discussion of this topic).

Although 95 years of experience with the Pendleton Act's institutional arrangements showed mixed results, by the mid- to late 1970s it became clear that the existing federal personnel system aimed at efficiency was, paradoxically, often inefficient. Among the problems were entrenched civil servants hindering executive initiatives, difficulty getting rid of incompetent employees, ease of circumventing merit system requirements, managerial frustration at cumbersome rules and red tape, and conflict in the roles of the Civil Service Commission. President Jimmy Carter proposed reforms to address these problems.

The Civil Service Reform Act of 1978 is built on the Pendleton Act and altered the institutional arrangement for federal personnel management. In place of the Civil Service Commission, two new institutions were created: the Office of Personnel Management (OPM) and the **Merit Systems Protection Board** (MSPB). The OPM is charged with the "doing" side of HRM—coordinating the federal government's personnel program. The director is appointed/removed by the president and functions as his principal advisor on personnel matters. The MSPB is the adjudicatory side, hearing employee appeals and investigating merit system violations. Two other important provisions in the CSRA were the creation of the **Federal Labor Relations Authority** (FLRA) and the establishment of the **Senior Executive Service** (SES). The FLRA functions as the federal sector counterpart to the private sector's National Labor Relations Board (NLRB). It is charged with overseeing, investigating, announcing, and enforcing rules pertaining to labor-management relations. The SES comprises top-level administrators—mostly career civil servants and a lesser number of political appointees. It sought (but failed to achieve) a European-like professional administrative class of senior executives who may be assigned or reassigned based on performance and ability. The structures created by the CSRA for human resource management are depicted in Exhibit 1.5.

State and local jurisdictions have varied institutional arrangements, but in many cases these governments have patterned their structures after those at the federal level. In some instances, state and local governments provided a model for federal HRM reforms. Parallelism between federal and subnational governments is seen in the existence of civil service commissions, guardian appeals boards protecting the merit system, executive personnel systems, and employee relations boards, among other features. **Civil service reform** refers to efforts undertaken by groups or individuals to alter the nature of government service. Exhibit 1.6 provides differing perspectives from local HR managers on whether civil service is outdated or necessary. The CSRA and its state and local counterparts have been the subject of recent criticism from those who wish to reform policies and practices. The next section briefly addresses their actions and proposals.

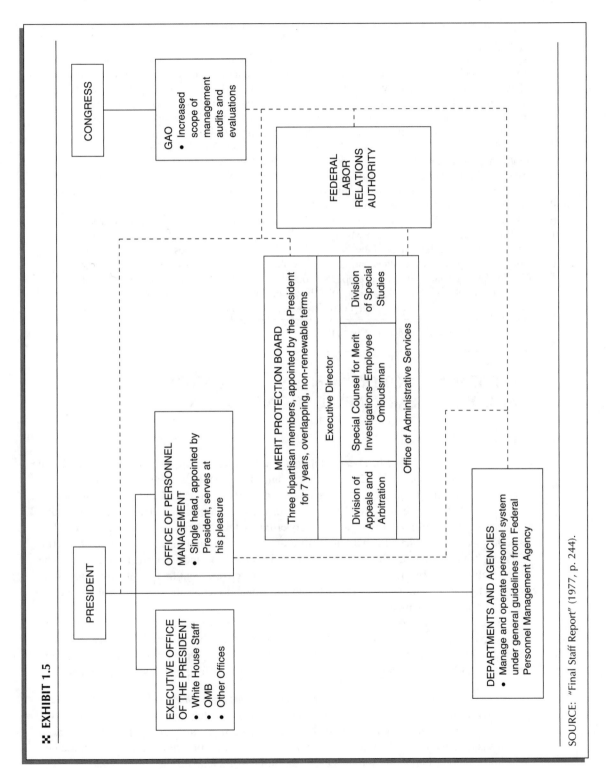

CONGRESS

GAO
• Increased scope of management audits and evaluations

FEDERAL LABOR RELATIONS AUTHORITY

MERIT PROTECTION BOARD
Three bipartisan members, appointed by the President for 7 years, overlapping, non-renewable terms

Executive Director

Division of Appeals and Arbitration

Special Counsel for Merit Investigations—Employee Ombudsman

Division of Special Studies

Office of Administrative Services

PRESIDENT

OFFICE OF PERSONNEL MANAGEMENT
• Single head, appointed by President, serves at his pleasure

EXECUTIVE OFFICE OF THE PRESIDENT
• White House Staff
• OMB
• Other Offices

DEPARTMENTS AND AGENCIES
• Manage and operate personnel system under general guidelines from Federal Personnel Management Agency

SOURCE: "Final Staff Report" (1977, p. 244).

17

✖ EXHIBIT 1.6   Civil Service: Outdated or Necessary?

The civil service system is one of the last bastions of democracy, according to James Hutt, personnel administrator for Waterbury, Connecticut. Everyone should have an equal right to compete for public jobs, and he believes that the civil service system protects that right. On the other hand, Mark Gregersen, human resource director of Vallejo, California, finds the civil service system outdated. In his opinion, employment laws and collective bargaining units today provide the same protections once offered by civil service systems. Gregersen also believes that civil service rules reduce the number of people considered for government jobs rather than "screen in" employees with the highest potential for success. New Britain, Connecticut's personnel director, John Byrne, believes civil service systems are still useful, providing continuity and consistency while newly elected officials become oriented to government operations.

Olufemi Folarin, director of human resources for Elgin, Illinois, thinks it is difficult to develop an effective affirmative action program when there is a civil service system, although he acknowledges that his government has successfully increased the number of minorities and women it employs through more aggressive recruiting efforts. Finally, Vallejo's Gregersen notes that civil service commissions do play one valid role: hearing employee appeals. The civil service commission not only protects employee interests by providing an impartial third-party opinion in the matter of employee suspensions, demotions, and discharges, but it can also reduce the cost and time of arbitration and litigation.

SOURCE: "Focus on Civil Service" (1996, p. 4).

REFORMING GOVERNMENT IN THE CLINTON AND BUSH YEARS: IMPLICATIONS FOR HR

Federal Level

Administrative change has been a recurring item on the public agenda for the past dozen or more years. Spurred by David Osborne and Ted Gaebler's (1992) book, *Reinventing Government,* reforms at the federal level started in 1993 with the Clinton administration's National Performance Review (NPR, later renamed National Partnership for Reinventing Government). The goal was to achieve government that "works better and costs less." In Light's framework, the NPR was an illustration of the liberation management tide of reform, although it also contains elements of "Hamiltonian activism" and scientific management. The key features of reinvention and NPR were to achieve government that is catalytic, empowering, enterprising, competitive, mission and customer driven, anticipatory, results oriented, decentralized and market oriented.

Reformers identified the link between performance improvement and the personnel system. In general, they detected flaws in the system rather than the individual civil servants and harshly criticized the counterproductive civil service system that they viewed as beyond redemption. Bilmes and Neal (2003, pp. 115–116) summarized problems facing civil service systems:

> . . . hiring, firing, promotion, organizational structure, lack of lateral opportunities, insufficient training, poor compensation, limited awards and recognition, few fringe benefits, lack of career development, legalistic dispute resolution, inflexibility, poor performance measurement and evaluation, use of contractors for mission-critical activities, antiquated information technology, and unhealthy, unsanitary office facilities . . .

Academics and professional groups proposed administrative changes in response to such problems (see, e.g., Donahue & Nye, 2003; National Academy of Public Administration [NAPA], 2004). Some of these reform proposals echoed past calls for governmentwide reorganization (e.g., the 1989 National Commission on the Public Service, or Volcker Commission) and anticipated more recent reform recommendations as well (e.g., the 2003 Volcker Commission, see Exhibit 1.7). The earlier report identified the "quiet crisis" facing civil service and recommended several familiar changes, including increased salaries, performance-based pay, simplified hiring, fewer political appointees, improved training, and so forth. The latter report followed characterizations of the federal civil service as a "system at risk" (Blunt, 2002; Lane, Wolf, & Woodward, 2003). Indeed, in 2001 U.S. Comptroller General David Walker elevated human capital to the GAO's list of "high-risk" government operations, stating that agencies are vulnerable to mission failure when they lack a focus on human capital development.

A retrospective on civil service reform during the Clinton years argues that the 1990s witnessed the disaggregation of the federal civil service. This little noticed phenomenon resulted

---

✕ EXHIBIT 1.7   Recommendations From the National Commission on the Public Service

Organization

- Reorganize the executive branch into a limited number of mission-related departments.
- Select agency managers based on their operational skills and give them authority to develop management and personnel systems appropriate to missions.
- Give the president expedited authority to recommend agency and departmental reorganization.
- Realign congressional committees to match mission-driven reorganization of executive branch.

Leadership

- Streamline and speed up the presidential appointment process.
- Reduce executive branch political positions.
- Divide Senior Executive Service into management corps and professional and technical corps.
- Examine employee ethics regulations and modify those with little public benefit.
- Increase judicial, executive, and legislative salaries to be comparable with other professions.
- Break the statutory link tying the salaries of judges and senior political appointees to those of congressional members.

Operations

- Develop more flexible personnel management systems.
- Continue efforts to simplify and accelerate employee recruitment.
- Allow agencies to set compensation related to current market conditions.
- Set outsourcing standards and goals that advance the public interest and do not undermine core government functions.

SOURCE: National Commission on the Public Service (2003).

in slightly fewer than half of all executive branch employees becoming part of the "excepted service," thereby relinquishing traditional civil service protections. In the quest for "hyper-flexibility," the Clinton administration pursued a three-prong strategy: authorizing personnel demonstration projects, creating "performance based organizations, and constructing modified personnel systems for malfunctioning agencies" (Thompson, 2001).

The George W. Bush administration had its own management reform agenda to address management dysfunctions. Five key areas were highlighted: human capital, competitive sourcing, financial performance, E-government, and budget-performance integration.

The first two are most relevant to human resource management. The administration's initiatives address people-related problems, giving greatest attention to the need for organizational restructuring, performance measurement, performance-based pay, hiring and development plans to fill key skill gaps, competitive sourcing, and information technology. For example, the 2001 Freedom to Manage initiative and Managerial Flexibility Act sought to "eliminate legal barriers to effective management" just as Clinton's reinvention reforms sought to move "from red tape to results." The Federal Activities Inventory Reform (FAIR) Act required agencies to assess the susceptibility to competition of the activities performed by their workforce in anticipation of placing federal workers in competition with the private sector. In the words of one analyst, these reforms "contain the excesses of Madisonian protection" and "promote the opportunity for Hamiltonian performance" (Behn, 2003).

The Bush administration stresses the need for strategic management of human capital by obtaining the talent to get the job done, seeking continuity of competent leadership, and creating a results-oriented performance culture (OMB, 2004). To monitor implementation of the agenda, it developed a simple grading system—red, yellow, and green. Key federal agencies are assessed regarding achievement of standards for success. Exhibit 1.8 reports the scorecard for 28 agencies during the quarter ending on June 30, 2003 (latest available) on the dimensions of human capital and competitive sourcing. A green designation indicates progress in implementing the president's management agenda. This is more evident on human capital than it is on competitive sourcing, and although a green designation is evident for many agencies on the progress dimension, no agency has yet to receive such a designation on the current status dimension for either human capital or competitive sourcing.

Recent reforms have been the target of critics. For example, the second Volcker report was opposed by the American Federation of Government Employees and the National Treasury Employees Unions, the two largest federal employee unions, but was warmly received by the Bush administration, which favored the increased flexibility resulting from restructuring (Kauffman, 2003a). Similarly, the Bush administration's outsourcing initiative, which seeks to subject as many of the government's approximately 850,000 "commercial" jobs as possible to privatization, has been opposed by the American Federation of Government Employees, other unions, and some lawmakers. Opponents claim the privatization/contracting-out agenda would diminish service quality in search for the lowest price (Phinney, 2003a). They protest the designation of certain positions as "commercial jobs" and seek to shield selected jobs from privatization (Phinney, 2003b).

Some of the proposed and adopted reforms have been particularly contentious, including the increased flexibility of personnel policies in the Departments of Homeland Security and Defense, the overhaul of pay for the Senior Executive Service, performance-based contracting, reducing the number of political appointees, and competitive sourcing (Kauffman, 2003a, 2003b, 2003c; Phinney, 2003a, 2003b; Robb, 2003).

✖ **Exhibit 1.8**   Executive Branch Management Scorecard

Agency	Current status as of June 30, 2003		Progress in implementing President's management agenda	
	Human Capital	Competitive Sourcing	Human Capital	Competitive Sourcing
Agriculture	Red	Red	Green	Yellow
Commerce	Yellow	Red	Green	Yellow
Defense	Yellow	Yellow +	Green	Yellow
Education	Yellow	Yellow +	Green	Green
Energy	Yellow	Red	Green	Green
EPA	Red	Red	Yellow	Green
HHS	Red	Red	Green	Green
Homeland	Red	Red	Yellow	Green
HUD	Red	Red	Green	Yellow
Interior	Red	Red	Green	Green
Justice	Red	Red	Green	Green
Labor	Yellow	Red	Green	Yellow
State	Yellow +	Red	Green	Yellow
DOT	Yellow +	Red	Green	Green
Treasury	Red	Red	Green	Green
VA	Red	Red	Green	Green
AID	Red	Red	Yellow	Yellow
Corps	Yellow +	Red	Green	Red
GSA	Red	Red	Green	Yellow
NASA	Yellow	Red	Green	Green
NSF	Red	Red	Green	Red
OMB	Red	Red	Green	Yellow
OPM	Yellow	Yellow +	Green	Green
SBA	Yellow +	Red	Green	Red
Smithsonian	Red	Red	Red	Red
SSA	Yellow	Red	Green	Green

Plus (+) indicates change in status since evaluation on March 31, 2003.

SOURCE: OMB (2004).

State and Local Levels

The National Commission on the State and Local Public Service report (National Commission on the State and Local Public Service [Winter Commission], 1993) outlined an agenda that targeted, among other institutions, civil service systems. The human resource portion of this report diagnosed "civil service paralysis" as a problem and prescribed deregulation of government's personnel system. Favoring a more flexible and less rule-bound system, the commission's recommendations included the following:

- More decentralization of the merit system
- Less reliance on written tests
- Rejection of the rule of three and other requirements that severely restrict managerial discretion in selecting from a pool of eligible applicants
- Less weight given to seniority and veteran's preference
- Fewer job classifications
- Less cumbersome procedures for removing employees from positions
- More portable pensions enabling government-to-government mobility
- More flexibility to provide financial incentives to exemplary performance by work teams

These recommendations for increased managerial flexibility echoed earlier and more recent suggestions from the National Commissions on the Public Service (1989, 2003) and resembled parallel observations from the Clinton administration's National Performance Review and the Bush administration's Management Agenda (Thompson, 1994).

Subnational reforms have included significant changes to the civil service system. Indeed, one state, Georgia, has undertaken radical reform—withdrawing merit protection for all new state employees beginning in 1996. Florida's 2001 radical reform withdrew civil service protection from more than 16,000 managers making them at-will employees who could be terminated for any or no reason not contrary to law (West & Bowman, 2004). Six other states have experienced notable reform (Massachusetts, Minnesota, New Jersey, Ohio, Oklahoma, and South Carolina). Reforms are most common in classification (reducing or increasing the number of job classifications, consolidating or broadbanding classifications), compensation (pay for performance, noncash incentives, bonuses, incentive-based pay), and performance evaluation (performance plans and standards). Managers' ability to complete their tasks successfully depends, in large measure, on their ability to attract, develop, motivate, and retain top-quality employees—the essential functions of human resource management. Reform efforts are designed to help meet these responsibilities.

The prognosis for reform efforts is more mixed than might be suggested from the emerging consensus that formed in the mid- to late 1990s. Efforts to reform human resource management were not without their critics and skeptics (Bowman, 2002; Bowman, West, & Gertz, in press; Hays & Kearney, 1999; Kearney & Hays, 1998). A sampling of some criticisms and shortcomings included the following:

- The role of public servants (e.g., privatization, downsizing) is undermined.
- Results fail to meet expectations (e.g., pay for performance).
- Too few people with the necessary skills (e.g., contract negotiating, auditing) are attracted to public service.
- Performance rewards are underfunded (bonuses).

- Oversight of the public service (decentralization, deregulation, outsourcing) is reduced, inviting corruption.
- In-service training for continuous learning and planning is frequently inadequate.
- Pursuit of quick successes via downsizing too often takes precedence over improving performance.
- Ideas borrowed from the private sector and accepted blindly often create more problems than solutions.
- Empowerment initiatives frequently are uneven.

Overall, civil service reform efforts have experienced a combination of successes, failures, and something in between (Ban & Riccucci, 1994; Bowman, Gertz, Gertz, & Williams, 2003; Cohen & Eimicke, 1994; Condrey & Maranto, 2001; Perry, Wise, & Martin, 1994; Pfiffner & Brook, 2000; Stein, 1994; Suleiman, 2003; Wechsler, 1994; West, 2002). One lesson is that when change advocates leave office, reform quickly loses salience as an issue. This result is likely to occur in regard to reform initiatives from the White House, state house, or city hall.

The impetus to improve performance and reduce costs, stated goals of the Clinton and Bush administrations and implied objectives of the Winter Commission, will continue in the future even if the strategies for achieving such goals change. Similarly, it is likely that experimentation in some form with new approaches to human resource management will proceed. These tides are part of the public service heritage and contain strains from earlier eras—scientific management, war on waste, watchful eye, and liberation management—but changing social, economic, technological, and political forces are likely to introduce new tides as well.

The final section of this chapter shifts attention from administrative reforms to the normative issues of values, ethics, and ways to manage them. This focus is important because managers need a clear understanding of the values of their community, government, and employee groups. Values serve as decision criteria when managers face choices among competing alternatives. They shape perceptions and interpretations about issues like downsizing and managing diversity. They also limit available choices by leading administrators to exclude certain alternatives as not viable. Finally, values help define the inducements (positive or negative) that managers may apply to actions of employees. Ethics helps address the question, "What should I do?" when confronting issues of right and wrong behavior. Although officials might feel that values and ethics are beyond their proper domain, they play an important, though not always obvious, role in virtually every decision of management.

VALUES, ETHICS, AND MANAGEMENT

Values

Public managers walk a tightrope seeking to balance the jurisdiction's basic values, the needs of workers, and the organization's financial resources. When there is uncertainty about fundamental values, managers lack guidance and direction in dealing with workplace issues. To address this matter, some jurisdictions and agencies have adopted a statement of values. For example, the Miami Department of Veterans Administration Medical Center (VAMC) has developed mission, vision, value, and pledge statements (Exhibit 1.9). Such statements have relevance because they typically contain content regarding managing the public service. The following are some important values of modern human resource management:

✖ EXHIBIT 1.9 Mission, Vision, Values, and Pledge of the Miami Department of Veterans Administration Medical Center

Mission

To provide timely, quality health care, individualized to meet the specific needs of our veterans and military patients. The mission is supported by our committed efforts to

Customer satisfaction

Advancements in research and education

Respect for all

Excellence

Vision

We will become a center of excellence in comprehensive, compassionate health care, continuing graduate education, and health care research

Values

Customer satisfaction

Continuous improvement

Quality care

Teamwork and partnership

I pledge to

Smile and be courteous, kind, caring, and compassionate

Go beyond the limits of my job to find solutions

Have a positive attitude

Have respect for all

Make a difference!

Please ask ME!

Our core values

Trust

Respect

Commitment

Compassion

Excellence

SOURCE: Adapted from materials used by the Miami Department of Veterans Administration Medical Center. © Copyright by Miami Department of Veterans Administration Medical Center. Reprinted with permission.

NOTE: Miami VAMC employees wear the above information on plastic cards attached to their identification badges.

- Valuing employee talents
- Encouraging professional growth
- Promoting fairness
- Providing productive work environments
- Increasing efficiency
- Developing teamwork
- Demonstrating concern for others
- Fostering openness
- Maintaining ethical principles
- Ensuring high-quality service
- Meeting customer needs

Prominent among these values are the goals of various prior reform tides that constitute the public service heritage—efficiency, economy, fairness, and high performance, among others. Managers and employees need to be conscious of such values as guides to behavior.

Clarification of basic values is important, but it requires education about values. There is considerable variation among employees regarding the degree of individual or organizational value consciousness. Van Wart (1998) divides this value consciousness into three levels: unconsciousness, elementary consciousness, and advanced consciousness. Administrators at Level 1—values unconsciousness—lack understanding or basic awareness of agency values, missions, or standard operating procedures (SOPs), and they may knowingly or unconsciously take inappropriate or illegal actions. At Level 2—elementary values consciousness—managers have a basic grasp of the mission, laws, and rules, and they focus on conforming in order to avoid legal violations or inappropriate actions. Managers at Level 3—advanced values consciousness—have a thorough understanding of their unit's mission, values, and mandate, and they can take actions that reflect the ideals associated with good government, such as efficiency, economy, ethics, fairness, and the public good.

The distinctions between various levels of values consciousness have important implications. If employees lack awareness of agency values, missions, laws, or SOPs, managers need to educate them. For example, ignorance of sexual harassment laws, affirmative action requirements, or workplace safety procedures (Level 1) can be very costly to an organization; managers must not tolerate such ignorance. Furthermore, mere conformity to laws, rules, and SOPs (Level 2) puts managers in the role of compliance officers who spend their time detecting and correcting wrongdoing. This is an important role, but a more expansive perspective is found at Level 3, where managers are fully conversant with agency values, missions, and requirements and view human resources as a precious resource for improving governmental performance.

Conflicts among fundamental values create dilemmas once values are applied. For instance, Americans value both liberty and equality; however, programs such as affirmative action may promote equality by preventing discrimination but infringe on the liberty of managers to hire or promote whomever they prefer. Other administrative values are also in tension: change and continuity, unfettered flexibility and unbending centralized control, and responsiveness to elected officials and respecting institutional memory (Smith, 1998). Seeking the proper balance among competing values is a major challenge. For example, timeliness and openness are competing values in hiring that are particularly intractable: It is difficult to hire quickly when jurisdictions require that all citizens have access to jobs. An additional example of conflicts is filling a vacancy quickly when a qualified candidate is already known but laws and organizational values require public announcement, open competition, and recruiting to ensure a diverse talent pool.

Ethics

Clarifying values, raising consciousness of values, and balancing conflicting values must be accompanied by an emphasis on ethics. Ethics involves behavior that is concerned with doing the right thing, or acting on the right values.

Here, too, managers have a difficult task: Discretion must be exercised in addressing specific ethical issues. Ethical judgment is required of managers facing complex issues such as the following:

- Responding to instructions to fire a public health nurse for refusing on religious grounds to distribute condoms and/or birth control pills to unmarried individuals
- Honoring a request to refuse to consider female job applicants age 30 or older
- Censuring a military officer for publicly opposing a ban on gays in the military
- Investigating a report by a third party that an employee was abusing legal substances (prescription drugs, alcohol) at work
- Reporting to coworkers who accidentally discovered information about pending layoffs
- Resolving a struggle between the benefits administration and the medical department over the length of time an employee can be absent from work following a surgical procedure
- Disciplining an employee for going on a "fiscal binge" of purchasing activity at the end of the fiscal year
- Reprimanding those who shirk distasteful responsibilities or scapegoat personal failures
- Reporting to supervisors observations of loafing and loitering
- Coping with pressure to fire newly hired minority supervisors because they do not "fit" the prevailing organizational culture
- Questioning the high pay levels and job security given to core staff when employees on the periphery are paid low wages and offered minimal job security (Brumback, 1991; Grensing-Pophal, 1998; Legge, 1996; Theedom, 1995)

In dealing with the above issues of legality, ethics, and fairness, managers are indeed required to weigh competing pressures. They are often squeezed from above and below in resolving such matters. Officials are also expected to conform to the organization's stated values and ethics codes. At a minimum, they must communicate the organization's policies and codes to employees (Level 1). Ideally, such policies or codes should be brief, clear, and provide practical guidance to help managers and employees deal with problems. Typical provisions might include conflict of interest, gift giving/receiving, confidentiality, sexual harassment, political activity, equal employment opportunities, and moonlighting (Pickard, 1995; Van Wart, 2003; West, Berman, & Cava, 1993). If policies or codes are adopted, they need to be observed so that there is no gap between expectations and behavior. Exhibit 1.10 reports the extent to which various ethics management strategies are used in city government and the changes in their use. It is paradoxical that ethical behavior is expected of municipal employees and stressed by their professional associations (the American Society for Public

EXHIBIT 1.10 Use of Ethics Management Strategies 1992 and 2002

	(N=427) *1992* *(A)*	*(N=129)* *2002* *(B)*	*Change from* *1992 to 2002*
Exemplary moral leadership by senior management	73 %	81.3 %	8.3 %
Adopting a standard of conduct	41	68.2	27.2
Exemplary moral leadership by elected officials	57	62.5	5.5
Adopting a code of ethics	41	60.0	19.0
Requiring financial disclosure	53	55.9	2.9
Monitoring adherence to a code of ethics	29	55.5	26.5
Requiring approval of outside activities	56	53.9	−2.1
Required familiarity with code of ethics	29	53.5	24.5
Regular communication to employees about ethics	29	50.4	21.4
Using ethics as a criterion in hiring and promotion	27	48.4	21.4
Voluntary ethics training for employees	41	43.5	2.5
Making counselors available for ethical issues	22	37.2	15.2
Mandatory ethics training for all employees	29	37.2	8.2
Mandatory ethics training for violators	6	25.3	19.3
Surveying opinions about ethics issues	7	14.6	7.6
Establishing an ethics hotline	3	11.6	8.6

SOURCE: Adapted from West & Berman (2004).

Administration, International City/County Management Association), but ethics management strategies are generally underdeveloped in local government: Most jurisdictions have no ethics training programs (West & Berman, 2004).

Ethics and Human Resource Management Subsystems

Ethics in HRM can be further considered by focusing on two key subsystems: (a) selection, socialization, and performance and (b) appraisal, reward/recognition/incentive, and development. Most administrators are involved in selection, socialization, and performance management of their employees. Managing the "joining up process" in a Level 1 work culture would be handled differently than it would be in a Level 2 or Level 3 culture. When workers lack basic consciousness about values and appropriate ethical conduct, then ethics and integrity are often managed using fear, threats, and punishment. At Level 2, there is an effort to have employees conform to work processes and comply with externally mandated standards. When employees and managers have a well-developed sense of ethics and the reasoning behind such standards (Level 3), there is an emphasis on democratic participation and collective responsibility for setting moral standards.

Similar observations can be made about the second subsystem—appraisal, rewards, and development. In a Level 1 culture, responses are nonexistent, selective, or reactive. Managers disregard or are slow to punish/reward unethical/exemplary conduct. Such an environment is characterized by the absence of any career guidance (no feedback, career ladder, organizational development efforts) and by the absence of empowerment or other initiatives to develop intrinsic motivation in workers. In a Level 2 culture, this subsystem is characterized by policies to appraise, reward, and develop employees. Conformity to conventional standards and legal compliance is commended and hailed as superior ethical behavior. The work environment provides occasional career guidance and fosters some empowerment and intrinsic motivation. Level 3 work cultures take into account ethical behavior in individual and group appraisal and in allocating rewards and recognition. Career development systems are pervasive, are fair, and exceed legal requirements. Moral exemplars are praised and ethical wrongdoers are criticized. Performance feedback, empowerment, and intrinsic motivation are found throughout the workplace (Petrick & Quinn, 1997).

Understanding the work culture and the ethical imperatives of public service is crucial. Cultures vary from agency to agency and government to government, but the ethical imperatives remain constant and provide continuity. Managers are expected to help their units develop from Level 1 to Level 3 consciousness. Doing so increases ethical awareness, which may reduce ethical shortfalls as well as create a positive climate for professional development. The strategies for ensuring integrity at work might differ from setting to setting and from one subsystem to another, but ethics management is an important responsibility for administrators. The following approaches to ethics management are repeatedly suggested in the personnel literature (Berman, West, & Bonczek, 1998; Bonczek, 1998; Brumback, 1991; Van Wart, 1995):

1. Modeling exemplary moral leadership to top officials

2. Adopting an organizational credo that promotes aspirational values

3. Developing and enforcing a code of ethics

4. Conducting an ethics audit

5. Using ethics as a criterion in hiring and promotion

6. Including ethics in employee and management training programs

7. Factoring ethics into performance appraisal

Finally, those with responsibilities for human resource and ethics management need to bear in mind three misconceptions identified by Thompson (1992) as "paradoxes of government ethics." First, *because other issues are more important than ethics, ethics are more important than any issue.* Here he highlights the relative importance of government ethics as a precondition for good government, a way to restore confidence in government, and a guideline to maintain focus on policies and practices rather than disputes about wrongdoing. Second, *private virtue is not public virtue.* In this paradox, Thompson is making a key distinction: Personal morality and political ethics are different; restrictive standards of behavior are required for those in public life (e.g., avoid giving preference to close friends, observe postemployment practices, disclose financial holdings, comply with conflict-of-interest provisions). Third, *appearing to do wrong while doing right is really wrong.* Although the appearance-of-impropriety standard may seem subjective, Thompson reminds us that it is important to recognize that in ethics as in politics, "appearances matter." Those who serve in government and manage employees need to heed the messages: Ethics is of central importance, adhering to restrictive ethics standards is expected, and appearances count. These lessons are not learned intuitively, and the seven approaches will help to reinforce them: Those with human resource responsibilities must push for their implementation.

SUMMARY AND CONCLUSION

Managers need to be prepared for the challenges that will confront them. Human resource issues involve improving the ways people contribute to organizations and concern such values as efficiency, economy, fairness, and high performance. Fundamental is the recognition that many issues and the alternatives for addressing them are not new but rather are recurring manifestations of problems and solutions from earlier historic periods. The tides from the past—scientific management, war on waste, watchful eye, and liberation management—provide lessons for the present and future. Good managers will heed these lessons and pursue best practices. Failure to do so will be costly. As Franklin D. Roosevelt observed, "A government without good management is a house built on sand."

As they seek to improve performance and rebuild a firm foundation of public trust, government managers need to hark back to the basic principles of reformers from years past and reexamine the heritage of public service. They must continue to exhibit professionalism, promote merit, ensure accountability to political leaders, and avoid partisan bias. Beyond this, managers should also work to reduce waste, demonstrate vigilance in pursuit of the public interest, reconcile competing demands for flexibility and consistency, and advance a strong sense of public service ethics. Reformers of today are still searching for ways to improve the "system" by which people are managed; this too requires continued creative effort. These are tall tasks, but Alan Ehrenhalt has it right in the quotation that opened this chapter: Good things are possible when government has "the right people, and the right system, and the right intentions." A vision for the future of the public service emerged from the Wye River Conference, which points to a shift from a traditional public sector system to a system for this century (see Exhibit 1.11).

Effective human resource problem solving also requires that managers combine right intentions with personal integrity and that they engage in careful values assessment. Defining core values and being guided by bedrock principles helps administrators make the critical ethical judgments often required in resolving nettlesome human resource issues. Public values are continuously changing, and managers must recognize and guide that change process. Thomas Jefferson said, "In matters of style, swim with the current, in matters of principle, stand like a rock."[2] Managers must decide, amid the turbulence in the public sector environment, when to "swim" with prevailing tides and when to "stand," not succumbing to pressures that would compromise core values and ethical principles.

Changes are also occurring in the way government does business and the way the public service is managed. Reforms at all levels of government are being proposed and implemented at a dizzying pace. These reforms influence the ability of administrators to do their jobs—favorably or unfavorably—so it is incumbent on them to keep abreast of new developments and guide this change process as well. The chapters that follow will highlight best practices, paradoxes, problems, and solutions to the tricky *human resource* challenges facing managers as change agents in the 21st century.

✖ EXHIBIT 1.11 Shifting from a Traditional Public Sector System to a System for the 21st Century

Traditional Public Sector System	Public Service for the 21st Century
1. Single system in theory; in reality, multiple systems not developed strategically	1. Recognize multiple systems, be strategic about system development, define and include core values
2. Merit definition that had the outcome of protecting people and equated fairness as sameness	2. Merit definition that has the outcome of encouraging better performance and allows differentiation between different talent
3. Emphasis on process and rules	3. Emphasis on performance and results
4. Hiring/promotion of talent based on technical expertise	4. Hire, nurture, and promote talent to the right places
5. Treating personnel as a cost	5. Treating human resources as an asset and an investment
6. Job for life/lifelong commitment	6. Inners and outers who share core values
7. Protection justifies tenure	7. Employee performance and employer need justifies retention
8. Performance appraisal based on individual activities	8. Performance appraisal based on demonstrated individual contribution to organizational goals
9. Labor-management relationship based on conflicting goals, antagonistic relationship, and ex post disputes and arbitration on individual cases	9. Labor-management partnership based on mutual goals of successful organization and employee satisfaction, ex ante involvement in work design
10. Central agency that fulfilled the personnel function for agencies	10. Central agency that enables agencies, especially managers, to fulfill the personnel function for themselves

SOURCE: Adapted from Patricia Ingraham, Sally Selden, and Donaled Moynihan, (2000). "People and Performance: Challenges for the Future Public Service: The Report From the Wye River Conference, in *Public Administration Review 60(1)*, p. 58. Reprinted with permission of the American Society for Public Administration (ASPA), 1120 G Street NW, Suite 700, Washington, D.C. 20005.

KEY TERMS

Civil service
Civil service commission
Civil service reform
Civil Service Reform Act of 1978
Ethics Reform Act (1989)

Federal Labor Relations Authority (FLRA)
Human resource management
Liberation management
Merit system
Merit Systems Protection Board (MSPB)

National Partnership for Reinventing
Government
Neutral competence
Pendleton Act (1883)
Personnel administration
POSDCORB
Scientific management

Senior Executive Service
Spoils system
Tides of reform
U.S. Office of Personnel Management (OPM)
War on waste
Watchful eye
Whistleblower Protection Act (1989)

EXERCISES

Class Discussion

1. Do you think Maria Hernandez is an example of a good human resource director? Why? What advice would you give her? Explain.

2. Identify and discuss some paradoxes and contradictions in the public service heritage. Why are they significant? To what extent do they reflect the two underlying paradoxes discussed in the Introduction?

3. What are some fundamental differences between the public and private sectors that influence how human resources are managed?

4. Using "da Vinci's parachute" (Introduction, Exhibit 0.3) as inspiration, which trends in the government environment are likely to continue in the future? Why? How will future trends influence human resource management?

5. Identify the "tides of reform." What are the implications of these four philosophies for human resource management? Evaluate the tides—which do you consider to be the most valuable philosophy for human resource management?

Team Activities

6. Employing the "25 in 10" technique (Exhibit 0.3), brainstorm the types of ethical dilemmas related to human resource management you think line and staff managers are likely to encounter at work.

7. Discuss the lessons from each of the four historical tides of reform and how they can influence human resource management decisions today.

8. What are the human resource management consequences of different levels of value consciousness?

9. Which ethics management strategies do you think are most effective? Why?

10. Evaluate the Miami VAMC values statement. Does it communicate the values of the government or department adequately? How would you modify the statements to make them better?

Individual Assignments

11. Identify several trends that affect managers and show how the seven principles of human resource management might influence the way you respond to the trend.

12. What is the purpose of a value statement, and how does it further the goals of an organization?

13. Interview a public manager and ask him or her to describe the most difficult human resource issues he or she has had to deal with. What areas of human resource management do they fall into? How were they handled?

14. Has the public service been significantly affected by civil service reform initiatives? How? Why?

15. Select one of the four tides of reform and (a) identify a public organization that demonstrates the characteristics of this reform philosophy, and (b) describe these characteristics and their consequences for government performance.

NOTES

1. For example, reforms that simultaneously reflect and cause distrust in government, national policies that contradict reform tides, restructuring proposals advanced by structureless "virtual" organizations, and conflicting themes embedded in the same statute.

2. Thomas Jefferson, as quoted on the World Wide Web: www.quotationspage.com/quote/27616. html

REFERENCES

Abramson, M., & Gardner, N. (2002). *Human capital 2002.* Lanham, MD: Rowman & Littlefield.

Ban, C., & Riccucci, N. (1994). New York State: Civil service reform in a complex political environment. *Review of Public Personnel Administration, 14*(2), 28–39.

Behn, R. (2003). Creating leadership capacity for the twenty-first century: Not another technical fix. In J. Donahue & J. Nye (Eds.), *For the people: Can we fix public service?* (pp. 191–224). Washington, DC: Brookings.

Berman, E., & West, J. (1998). Responsible risk taking. *Public Administration Review, 58*(4), 346–352.

Berman, E., West, J., & Bonczek, S. (1998). *The ethics edge.* Washington, DC: International City/County Management Association.

Bernardin, J., & Russell, J. (1998). *Human resource management.* New York: Irwin McGraw-Hill.

Bilmes, L., & Neal, J. (2003). The people factor: Human resources reform in government. In J. Donahue & J. Nye (Eds.), *For the people: Can we fix public service?* (pp. 113–133). Washington, DC: Brookings.

Blunt, R. (2002). Organizations growing leaders: Best practices and principles in the public service. In M. Abramson & N. Gardner (Eds.), *Human capital* (pp. 111–162). Lanham, MD: Rowman & Littlefield.

Bonczek, S. (1998). Creating an ethical environment. In E. Berman, J. West, & S. Bonczek (Eds.), *The ethics edge* (pp. 72–80). Washington, DC: ICMA.

Bowman, J. (2002). At-will employment in Florida: A naked formula to corrupt public service. *WorkingUSA 6*(2), 90–102.

Bowman, J., Gertz, S., Gertz, M., & Williams, R. (2003). Civil service reform in Florida state government: Employee attitudes 1 year later. *Review of Public Personnel Administration, 23*(4), 286–304.

Bowman, J., West, J., Berman, E., & Wan Wart, M. (2004). *The professional edge: Competencies in public service.* New York: M. E. Sharpe.

Bowman, J., West, J., & Gertz, S. (in press). Florida's "service first": Radical reform in the sunshine state. In E. Kellough & L. Nigro (Eds.), *Civil service reform in the states.* Albany: SUNY Press.

Brackey, H. J. (2000, March 3). Generation X determined to charge ahead in the workplace. *Tallahassee Democrat,* pp. E1, 2.

Brumback, G. (1991). Institutionalizing ethics in government. *Public Personnel Management, 20*(3), 353–363.

Cohen, S., & Eimicke, W. (1994). The overregulated civil service. *Review of Public Personnel Administration, 14*(2), 10–27.

Condrey, S. (2005). *Handbook of human resource management in government* (2nd ed.). San Francisco: Jossey-Bass.

Condrey, S., & Maranto, R. (Eds.). (2001). *Radical reform of the civil service.* Lanham, MD: Lexington.

Donahue, J., & Nye, J. (2003). *For the people: Can we fix public service?* Washington, DC: Brookings.

Edwards, G., Wattenberg, M., & Lineberry, R. (2004). *Government in America: People, politics, and policy.* New York: Longman.

Ehrenhalt, A. (1998, May). Why governments don't work. *Governing,* 7–11.

Elliott, R. H. (1998). Human resource management. In J. Shafritz (Ed.), *The international encyclopedia of public policy and administration* (p. 1079). Boulder, CO: Westview.

Final Staff Report. (1977). *Personnel management project.* Washington, DC: Government Printing Office.

Focus on civil service. (1996). *HR Report, 4*(7), 3–8.

Gilles, J. S. (2000, March 13). Wired for work. *Washington Post Weekly,* p. 34.

Grensing-Pophal, L. (1998). Walking the tightrope, balancing risks and gains. *HRMagazine, 11*(43), 112–118.

Hays, S., & Kearney, R. (1999). A brief rejoinder: Saving the civil service. *Review of Public Personnel Administration, 19*(1), 77–79.

Hornestay, D. (1999, February). The human factor. *Government Executive,* 1–10. (www.govexec.com)

Ingraham, P., Selden, S., & Moynihan, D. (2000). People and performance: Challenges for the future public service: The report from the Wye River Conference. *Public Administration Review, 60*(1), 54–60.

Jones, J. (1998). *Virtual HR.* Menlo Park, CA: Crisp.

Kauffman, T. (2003a, January 13). Volcker's radical Rx. *Federal Times,* p. 1, 6.

Kauffman, T. (2003b, April 7). The new reform agenda: Congress takes up bills to overhaul pay, personnel rules. *Federal Times,* p. 1, 6.

Kauffman, T. (2003c, April 21). Overhaul at defense: Sweeping personnel authorities proposed for DOD secretary. *Federal Times,* p. 1, 11.

Kearney, R., & Hays, S. (1998, Fall). Reinventing government: The new public management and civil service systems in international perspective. *Review of Public Personnel Administration, 18,* 38–54.

Kirch, J. (2002, July 29). Age-diverse staff brings variety of skills, styles. *Federal Times,* p. 18.

Klingner, D., & Lynn, D. (1997). Beyond civil service: The changing face of public personnel management. *Public Personnel Management, 26*(2), 157–173.

Lane, L., Wolf, J., & Woodard, C. (2003). Reassessing the human resource crisis in the public service, 1987–2002. *American Review of Public Administration, 33*(2), 123–145.

Legge, K. (1996). Morality bound: Ethics in human resource management. *People Management, 25*(2), 34–39.

Light, P. C. (1997). *The tides of reform: Making government work 1945–1995.* New Haven, CT: Yale University Press.

Light, P. C. (1999). *The new public service.* Washington, DC: Brookings.

Light, P. C. (2000). The empty government talent pool. *Brookings Review, 18*(1), 20–23.

National Academy of Public Administration. (2004). *Conversations on public service: Performance-based pay in the federal government.* Washington, DC: NAPA.

National Commission on the Public Service (Volcker Commission). (1989). *Leadership for America: Rebuilding the public service.* Washington, DC: Author.

National Commission on the Public Service (Volcker Commission). (2003). *Urgent business for America: Revitalizing the federal government for the 21st century.* Washington, DC: Brookings.

National Commission on the State and Local Public Service (Winter Commission). (1993). *Hard truths/tough choices: An agenda for state and local reform.* Albany, NY: Rockefeller Institute of Government.

Office of Management and Budget. (2004). Progress implementing the president's management agenda. Retrieved February 9, 2004, from www.whitehouse.gov/omb/budget/fy2004/progress.html

Osborne, D., & Gaebler, T. (1992). *Reinventing government: How the entrepreneurial spirit is transforming the public sector.* New York: Penguin.

Perry, J., Wise, L., & Martin, M. (1994). Breaking the civil service mold: The case of Indianapolis. *Review of Public Personnel Administration, 14*(2), 40–54.

Petrick, J. A., & Quinn, J. F. (1997). *Management ethics: Integrity at work.* Thousand Oaks, CA: Sage.

Phinney, D. (2003a, June 16). Employees step up resistance to outsourcing efforts. *Federal Times,* pp. 1, 6.

Phinney, D. (2003b, September 22). Opposition to outsourcing builds in Congress. *Federal Times,* pp. 6, 7.

Pickard, J. (1995). Prepare to make a moral judgment. *People Management, 9*(1), 22–31.

Piffner, J., & Brook, D. (Eds.). (2000). *The future of merit: Twenty years after the civil service reform act.* Baltimore, MD: Johns Hopkins University Press.

Robb, K. (2003, October 27). Still micromanaging: Managers slow to embrace performance-based contracting. *Federal Times,* pp. 1, 4.

Smith, C. (1998). Reinventing our understanding of merit. *Administration & Society, 20*(6), 620–623.

Stein, L. (1994). Personnel rules and reforms in an unreformed setting. *Review of Public Personnel Administration, 14*(2), 55–63.

Suleiman, E. (2003). *Dismantling democratic states.* Princeton, NJ: Princeton University Press.

Sylvia, R. (1998). Public personnel administration. In J. Shafritz (Ed.), *The international encyclopedia of public policy and administration* (pp. 1843–1847). Boulder, CO: Westview.

Theedom, R. (1995). Employee recognition and a code of ethics in the public service. *Optimum, 25*(4), 38–40.

Thompson, D. (1992). Paradoxes of government ethics. *Public Administration Review, 52*(2), 255–256.

Thompson, F. (1994). Deregulation and public personnel administration: The Winter Commission. *Review of Public Personnel Administration, 14*(2), 5–10.

Thompson, J. (2001). The civil service under Clinton: The institutional consequences of disaggregation. *Review of Public Personnel Administration, 21*(3), 87–113.

U.S. Bureau of the Census. (1993). *Public employee data.* (www.census.gov/govs/apes/93stlus.txt)

U.S. Bureau of the Census. (2002). *Public employee data.* (www.census.gov/govs/apes/02stlus.txt)

Van Wart, M. (1995, September/October). The first step in the reinvention process: Assessment. *Public Administration Review, 55,* 425–438.

Van Wart, M. (1998). *Changing public sector values.* New York: Garland.

Van Wart, M. (2003). Codes of ethics as living documents: The case of the American Society for Public Administration. *Public Integrity, 5*(4), 331–346.

Wechsler, B. (1994). Reinventing Florida's civil service system: The failure of reform. *Review of Public Personnel Administration, 14*(2), 64–76.

West, J. (2002). Georgia on the mind of radical civil service reformers. *Review of Public Personnel Administration, 21*(2), 79–93.

West, J., & Berman, E. (2001). From traditional to virtual HR: Is the transition occurring in local government? *Review of Public Personnel Administration, 21*(1), 38–64.

West, J., & Berman, E. (2004). Ethics training in U.S. cities: Content, pedagogy, and impact. *Public Integrity, 6*(3), 189–206.

West, J., Berman, E., & Cava, A. (1993). Ethics in the municipal workplace. In *Municipal Yearbook* (pp. 3–16). Washington, DC: International City/County Management Association.

West, J., & Bowman, J. (2004). Stakeholder analysis of civil service reform in Florida: A descriptive, instrumental, normative human resource management perspective. *State and Local Government Review, 36*(1), 20–34.

2

LEGAL RIGHTS AND RESPONSIBILITIES

Doing the Right Thing Right

If people were angels, laws would be unnecessary.

—James Madison

After studying this chapter, you should be able to

- Identify the framework of HRM law and understand its paradoxes and problems
- Recognize employee rights, responsibilities, and liabilities
- Explain current practices and trends in affirmative action
- Develop a legal perspective on lifestyle and privacy issues

People do not have the same rights to liberty on their jobs as they have as citizens. Employees must arrive on time, must follow orders and requests, accept limited freedom of speech, and conform to a host of regulations. A key issue—the paradox of freedom—is that people give up some of their civil rights when they join organizations: To get something (money, opportunity to make a difference), you may have to give up something (liberty and time).

Although workplace laws give managers wide discretion in many matters, the rights of employees cannot be trampled on without fear of legal repercussions. Being legally informed helps both managers and staff to do the right thing, in the right way. Employment law also prescribes how officials must act to further a variety of social objectives such as ensuring equal opportunity.

Much of the framework for understanding the legal requirements of human resource management in the public sector is based on the U.S. Constitution and various statutory laws. Changes come about by passage of new laws and court decisions. No matter how complex or highly detailed employment statutes appear to be, they are typically grounded in the balance of three often competing interests: (a) the need of employers to manage their workforce and operations in efficient ways, (b) rights that employees have in their jobs, privacy, and other matters, and (c) the interest of governments to pursue social objectives through public policy. The resulting balance that is found varies from situation to situation and changes dynamically over time. Indeed, as attitudes, social norms, and economic conditions change, the resolution of old issues is challenged and new areas of contention are raised (e.g., privacy issues involving AIDS and "reverse discrimination" in employment decisions).

Challenges and paradoxes are plentiful in the legal arena. Five, in particular, are likely to confront public officials.

1. Managers are expected to uphold the law in their decisions; however, the complexities of constitutional, statutory, administrative, and common law make such compliance quite difficult.

2. Because of complex legal requirements, managers sometimes have the experience that "the more you know, the less you know"—once they become familiar with some laws, they realize how little they actually know.

3. Relatedly, they may contact legal counsel for assistance; however, formal opinions take a considerable time to obtain, and legal staff may be unwilling to stand behind initial, informal opinions.

4. Managerial decision making based on case law is often difficult because cases are usually decided using situationally specific facts that may mask more general principles useful for guiding decision making. The circumstantial facts of a case may lead administrators to draw erroneous conclusions because the basic principles underlying the decision may remain obscure. In addition, case law can be radically changed by a single legal opinion.

5. Legal requirements may be cross-cutting so that compliance with one directive conflicts with another. For example, negotiated labor agreements often mandate the use of seniority in making promotion decisions, whereas compliance with affirmative action and merit system requirements may lead to making promotion decisions on other criteria.

Managing effectively includes understanding how law affects individual and organizational goals, the essence of the paradox of needs. An administrator's job includes decisions affecting the employment conditions of her subordinates. Such judgments must be based on objective criteria directly linked to doing the work that needs to be accomplished, reflecting appropriate sensitivity and responsiveness to employee rights and public policy objectives described in this chapter. Personnel decisions should not be based on mere personal beliefs or preferences. Job-related, equitable decisions are usually not only legal but also right for both the agency and the employee. They likely will minimize personal and organizational legal liability (Shilling, 2002).

This chapter assists readers to become conversant with important, foundational aspects of relevant law. Awareness of the legal context of HRM is critical for agency managers, as functions from recruitment through evaluation are constrained by law. It helps them recognize when to seek assistance from human resource professionals (who can serve as informed neutral parties familiar with how the department has dealt with similar cases) and legal advisers (who help apply law to specific circumstances: case law is forever changing). A cavalier approach to employment law is a dangerous strategy. Managers taken to court incur high psychological, career, and sometimes financial costs. Others may be assigned to take over their responsibilities because they will be spending months in case preparation, despositions, affidavits, and court appearances. Such costs can be avoided by managing in a manner that prevents lawsuits and by being familiar with the law. Exhibit 2.1 discusses some additional strategies for staying up to date, and Exhibit 2.2 identifies some important statutes. In light of the trends and paradoxes above, attention now turns to legal rights and responsibilities as they pertain to a variety of significant privacy and job rights issues.

⊠ EXHIBIT 2.1   Keeping Abreast

How do administrators stay up to date with legal changes? Many managers prefer to await policy directives from their organizations. This may be a sensible approach, but employers are sometimes behind the curve, and managers may face situations for which they need specialized legal advice. This situation requires a proactive strategy.

The human resource department may be a good source of legal information. Human resource managers face many situations involving employees; singular situations for line managers are sometimes routine events for HR managers who are networked well with other personnel specialists and lawyers in the community.

Still, it pays to develop an independent perspective. Leading newspapers follow new legal developments, and professional conferences are ideal for learning about the latest trends. Some law firms give seminars on related topics. Lexis-Nexis can search major newspapers and court rulings on legal topics. *The Employment Law Report* (Rosemont, MN: Data Research, Inc.) is a monthly update and review of case laws and new rules. Legal advice also can be found on the Internet, such as at Nolo (www.nolo.com). The Emory University law library (www.law.emory.edu/erd/index.html) includes a very useful portal by subject area (www.law.emory.edu/erd/subject/megasite.html#a). The International Personnel Management Association (IPMA) publishes a manager-friendly newsletter that covers legal issues (www.ipma-hr.org).

⊠ EXHIBIT 2.2   Overview of Selected Labor Laws

Civil Rights Act of 1964

Prohibits employers from discriminating against employees in hiring, promotion, and termination decisions based on their race, color, religion, national origin, or gender.

Age Discrimination in Employment Act

Protects workers over 40 years of age in hiring, promotion, and termination decisions.

Americans With Disabilities Act

Requires employers to provide persons with disabilities reasonable access to buildings and reasonable accommodations of their work spaces.

Fair Labor Standards Act

States minimum wage and overtime pay standards, and record keeping for child labor laws.

(Continued)

(Continued)

Occupational Safety and Health Act

Regulates safety and health conditions, including exposure to a variety of health hazards.

Family and Medical Leave Act

Requires employers of 50 of more employees and all public agencies to provide up to 12 weeks of unpaid, job-protected leave to eligible employees for the birth and care of a child, adoption and placement of a child, or serious illness of the employee or immediate family member.

Uniformed Services Employment and Reemployment Rights Act

Protects the employment rights of National Guard and Reserve members called up to active duty and rights and responsibilities of members and their employers

Consumer Credit Protection Act

Limits the amount of an employee's earning that may be garnished and protects employees from being discharged by their employers because their wages have been garnished to pay debt.

Employee Polygraph Protection Act

Prohibits most uses of lie detectors by private employers on the employees and job applicants with exception of consultants and others contracted by defense or national security agencies. The law does not apply to governmental employers.

JOB RIGHTS AND RESPONSIBILITIES

Civil servants have extensive rights and protections. The balance between employer interests and employee rights is clearly reflected in the cases below as well as in the broader public interest to ensure a professional and efficient workforce. This section examines the following: (a) due process, (b) freedom of speech, (c) political activities, (d) freedom of association, (e) constitutional liability and responsibility, (f) adverse action, and (g) compensation. The subsequent section focuses on employee privacy.

Civil servants have rights today, but historically this has not always been true. Traditionally, public employment has been regarded as a privilege rather than a right; employers and employees could terminate their relationship without any reason or justification. Such **at-will employment** relationships were, perhaps oddly, viewed as a fair balance of interests because either party was free to sever the relationship. Of course, many personnel need their employers more than vice versa, thereby opening the door to formidable abuse and discrimination. It is clear, that employees (as well as citizens) need protection from potentially unconstitutional misuse of government power (Rosenbloom & Bailey, 2003).

Since the 1950s, two trends have greatly increased individual rights by eroding the at-will doctrine. First, the Supreme Court has ruled that public employees do not lose individual constitutional rights as a result of accepting government employment. A variety of claims were brought before the courts involving freedom of speech, freedom of association, and the right to privacy, and the resolution resulted in significant employee rights. Second, the Court, stating that personnel have "substantial interest" in their jobs (namely, their reputations and careers), interpreted the Fifth and Fourteenth Amendments concerning due process as affording public employees a right to a hearing when faced with dismissal or adverse disciplinary action. The result of these rulings is rejection of the at-will doctrine in favor of a model that balances employee, employer, and government interests.

Due Process

The Fifth and Fourteenth Amendments state that no person can be deprived of life, liberty, or property without due process of law. Due process for public employees is grounded on the idea that staff members with permanent nonprobationary status have "substantial interests" in their jobs. In *Board of Regents v. Roth* (1972), the Supreme Court enumerated conditions that may trigger the right to a hearing, such as when employees with tenure or a contract are involved or when dismissal is based on retaliation for exercising constitutionally protected rights. **Due process rights** pertain to employees' rights to a hearing when faced with adverse actions. Later cases clarify that the right to a pre-termination hearing is a constitutional right that supersedes state laws that might limit such hearings.

The notion of a required pre-termination hearing is affirmed in the *Cleveland Board of Education v. Loudermill* (1985) decision. This case involves the dismissal of a law enforcement officer who was found to have lied on his job application. Loudermill was dismissed without a pre-termination hearing, following Ohio state statutes. The Supreme Court ruled that doing so was unconstitutional. The right to a pre-termination hearing is known as "**Loudermill rights**" and requires that employers provide notice of the charge and time of the hearing, an explanation of the evidence, and an opportunity for the employee to cross-examine and present other evidence, thereby presenting his or her side. The hearing does not need to resolve the appropriateness of the termination but should establish whether there are, in fact, reasonable grounds. The courts do not mandate the exact nature of the hearings, but procedures are often spelled out in collective bargaining agreements, statutory laws, or administrative rules. Finally, using the balancing test of interests, the Supreme Court has ruled that Loudermill rights were not present in another case of a law enforcement officer receiving a suspension, rather than termination, in this instance because the postdeprivation hearing was prompt and the loss of income relatively insignificant.

An individual's right to a hearing does not imply that an organization must conduct a hearing. Organizations typically try to avoid having hearings. One strategy is to present evidence in a timely way and to obtain agreement with the facts that underlie an adverse action. When employees agree with the facts, they are less likely to challenge them later. Due process procedures can take 6 to 18 months, and sometimes longer, because arbitration is often backlogged and more fact-finding may be required. Employees have additional rights to appeal and sue in court. This causes employers to seek alternatives to termination such as reassignment. In recent years, many jurisdictions have adopted expedited processes. For example, New York State gives employees 14 days to file a challenge to the proposed discipline, and it provides decisions by arbitrators within 45 days thereafter.

Freedom of Speech

In *Pickering v. Board of Education* (1968), the U.S. Supreme Court sought to weigh the need for workplace efficiency against employees' **free speech rights** to speak out as citizens in matters of public debate. This case concerned a teacher who wrote a letter critical of the school board published by the local newspaper. The Court found that the teacher could not be dismissed without showing that he made recklessly false statements or otherwise adversely affected working relations or the job performance of others. In short, public servants do not relinquish their First Amendment free speech rights when they accept employment (Koenig, 1997; Lindquist & Wasby, 2002).

Other cases show that although employees can speak out on policy matters, they cannot claim their First Amendment rights as a basis for activities that disrupt work processes. They must, instead, accommodate their employer's interests for efficiency. Various cases concern frustrated, disgruntled personnel who vent their disagreement over internal agency matters to other employees or the public. In these instances, the courts have upheld adverse actions. For example, the Fourth Circuit Court upheld the demotion of a policeman who brought administrative problems to the attention of a local newspaper. The court argued that the officer went outside proper channels and, given his position, should have exhibited restraint. Another case concerned a worker who conducted a survey among agency personnel about their views on departmental policies. The Supreme Court ruled that for the most part the survey concerned matters of personal grievance rather than public policy. Employee speech, in short, that involves work-related matters or disrupts the workplace may *not* be protected under the First Amendment.

Almost all jurisdictions offer protection for the free speech of whistleblowers. Staff members are protected when, in good faith, they come forward with concerns of gross mismanagement, illegal acts, misuse of funds, or danger to public safety or health. Protection is sometimes limited, however. For example, the Whistleblower Protection Act of 1989 requires federal employees to seek protection against an agency's adverse action in response to **whistleblowing** through the Office of Special Counsel. If this course is unsatisfactory, plaintiffs may appeal to the Merit Systems Protection Board, but they may not themselves initiate action against agencies. Employees must show, by preponderance of evidence, that retaliation is a contributing factor in any adverse action. Even when they prevail, whistleblowers may find their careers jeopardized through meaningless assignments and distant relations with coworkers. Exhibit 2.3 discusses, in broader perspective, some issues regarding ethics and the law.

Political Activities

During the 19th century, public employees often participated in partisan activities such as campaigning and fund-raising for the party that appointed them. These activities are contrary to the principles of political neutrality embedded in the Pendleton Act of 1883, which protects federal employees from dismissal on partisan grounds but also limits participation in electioneering (see Chapter 1). In 1907, President Roosevelt prohibited civil service employees from actively taking part in campaigns or party management, and case law about the exact nature of prohibited practices evolved. The **Hatch Act of 1939** consolidated these rulings and extended prohibited political activities to all federal employees because legislators were concerned that the bureaucracies would become part of the political machine. The second Hatch Act of 1940 extended these provisions to state and local personnel in functions that received federal funding. Employees were prohibited from being candidates for elective political office, soliciting or handling political contributions, speaking at political meetings, being officers of political organizations, and electioneering. The Hatch Act as amended in 1993 allows

---

⊠ EXHIBIT 2.3   Ethics and the Law

Efforts to promote ethics in organizations are supported by rules and regulations that focus narrowly on avoiding conflicts of interest and misuse of public property. Many jurisdictions have policies that prohibit employees from (a) "moonlighting" when this activity might impair the independence of judgment and discharge of official duties, (b) negotiating with firms in which they have a financial interest, (c) participating in discussions about pending legislation that involves organizations in which employees have financial interest, and (d) accepting gifts larger than $25, lobbying former employers, and using public property for private purposes. The Ethics in Government Act of 1978 also requires certain high-level federal officials to provide financial disclosure.

The Supreme Court has adopted a model of individual responsibility that aims to deter public employees from official conduct that may reduce trust in government. Court decisions now give employers broad discretion in investigating allegations of employee misconduct. Personnel are not, however, required to cooperate with such investigations; they may claim their Fifth Amendment rights against self-incrimination. The Court has also made it easier for the federal government to pursue charges of corruption and bribery against officials. For example, prosecutors no longer need statements from officials that link gift taking to the exchange of favors. The acceptance of payments that are known to be made in exchange for favors suffices (Roberts, 1998).

The legal approach to ethics is limited in both financial and regulatory terms. It does little to promote an aspirational orientation toward public service ethics, and there is scant evidence that the deterrent objective is realized. Also, the ethics commissions of many states often have very limited resources and limited powers to impose substantial penalties (Smith, 2003). They are not always seen as effective in pursuing allegations of wrongful behavior by local officials. In addition, it is sometimes difficult to see how increasing public awareness of ethical wrongdoing by officials enhances citizen trust. Many highly visible investigations into misdeeds seem motivated by politics rather by than interest in good government, which further decreases confidence. The legal approach to ethics is necessary but is insufficient to ensure public trust.

---

personnel to participate in political campaigns but further restricts on-the-job activities such as engaging in political activities while on duty or in uniform (being on or off duty) or on government property; soliciting financial or manpower contributions from any political organization or candidate; campaigning for partisan positions in government; or using authority to influence or interfere with election results (Gely & Chandler, 2000).

Although political expression is a First Amendment right, the courts dismissed challenges to these restrictions in favor of the efficiency of government. Over time, however, Congress relaxed some restrictions. The Federal Elections Campaign Act of 1974 eliminated many prohibitions for state and local employees. Importantly, the Federal Employees Political Activities Act of 1993 now allows federal employees to raise funds, manage campaigns, and hold office in political parties, but they are still barred from running for partisan office and from distributing campaign literature in the workplace (Brown, 2000; O'Brien, 1997).

Freedom of Association

Civil servants cannot be forced to join a political party as a condition of their employment, but they can be compelled to pay union dues in union shops (Chapter 10). Although such arrangements are coercive, the courts believe that they are the price to be paid for stable labor relations, similar to those found in the private sector. As a protection of First Amendment rights, nonunion members cannot be forced to pay for the political activities of unions in union shops. Unions are thus prohibited from using nonmember dues for these purposes.

Political affiliation is also an unconstitutional basis for making personnel decisions relating to hiring, promotion, transferring, and termination. In *Branti v. Finkel* (1980), the Supreme Court ruled that employers must show that party affiliation is an appropriate requirement for effective performance, not merely whether the position involves policy making. This ruling was later upheld and extended to other aspects of personnel management. The rule protects civil servants from pressures of political patronage and further distinguishes political appointees who serve at the pleasure of their superiors from those with civil service job rights.

Constitutional Liability and Responsibility

Public employees are personally liable for actions, undertaken in their line of duty, that violate the constitutional rights of others. Such actions can be remedied through civil suits. For example, violations of privacy due to unreasonable search and seizures can draw lawsuits. Cruel and unusual punishment, as well as denial of due process rights of others, is also a source of personal liability.

Until the 1970s, public employees usually enjoyed absolute immunity from their actions. This doctrine is based on the belief that the actions should not be crippled by threats of later lawsuits. The doctrine of absolute immunity has been steadily eroded since the 1950s as citizens gained procedural and other protections in their dealings with agencies. **Qualified immunity** states that public officials are immune from civil litigation only if they act in good faith and not "unreasonably." This means that they reasonably should know that their actions would violate any statutory or constitutional rights, such as the use of cruel punishment in corrections facilities (*Wood v. Strickland,* 1975). Many subsequent cases have upheld that public employees are liable for violating clearly established rights of those affected by their actions (Gibson, 2001).

Liability exists for compensatory as well as punitive damages. The courts view punitive damages as a deterrent that, they hope, will cause officials to be cautious in dealing with constitutional rights. According to Hartman, Homer, and Reff (2004), thousands of liability cases have been brought against government officials. Many concern public employment practices and due process violations. Although judges have absolute immunity for their judicial acts, this immunity does not cover other acts such as hiring staff. Although the odds of individuals personally paying such costs are slim, these court cases are a concern.

Generally, public employees are shielded from such lawsuits. The Federal Employees Liability Reform and Tort Compensation Act of 1988 gives employees the right to request that the suits against them be converted into suits against the government. Many states shield their personnel from tort liability as well. Of course, this does not give officials free rein, as they may be punished for wrongful acts through the disciplinary actions of their organizations. Employees are also personally liable for statements about coworkers, superiors, or subordinates that are libelous or slanderous. It is difficult, however, to recover damages because plaintiffs must show that statements are committed with malice, that is, with reckless disregard for the truth or intentional use of false statements. In addition, courts often characterize defamation as "opinion" rather than fact. Although it is difficult to prevail in such suits, being

---

✖ EXHIBIT 2.4   Constitutional Constraints on Privatization

The Constitution poses a number of constraints on privatization, an important strategy said to improve government performance. Privatization usually involves the use of private sector contractors in an effort to reduce costs or reward campaign contributors. According to Rosenbloom (1998), one constraint is that government agencies cannot privatize public responsibilities. In *West v. Atkins* (1988), the Supreme Court noted that "contracting out prison medical care does not relieve the State of its constitutional duty to provide adequate medical treatment to those in its custody." Policy-making duties cannot be privatized. Likewise, when the State of Colorado attempted to privatize its University Hospital, the Colorado Supreme Court ruled this effort to be unconstitutional because public health agencies cannot abandon their responsibilities for indigent care and public health.

A second constraint is that private companies that are "clothed with the authority of state law" can be held liable for constitutional torts. Unlike public employers, these private organizations have no immunity and may have deep pockets. Examples include private debt collection agencies, background investigation companies or drug-testing laboratories, and security firms. Such responsibilities increase the cost of doing business, hence making privatization less attractive.

A third constraint is a tendency of the Supreme Court to extend constitutional protections to independent contractors. In some instances, they are afforded the same rights as public employees. In one case, the Court ruled that it was an unconstitutional violation of free speech when a municipality failed to renew a vendor's contract because the vendor spoke out against the agency that issued the contract.

Finally, where government creates private organizations for the fulfillment of its functions, courts may hold such organizations and its employees to the same standards as public organizations and their staff. In one instance, Lycoming County (PA) created a nonprofit organization to run a nursing home that received start up funds from the county and on whose board the county commissioners sat. The courts ruled that extensive control by the county created a *de facto* arm of the county and that therefore the nursing home employees were entitled to pay that was consistent with public sector wage laws (Lindquist, 2003).

---

sued for libel or defamation can by itself damage a managerial career. Exhibit 2.4 examines some other constitutional responsibilities, namely those involving privatization and private organizations involved in public purposes.

Finally, employees have the **right to disobey** orders that an individual, in good faith, believes to be unconstitutional. *Harley v. Schuylkill County* (1979) concerns a prison guard who refused a directive that would violate an inmate's Eighth Amendment rights against cruel and unusual punishment. The refusal was upheld in court; the ruling stated that it was the guard's duty to refrain from unconstitutional behavior. A practical problem is that employees cannot be certain whether their claims will be upheld and whether they would face adverse action (Rosenbloom, 2001).

Adverse Action

Employees can face **adverse action** for both unsatisfactory performance and job misconduct. Such actions are formal, administrative actions that are taken to correct an employee's job performance, including behaviors associated with such performance (see Chapter 9). They may involve reprimands, suspensions, salary reduction, demotions, or terminations. Prior to adverse action for unsatisfactory performance, employees have a right to be informed (such as by being given written warning or notice) about the alleged existence of unsatisfactory performance and any documentation and evidence pertaining to it. They also have a right to be informed of the performance standards prior to the period in which their work is being evaluated, hence the importance of appraisal. Employees also have a right to improve their performance after they have received notice. Only then can adverse action occur, if the performance remains deficient.

Adverse action can follow from both personal and public forms of misconduct. Misconduct includes the use of a public position for private gain, acceptance of favors or bribes, conflicts of interest, abuse of authority, release of confidential information, favoritism, or nepotism. It may also involve actions that affect one's job or the reputation of the agency, affecting its ability to perform. For example, conviction for tax evasion may be a cause for dismissal of employees working in tax revenue agencies. Law enforcement officials are held to high standards and may be terminated for off-duty use of illegal substances or sex crime violations. The term misconduct is broad, and it must be demonstrably related to job or agency performance.

Compensation

In addition to the above constitutional rights, workers also have statutory rights. Under the 1938 Fair Labor Standards Act, personnel are entitled to overtime pay after 40 hours per week at time-plus-1/2 of the regular rate. This law applies to hourly staff but exempts executive, administrative, and professional employees who are compensated on a regular salary basis that does not depend on quality or quantity of work performed. Employers are not permitted to "make up" overtime of nonexempt workers by giving employees time off on an hour-for-hour basis. Employers are also required to keep accurate time records for all nonexempt employees and to pay minimum hourly wages and specified fringe benefits. They must offer employees the option to continue coverage under the employer's group health plan upon termination (Consolidated Omnibus Budget and Reconciliation Act of 1985, also known as "COBRA").

PRIVACY ISSUES

Public employees have considerable rights to privacy. These rights are relevant to search and seizure, alcohol and drug testing, personal habits, grooming and **dress codes**, pre-employment background checks, and religious freedom. Each of these areas is examined below.

Search and Seizure

The Fourth and Fourteenth Amendments protect individuals against unreasonable government search and seizure. Conflicts arise when public employees feel that managers unreasonably intrude into their private life or work spaces. These conflicts may take place in the normal course of business, such as when a manager calls a subordinate at home. Privacy issues also arise when a supervisor searches through someone's briefcase to retrieve job-related material.

In *O'Connor v. Ortega* (1987), the U.S. Supreme Court established that public employees have constitutional protections against unreasonable searches. Ortega was a doctor whose superiors seized the contents of his office, including a personal photograph and a Valentine's Day card. The court stated that a reasonable search must balance the work-related purposes of the government against socially accepted expectations of privacy. It acknowledged that such expectations create privacy rights but that "reasonableness" does not require employers to get a warrant in order to conduct a search or even to give employees prior notice, as Ortega sought. Indeed, the need to retrieve job-relevant material did override Ortega's privacy rights.

Employers can reduce expectations of privacy by eliminating personal work spaces and adopting pertinent workplace policies. Fourth Amendment protections against unreasonable searches and seizures exist only where **privacy expectations** exist. It is paradoxical that trust between employees and managers, a cornerstone of effective managing, can be at risk. Privacy issues are also raised in matters of e-mail and technological surveillance. Courts have ruled that employees do not have privacy expectations regarding e-mail: They should expect their files to be widely read, such as when messages are forwarded to third parties. Employers may adopt policies of technological and telephone surveillance, but these policies must be communicated to employees to eliminate privacy expectations. There are very few restrictions on the rights of organizations to monitor personnel; although private, non-work-related information gathered through telephone monitoring and surveillance generally may not be used against employees, the use of employer resources for private purposes can be ground for disciplinary action when, for example, such use adversely affects employer efficiency or reputation or otherwise involves "excessive," nonincidental use. In the end, "reasonableness" of searches is determined on a case-by-case basis because it is not possible to foresee all instances in which individuals may have valid expectations.

Testing for Alcohol or Drug Use

Executive Order 12564 prohibits drug use, while on or off duty, by federal civil servants; and many state and local governments have similar policies. Privacy issues are triggered by the fact that urine analysis (the most common drug-testing method) requires samples that obviously are private. In *National Treasury Employee's Union v. Von Raab* (1989), the Supreme Court ruled that collecting these samples is a search and seizure under the Fourth Amendment. Except in the case of some public safety functions, managers are required to show "probable cause" of suspected wrongdoing, specifically by observing the use of illegal drugs or behaviors reflecting drug use, or when an employee has been arrested for drug use. Individuals have due process rights (discussed below), which entitle them to know test results and to challenge them; if drug use is the basis of termination, then they have the right to a pre-termination hearing as well.

Courts have ruled that universal drug testing is not allowed in the absence of safety, administrative, or national security issues. For instance, the Omnibus Transportation Employee Testing Act of 1991 requires testing those in safety-sensitive jobs such as operators of vehicles, trains, or planes. Employees who work in areas of national security and public safety, such as law enforcement and correctional personnel, also may be subject to random tests. Legally, then, such staff have fewer expectations of privacy than other public employees. Finally, because courts have ruled that job applicants are not legally considered employees, they may be subject to testing.

Following these principles, many policies direct supervisors, together with a manager, to interview and observe employees when they have "reasonable cause" to believe that job performance may be affected by drugs or alcohol. According to the Local Government Institute (2002), indications include staggering or irregular gait, odor of alcohol on breath, slurred speech, dilated or constricted pupils, inattentiveness, listlessness, hyperactivity, illogical speech and thought processes, poor judgment, or any unusual or abnormal behavior. Some work-related accidents may require drug testing. Employees can be required to take a drug or alcohol test at the jurisdiction's expense. Failure to submit is cause for disciplinary action. Typically, if the test is negative, the employee is advised to undergo further medical evaluation. If the result is positive, then he or she may be terminated or placed on unpaid leave and required to participate in a rehabilitation program. On the return to work, the personnel remains subject to disciplinary action for failing to comply with the terms of the continued treatment.

Personal Habits/Grooming and Dress Codes

Many personnel feel that they should be allowed wide latitude in how they dress for work. Can policies that promote diversity be matched by tolerance for diversity in fashion statements? If women can wear pants, can men wear earrings and skirts? *Kelley v. Johnson* (1976) challenged a police department's facial hair rule as violating rights to free expression (i.e., liberty) and serving no legitimate department interest. The Supreme Court ruled that employers need not show any public interest, only that the requirements were not arbitrary or irrational.

Litigation has also examined **disparate impacts**. For example, certain hairstyling requirements may have disparate impact on African Americans, whereas other makeup limitations or requirements will almost exclusively affect women. In such instances, courts have looked favorably on reasons for restriction that are based on promotion of professional bearing and health. Disparate impact can occur when grooming and dress rules affect both sexes. For example, it is illegal to forbid women to wear glasses when the same requirement is not also made of men; however, females can be allowed to wear dresses, but males are forbidden to do the same because dresses are usually not considered appropriate for men in most jurisdictions. Dress codes are further discussed in Exhibit 2.5.

One issue that sometimes surfaces is basic hygiene. Someone who, for example, repeatedly wears the same clothes may eventually foul the breathing air of others. Some workers bring foul-smelling food to the workplace. Managers might make a case that such behaviors distract coworkers, thereby reducing the efficiency of work. Although it seems reasonable that workers could be required to follow basic hygiene, recent case law is absent on this matter. Rather, administrators need to follow managerial strategies, such as emphasizing the need to maintain positive relations among personnel (McKee, 2000).

Pre-Employment Background Checks

Pre-employment background checks often reveal private information about past conduct and personal preferences. Interview questions as well as background investigations must be job related. Thus, employers may not inquire about such personal matters as sexual orientation, marital status, or even the willingness of a working spouse to relocate. Although the latter may have a bearing on job acceptance, it is not germane and may discriminate against those with working spouses. Rather, interviewers should ask whether there are any barriers to relocation, thus finding out what the organization really needs to know. The cardinal rule is job

✖ EXHIBIT 2.5 Dress and Grooming Regulations in the Public Service

Clothes make the man. Naked people have little or no influence in our society.

—Mark Twain

Written and unwritten dress and grooming codes are common in the private and public sectors because a suitably attired and groomed workforce is an integral part of a professional, productive organization. As vital mediators in social relations, clothing and hairstyle choices can reflect complex feelings about power, money, autonomy, and gender, feelings that often have significant interpersonal consequences. Although few would deny the obvious superiority of personal character and inner values, too much credence may be given to glib assertions that images are without moment; empirical evidence demonstrates that people readily form opinions—right or wrong—about the social and professional desirability of individuals based largely on their appearance.

As a highly visible employer, the government is a prominent model of employment relations practices. Dress and grooming codes are significant because they can have both subtle and obvious implications for management philosophies (e.g., participative management), task organization (employee teams), personnel functions (selection, placement, evaluation), quality of work life (self-confidence and mutual respect), and constitutional issues (freedom of speech, equal treatment, sex discrimination). In government, dress and grooming can also represent the mantle of state authority.

Accordingly, managers should be aware of the instrumental role played by dress and grooming in communicating credibility and responsibility. Indeed, 75% of a national sample of state managers thought that "well-dressed and groomed people are often perceived as more intelligent, hardworking, and socially acceptable than those with a more casual appearance," and 85% rejected the contention that "an employee's appearance is unimportant to the organization" (Bowman, 1992, p. 38). One Oklahoma agency dress code, for example, affirms that "All employees . . . are representatives of the State . . . and shall dress accordingly, in a manner that presents a good image" (Bowman, 1992, p. 38).

These data suggest that certain norms, or formal and informal dress rules, are part of the fabric of most agency cultures. Indeed, the courts generally have found that personal appearance expectations—explicit and implicit—are a legitimate management concern if they are job related, gender and racially neutral, reasonable, and evenly applied. Courts have maintained, however, that the prerogative to determine one's appearance is a fundamental right requiring the application of a strict standard of judicial review. That is, state interests found sufficiently compelling to justify infringement of this right include health, safety, and business necessity. The standard must have, in other words, a rational basis that balances competing rights.

Applying such a standard, courts have found some regulations to be arbitrary and unreasonable and therefore a denial of due process. Thus, public schools have consistently failed to prohibit faculty from wearing beards because such regulations could not be shown to be job related. The trend seems to be toward greater employee freedom provided there is no legitimate public interest that outweighs individual rights.

Ignoring commonly held standards of neatness and adaptability may suggest insensitivity to one's milieu or could demonstrate personal obstinacy, both of which can affect job performance. As one manager observed, "If employees can't figure out what clothes are appropriate for their work, they probably can't do the work!" An employee of the Equal Employment Opportunity Commission thus would likely encounter difficulties in rendering service to the public if he or she wore Nazi or Ku Klux Klan insignia to work.

Some readers may be disappointed that a clear, one-size-fits-all standard of dress and grooming is not recommended here. Given wide variations of occupations and agencies, not only would such a code be difficult to promulgate, but it also would be contrary to the agency-initiated, participative management approach needed to develop useful standards; a contingency approach seems warranted.

SOURCES: Adapted from Bowman and Hooper (1991, pp. 328-340); Bowman (1992, pp. 35–51).

relatedness. Courts do allow questions about hobbies and other off-duty activities that may have relevance to job performance.

The Employee Polygraph Protection Act of 1988 bans the use of most such tests in business, except where a reasonable suspicion exists that employees are involved in theft or where used in conjunction with other methods in prehiring screening in selected industries that deal with national security, public safety, or money. Although the law explicitly exempts all public agencies, the courts will carefully scrutinize polygraph questions if these are challenged. For example, in *Hester v. City of Milledgeville* (1985), a circuit court allowed the use of polygraph tests to investigate drug use in a fire department. Questions about sexual orientation, however, were viewed as discriminatory and disallowed. In some instances, applicants have refused polygraph tests on the grounds that they might incriminate themselves. In these cases, courts have ruled that pre-employment information may not be used for any purpose other than employment decisions (White, 2001).

Some organizations use personality inventory tests to assist with employment decision making. The Myers-Briggs test, for example, provides information about decision-making styles and interpersonal interactions that, along with other information, can help determine an individual's fit with the organization. Courts have ruled that employers may use these tests but also that they will scrutinize each question to ensure that it is job relevant and nondiscriminatory. Because such tests generally do include items of personal, non-work-related matter, in practice personality tests should not be used in public sector settings.

Finally, **medical testing** is sometimes required for drug and alcohol use as well as for tuberculosis and other communicable diseases. Generally, employers may not use them for pre-employment screening, but they may be used as a condition to hiring after an offer has been made. Thus, medical tests should not be discriminatory in the selection process, and employers must demonstrate that such tests are relevant for protecting the public health of coworkers. For example, candidates for public safety functions may be required to pass fitness tests, but AIDS tests may be used only where transmission of the HIV virus is a demonstrable risk. HIV-positive persons are protected under the Americans With Disabilities Act, discussed below. An emerging concern may become the use of genetic testing for illnesses that might affect job performance, such as Alzheimer's disease.

Religious Freedom

Although it is illegal to discriminate on religious grounds, the First Amendment right to free exercise of religion creates competing demands. Problems arise when religious requirements, such as the observance of holidays or respecting proscribed and prohibited practices, conflict with employee duties. In *Sherbert v. Verner* (1963), the Supreme Court ruled that employees cannot be put in a predicament of having to choose between their employment and religious beliefs. Employers are required to make "reasonable accommodation" for all aspects of religious beliefs and practices that do not impose "undue hardship" on the business. **Reasonable accommodation** is interpreted to mean that which is minimally necessary for the employee to fulfill his or her religious obligation or conscience, whereas **undue hardship** is the least burdensome accommodation that employers might make. Organizations are not required to accept employees' suggestions of accommodation, and they may require that religious duties be fulfilled without receiving compensation for time spent off the job. Agencies do not have to alter work schedules or duty assignments to accommodate religious attendance.

Regarding the issue of religious clothing, courts generally have ruled in favor of employers who prohibit the use of religious garb such as skullcaps or robes. Even when religious dress does not interfere with work-related duties, courts may still side with employer interests. For example, the Court has found that prohibition of religious dress was consistent with the need of the military to maintain discipline. Congress passed a law in 1987, however, that allows armed forces personnel to wear religious apparel if "neat and conservative." Nevertheless, the interpretation of these terms is unclear and could be the subject of future litigation.

To summarize this section, managers often desire universal generalizations that help them do their job, but what is legal is often based on case law, which in turn depends on specific circumstances. Generally, public employees have considerable Fourth Amendment privacy and lifestyle rights, but courts often give employers wide latitude in limiting these rights when their reasons are job related and nondiscriminatory. Many gray areas are not settled by law. Administrators do well to develop a keen sense of employee expectations concerning life-styles and privacy in order to avoid unnecessary legal entanglements.

DISCRIMINATION

The **Civil Rights Act of 1964** prohibits employers from discriminating against employees in hiring, promotion, and termination decisions based on their race, color, religion, national origin, or gender. Although some of these provisions applied to the federal government through earlier statutes, this law is broader and was soon extended to private and all public employers. The 1967 Age Discrimination in Employment Act (ADEA) extended protection to all workers over 40 years of age, and the **Americans With Disabilities Act** (ADA) of 1990 protects persons with disabilities and requires employers to make reasonable accommodation. These laws are discussed below.

It should be noted that various studies question the effectiveness of these statutes. For example, the **Equal Employment Opportunity** Act of 1972, expanding coverage of Title VII of the Civil Rights Act of 1964, sought to create equal employment opportunities in public employment for African Americans (among other groups), but their representation in executive, administrative, and managerial positions relative to whites has not improved markedly (Guy & Newman, 1998). Nevertheless, managers must be familiar with both the provisions and intent of these and other related laws and seek to aggressively implement them.

Race and Gender

Since the 1940s, the federal government has sought to absorb African American and female workers in its workforce through antidiscrimination laws and efforts to increase the fairness of recruitment practices. It was not until well after the Civil Rights Act of 1964 that current practices were solidified. **Disparate treatment discrimination** cases are those in which plaintiffs claim that adverse personnel actions are based on race, gender, or other protected conditions. Many employers avoid blatantly discriminatory policy statements (e.g., "women with children cannot be promoted"), and plaintiffs must show that adverse employment actions were illegally motivated—a very high standard. The presence of racial- or gender-biased statements alone is insufficient, and even when employees demonstrate that adverse action was based on race or

gender discrimination, employers need only show that they have other, job-related performance reasons that would have led them to the same action. Even when plaintiffs rebut such
reasons as being pretextual, employers may offer additional, nondiscriminatory reasons. Thus,
the standard for proving racial or gender discrimination is high.

A claim of unfair treatment begins by filing a complaint with the **Equal Employment
Opportunity Commission** (EEOC), the federal agency that processes complaints of discrimination and reviews affirmative action plans. Only after the EEOC has investigated the
allegation and finds reasonable cause to believe that the discrimination occurred and was
directed at the employee may an individual sue in federal court.

Courts, however, have recognized that workplaces are hostile toward the above protected
conditions and that groups can create demoralizing conditions that have the same effect as
illegally motivated personnel actions. Environments in which racially or sexually motivated
derogatory behavior is an ongoing, frequent pattern constitute violations of the Civil Rights
Act: They are racially or sexually "intimidating environments." Recognizing the importance
of furthering fairness in working conditions and employment decisions, many organizations
have adopted **diversity policies** that promote an environment that allows all employees to
contribute to the organization and prohibit all forms of harassment based on the full range of
above conditions. These policies mandate that organizations investigate and provide relief to
individuals who are victims of harassment, including those who are victims of false accusations of harassment (Local Government Institute, 2002).

The Supreme Court also allows plaintiffs to show discrimination against a class of employees rather than against individuals. In *Griggs v. Duke Power Co.* (1971), the Court determined
that employment selection criteria that had an adverse impact on African Americans were discriminatory. Businesses can rebut charges of adverse impact on protected groups, however, by
showing that the practice in question is a business necessity. In *Wards Cove Packing v. Atonio*
(1989), the Court clarified that companies need only to show that these practices further business efficiency, not that they are indispensable. This standard, however, was overturned by
Congress in the Civil Rights Act of 1991. In recent years, some minority and female employees
have successfully claimed that, as a group, they received less favorable assignments than white
males and thus suffered discrimination in promotion. In instances where plaintiffs could support
their claims, courts ordered agencies to adopt policies and procedures to avoid adverse impact.

In *Griggs,* the Court defined discrimination as any selection process that resulted in qualification rates of protected groups that are less than 80% of those of the highest group (the
80% rule). The Court adopted this standard from the Equal Employment Opportunity
Commission, which processes complaints of discrimination and reviews affirmative action
plans. Employers are required by the Commission to maintain records of all hiring, promotion, and firing by race, sex, and national origin. EEOC investigations usually focus on dis-
proportionate representations of protected classes. Employers bear the burden of proof to
show that selection processes that result in qualification rates of less than 80% for protected
groups are not caused by discriminatory intent. Business can show this either by marshalling
empirical evidence that the selection criteria are associated with higher job performance of its
employees or, more commonly, by showing that the criteria are based on an empirical analysis of job-related skills, knowledge, and abilities. Such analysis is usually based on extensive
interviews with employees and managers. **Race-norming** is the practice of adjusting test
scores of minority groups to ensure that a sufficient number of candidates can be hired. This
is a generally disallowed practice, but it was allowed in the narrow case of the Chicago Police

Department, which showed that diversity was critical to its effective functioning and which instituted such norming for a limited time, in only certain positions, in order to ensure adequate diversity and, hence, effective functioning.

Affirmative action is defined as actions undertaken to overcome barriers to equal employment opportunities and to remedy the effects of past discrimination. These usually include comparing demographic characteristics of the potential labor pool with those of the organization's job applicants and employees. Imbalances are identified according to the 80% rule, and programs are developed that affirmatively reach out to minorities and women in the relevant job categories and encourage them to apply. This should not be confused with quotas, which courts may impose on recalcitrant organizations as a temporary policy to correct historic imbalances. Most agencies have also adopted **voluntary affirmative action plans**, but courts have ordered that such plans are legal only if they are temporary, aim to break down an existing pattern of discrimination, and do not trample on the interests of employees not covered by the plans. The above example of the Chicago Police Department is one such instance. By contrast, in *Adarand Contractors v. Pena* (1995), the court ruled that race-based preferences in government contracts were unconstitutional because they were not narrowly tailored to serve a compelling government interest. Similarly, the U.S. Supreme Court ruled in 2003 that the University of Michigan's undergraduate admissions policy was unconstitutional because it did not include adequate individual assessments and was not narrowly defined to create classroom diversity. The University of Michigan's law school admission policy, however, was allowed because it was narrowly tailored to further the compelling interest of classroom diversity and the practice assessed each applicant according to a broad range of academic and other criteria in order to achieve diversity.

Managers must be careful not to promote affirmative action in ways that are discriminatory against majority groups. Such **reverse discrimination** cases are numerous. From the beginning, affirmative action has been a controversial policy. Although it was designed to correct past discrimination, its implementation has often drawn the ire of those who feel that it discriminates against men and majorities in order to make room for minorities and women (i.e., "reverse discrimination"). It is also opposed by those who feel that affirmative action does not aim to recruit the "best and the brightest" job candidates but only those who are "qualified" and belong to a protected class. When organizations have adopted a bona fide voluntary affirmative action plan to address underrepresentation, they may hire qualified minority or female candidates over better-qualified majority or male candidates; organizations are not required to use good business sense or to promote efficiency over equity. If no prior finding of gender or racial imbalance exists, however, employees who belong to the majority class may have a case for pursuing reverse discrimination charges.

In the early history of the Civil Rights Act of 1964, organizations were permitted to develop bona fide occupational qualifications (BFOQs) that could allow employers to make gender or race a relevant qualification—if it is job related. Thus, it is illegal for male correctional institutions to require being "male" as a job qualification; all positions must be open to both men and women, unless employers can show that for job-related reasons one sex must be excluded. Today, BFOQs are seldom utilized because they are difficult to defend.

In recent years, **sexual harassment** developed from a growing social concern to a subject of public policy. It involves (a) any sexual submission that is a quid pro quo affecting employment condition or (b) any unwelcome verbal, visual, or physical contacts of a sexual nature that create a hostile or offensive environment. The vagueness of the latter has resulted in many lawsuits. At present, a person may claim almost anything to be sexually offensive, but (a) the allegations must be made to the alleged offender, who then has an opportunity to address the concern, and (b) the sexually offensive behavior usually must be part of a pattern, not an isolated incident. These standards balance the interests of the alleged victim and those of alleged offenders. The requirement that behaviors are part of a pattern also protects alleged offenders against frivolous accusations based on accidental events (Wise, 2002). Such accusations might be used as a means of rivalry between members of opposite sexes. Although offenders can be held accountable by employers under their diversity and misconduct policies, some studies show that victims do not always come forward for fear of retaliation (Reese & Lindenberg, 2003).

In March 1998, the Supreme Court ruled unanimously that federal laws protect employees from being sexually harassed by members of the same sex. Justice Scalia stated that it was the conduct itself, and not the sex or motivation of the people involved, that determined sexual harassment. Previously, many lower courts had rejected same-sex harassment claims as a matter of law or had limited them to cases where one employee was homosexual. The case involved an oil rig worker, John Oncale, who alleged that he was the target of unwanted touching and threats of rape by several members of an all-male crew. Oncale resigned after company officials refused to help him. In another case, a federal appeals court allowed a same-sex sexual harassment case involving a teenage boy who wore an earring and was being harassed by a municipal work crew in Belleville, Illinois, for not being sufficiently masculine ("High Court," 1998).

Finally, the **Family and Medical Leave Act** (FMLA) of 1993 requires employers to give employees up to 12 weeks of unpaid leave for childbirth, adoption, or care of ill children, spouses, or parents. Ill persons can also take the same amount of unpaid leave. If the individual's illness constitutes a disability, then the employee may trigger the provisions of the ADA after the 12 weeks of leave have been exhausted.

Age and Disability

The Age Discrimination in Employment Act (ADEA) of 1967, as amended, protects workers over 40 years of age in hiring, promotion, and termination decisions. The act also prohibits mandatory retirements based on age, with the exception of those in executive policy-making positions. It is often difficult to prove that age is a discriminating factor; like racial and gender cases, employees must show that age is the reason for demotion or termination, whereas employers need only show that it was not a factor and provide some other non-age-related reason for their actions. A major concern is organizational restructuring and reductions in force (RIFs); employers must show that job-related criteria are the reason for any disparate impact that may occur.

Finally, the federal government has prohibited discrimination against persons with disabilities in its own employment decisions since 1948. The Americans With Disabilities Act (ADA) of 1990 broadened coverage to all employers and requires employers to provide persons with disabilities reasonable access to buildings (including testing accommodations) and accommodations of their work spaces. As one might imagine, the term "reasonable" has been subject to considerable litigation. Employer accommodations should be determined on a case-by-case basis and may include reserved parking, providing special equipment or personal aides, part-time or flextime work schedules, and building renovations. Accommodations that cause undue hardship to the employer are not required, and most accommodations can be made with relatively low expenditures.

The ADA also limits medical tests that may be used in job selection. Employers may ask only job-related questions and cannot use medical information to disqualify candidates if they are able to do the job. Administrators should not ask in their interview process whether applicants have a disability (Steingold, 2002). Persons with prior alcoholism are protected under the Rehabilitation Act of 1973, and those with HIV and AIDS are covered under the ADA. Thus, it is usually illegal to ask applicants about these conditions or to subject them to medical tests, but interview questions can be asked about the ability to perform job-related tasks (without inquiring into disabilities). The 1970 Occupational Safety and Health Act requires that employers provide a safe working environment. Organizations can subject employees to medical tests when public health issues arise, such as from contagious diseases. Thus, hospitals may require nurses to take HIV tests. The U.S. State Department requires applicants to provide a range of medical information about themselves, citing the impracticality of providing adequate health care in some of their overseas postings. In recent years, court cases have dealt with the nature of disabilities that qualify under the ADA. Individuals must be substantially limited in major life activity; it is insufficient to "merely" need glasses or have carpal tunnel syndrome (Crampton & Hodge, 2003).

SUMMARY AND CONCLUSION

The laws of the workplace are quite different from those of other spheres of life. Although employees enjoy far fewer rights than citizens, public personnel generally have more rights than those in business because they are not required to surrender their constitutional rights simply because they work for government. These rights include those pertaining to privacy, grooming, due process, free speech, and disobedience. They have fewer rights than citizens, however, with regard to political participation and, in some instances, drug and polygraph testing. Federal laws prohibit discrimination against both public and private employees on the basis of race, gender, national origin, religion, color, age, disability, or marital status; and employees have rights to workplaces free from racial or sexual harassment as well as other forms of harassment and intimidation indicated in the diversity policies of selected jurisdictions.

Workplace laws reflect a balance among three competing interests: managerial efficiency, employee rights, and social aspirations of the law (such as nondiscrimination). This balance is not written in stone; rather it is a reflection of lawmaking and the outcomes of many court cases over time. At present, a trend exists to interpret laws in favor of managerial efficiency, as employee rights are becoming ever more narrowly defined.

Case law deals with specific conduct, under specific conditions. Managers who look to such law and statutes to define an exhaustive set of prohibited or proscribed behaviors will be disappointed. It is seldom applicable to situations that are not exactly like the ones that are litigated—as is true with many situations that officials encounter. The basis for judgment is then the intent of the law—the values that underlie the cases and laws discussed in this chapter. For example, if supervisors must respect employee privacy, then it follows that they should ask permission when they think that it might be violated—even if legally they are unclear whether a right exists. If employees refuse to cooperate, then resolution might be sought in a collaborative manner, perhaps with assistance from other managers. Paradoxically, if case law is too specific, then statutes are too broad and vague: They often lack standards for interpretation and application. What are managers to do when both the law and their own employers and attorneys fail to provide definitive guidance? It is clear that they must form their own judgment. Administrators cannot expect legal standards to settle uncertainty in each and every instance: Cases and laws often provide only guideposts. Administrators must ensure that their actions are consistent with the spirit and aims of employment cases, law, and policies.

KEY TERMS

Adverse action
Affirmative action
Age discrimination
Americans With Disabilities Act of 1990
At-will employment
Civil Rights Act of 1964
Disparate impact
Disparate treatment discrimination
Diversity policies
Dress codes
Due process rights
80% rule
Equal Employment Opportunity Commission
Family and Medical Leave Act
Free speech rights

Hatch Act of 1939
Laudermill rights
Medical testing
Pre-employment background checks
Privacy expectations
Qualified immunity
Race-norming
Reasonable accommodation
Reverse discrimination
Right to disobey
Sexual harassment
Undue hardship
Voluntary affirmative action plans
Whistle-blowing

EXERCISES

Class Discussion

1. Some departments in universities believe that their faculty should mirror the demographic composition of the student body and that faculty recruitment should use "diversity" policies to pursue this objective. Assess the merits of this proposition.

2. Many people are increasingly conducting part of their work at home through telecommuting. Which privacy rights and responsibilities, if any, might this activity raise, and how might managers deal with these?

3. Identify a controversial workplace topic, and then use the test of balancing employee, employer, and society's interests to develop a range of possible policies addressing it.

4. A person with a mobility disability applies for a job in your office. Which interview questions can be asked about this disability without violating ADA provisions? Which questions should not be asked? How does this problem exemplify the paradox of needs?

Team Activities

5. Design a work group seminar to inform employees about their rights and limits when using e-mail and the Internet. What paradoxes protrude, and how can they be dealt with?

6. A coworker informs you, in confidence, that she feels attracted to another coworker in your office. What legal or policy advice would you give?

7. An employee requests a leave of absence to observe a religious event. He is important to the success of an effort that you are undertaking as a manager, and the employee's leave is likely to cause some delay and cost. What do you do?

8. Develop a policy for increasing workplace diversity that meets the constitutional standards.

Individual Assignments

9. Explain employees' rights to free speech. Are there any limits?

10. For what actions can public employees be sued?

11. Define and explain the 80% rule.

12. Which substantial interests do public employees have in their jobs?

13. What accommodations must employers make for disabled persons?

14. Based on your experience, give an example of either the paradox of democracy or the paradox of needs, as they apply to this chapter. Both paradoxes are mentioned in the Introduction.

15. What restrictions are imposed by the various Hatch Acts?

16. Roman playwright and carpenter Plautus (254–184 B.C.E.) offered the advice that one should "Practice what you preach." Discuss this advice in the context of this chapter.

REFERENCES

Adarand Contractors v. Pena, 115 S. Ct. 2097 (1995).

Board of Regents v. Roth, 408 U.S. 564 (1972).

Bowman, J. S. (1992, Fall). Dress standards in government: A national survey of state administrators. *Review of Public Personnel Administration, 15,* 35–51.

Bowman, J. S., & Hooper, H. L. (1991, Fall). Dress and grooming regulations in the public service: Standards, legality of enforcement. *Public Administration Quarterly, 15,* 328–340.

Branti v. Finkel, 445 U.S. 507 (1980).

Brown, A. (2000). Public employee political participation. *Public Integrity, 2*(2), 105–120.

Cleveland Board of Education v. Loudermill, 470 U.S. 532 (1985).

Crampton, S., & Hodge, J. (2003). The ADA and disability accommodations. *Public Personnel Management, 32*(1), 143–154.

Gely, R., & Chandler, T. (2000). Restricting public employees' political activities: Good government or partisan politics? *Houston Law Review, 37*(3), 776–822.

Gibson, C. (2001). Luder v. Endicott: The Fair Labor Standards Act and individual liability of public managers. *Review of Public Personnel Administration, 21*(2), 152–158.

Griggs v. Duke Power Co., 401 U.S. 424 (1971).

Guy, M., & Newman, M. (1998). Toward diversity in the workplace. In S. Condrey (Ed.), *Handbook of human resource management in government* (pp. 75–92). San Francisco: Jossey-Bass.

Harley v. Schuylkill County, 476 F. Supp. 191 (1979).

Hartman, G., Homer, G., & Reff, A. (2004). Human resource management legal issues: An overview. In S. Condrey (Ed.), *Handbook of human resource management in government* (ch. 17). San Francisco: Jossey-Bass.

Hester v. City of Milledgeville, 777 F2d 1492 (11th Cir 1985).

High court widens workplace claims in sex harassment. (1998, March 5). *New York Times,* p. A1.

Kelley v. Johnson, 425 U.S. 347 (1976).

Koenig, H. (1997). Free speech: Government employees and government contractors. *Public Administration Review, 57*(1), 1–3.

Lindquist, S. (2003). Privatizations through related corporations. *Review of Public Personnel Administration 23*(4), 323–327.

Lindquist, S., & Wasby, S. (2002). Defining free speech protections for public employees. *Review of Public Personnel Administration, 22*(1), 63–66.

Local Government Institute. (2002). *Model personnel policies and procedures for local government.* Tacoma, WA: Author.

McKee, V. (2000, March 12). Sex and work. *New York Times,* Sec. 3, p. 1.

National Treasury Employee's Union v. Von Raab, 489 U.S. 656 (1989).

O'Brien, D. (1997). The first amendment and the public sector. In P. Cooper & C. Newland (Eds.), *Public law and administration* (pp. 259–273). San Francisco: Jossey-Bass.

O'Connor v. Ortega, 480 U.S. 709 (1987).

Pickering v. Board of Education, 391 U.S. 563 (1968).

Reese, L., & Lindenberg, K. (2003). The importance of training on sexual harassment policy outcomes. *Review of Public Personnel Administration, 23*(3), 175–191.

Roberts, R. (1998). The Supreme Court and the law of public service ethics. *Public Integrity, 1*(1), 20–40.

Rosenbloom, D. (1998). Constitutional problems for the new public management in the U.S. In K. Thai & R. Carter (Eds.), *Current public policy issues: The 1998 annals.* Boca Raton, FL: Academic.

Rosenbloom, D. (2001). Public employees' liability for "constitutional torts." In C. Ban & N. Riccucci (Eds.), *Public personnel management: Current concerns, future challenges* (3rd ed., pp. 237–252). New York: Longman.

Rosenbloom, D., & Bailey, M. (2003). What every public personnel manger should know about the Constitution. In S. Hays & R. Kearney. *Public personnel administration: Problems and prospects* (4th ed., pp. 29–45). Upper Saddle River, NJ: Prentice Hall.

Shilling, D. (2002). *The complete guide to human resources and the law* (2nd ed.). New York: Aspen.

Sherbert v. Verner, 374 U.S. 398 (1963).

Smith, R. (2003). Enforcement or ethical capacity: Considering the role of state ethics commissions at the millennium. *Public Administration Review, 63*(3), 283–295.

Steingold, F. (2002). *The employer's legal handbook* (5th ed.). Berkeley, CA: Nolo Press.

Wards Cove Packing v. Atonio, 490 U.S. 642 (1989).

West v. Atkins, 487 U.S. 42 (1988).

Wise, C. (2002). Setting the boundaries for public employer liability for sexual harassment. *Review of Public Personnel Administration, 22*(4), 320–325.

White, R. (2001). Ask me no questions, tell me no lies: Examining the uses and misuses of the polygraph. *Public Personnel Management, 20*(4), 483–493.

Wood v. Strickland, 420 U.S. 303 (1975).

Part II

PROCESSES AND SKILLS: FROM START TO FINISH

3

RECRUITMENT

From Passive Posting to Head-Hunting

Your recruiting process should say to the candidate, "How'd you like to be part of our community, do neat things together, grow individually and with your peers?"

—Tom Peters, *The Pursuit of WOW!*
Every Person's Guide to Topsy-Turvy Times

After studying this chapter, you should be able to

- Identify the key paradoxes and challenges in recruitment from an organizational viewpoint
- Explain the three recruitment steps in the civil service staffing process
- Pose probing preliminary staffing questions such as whether to hire internally or externally and whether to duplicate the previous **recruitment process** or to restructure the position
- Write a customized job announcement
- Spot the strengths and weaknesses of various strategies and be able to determine an effective mix for specific staffing
- Describe some of the "do's and don'ts" of the recruitment process from an applicant's standpoint
- Incorporate tactics for enhancing diversity

Having examined human resource management's context and challenges—the civil service heritage and the legal environment—the essential functions of HRM are explored beginning with recruitment, arguably the most important of them all. From an applicant's perspective, recruitment is often daunting and esoteric. Ultimately, it can be life changing, as one must navigate through what is sometimes a bewildering variety of procedures. From the organization's perspective, recruitment is a process of soliciting the most talented and motivated applicants, and as such it is a bedrock function. Only with highly skilled staff—human capital—do organizations have the opportunity to thrive in an era in which work tends to be complex, customized, and rapidly changing. This chapter, then, discusses an array of concerns that agencies and applicants encounter and explains why the public sector confronts unique challenges.

One paradox is that procurement strategies and techniques, despite their importance, may be relatively insignificant compared to the American sociopolitical environment within which this function takes place. That is, three cultural forces—the historical recruitment philosophy, the social status of public employment, and political leadership—form a powerful context within which government seeks employees. Historically, recruitment has been passive, and until the 1950s it was not legal for the federal government to advertise in newspapers. It has also been highly negative and legalistic, often "turning off" would-be job applicants and contributing to the perception of excessive red tape (U.S. Merit Systems Protection Board [U.S. MSPB], 2000). Further, the loss of prestige of the public service from its high-water mark in the 1930s and 1940s is a constant concern (Lewis & Frank, 2002). Finally, politicians may make public employment harder by both "bashing the bureaucracy" (which they are in charge of) and starving the administration of the resources for high-quality recruitment (such as pay and hiring flexibilities).

For the job seeker, another stark paradox is the seeming abundance of employment opportunities but scarcity of desirable positions. There are several reasons for this. Not only is there a tendency to increase the span of control and eliminate whole layers of middle management, but there is also a propensity to reduce the number of specialists who have management rank and perquisites; as a result, positions with attractive professional opportunities can easily elicit scores of qualified candidates.

Applicants are also often perplexed by the mixed messages. Is recruitment a politically neutral, skill-based process, as it purports to be, or is it frequently a personalistic, "underground" hiring system with "wired" jobs subject to subtle, modern-day patronage? As discussed below, the public service was once largely based on patronage, and even today patronage positions are among the most influential in government. The bulk of those senior positions, however, are supposed to be based strictly on technical merit, yet the influence of "political" or personal factors is common. Yet below the policy level, personal factors cannot be discounted. Local government has always prided itself on a balanced approach using technical merit and a "good fit." Even at the federal level, entry-level job applicants hear about a job more frequently from friends and relatives than any other source (U.S. MSPB, 2000), and internal promotions are affected by personal factors (U.S. MSPB, 2001). Thus paradoxically, depending on the position, both perspectives can be true, and it is often impossible for the applicant to know how best to proceed.

In addition, should management aspirants prepare themselves as specialists or as generalists? Paradoxically, the answer is sometimes "yes." Applicants for better positions must be both. Until recently, the American tradition has largely favored specialists. The best caseworkers in social service agencies would often be promoted to supervisors, the best engineers in transportation agencies would be appointed as managers, and good researchers in state universities would become administrators. Advanced positions seldom required either generalist management training or experience in rotational assignments to gain broad experience. Although organizations seem to appreciate generalist training, it is usually on top of specialist training—for those few who are advanced in today's flatter hierarchies. Generalist training, however, is critical for managers who deal with diverse functions and who rarely have the time to maintain specialist expertise.

Paradoxes and challenges also exist from an organizational perspective. They start with the notion that recruitment is the most compelling human resource function, but it is generally acknowledged to be the weakest (General Accounting Office [GAO], 2003). It is pivotal because if recruitment is done poorly, then all subsequent human resource functions will be negatively affected. It is weakest because when done properly, it is a time-consuming, expensive process that busy administrators may try to circumvent. A challenge, given the contemporary demand for well-paying jobs, is that staffing practices may not consistently produce the "best and brightest" (Crewson, 1997). Perceptions of lower pay and job quality haunt the public sector (GAO, 2003; U.S. MSPB, 1988). Therefore, recruitment must be better to compensate, but recruitment resources pale compared with those available in leading corporations. Selected jurisdictions, however, realize that success in a competitive environment cannot occur without entrepreneurial recruitment practices such as better hiring location and test flexibility (Lavigna, 2002) and use of Internet efficiencies for disseminating information and gathering/evaluating applicant data (Kauffman & Robb, 2003).

Another challenge is the focus of recruitment: Should it be on current skills or future potential? Traditionally, procuring personnel emphasized technical skills[1] and longevity. More and more, however, organizations are interested in employee potential. The ability to adapt to new responsibilities and positions is critical as agencies reorganize and decentralize decision making (Kanter, 1989; Keenoy & Noon, 1992). Detecting future ability and identifying flexible employees takes a staffing process that seeks a different set of skills than has commonly been the case (Redman & Mathews, 1997).

Next is the paradox of balancing competing values: the need for timely recruitment—generally the biggest single concern of applicants and hiring supervisors alike—while maintaining lengthy processes in the name of fairness and openness. Although on-the-spot hiring occurs in government (see below), months can elapse between the job announcement and an offer of employment (GAO, 2003).

Another paradox is what to emphasize in the recruitment process. Which of the following are most significant: (a) knowledge, skills, and abilities; (b) motivation; (c) diversity and broad representation of minority and protected classes in the workforce; or (d) loyalty? Certainly technical skills are important, but it is quite possible to hire an employee who is well qualified yet who is poorly motivated, contributes to a racial/gender imbalance, and is not loyal. Nontechnical emphases have several challenges as well. Motivation is hard to predict, although it can transform a workplace. Diversity has an important management and ethical dimension, although some affirmative action programs have been downgraded. Organizations that lack employee loyalty likely lack trust, innovation, or dedication as well. Similarly, there is the dilemma of whether to use open recruitment, which encourages a broader pool and fresh ideas, or closed recruitment limited to the organization, which rewards service and loyalty as well as generally being faster.

Finally, what responsibility does the organization have to the applicant? Job seekers spend a great deal of energy and time. For example, is it ethical to use open recruitment to fulfill a legal requirement when an internal candidate has implicitly been selected for the position? **Sham recruitment** processes are infuriating for the candidate and are a drain on the resources of the organization. Or is it fair to ask for job references in the initial job application process when only those of the most highly ranked candidates will be read?

Such paradoxes are woven into the analysis below. Although there are few definitive answers to these queries, an examination of best practices suggests the need for balanced approaches. The chapter first identifies the overarching factors affecting recruiting success and then introduces specific steps in the recruitment/selection process. Then, three steps—planning and approval, position announcements, and recruitment strategies—are probed in more detail. Additional discussions include recruitment and diversity, the division of recruitment responsibilities, and job seeker advice. The chapter closes with a summary and concluding recommendations.

FACTORS IN RECRUITMENT: EMPLOYER AND APPLICANT PERSPECTIVES

Recruitment can be seen from two perspectives. What are the factors that affect success for the organization? And just as important, what are applicants' perspectives on what a quality process is, even if they are not selected?

Employer Recruitment

At least five major elements influence the effectiveness of recruitment: the breadth and quality of the process, the size of the labor pool and the location of jobs, pay and benefits (discussed in Chapters 6 and 7), job quality, and organizational image.

Having a sound recruitment philosophy means asking the right and wise questions from the outset (Breaugh & Starke, 2000). Is the entire procedure well conceived and supported so that it fully embodies vital organization goals? Are enough—and the correct—strategies used to reach a broad range of those who might be qualified and interested? Is the process aggressive enough to encourage the best candidates to apply? Is it clear and nonbureaucratic so that would-be applicants will not be discouraged? Is the process free from legal challenges yet not excessively legalistic or stultifying? Do applicants feel good about the recruitment? Finally, is the overall procedure cost-effective for the position being considered and the recruitment environment, both of which vary enormously?

Although other factors are not emphasized in this chapter, they have influence on the context within which the technical process operates. Labor pool size and job location play a role in recruitment (Smith, 2000). For instance, in the last generation, thousands of public sector jobs have been privatized with the result that they have gone to private domestic and overseas contractors. Economic boom or bust cycles also affect recruitment. For school districts, for example, this means that sometimes HR offices may be inundated with high-quality candidates; yet in times of shortages districts may travel out of state to job fairs and offer signing bonuses and moving allowances to fill vacancies. Good economic times generally mean that professionals of all types—lawyers, accountants, doctors, engineers, and others—may be in short supply; when the economy is weak, employee supply expands to the advantage of employers.

Job quality may or may not be an element that applicants are immediately aware of, but top candidates invariably become proficient analysts of the organization they are considering. The best ones investigate with a critical eye such aspects as job security, challenges and potential, working conditions, and professional perquisites such as travel and training. Although much of this understanding is sought and verified in the selection process (Chapter 4), it begins with recruitment.

Finally, organizational status plays a significant role (Gatehouse, Gowan, & Lautenschlager, 1993). Being an auditor in a social service agency beleaguered with a series of child protective service and welfare scandals may not be as appealing as working as an auditor in a large accounting firm. When the pay differential is factored in as well, it means that one organization may have Ivy League graduates competing for interviews, whereas the other does not. Laudable as the public service ethic may be, it can wear people out if agencies do not contribute to employee welfare in important ways. To illustrate, although most public defender offices pay poorly and overwork assistant public defenders, some have fine candidates because the training afforded is excellent and the work is as exciting as it is challenging. Interestingly, because of the surge in popularity of a strong public service ethic after the terrorist attacks of 9/11, interest in public service employment is up (Kaufman, 2004). Also, there has been increased attention on polishing agencies' images—called "branding"—which is often done in tandem with recruiting (Bailes, 2002).

High-Quality Recruitment: An Applicant's Perspective

According to recruitment expert Sara Rynes (1993), too often employers neglect to think of the applicant's perspective in the recruitment process. Instead of candidates being impressed by the organization whether they are hired or not, most feel resentment because of cold, unthoughtful, and/or dilatory treatment. Rynes offers four suggestions for employers who want people to have a good impression of the agency:

1. *Timing to minimize anxiety.* Good candidates expect recruitment processes to result in timely notification of being in contention, prompt follow-ups, and enough time to make a reasonable choice among offers.

2. *Feedback to optimize scarce job search resources.* "Withholding of negative feedback is often interpreted as 'stringing applicants along' to preserve complete freedom of *organizational* decision making" (Rynes, 1993, p. 31). In other words, as soon as agencies have eliminated applicants by narrowing the field to a short list, they should consider notifying candidates rather than wait until the final person has been selected.

3. *Information that makes distinctions.* People prefer to have information that is detailed enough to allow realistic assumptions about the specific job content rather than the single-sentence descriptions common in many announcements. In the interview process, candidates appreciate a realistic job preview because they understand Malcolm Forbes's statement, "If you have a job without aggravation, you don't have a job."

4. *Enthusiastic, informative, and credible representatives.* In the initial recruitment process, applicants respond much better to warm and enthusiastic recruiters. In the interview process, candidates not only notice whether they meet top organizational leaders and coworkers but also are sensitive to how their time is used. Dead time in the schedule or a casual interview schedule is seen as a negative factor from the candidate's perspective.

Overall, treat applicants as customers, and manage the recruitment process in a professional manner. With the backdrop of these recruitment factors and applicant preferences, our attention now turns to the technical processes.

RECRUITMENT STEPS

Recruitment provides information about available positions and encourages qualified candidates to apply. It has three stages: planning and approval of the position, preparation of the position announcement, and selection and use of specific strategies. The process should be seamlessly connected with selection (the next chapter), and together they are known as **staffing** (the receipt

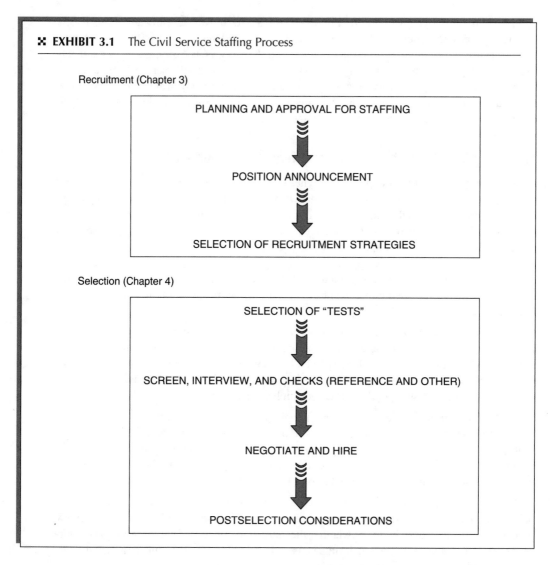

✖ **EXHIBIT 3.1**   The Civil Service Staffing Process

Recruitment (Chapter 3)

PLANNING AND APPROVAL FOR STAFFING

POSITION ANNOUNCEMENT

SELECTION OF RECRUITMENT STRATEGIES

Selection (Chapter 4)

SELECTION OF "TESTS"

SCREEN, INTERVIEW, AND CHECKS (REFERENCE AND OTHER)

NEGOTIATE AND HIRE

POSTSELECTION CONSIDERATIONS

of applications and the closing date of the position signal the end of recruitment and the beginning of the selection process). The staffing procedure is highlighted in Exhibit 3.1.

Generalizations are necessary but difficult, because substantial variations exist.[2] Thus, the process for an entry-level position may be quite different from that used for a midlevel manager, which in turn may be unlike that for an administrative head. Further, small and large organizations will vary substantially. Even large agencies will range between centralized processes and decentralized practices. Finally, departments often rotate between individual recruitment for a particular position and institutional recruitment to procure many people for a job classification such as entry-level secretaries, accountants, laborers, forest rangers, or caseworkers.

An important long-term trend in the last century was **proceduralism** ("red tape"). It connotes processes that have become excessively detailed, complicated, protracted, and/or impersonal (e.g., filling out different forms requesting the same information, having to go to multiple locations, or lengthy procedures that could be accomplished in a short time). Ever since the widespread use of civil service systems, the ideal has been to be as neutral as possible to make the process fair and unbiased. To accommodate numerous applicant requests for a large range of positions, centralized systems emerged in the federal government in the 1920s and elsewhere thereafter (Hamman & Desai, 1995, p. 90). Certainly this was sensible, helping to combat excessive political cronyism and managerial personalism and to overcome a lack of hiring expertise dispersed among various units. It led, however, to rigidity and formalism as well. Adding to proceduralism in the mid-1960s was the interest in providing greater employment accessibility for minorities, women, and other protected classes.[3]

The trend today seeks to ease the effects of proceduralism by decentralizing to allow hiring managers more control and to try innovative methods to compete in the new employment environment. For example, Hays (1998) notes that the recent government reform initiatives have affected staffing in three ways:

First, there is a strong drive to decentralize staffing activities. To the extent feasible, line managers are being provided with greater influence over recruitment and selection efforts. Second, government appears to be making a sincere effort to simplify and invigorate intake functions. More energy is being spent on selling public agencies to prospective workers and on easing their passage into the workforce. Finally, personnel offices are beginning to demonstrate an unaccustomed willingness to experiment with new staffing strategies (p. 303).

Thus, for instance, Congress approved the use of direct hiring authority in the wake of 9/11 for 2-year emergency appointments. As well, an agency in the U.S. Department of Health and Human Services recruits 50 college graduates each year in its scholarship program as full-time employees who receive special training, mentoring, and job rotation experiences.

PLANNING AND APPROVAL

At least two different types of planning occur in well-managed organizations (Mintzberg, 1994). First, they engage in strategic thinking about the future needs, challenges, and opportunities of their incoming workforce. True strategic planning requires research, original thinking, and a willingness to change. Second, agencies operationalize strategic plans as concrete positions become available. In other words, preliminary, vital questions should be rigorously asked about available positions before the actual recruitment process takes place.

Strategic Planning and Management of Vacancies

A plan for staffing begins with a **labor market survey** or overview of the labor market as it affects agency job clusters. What are trends in terms of availability, salaries, and education levels? Public organizations often suffer most in employment cycles because of the difficulty of implementing policies to compete for workers in tight labor markets. In addition to a market analysis, a needs assessment should be done. What does the organization anticipate its requirements will be for new positions, restructured positions, and eliminated positions? If an agency is required to strengthen its educative/facilitative role and decrease its regulative role (such as occurred at the U.S. Department of Housing and Urban Development in the 1990s, for instance), then it takes new skills and even different types of staff. It is nevertheless quite common to find workforces lacking the requisite technical, interpersonal, and problem-solving skills needed by the contemporary organization. Such mission transitions are common today. Although the decentralization of human resource functions overall has made planning at the systems level more difficult for states and cities, it has made it more flexible at the department and unit level.

Planning can take a number of different forms. Organizations can make sure that the staff intake function is properly funded. They can work on institutional image to positively affect recruitment. Agencies can provide flexible schedules, family support policies like child care, comparable pay, and technology upgrades. Such planning and action take place long before any particular position is advertised. A final aspect of planning is to make sure that the process is timely and user friendly.

Ultimately, each position that opens may have special problems and opportunities. Administrators need to be able to assess whether a routine protocol is best or whether closer examination is necessary. If any of the following red flags are present, the hiring manager should probably give special attention to a new or customized process:

- Applicants for recent positions have been poorly qualified.
- Supervisors complain that new workers do not fit into the department well.
- The best candidates do not apply.
- Better applicants have already found positions by the time the position is offered.

When strategic issues are involved, it is time to consult with the human resources department, colleagues in the agency and other organizations, and professional trade journals. Systemic concerns should trigger the use of decision-making tools such as cause-and-effect charts, statistical analysis, and Delphi techniques (i.e., the pooling of expert opinions on a problem or issue) so that solutions can be found.

An example of a strategic problem comes from a midlevel information technology manager arguing with his supervisor about whether to hire an underqualified but high-potential candidate. The supervisor's view was that such employees take at least 3 months to have marginal utility and 6 months to perform at standard. Furthermore, some never come up to speed but rather plateau at a low performance level. The midlevel manager's position was that the unit had five open positions, was struggling to keep up with a rapidly expanding workload, and found that fully qualified personnel were simply not applying, despite a new, higher pay level.

By discussing the systemic problem with human resource experts, however, the manager and supervisor uncovered a strategic opportunity. Why not hire five technically underqualified but high-potential candidates (who were relatively plentiful) and offer a special training class? This would be worth the effort because its size would justify a full-time trainer, which would, in turn, ensure higher-quality training than the ad hoc on-the-job training provided to single hires. Furthermore, furnishing a trainer would reduce the demands on the already overworked personnel in the unit for whom training was generally a distraction. Another case of a strategic decision is the outsourcing of governmental jobs in recent years to contractors and subcontractors operating overseas to avoid improving working conditions and compensation for American employees.

Preliminary Decisions About the Specific Position

Before the recruitment for a position begins, some thought must be given to staffing fundamentals. Is it advisable to fill the position at all? Sometimes it is better to leave one position unfilled so that the spare capacity can be used elsewhere in the unit or organization. Another question is whether the position needs to be restructured or if expectations need to be adjusted (see also Chapter 5 on classification). Has the position become over- or underclassified? Is it too narrowly or too broadly defined? Have fundamental job skills shifted because of technology or program maturation? Sometimes one or two vacancies provide a good opportunity to address such questions.

If the position is not entry level, should it be filled from the inside only or should outside applicants be solicited? Morale, it is generally argued, is improved by inside hiring, whereas depth and diversity are improved by an open search. Generally, "inside only" decisions are used by departments that rely on rank classification (such as the military and public safety organizations) and by strong union agencies in which priority application provisions for existing employees are tantamount to property rights. Whereas government tended to have a preference for internal promotion in the past, even at the federal level new flexibilities ("hiring authorities") are making greater use of external candidates (Kaufman, 2003).

The type of recruitment process is yet another issue: **individual versus "pool" or institutional recruitment**. At the federal level, these categories are called case examining versus standing inventories. Broad, entry-level classifications in moderately large organizations generally use pool hiring. For example, a personnel department may generically advertise for numerous entry-level secretaries, computer programmers, and accountants to be placed on a standing certified list to be used by numerous state agencies in the selection process. The advantages are increased efficiency, low cost, and multiple considerations of qualified applications; disadvantages are primarily the difficulties of keeping the list up to date. Common or hard-to-fill positions may be on a continuous list in order to constantly replenish candidates. Individual recruitment is used for most positions above the entry level, jobs in smaller organizations, and less common classifications.

A critical decision is the breadth of involvement of those in hiring and related units. Sometimes, typically for entry-level slots, the supervisor is the sole decision maker and works exclusively with the personnel authority. At the other extreme—commonly in senior level and professional positions—is a search committee that selects the finalists for an interview and recommends a best candidate to the hiring supervisor. A midpoint is often struck for middle management jobs in which input is solicited from the affected subordinates and colleagues, but the final decision is still primarily the domain of the supervisor.

For many positions, especially those involved in first-line management, the question of the generalist versus the specialist arises. Of course, there is no definitive answer; it depends on the needs of the position. Specialists may relate to line workers well and understand technical issues; however, as the philosopher Shunryu Suzuki noted, "In the generalist's mind there are many opportunities; in an expert's mind there are few." Generalists tend to have a broader perspective that is valuable in management positions. On the whole, they can "see the forest for the trees," have superior people skills, and are easier to cross-train. Specialists, on the other hand, can be more efficient because of their technical background, be easier to justify in the budget in frontline supervisory positions, and require relatively little training for the production work that many supervisors today continue to do. The challenge is that frontline positions need specialist abilities, but when those same people are promoted, their new management responsibilities tend to focus on generalist competencies. For the 21st century, it may be less important what one knows and more important what one has in the way of potential to respond to unknown challenges.

The final preliminary issue is getting authority for hiring and approval for any job adjustments that may be needed. Positions are a carefully guarded resource, with hiring freezes instituted directly by presidents, governors, county commissioners, and mayors. Paperwork must be carefully completed, adjustments must be documented, and acquiring formal union approval or informal approval by colleagues is prudent. Hiring supervisors who are sloppy or impatient with the process or inarticulate with their rationale may find their hiring opportunities hamstrung by human resource specialists or stymied by superiors. As often as not, managers who demand expedited processes have simply neglected to plan properly or learn long-established procedures.

In summary, recruitment begins before a position becomes available. An agency that wants to appeal to the best candidates will make sure that it is competitive in terms of pay, reputation, working conditions, and collegiality and that its personnel procurement process has resources to identify and attract the finest people available. As positions become available, proper planning requires a series of preliminary questions related to job currency and restructuring, **inside-only** versus **outside recruitment**, pool versus targeted hiring, scope of involvement, specialist-generalist characteristics, and timeliness. This planning occurs prior to designing the job announcement, discussed below.

POSITION ANNOUNCEMENTS

Because there are no standard legal requirements about minimum information in **job (position) announcements**, they vary from jurisdiction to jurisdiction, from entry level to professional recruitment, and from source to source. For example, one jurisdiction may routinely include information about its benefits package, whereas another may not. Or a professional level announcement in a national trade journal may insert a promotional paragraph about the agency or its jurisdiction that would rarely appear in an entry-level announcement in a local newspaper. Many agencies use advertisements that have relatively little detail but rather are aimed at notifying applicants of opportunities that can be more fully explored by requesting more information. A cost-effective compromise may be to post an ad in a national job search Web site like Monster.com or Careerpaths.com; such ads include a series of questions that screen qualified people as they read them. In any event, the announcement should be designed initially using a full format, which subsequently can be modified for a variety of purposes (see Exhibit 3.2).

✖ EXHIBIT 3.2   The Elements of a Job Announcement

The following types of information are relatively standard in a full announcement:

1. *Title and agency/organization affiliation.* This can include the official title and/or the working title. The agency/division affiliation is mentioned except when recruitment is being conducted on a centralized basis (e.g., statewide or citywide).

2. *Salary range.* The range generally indicates the starting salary as well as its ceiling. Professional and executive positions may simply state that a "competitive salary" is offered depending on experience and credentials.

3. *Description of job duties and responsibilities.* This is essentially a short job description. What will the incumbent actually do and be responsible for? Supervisory responsibilities, financial duties, and program responsibilities are especially useful in nonentry positions. Work hours are also standard information, although sometimes omitted when conventional.

4. *Minimum qualifications.* What education, skills, and experience are required, as a minimum, to qualify for the job? Education requirements could be a degree in select fields or a specialized certification. Skills could be as specific as typing speed or as general as communication facility. Many positions require specific experiences such as at least 3 years as a planner or 7 years in positions with progressively more responsibility (e.g., managerial). Minimum qualifications must be job related; employers should not arbitrarily raise such qualifications just to reduce the number of job applicants.

5. *Special conditions.* These often signal applicants to aspects of the job that some people (but not necessarily all) may find unappealing. Common special conditions include travel requirements, being stationed at outlying locations, a harsh or dangerous work environment, requirements for background checks, unusual hours, and residency requirements.

6. *Application procedures.* What exam method will be used? If there is a specific test, when is it administered? Or is examination done by rating the education and experience of candidates? To whom and where does one apply, and with what exact materials? A closing date for the recruitment period is necessary, although sometimes positions "remain open until filled" after the closing date. Re-advertised positions may "begin interviewing immediately." Otherwise, most jurisdictions require 3 weeks or more to close the recruitment period. Minimum periods for advertising are often in the legal code or statute and should be scrupulously followed. Emergency and temporary hiring practices are always possible but generally require exceptional justification and authorization.

7. *Equal Opportunity Employment.* Standard phrases are used to indicate the organization's commitment to equal opportunity employment and affirmative action.

Beyond these standard types of information, some other kinds are not routine but are nevertheless common.

1. *Classification.* The specific ranking of the position in the organizational system (grade level) is often not included in external postings because it may confuse outsiders. When it is relatively easy to understand, such as the federal General Schedule, it should be listed. Grade level is invariably of interest to organizational members, so internal postings should always include this more technical data.

2. *Career potential.* A good job posting should discourage poorly qualified applicants, but it should also encourage those who are well qualified. Candidates often are looking at not only the position but its career potential. Mentioning career potential generally helps recruit better and more ambitious applicants. Examples include opportunities for promotion, training and education, and special experience.

3. *Special benefits.* Some positions have special benefits. Examples might be seasonal vacations (such as summers for teachers and faculty), opportunities for extra pay, availability to work with distinguished people, or exceptional retirement programs (such as the military and paramilitary organizations).

Style and tone matter more in announcements today than in the past because of a tight labor market and the difficulty of getting well-qualified people. Although announcements were once expected to be solemn, standardized, and neutral, now they must, at least to some degree, be inviting and interesting (Zeidner, 2001). In an in-depth analysis of vacancy announcements, the U.S. Merit Systems Protection Board criticized federal recruitment in this area:

> Our systematic review of a random sample of vacancy announcements found that at least half of them are poorly written and that they make little or no attempt to sell the government, the agency, or the positions to be filled. Far too often vacancy announcements are difficult to understand and use threatening and insulting language, characteristics that are more likely to drive applicants away than attract them. (U.S. MSPB, 2003)

Some of the recommendations from that study that apply to all public sector organizations include the following:

- Greatly reduce the length of vacancy announcements.
- Reduce the use of negative, threatening, and legalistic language.
- Design a message to sell the job and the agency and, to the extent possible, present the agency as the employer of choice.
- Describe the job and its requirements clearly and realistically.
- Require the least amount of information needed to make basic qualification determinations and then request more information as needed later in the process.
- Give straightforward instructions on how to apply.

Finally, announcements should always be reviewed carefully for both accuracy and currency because misstatements become legally binding and errors make the organization look unprofessional. Of course, they should tie directly to the official job description, which in turn is often based on a formal job analysis (see Chapter 5). Although conceptually job analyses and descriptions precede announcements, it is not unheard of that preparation of an announcement sparks changes in a description or causes a new job analysis. Once an announcement is completed and authorized, the department can focus on an appropriate set of recruitment strategies.

RECRUITMENT STRATEGIES

There are numerous **recruitment strategies**—methods of contacting and informing potential applicants—but they are seldom used simultaneously. Of course, it is not the sheer number that determines a quality intake process but the choice of an appropriate combination. Unfortunately, governments historically eschewed aggressive recruitment practices. There is a new activism today (GAO, 2003), which means that agencies are using more approaches and trying to do so with more effect. Ten strategies are discussed here, each of which has strengths and weaknesses and, therefore, various utilization patterns. Four major factors (relative ease of use, effectiveness, cost, and common usage) will be identified for each strategy.

Job posting was originally the placing of the announcement on walls in prominent places such as post offices or city halls. Many civil service systems still require physical posting in a minimum number of public places. Posting is considered the most basic of all recruitment strategies; it is easy to do because the entire announcement can be used without modification. Its effectiveness is largely limited to organization members and aggressive job seekers who come to the agency's employment office(s). For a job that must be filled internally, say a fire lieutenant's position, posting alone can be sufficient. Many positions, however, are recruited outside the organization, and traditional posting is unlikely to be effective. As Eleanor Trice (1999) of the International Personnel Management Association says, "The days when government organizations could recruit by simply posting a vacancy announcement, then sitting back and assuming that enough qualified applicants would apply, are gone" (p. 10).

Today posting also refers to **electronic posting**—listing jobs on agency Web sites or Web sites exclusively dedicated to job seekers. The Internet is an enormously important recruitment tool whose cost is minimal. Some examples are the following:

- U.S. Office of Personnel Management in *USAJOBS*   www.usajobs.opm.gov
- Federal jobs   www.fedworld.gov
- *Federal Times*   www.federaltimes.com
- Jobs in government   www.JobsInGovernment.com
- International Personnel Management Association   www.publicsectorjobs.com
- Local government jobnet   www.lgi.org
- Career Mosaic (private sector)   www.careerbuilder.com

Electronic posting is now required by law for federal positions that are competitively recruited and is the baseline for all but the most specialized jobs or smallest agencies. The ease of placing job advertisements has become a substantial advantage, as has the ability to reach an enormous pool at minimal cost. Despite its growth and popularity as the recruitment tool, there are studies that indicate electronic posting is already probably overused. The U.S. Merit Systems Protection Board cautions against overreliance on electronic methods (2003) because of concerns about digital access. Research on Internet recruitment by Feldman and Klass (2002) indicate that only 16% of those identifying the most effective recruitment tools name the Internet, whereas 22% indicated that it was among the least effective. Although improved digital access will certainly increase these percentages over time, the point is that it is not necessarily the most effective strategy for securing the most high-quality talent.

Newspaper recruitment focuses on local or regional openings. The employment section of the largest area Sunday paper is the most common vehicle for job announcements, but some jurisdictions use daily employment sections as well. Smaller local papers may be ideal for a local job, especially those that are entry level, low-paying, or part-time. Despite cost, newspapers can be relatively effective in external recruitment.

Trade journals are the newsletters and magazines that inform members of professions about activities on a regular basis (e.g., *PATimes, ICMA Newsletter,* and *IPMA Newsletter*). The audience is narrower than that of a newspaper in terms of professional range but broader in terms of national scope. Trade journals are used extensively for professional and senior management positions in which high levels of specialized expertise are desired and generally available only on the national market. If a federal agency is looking for a senior math statistician, a state agency is seeking a director for its lottery department, or a city is searching for a city manager, they are all likely to list these positions in relevant journals where candidates can easily scan the entire job market. To the degree that appointive positions use open procedures, trade journals are also a strategy of choice, despite the associated cost.

Recruitment by **mail** is a highly personalized approach in which individuals are encouraged by letter to apply. Aggressive private sector corporations use this strategy to contact students who are in the top few deciles of a handful of institutions identified as sources of exceptional candidates. Even more targeted recruitment occurs when a search committee identifies a select number of individuals who are exceedingly qualified and then personally encourages them. Such an approach "seeds" the recruitment pool with candidates who may not otherwise apply. It is rarely used in the public sector but is a mainstay strategy for Fortune 500 companies. Both sectors use search firms that rely on such personalized approaches. In addition, e-mail provides an inexpensive, informal, and rapid outreach technique.

Other mass communications (excluding the print and electronic methods already mentioned) include dedicated phone lines, government access TV, institutional advertising, and positive public relations stories. Dedicated phone lines are used by centralized personnel agencies to accommodate the standardized information needs of applicants who can call about jobs 24 hours a day. Government access TV is most commonly used by cities and counties that have a controlled-access government station provided by the authorized cable company. It is common for these stations to list available jobs at various times. Some organizations do institutional advertising, especially when they have a service to sell (e.g., state universities). This advertising increases awareness and prestige, even though it does not target select positions. Positive media coverage can have a similar effect on recruitment efforts.

Personal contact recruitment occurs when recruiters, managers, or search panel members attend job fairs, conduct on-campus recruiting, or individually contact top candidates for positions. Recruiters generally travel to such events, perhaps across town but sometimes to other states, or make targeted calls to potential candidates who have not applied. Such tactics are routine for some corporations, professional sports teams, and elite law firms but are less common for all but the largest government agencies. Job fairs provide candidates a chance to talk to prospective employers and provide the organization an opportunity to increase its visibility and scout for suitable talent. The practice of managers personally contacting candidates is common in business; it is less so in the public sector, which is considered vulnerable to accusations of cronyism and bias.

Internship programs are a common practice in many midsized and large jurisdictions (see Exhibit 3.3 for two examples). Elite organizations screen interns nearly as closely as job applicants because of program cost and subsequent high hiring rates. Consequently, such opportunities are a standard element of almost all master of public administration curricula, and program quality can be quite high. Organizations that make large-scale and effective use of this strategy report that the benefits in terms of training, acculturation, job preview, and job longevity are unequaled by other methods.

The federal government has well-known initiatives such as the Presidential Management Fellowship (formerly the Presidential Management Internship program), Federal Career Intern program, AmeriCorps, National Health Service Corps, and Reserve Officer Training Corps (ROTC), including high school junior ROTC. Cooperative education programs are endorsed by the federal government as well (called the Student Educational Employment Program). In such programs, agencies employ students while they are completing a degree program (such as an MPA) without going through a competitive process. Federal law permits conversion of these positions to regular positions if the agency is so inclined. States and cities have set up similar undertakings (National Commission on the State and Local Public Service, 1993). Ties between master of public administration programs and local/regional

✖ **EXHIBIT 3.3**   Examples of Internship Recruiting

Both of these examples appeared in the *PA Times.*

MANAGEMENT INTERNSHIP
CITY OF PHOENIX, ARIZONA

Three Management Intern positions are available beginning July 1, 1999, for a minimum twelve month period. Present starting salary is $27,851, plus comprehensive employee benefits. Management Interns are assigned in the Budget and Research Department and serve rotational assignments in the City Manager's Office and a line department. This will be the 50th class of the City's Intern Program, which has proven to be an excellent training ground for higher-level administrative and managerial positions.

Applicants must have completed courses required for a master's degree in public administration or business administration, or related field by July 1, 1999. Applications must be postmarked by January 15, 1999. Application materials are available on our Web Site at: http://www.ci.phoenix .as.us/EMPLOY/empidx.html, or write or call:

Management Intern Search, 135 N. 2nd Avenue, Phoenix AZ 85003-2018

(602) 262-6277   AA/EEO/D Employer

JUDICIAL FELLOWS PROGRAM

The Judicial Fellows Commission seeks outstanding individuals interested in working within the federal judiciary in Washington D.C. Fellows spend one calendar year (beginning late August/ early September) at the Supreme Court of the United States, the Federal Judicial Center, the Administrative Office of the United States Courts, or the United States Sentencing Commission working on various projects concerning the federal court system and the administration of justice.

Number of Fellowship Positions: Four

Qualifications: Candidates must be familiar with the judicial system, have at least one postgraduate degree, two or more years of professional experience with high achievement. Multidisciplinary training and experience, whether in law, administration, the social sciences, or the humanities, are desirable.

Salary: based on education and experience, not to exceed government pay schedule GS-15, step 3, presently $80,789.

Application Requirements: Candidates must submit resume, 700 word essay explaining interests in the Program, copies of two publications or other writing samples, and three reference letters forwarded directly to the Program.

Application Deadline: November 6.

Interested candidates should submit materials to: Judicial Fellows Program, Supreme Court of the United States, Washington, D.C. 20543. (202) 479-3415.

An Equal Opportunity Employer

agencies enhance academic curricula and are appreciated by both students and agencies. Internship and shadowing programs at the high school level are a long-term recruitment strategy but certainly can make strong impressions while providing a useful service component for the host agency. Fellowships, which can be extremely competitive, are generally aimed at mid- to senior level candidates interested in new or broader professional experiences.

Head-hunting, or external recruitment, occurs when the staffing function is farmed out to a third party that makes the initial contact or even provides the hiring contract. Ironically, it is used most for both the lowest and highest, but not the middle positions in government. Public agencies contract employment firms, especially in a tight labor market, for basic labor, clerical, and temporary positions (generally en masse). At the top end of the spectrum, private sector organizations have long relied on head-hunting strategies to fill executive and senior management positions, but this is less prevalent in government, which places a premium on open processes from beginning to end. Executive head-hunting is on the upswing as new practices in states like Michigan (Kost, 1996) and Washington (which uses internal executive recruiters); it has always been common for city and county management positions.

Noncompetitive recruitment means that a single official completes the process without a formal comparison of candidates. Therefore, recruitment may be "open" for certain jobs or types of applicants. Sometimes it means that immediate hiring is allowed if candidates meet certain standards; at other times the decision maker simply has the authority to select those people deemed appropriate. An illustration of the first instance is when the federal government has allowed its campus recruiters to hire students immediately if they met certain grade point standards (e.g., the Outstanding Scholar Program and Schedule B appointments, which do not require a competitive examination). This practice has become so popular, in fact, that it was challenged because of affirmative action concerns (Rivenbark, 1998). An example of the second instance is the process of appointing confidential staff; elected and senior appointed officials can hire advisers, deputies, and personal assistants without either a formal merit or legislative consent process. Of course, a noncompetitive process is easier and less costly than other methods. The practice is effective in a limited number of cases such as hard-to-fill positions where meeting a given standard is sufficient for hiring or where political and personal loyalty is an appropriate factor.

Which strategies are best for which jobs? For positions in police, fire, and paramilitary organizations with strong seniority policies, there is little reason to go much beyond physical and virtual posting. Organizational members wait for these opportunities, and internal recruitment is usually sufficient. The situation is quite different elsewhere, when competition for high-quality candidates can often be fierce. The question is not *which* strategy to use but *how many*, given financial and personnel resources. Following its strategic plan, the U.S. State Department uses both cutting-edge technology and interpersonal relations. By integrating traditional marketing, outreach techniques and public relations with Web-based technology, its Diplomatic Readiness Initiative made the department's recruitment program a model (Pearson, 2004).

The strengths of public sector recruitment have been in notification strategies—job posting, electronic posting, newspapers, trade journals, and some mass communication methods. Traditional weaknesses have been the lack of expensive, proactive strategies—well-paid internship programs (with the notable exception of the federal government), systematic personal contacts, mail recruitment, head-hunting, and noncompetitive hiring. Future innovations are more likely to be in these latter strategies (see Exhibit 3.4). Current innovations cluster around increasing timeliness, in general, and flexibility where positions are hard to fill (see Exhibit 3.5). In 2004, for instance, the U.S. Office of Personnel Management developed Recruitment One-Stop, an integrated, governmentwide online recruitment system. A critical aspect in selecting recruitment strategies is determining whom they target and whether they encourage diversity in the organization, which is examined below.

> ✖ **EXHIBIT 3.4**   Just How Aggressive Should Public Sector Organizations Become?
>
> Government is often urged to act more like business. Should it adopt private sector strategies about recruitment? For example, should it abandon competitive hiring (comparing multiple candidates) for selected "hot" fields and substitute minimum standards coupled with on-the-spot hiring in order to make timely offers? Should it use signing bonuses, common in the private sector for difficult-to-hire positions? Although there was a time when this strategy was unheard of, it is now used by school districts desperate to fill positions and by agencies hiring for information technology positions. Should government follow the example of those corporations that target select institutions where the graduates are known to be superior, often tracking specific students during the latter part of their academic study? Should agencies actively hire specific high-performing employees away from other organizations, even though they have not applied for positions? Corporate raiding of employees is common practice, often with public sector employees being the target. Is it appropriate and ethical for public agencies to use such an approach? Finally, should the inducements for outstanding candidates be enhanced by special contracts promising advantageous opportunities? An example might include rotational fast-track assignments for junior applicants (this has always been done to some degree in the military with academy officers). Instances of these proactive strategies exist in the government, but they are all unusual. How common should they be? Just how aggressive should public organizations become?

> ✖ **EXHIBIT 3.5**   Recruitment Innovations in Wisconsin
>
> The state of Wisconsin has been widely regarded as an innovator in procurement practices. Like many organizations that have assessed their recruitment practices, it found that the major complaints from customers (both hiring agencies and applicants) were timeliness and *flexibility*. Three programs targeted these problems. The walk-in civil service testing program allows applicants to take almost any civil service test each week in 14 different locations across the state without having to apply in advance. This has cut down the waiting time for applicants by half and has reduced overall administrative costs. The Entry Professional Program allows agencies to customize recruitment strategies for select entry professional positions, often deleting a multiple-choice civil service exam (which reduces the application time and applicant frustration) and substituting rigorous education and experience reviews and more extensive interview programs. Where applicable, this program allows interviewing of all eligible candidates, exceeding the normal top 5 or 10 candidates. Agencies must simply justify their rationale for adjusting standard recruitment procedures for those targeted professional positions. The critical recruitment program targets those positions in which fewer than 10 applicants are expected. Rather than require multiple-choice testing, the program allows use of evaluations of experience and training, job task checklists, or academic crediting schedules (Lavigna, 1996, pp. 428–429). Interviews are allowed immediately for all who meet minimum standards. In some cases, it is possible for applicants to apply, be evaluated, be interviewed, and be offered a job all on the same day.

Unity Through Diversity in Recruitment

Even though affirmative action has been de-emphasized in recent years (Ewoh & Elliott, 1997; Riccucci, 1997; Slack, 1997), a diverse workforce is both ethical and a management necessity. There are three factors to consider. First, does the agency provide an environment compatible for diversity through its promotion processes and organizational culture? A department that insists on standard working hours, does not provide child care assistance, and subtly penalizes leaves of absence for family reasons does not create a suitable atmosphere for employee-parents. Such issues might be subtle but are critical if a diverse environment is to be created and to be optimally productive.

An illustration of providing a hospitable environment for families is the creation of spousal assistance programs. Spousal assistance may be offered to help reduce the trauma of relocating families. Such plans are more common in the private sector (28%), especially in large corporations (52%), than in the public sector (Galinsky, Friedman, & Hernandez, 1991; Mercer, 1996). For dual-career couples, a transfer or relocation of one spouse is highly disruptive to the other's career plans. This has led to refusals to accept jobs, promotions, or transfers to avoid family disruptions. Research highlights the need for such assistance: More than one third of formerly employed spouses lacked opportunities 3 months after relocating; 1 out of 5 dual-career spouses was assisted by the employee's firm; and 8 out of 10 desired such assistance in a future relocation (Rukeyser, 1996). Organizations that do not provide spousal assistance may find themselves accepting less than ideal candidates for positions because their preferred candidate declined to move.

Second, is there a conscious attempt to maintain a well-rounded workforce so that no group, including white males, has a legitimate complaint? Are resources made available to minority members in the organization? All things being equal, qualified women and minorities should be given priority if they are clearly underrepresented in proportion to the available, eligible workforce. Research indicates that minorities are highly sensitive to the presence of role models in the recruitment process and to the comparative level of resources available (Gilbert, 2000). Although the public sector has generally done better than business in this regard, there are many workplaces that are still negligent in promoting unity through diversity. Common examples include not hiring women in paramilitary agencies, lower employment of Latinos in the federal workforce (U.S. MSPB, 1997) and a low representation of African Americans in senior management positions across all levels of government.

Third, there should be awareness that where and how recruitment takes place will have an effect (Thaler-Carter, 2001). Sometimes procurement practices need to target locations where diverse candidates are more likely to congregate (perhaps particular schools or job fairs) and sources that such individuals are likely to read (such as ethnically oriented newspapers and newsletters).

Dividing Responsibilities

There is no hard-and-fast rule about who is responsible for what aspects of recruitment. As discussed in the Wye River Conference (see Exhibit 1.11), the central agency should enable individual units and managers to better perform the human resource function. In larger government agencies, the responsibility has been divided among three entities. The centralized human resource office is often responsible for (a) overseeing diversity plans, (b) providing a comprehensive listing of recruitment sources, (c) supplying coordination of institutional recruitment (such as mass entry-level positions) and personal procurement (such as job fairs and college recruitment), and (d) furnishing a centralized recruitment source when departments elect not to handle it on their own. These offices function as expert sources of assistance for departments. A second approach is that agencies either have full-time human resource experts or coordinators with personnel responsibilities. These specialists provide support to operational units and monitor hiring practices. Finally, organizations may conduct much of their recruitment directly, especially for midlevel and senior positions. This has the advantage of increased buy-in and involvement from departments in the entire process; it also may mean that there is an opportunity for inappropriate practices if hiring units do not take the responsibility seriously or plan for it properly. Exhibit 3.6 is an example of the division of responsibilities in the state of Iowa.

✂ EXHIBIT 3.6   An Example of Dividing the Work of Recruitment in a Large System

---

The recruitment of qualified applicants for state employment is the joint responsibility of the following:

- Managers and supervisors
- Personnel officers (assigned to specific agencies)
- Employment specialists at the Iowa Department of Personnel (IDOP)

Departments' recruitment efforts include the following:

- Review their affirmative action plans to understand the status of their progress.
- Project the number of upcoming vacancies and when they will be filled.
- Submit an annual and quarterly vacancy forecast to the IDOP.
- Identify exact recruitment needs (job title; class code; selective areas, if appropriate; job location).
- Contact all potential sources of applicants.
- Determine the best methods for informing applicants.
- Determine what resources to commit to recruitment efforts.
- Contact personnel officer and employment specialist for assistance.

Personnel officer's recruitment efforts include the following:

- Be familiar with the department's affirmative action plan and progress toward its goals.
- Assist the department in locating local, specialized recruitment sources for their specific needs to supplement the employment bureau's list.
- Assist the IDOP Employment Bureau on recruitment trips and keep it informed of the department's recruitment plans.

IDOP Employment Bureau efforts include the following:

- Determine relevant recruitment areas (local, statewide, national).
- Develop a comprehensive recruitment source list and keep it up to date.
- Assist departments and the personnel offices on how best to inform potential applicants of vacancies.
- Coordinate career days, job fairs, and information sessions and include the participation of departments and personnel officers.
- Mesh recruitment efforts with the overall employment process.

SOURCE: Iowa Department of Personnel (1994).

ENHANCING RECRUITMENT PROSPECTS: THE SEEKER'S PERSPECTIVE

The basics of job seeking may be widely known but are not necessarily commonly practiced.

- The first suggestion is to *know the recruitment process* and *know what resources are available*. Reading this chapter accomplishes the first aspect. Learning where recruitment occurs in a targeted profession includes consulting with practicing professionals who can identify the standard trade journals, knowing the newspapers that carry the appropriate advertisements, and exploring to find additional sources through the Internet and elsewhere. Developing personal contacts—networking—can make an enormous difference in discovering good prospects. See Exhibit 3.7 for a discussion of networking.

✂ EXHIBIT 3.7   Recruitment for Job Seekers: Networking

The mantra for any job seeker is networking, networking, networking. Professional acquaintances help job seekers by giving them advanced notice of upcoming openings and agency needs. They can also act as advocates for those they would like to see fill positions in their agency or department or serve as references who can vouch for the job experience, performance, and personal attributes of job seekers. It is well known that jobs may have been wired for others; these people often had a network of advocates working for them. Most professionals belong to several networks. On the national level, for example, you may belong to a national association in your specific line of work. Other networks are statewide or regional associations for more in-depth or frequent interaction with other professionals in your field. And still others are local groups of all types, formal and informal.

Networks are not built overnight. They are often the result of attending professional conferences for several years and building ties with similar professionals in other agencies. Such ties often are formed among those with similar professional interests, commitments, and values. Indeed, a basic, prerequisite skill for any professional is the ability to articulate these in a relatively concise and coherent fashion: People need to know what others stand for. How else do humans form enduring bonds?

It is unclear how large a professional network needs to be in order to be effective, but most professionals who feel part of a network would know about 30 to 60 people fairly well and probably know a couple hundred by face or name. How do people get to know so many people? First, most individuals know more people than they realize and even more people who could introduce them to others if only they were asked to do so. Second, a large network requires a commitment to go to venues such as conferences where people meet others. Attending a conference once may lead to knowing only a very few others, but attending for 4 years may lead to knowing half the attendees. Maintaining a professional network requires an investment of time to keep others informed of your professional self. Third, another great way to network is to volunteer. Often people at lower levels in the organizations know what they want to do, but their job or boss does not provide for that. Volunteering for a nonprofit is a great way to gain experience and meet people. Doing good, professional work outside the scope of employment might even get back to a current employer who then may consider the volunteer "management material" because of the extra commitment shown.

Having a strong network, and helping others in the network, brings numerous rewards. Networking is also helpful for other purposes such as to increase professional resources for doing one's job (getting advice, help with a problem). Through networking, job seekers also learn about employers: Are they really as good as they claim? Are others happy working there? Or is the department a snake pit, best to be avoided? People in a network often have information about these matters. Find out where people who have similar interests go. Join with them. It will be worth the cost.

- Next, *carefully screen jobs before applying*. Although it may cost little to send out 100 resumes, it is discouraging to hear nothing from so many, which is likely to happen with a shotgun approach. If one does not already bring some appropriate expertise or some special experience to a job, there is little likelihood of being a finalist. If necessary experience is lacking, there may be a need to either get more experience in an internship or take a lower-level position.

- *Make sure that all the information about the job is available*. Short newspaper and trade journal advertisements are generally reduced versions of the full announcements. Contact the appropriate source to see if there is additional information available.

- *Take the time to write a customized, flawless cover letter*. A letter that is simply "good" will not be noticed. A substantive one is highly focused, responding to the exact points covered in the job announcement. Although all the elements indicated in the announcement may be in the resume, be sure that they are spelled out in the sequence requested in the cover letter. Failure to do so indicates a lack of seriousness.

- *Write a carefully crafted résumé*. Certainly a candidate must not make things up, but be sure the résumé has all the relevant experience and that the presentation is professional in content. Résumé writing is an art, and those making distinctions at the reviewing end quickly become master critics. Many "how-to" guides are available. Generally, they discuss variations of two types of résumés (the chronological and the functional), as well as presentation styles. The résumé should always be reviewed by an expert for advice. Be sure to have a disk copy that can be altered for specific jobs. Use the term *curriculum vitae* (Latin for course of life) if the job has a research or academic component.

- *Do not spend much time either researching the organization or contacting the hiring authority in the early stages,* as you might for a business position. Public sector organizations tend to focus almost exclusively on the job qualifications initially, often to a fault. If called for an interview, then immediately do quick research on the organization via the Web and via information provided by the initial point of contact, friends, and any other sources.

Advancing From Job Seeking to Career Development

Midcareer professionals (including most completing MPA degrees) are beyond such basics. They have had one or more positions and perhaps have been a part of the hiring process themselves. Those retooling their skills and looking at entry positions are seeking jobs whose career potential is exceptional. They understand that the competition for good management and technical jobs is generally quite intense. For example, in one study of public sector hiring practices, 85% of the hiring managers reported that they use the quality of the candidate's application itself to a great or moderate extent in selection (U.S. MSPB, 2003). For the ambitious midcareer professional, by necessity, job seeking needs to evolve into carefully planned career development.

- In addition to passively hunting for positions, the midcareer professional needs to *envision the ideal position*. Such a process requires the candidate to distinguish critical job characteristics from those that are unimportant. It also helps the career developer focus on the most appropriate prospects.

- At the same time, individuals need to *assess their strengths and weaknesses candidly.* Of course, the initial question is rating one's own technical competence and experience. Technical competence and experience are only part of what employers seek, however (Hicks, 1998). Frequently, the single most desired characteristic is communication skills (written, oral, listening, persuasiveness). Does the candidate have basic computer literacy skills such as competence in word processing, spreadsheet programs, Internet usage, and the standard programs utilized in the field? Also high on employers' lists are team skills, facility with inter-personal relations, and the ability to be creative and innovative. Those seriously developing their career today need to make sure that they have not only developed these skills but also have examples to demonstrate competency.

- A rigorous self-assessment should lead one to *enhance the ability to demonstrate one's strengths.* One of the best ways is to develop a portfolio of materials, examples, and refer-ences. Copies of successful projects, job evaluations, photographs where visual representa-tions are useful, and letters of reference are examples of the types of materials to be collected and shared as needed.

- The self-assessment should also lead a career developer to *improve weaknesses.* Weaknesses can be improved by self-study and reading, by training inside or outside the organization, and by formal education. Strengthening weaknesses takes considerable self-discipline because it is easier to ignore or hide them; yet not addressing them damages both job prospects and performance. In a competitive market, lack of exceptional or unusual KSAs (knowledge, skills, and abilities) may be a weakness because basic qualifications are assumed. For instance, although police chiefs (and senior police commanders) in large municipal, county, and state law enforcement agencies may not technically be required to have master's degrees, management and executive training at the FBI and national command schools, and areas of extraordinary competence, the reality is that such jobs are inundated with exceptional candidates who do possess all these characteristics.

- Better jobs always include a substantial interview process in which the position is often won or lost. *There is no substitute for practice.* When practiced, difficult questions offer a chance to shine. When unpracticed, these questions are just tough and cause elimination.

- Finally, even before the actual recruitment process begins, those seeking better posi-tions must *be realistic, practical, and disciplined.* Preparation for the position should begin long before the recruitment process. The procedure itself is generally a protracted effort, requiring a long-term devotion of personal resources, numerous attempts, and self-discipline in the face of challenges and disappointments.

SUMMARY AND CONCLUSION

Finding talented workers for the public sector organization is a function involving five factors, of which the quality of the recruitment process per se is only one. Pay, labor pool size, organizational image, and job quality are also important. A first-class intake process can optimize or minimize these other factors substantially. Historically, recruitment has not been a strength in many organizations. Of the seven staffing steps, the first three constituting recruitment often have been the more passively administered, whereas those that constitute selection have been the more rigorously pursued. If competitive candidates are not in the pool, however, then the value of a neutral and precise selection process is limited.

What steps can be taken to ensure that appropriate applicants are attracted? First, quality recruitment is affected by planning. This involves asking and answering key questions, in advance of hiring, so that the recruitment and selection processes do not waste time and resources. Errors include not anticipating vacancies and labor shortages, not providing proper funding, not mitigating negative factors, and not effectively identifying agency strengths. Competent planning involves asking pertinent questions about the position, such as whether it (a) is needed at all, (b) should be hired from within, and (c) should be restructured, as well as who should be involved in the process and whether necessary forethought has been devoted to the authorization process. The announcement should always be written out fully: It is unwise to rush an advertisement to press before it is carefully crafted and endorsed. The final consideration is which recruitment methods to use in combination, with the goal of producing a customized applicant pool. Strategies include physical posting, electronic posting, newspapers, trade journals, custom mailings, other mass communication methods, personal contact, internship programs, head-hunting, and noncompetitive recruiting. The variety of methods and the need for a diverse workforce place a major responsibility on the line manager, who is increasingly responsible for organizing and implementing the recruitment process.

Clearly, the recruitment of high-quality human capital is an area that is particularly susceptible to reform for those agencies serious about being "world-class organizations." Traditional passivity must give way to more aggressive strategies in which quality candidates are actively sought. There must be an insistence that most recruitment pools include truly exceptional, rather than just acceptable, candidates. This implies that organizations must devote more resources and energy to recruitment as the Armed Forces did when converting from a draft to a volunteer system in the 1970s. The business example of senior managers going on annual recruiting trips is unusual in the public sector.[4] Finally, it is critical that unit supervisors and employees take seriously their increased responsibilities in decentralized recruiting systems, for they directly affect the quality of the future workforce.

KEY TERMS

Electronic posting
Head-hunting
Individual vs. "pool" recruitment
Inside (internal) vs. outside (external) recruitment
Internship recruitment
Job (position) announcements
Job posting
Labor market surveys

Mail recruitment
Noncompetitive recruitment
Personal contact recruitment
Proceduralism
Recruitment process
Recruitment strategies
Sham recruitment
Staffing

Class Exercises

1. In your area, identify some of the factors affecting recruitment, *excluding the recruitment process itself.* That is, discuss the labor pool, pay and benefits, images of public sector organizations, and perceptions of jobs in government as they affect local agencies' recruitment capacity.

2. How broadly should members of the hiring unit participate in the staffing process? Does the nature of the position (entry vs. midlevel, technical vs. administrative) make a difference? When should a hiring unit vote on the best candidate (such as is common for state university faculty positions)?

3. What examples have class members witnessed, if any, of shoddy or inappropriate recruitment practices? How should those practices be modified or improved?

4. What internships are available in the state, county, and cities in your area? Which are paid? How does one apply? Are there any fellowship programs?

5. What is the typical size of the applicant pool for jobs in your organization (be it a public agency, university, or nonprofit organization)? Typically, how many applicants are minimally qualified? Well qualified? Are job searches ever canceled for lack of qualified applicants?

6. Divide the Web sites listed on page 71 and in Exhibit 0.2 among you. Which ones are the most helpful in thinking about recruitment? Which provide the best links to other sites?

Team Exercises

7. To what extent would you emphasize future potential over current skills in each of the following jobs: office manager, police recruit, division director, and agency director (appointive but nominated by a committee)?

8. Find out from group members what recruitment strategies they have personally experienced, as well as their perceptions of those sources (posting vs. newspapers vs. the Internet).

9. Using the "25 in 10" technique (Exhibit 0.3), what would agencies have to do to attract the most outstanding university students?

10. Identify and discuss some paradoxes from your own recruitment experience.

Individual Assignments

11. Rate each of the following factors, by percentage, in terms of importance in recruiting a social service case management supervisor. The unit is predominantly white females, characterized by lower pay, low morale, and high turnover.

    KSAs _____%
    Motivation _____%
    Diversity _____%
    Loyalty _____%

12. In the previous example, if you believed that there was only one well-qualified internal candidate, the only white male in the unit, would you recruit internally or externally? What would your

goal be? How would you use recruitment to achieve that goal? How would you publicize that goal to the hiring unit?

13. Clip some job advertisements for public sector jobs from several sources, including the local paper. What are the variations in format and style that you notice? How might the advertisements be improved?

NOTES

1. See the discussion on rank-in-job versus rank-in-person systems in Chapter 5. Rank-in-job positions have been the most common and emphasize technical skills. Rank-in-person systems (such as the military) emphasize employee development potential.

2. In true patronage positions, elected officials can select whomever they please without review. These often include staff positions. Appointive positions such as department heads and their chief deputies arguably are not true patronage positions because they are reviewed by the appropriate legislative body for confirmation. Of course, recruitment in elective positions is generally through the democratic process of primaries.

3. Employment statistics indicate that government has generally been a leader in hiring a diverse workforce; however, meeting the requirements and documenting compliance with equal opportunity, affirmative action, age discrimination, and disability accommodation has added to "bureaucratic red tape."

4. Some examples do exist, of course. The U.S. General Accounting Office has assigned senior executives to do campus visits annually for years.

REFERENCES

Bailes, A. L. (2002, Spring). Who says it can't be done? Recruiting the next generation of public servants. *Business of Government*, 51–55. (www.businessofgovernment.org/pdfs/EBG_Spring02.pdf)

Breaugh, J. A., & Starke, M. (2000). Research on employee recruitment: So many studies, so many remaining questions. *Journal of Management*, *26*(3), 405–435.

Crewson, P. C. (1997, June). Are the best and the brightest fleeing public sector employment? *Public Productivity & Management Review, 20,* 368–378.

Ewoh, A. I. E., & Elliott, E. (1997). End of an era? Affirmative action and reaction in the 1990s. *Review of Public Personnel Administration, 17*(4), 38–51.

Feldman, D. C., & Klass, B. S. (2002). Internet job hunting: A field study of applicant experiences with on-line recruiting. *Human Resource Management, 41*(2), 175–192.

Galinsky, E., Friedman, D., & Hernandez, C. (1991). *The corporate reference guide to work-family programs.* New York: Families and Work Institute.

Gatehouse, R. D., Gowan, M. A., & Lautenschlager, G. J. (1993). Corporate image, recruitment image, and initial job choice decisions. *Academy of Management Journal, 36*(2), 414–428.

General Accounting Office. (2003). *Human capital: Opportunities to improve executive agencies' hiring processes.* Washington, DC: Author.

Gilbert, J. A. (2000). An empirical examination of resources in a diverse environment. *Public Personnel Management, 29*(2), 175–184.

Hamman, J. A., & Desai, U. (1995). Current issues and challenges in recruitment and selection. In S. Hays & R. Kearney (Eds.), *Public personnel administration: Problems and prospects* (3rd ed., pp. 89–104). Englewood Cliffs, NJ: Prentice Hall.

Hays, S. W. (1998). Staffing the bureaucracy: Employee recruitment and selection. In S. Condrey (Ed.), *Handbook of human resource management in government* (pp. 298–321). San Francisco: Jossey-Bass.

Hicks, L. (1998, September 27). Central Iowa labor crisis looms. *Des Moines Sunday Register,* pp. 1G–2G.

Iowa Department of Personnel. (1994). *Personnel management for managers and supervisors,* Section 4.20. Des Moines: Author.

Kanter, R. M. (1989, November/December). The new managerial work. *Harvard Business Review,* 85–92.

Kauffman, T. (2003, June 16). OPM expands hiring, early retirement authorities. *Federal Times.*

Kauffman, T. (2004, July 2). Job seekers favor government, OPM surveys find. *Federal Times.*

Kauffman, T., & Robb, K. (2003, July 14). Online recruitment: New system promises more choice, faster hires. *Federal Times.*

Keenoy, T., & Noon, M. (1992). Employment relations in the enterprise culture: Themes and issues. *Journal of Management Studies, 29*(5), 561–570.

Kost, J. M. (1996). *New approaches to public management: The case of Michigan.* Washington, DC: Brookings.

Lavigna, R. J. (1996). Innovations in recruiting and hiring: Attracting the best and brightest to Wisconsin state government. *Public Personnel Management, 25*(4), 423–437.

Lavigna, R. J. (2002). Best practices in public-sector human resources: Wisconsin state government. *Human Resource Management, 41*(3), 369–384.

Lewis, G. B., & Frank, S. A. (2002). Who wants to work for government? *Public Administration Review, 62*(4), 395–404.

Mercer, W. M. (1996). *Mercer work/life and diversity initiatives.* Retrieved January 15, 2004, from www.dcclifecare.com/mercer/mercer-c.html

Mintzberg, H. (1994, January/February). The fall and rise of strategic planning. *Harvard Business Review,* 107–114.

National Commission on the Public Service (Volcker Commission). (1989). *Leadership for America: Rebuilding the public service.* Washington, DC: Author.

National Commission on the State and Local Public Service. (1993). *Hard truths/tough choices: An agenda for state and local reform.* Albany, NY: Rockefeller Institute of Government.

Pearson, R. (2004, July 12). Technology helps state recruit the best. *Federal Times,* p. 21.

Redman, T., & Mathews, B. P. (1997). What do recruiters want in a public sector manager? *Public Personnel Management, 26*(2), 245–256.

Riccucci, N. M. (1997). The legal status of affirmative action. *Review of Public Personnel Administration, 17*(4), 22–37.

Rivenbark, L. (1998, August 17). Scholar hiring investigated: Program should target Blacks and Hispanics, OPM says. *Federal Times,* p. 5.

Rukeyser, W. (1996, January 18). *Relocation brings anxiety to two-career families.* Retrieved January 15, 2004, from www.cnnfn.com/mymoney/9601/18/relocation/index.html

Rynes, S. L. (1993). When recruitment fails to attract: Individual expectations meet organizational realities in recruitment. In H. Schuler, J. L. Farr, & M. Smith (Eds.), *Personnel selection and assessment: Individual and organizational perspectives* (pp. 27–40). Hillsdale, NJ: Lawrence Erlbaum.

Slack, J. D. (1997). From affirmative action to full spectrum diversity in the American workplace. *Review of Public Personnel Administration, 17*(4), 75–88.

Smith, M. (2000, March). Innovative personnel recruitment/changing workforce demographics. *IPMA News,* pp. 12–14.

Thaler-Carter, R. E. (2001, June). Diversify your recruitment advertising. *HRMagazine,* 92–100.

Trice, E. (1999, June). Timely hiring: Making your agency a best practice. *IPMA News,* pp. 10–11.

U.S. Merit Systems Protection Board. (1988). *Attracting quality graduates to the federal government: A view of college recruiting.* Washington, DC: Author.

U.S. Merit Systems Protection Board. (1997). *Achieving a representative federal workforce: Addressing the barriers to Hispanic participation.* Washington, DC: Author.

U.S. Merit Systems Protection Board. (2000). *Competing for federal jobs: Job search experiences of new hires.* Washington, DC: Author.

U.S. Merit Systems Protection Board. (2001). *Attracting quality graduates to the federal government: A view of college recruiting.* Washington, DC: Author.

U.S. Merit Systems Protection Board. (2003). *Help wanted: A review of federal vacancy announcements.* Washington, DC: Author.

Zeidner, R. (2001, October 1). Do-it-yourself hiring process. *Federal Times.*

4

SELECTION

From Civil Service Commissions to Decentralized Decision Making

First-rate people hire first-rate people; second-rate people hire third-rate people.

—Leo Rosten

After studying this chapter, you should be able to

- Recognize and seek to resolve paradoxical dimensions in the selection process
- Articulate the different philosophical bases of selection
- Understand the history of civil service commissions and how they continue to affect thinking in employee selection despite their reduced roles
- Distinguish six historical eras of selection
- Discuss the "ideal" stages of the selection process and current trends to make it more flexible and decentralized
- Choose appropriate examination methods ("tests") for different selection stages and job search needs
- Understand the different types of validity related to selection processes
- Avoid illegal questions in the interview and reference check process
- Determine who will make hiring decisions and how they will be made and documented

Selection technically starts when applications have been received. Which of the applicants will be chosen, by what process, and by whom? Certainly the public sector is far stronger for having outgrown the excesses of 19th century patronage, which permeated jobs at all levels of government and resulted in widespread corruption and graft such as vote racketeering and kickbacks (Mosher, 1982). During the 20th century, merit principles replaced patronage as the most common, but by no means the sole, selection criteria. Today, patronage excesses are relatively rare—less common than in the private sector—and they constitute little problem for the bulk of positions in government (a position that has been strengthened in modern Supreme

Court cases such as *Branti v. Finkel,* 1980; *Elrod v. Burns,* 1976; and *Rutan v. Republican Party of Illinois,* 1990).[1]

The paradox is that political appointment—a form of patronage—is the primary selection method for most senior government positions. Appointees are often selected as much based on party and personal affiliations as on technical merit. The U.S. president selects not only all the agency and department heads but thousands of second- and third-layer executives as well, including up to 10% of the Senior Executive Service. Governors generally have hundreds of appointive positions in their control. "Strong" mayors and county boards of supervisors also generally have extensive appointive responsibilities that lend themselves to patronage. Nor is it unheard of for high appointees and elected officials to provide "character references" wherein career supervisors are "encouraged" to hire campaign workers and friends for low-level positions. This paradox—merit systems run by dilettantes—often contributes to cynicism by career employees who view political appointees as transitory, poorly trained, and inexperienced. Without that occasional fresh administrative leadership, however, the public service might become unresponsive, rigid, and self-serving.

A second irony is that although public sector selection is primarily an open application of merit principles, selection for many positions is determined largely by **seniority**. For example, agency policy or union contracts often require a strict ordering in selection rights that results in most of the better jobs being labeled "promotional" and therefore not available to "outside" candidates. It is common for many entry-level and nearly all midlevel vacancies to be filled internally. For example, the U.S. Merit Systems Protection Board (U.S. MSPB) reported that supervisors filled vacancies with current agency personnel 46% of the time, with other federal employees 25% of the time, and only 29% of the time did they select from outside the government (2001a).

Seniority does not necessarily conflict with merit, but it may limit its field of application. These two paradoxes—patronage appointments (both legal and legally dubious) and seniority selection—can mean that only entry-level positions (and sometimes not even those) tend to be selected on strict merit.

A third paradox is that despite the success of rigorous methods for ensuring merit principles (and sustaining seniority practices as well), the trend is to introduce more flexibility in, and localized determination of, the hiring process (Ingraham, Selden, & Moynihan, 2000). Predictions about the challenges of finding good public sector employees in the beginning of the 1990s have largely come true (Lane & Wolf, 1990); for instance, in 1999 the U.S. Air Force for the first time in its history started advertising for recruits and in 2000 added substantial hiring bonuses. Even as government becomes increasingly interested in a competency-based hiring/promotional model, it is more willing to expand the hiring discretion of agencies and their managers. Such discretion can also mean that they may abuse it out of haste or ignorance (U.S. MSPB, 1998) and/or engage in illegal practices (Condrey & Maranto, 2001).

Although the selection process has always been a significant role for managers and supervisors, that role has taken on far greater responsibility with the dramatic downsizing of human resource departments throughout government. For example, the Office of Personnel Management (OPM) was downsized by over 50% as it was being reinvented in the 1990s (U.S. MSPB, 2001b). Therefore, today it is important to recognize that human resource management skills are critical generalist competencies for *all* managers.

This chapter begins with a broad discussion of the criteria used in a selection process and how different principles have taken precedence in civil service positions in various historical eras. The majority of the chapter focuses on prominent technical aspects of selection related to application review, testing, interviewing, reference checks, the hiring decision, and posthiring issues. It concludes by reaffirming that this important human resource function is as easy to understand as it is difficult to carry out. Predicting human behavior, a goal in the selection process, is no easy task, as illustrated by the fact that former professional basketball superstar Michael Jordan was cut from his high school basketball team because he lacked potential.

THE BASES AND ORIGIN OF SELECTION

Selection Criteria

Selection is arguably the most momentous, politically sensitive aspect of human resource activities (Schuler, Farr, & Smith, 1993). Indeed, historical eras of human resource management are largely defined by the underlying philosophy of selection. There are essentially six possible criteria that can be used, separately or in combination, to provide the basis for the decision: electoral popularity, social class, patronage, merit, seniority, and representativeness. All except for social class are explicitly used in various arenas of the public sector. Although the terms *civil service* and *merit* are often used as synonyms, in common practice *civil service* is a broader term because it embraces elements of seniority and representativeness as well as merit.

Electoral Popularity

Electoral popularity is the basis of representative democracy. Citizens vote for those who they think will do or are doing a good job. What types of positions are reserved for the electoral popularity model? First and foremost, they are policy-making jobs that craft laws and the broad administrative missions of national, state, and local governments. Such officials occupy the legislative bodies at all levels of government—Congress, state legislatures, county boards of supervisors, city councils, and boards of townships, school districts, and other special units. To a substantially lesser degree, but still common, is the election of judicial personnel—judges, state attorneys general, county attorneys, and local justices of the peace are examples. Of course, elected executives such as presidents, governors, and mayors are significant and visible in the American democratic system. Although they share a policy role with legislators, they also have a critical administrative role in managing the agencies and departments of government. It should be noted, however, that some were intended to be primarily administrative and are so to this day (e.g., state level secretaries of state, education, and treasury, and county level sheriffs, treasurers, clerks of court, auditors, and recorders). For instance, in small jurisdictions the full-time elected official may come to the counter to assist in busy periods. Of course, the bulk of all elected officials serve on school boards and town councils with little or no pay. The strength of the electoral selection philosophy is its support of democratic theory through popular involvement as well as popular accountability. The limits of this strategy are also clear: Voters have natural limitations of knowledge, time, and interest. As the number of those who run for election increases and as the issues involved become more technical and complex, the attention of citizens becomes diluted and turnout declines. The highly fragmented structure of most county governments is a prime example of the accountability problem.

Social Class

Social class selection, the antithesis of democratic selection, is generally illegal as an explicit selection philosophy in the United States. In many societies, however, the administrative classes were "bred" so that they would have the requisite education to fulfill administrative functions. This remains evident in many European democracies and is one of the distinctive features of some rank-based systems (discussed in Chapter 5). In the United States during the Federalist period, education was more limited, and a strong upper- and upper-middle-class bias existed in administrative roles. In contemporary advanced democracies, with their high literacy rates and widespread access to universities, this philosophical base has limited virtue, although it is often argued by minorities and women that the dominant culture still subtly guides the selection process itself. For example, prestigious educational institutions sometimes become proxies for social class, with classic cases being the State Department's historical preference for select eastern institutions at the federal level and state governments giving preference to their flagship university at that level.

Patronage

Patronage applies to a broad class of selection decisions in which a single person is responsible for designating officials or employees without a requirement for a formalized application process. Such appointments may or may not be subject to a confirmation process. As a process, it tends to have a negative connotation because it assumes that loyalty will be to the patron or person making the selection rather than to the government at large. This is not always true, however, and it sometimes is not a negative feature. Supreme Court justices are often picked because of their political leanings and personal connections to presidents, yet they sometimes become remarkably independent. A different case is the political adviser who is hired on the public payroll by a political executive for personal loyalty and party-based affinity but of whom nothing more or less would be expected. Ultimately, those using such appointments employ three criteria: political loyalty, personal acquaintance, and technical competence or merit. In the ideal case for a political executive, the pool of possible candidates can be narrowed to those who are of the same party or have the same political preferences. The executive can identify people he or she has known or worked with in the past and then select people who are still highly experienced in the targeted area and competent for the duties to be assigned.

Problems occur when the first two principles are met but the third is not. For instance, well-connected policy generalists are sometimes installed as directors of large agencies when they lack either the in-depth policy background or the administrative experience to cope with their new responsibilities (e.g., a former Playboy bunny, with no relevant expertise, was appointed to run a large agency in a southern state in the late 1990s). To reduce the political and personal nature of many executive appointments at the city and county levels, professional manager systems have been installed so that technical merit rather than patronage becomes the primary factor for department heads.

Merit

Merit-based systems emphasize technical qualifications using processes that analyze job competencies and require open application procedures.[2] These systems require "tests," but they may consist of an education and experience review, performance evaluations, and/or licensure as well as written tests. **Merit selection** is the primary philosophy for civil service systems that dominate nonexecutive employment. The strengths of merit selection are its fairness to candidates, its availability to scrutiny, and its assurance of minimum competencies and qualifications. It also fits well with notions of democratic access and accountability.

Merit does not, however, always live up to its promise: Selection is often so mechanical and technical that the best candidates never apply, diversity of experience is inhibited, there is an excessive emphasis on tangible skills over future potential, and the time required to process becomes onerous. As the discussion here will highlight, the pursuit of precise and valid indicators of merit is challenging when considering what tests to use and how much weight to give to them. This has led to a decrease in some jurisdictions in the number of "true" merit positions in which a formal competitive process is required. For example, the state of Maryland moved 1,400 management positions from merit to "noncompetitive" and changed their termination rights from "just cause" to "for any reason" (see Exhibit 4.1). Likewise, the entire state middle management corps in Florida was also converted in 2001.

Seniority

Seniority is also a crucial selection principle in civil service systems. Philosophically, it asserts that those already employed in the agency (a) have already been through the merit process once, (b) have been screened in probationary periods and evaluation processes, and (c) have superior organizational insight and loyalty because of their employment. Seniority systems therefore either limit job searches to internal candidates or give internal candidates substantial advantages in the process, such as points for years of service or opportunities to fill positions prior to advertisement outside the agency. The effects are that civil service employment occurs primarily in selected entry positions and that external hiring is unusual at the supervisory level and above. This is particularly noticeable in highly unionized environments and paramilitary occupations such as public safety.

Seniority systems do ensure that organizations provide a sense of loyalty to their staff as well as career development paths; however, such systems also tend to lock employees into a single governmental system (often just their own division and unit) for career growth. Organizationally, they can lead to "inbreeding" and "groupthink," and they can prevent fresh management insights, which are a prime motivation for lateral hiring (see Edwards & Morrison, 1994, for an example of selection issues in Navy officer candidates and promotion). Even more insidious is that strong seniority systems can provide a milieu in which the "Peter principle" operates (people are promoted until they achieve a position in which they are incompetent; Peter & Hull, 1969).

Representativeness

The final principle of selection is **representativeness**, which can be interpreted in numerous ways such as by geography, social class, gender, racial/ethnic groups, prior military service, and disability. The Constitution supports geography in electoral issues through its federal system. Andrew Jackson and his supporters felt that too many federal jobs went to easterners and the social elite, and they therefore emphasized those from western states (of that day) and from less privileged classes. A contemporary debate is selection (or more generally nonselection) based on sexual orientation. Because veterans are taken out of the labor

---

✖ **EXHIBIT 4.1**   Personnel Reform in Maryland

In 1996, the Maryland General Assembly passed legislation that resulted in a restructuring of the State Government Management System. Prior to that time, the majority of positions were covered by the classified service merit system. The law diminished the number of those covered by the classified service and established four services for employees, as follows:

Skilled service: Positions are competitively selected, and termination must be for just cause. There are currently approximately 37,000 positions in the skilled service, most of which were previously in the classified service.

Professional service: Positions are competitively selected, and termination must be for just cause. These require a professional license or an advanced degree. There are some 4,500 positions in the professional service, most of which were previously in the classified service.

Management service: Positions are selected noncompetitively, and termination may be for any reason not prohibited by law. They must have direct responsibility for management of a program, including responsibility for personnel and financial resources. There are roughly 1,900 positions in the management service, most of which were previously in the classified service.

Executive service: Positions are selected noncompetitively, and employees may be terminated for any reason not prohibited by law. These include cabinet secretaries, deputy cabinet secretaries, assistant secretaries, and other officials of equivalent rank. There are approximately 190 executive service employees. These positions worked under similar nonmerit rules prior to reform.

Another category is strictly patronage based.

Special appointments: Positions are noncompetitively selected, and termination may be for any reason not prohibited by law. These include jobs that have a direct reporting relationship to an employee in the executive service or that have substantial responsibility for developing and recommending high-level agency policies. The majority of these 4,700 positions were in the unclassified service and did not have merit protection.

The impact of the new personnel reform changes, especially in relationship to the management service, has yet to be determined because there has not been a change in political parties or the state's fiscal condition since the legislation passed.

SOURCE: Martin Smith (personal communication), Personnel Services Administration, Maryland Department of Health and Mental Hygiene.

---

force and might have a liability in seeking employment upon leaving the military, they commonly receive a preference in civil service systems. **Veterans' points** are used by the federal government (Veteran's Preference Act of 1944) and are still common in many states. Typically, veterans serving during wars are eligible for extra points in ratings systems, and wounded veterans may be eligible for additional points.

In the last half century, there has been an emphasis on gender and racial representativeness, as evidenced by military integration (both African Americans and women), equal opportunity legislation, affirmative action plans, and, more recently, diversity programs. Generally speaking, affirmative action tries to encourage women and minorities to seek positions for which they are qualified, especially where the targeted rate of employment is low. *Ceteris paribus*—"all things being equal"—the targeted groups should get positions in areas of underrepresentation. That is to say, affirmative action generally has upheld merit as the premier value but has given representativeness a strong second-place consideration when merit principles are followed. In terms of implementation, affirmative action programs also require extensive analysis of **disparate impact** on women and minorities so that applicant pools can be restructured where underrepresentation appears to be a problem. Although many numerically based goal systems are being adjusted or phased out, chronic underrepresentation of some groups remains an important and legitimate consideration, especially in many formerly male- and white-dominated organizations where occupational segregation has merely given way to tokenism. Representativeness remains a legally appropriate consideration on a case-by-case basis as long as there is equivalent merit and documented imbalance. In more recent diversity programs, numerical representativeness has given way to an emphasis on a supportive environment that welcomes employment of different groups and embraces their heterogeneity.

The History of Selection: Six Eras

Selection philosophies—except for elected positions—have varied over time (Mosher, 1982; Van Riper, 1958); note that the later timeframes overlap.

Administration by Gentility: 1789–1829

From President Washington up to President Jackson, patronage (appointment based on connections and political views) was the primary system for selection but was muted by the ethic of "fitness of character" and genteel education (social class). President Washington was a strong force in shaping a tradition that balanced competence and political neutrality. Although he avoided appointing those openly hostile to his political views, he was careful in selecting from among all the states and from a range of political perspectives. He generally gave preference to those of education—hence class—although he only appointed those known for integrity and public spirit. He also did sometimes give preference to Revolutionary War military officers. With the evolution of political parties, Jefferson was faced with replacing enough Federalists to ensure responsiveness to his Democratic Republican Party. During the presidencies of Madison, Monroe, and John Quincy Adams, the ethic of fitness of character and political neutrality generally held sway but increasingly came under pressure as the party ruling Congress urged for more political determination of administrative posts at all levels of government.

Selection by Spoils: 1829–1883

Andrew Jackson insisted on better representation of all social classes and westerners. He also thought that rotation of government positions was healthy. He advocated keeping government jobs as simple as possible so that those with modest education could be eligible. He argued that greater political responsiveness would reduce corruption and complacency. Although he replaced only 20% of the federal workforce (a proportion not substantially greater than that replaced by Jefferson) and was himself not really an advocate of a **spoils system** (appointment of jobs as spoils of victory to those active in the victorious campaign—despite lack of qualifications), he did create the philosophical basis for widespread abuses in the following decades (Van Riper, 1958, p. 42).

Several problems with a solely patronage-based civil service became increasingly common over the next 40 years. First, appointments were often assigned with little regard for experience, knowledge, or abilities. Second, inequities in pay were frequent; compensation was as much a function of connection to a political patron as to specific job responsibilities. Third, it became common to require government workers to campaign for the reelection of politicians in office and to relinquish a portion of their pay to the party in power. Furthermore, spoils appointments often included jobs for those who did not work full-time (or at all), despite receiving a paycheck.

The rampant corruption of the patronage period spawned a public-driven government reform movement after the Civil War that lasted nearly 50 years. One of the early, if brief, successes was during the administration of President Grant, who signed a bill authorizing competitive examinations for some federal positions. It lapsed only 2 years later for lack of funding because of congressional fears of curbs on patronage opportunities. Many cities that had rampant political patronage and corruption saw the development of civil service reform associations at the municipal level. The pressure continued to build as governmental incompetence and abuse became more blatant and government responsibilities expanded.

Technical Merit Systems: 1883–1912

The **Pendleton Act** of 1883 signaled a new era in personnel management, although it was more than 50 years before the system evolved into one that was comprehensive in the federal government, widely adopted across other levels of government, and was generally rigorously applied. Although the act was prompted by the assassination of President Garfield by a disappointed job seeker in 1881, it responded to the growing perception that the functions of government had become too large, complex, and important to be handled entirely by a patronage system. The new system incorporated the following:

- Open, competitive examinations based on technical qualifications
- Lists of those eligible or "certified" to the hiring authority
- Rules against politicians intervening in civil service selection, coercing civil servants to work in campaigns, or requiring employees to provide kickbacks for civil service employment
- An independent **Civil Service Commission**, which administered practical competitive examinations (essentially a central job register) and acted as a judicial review board for abuses

This new model required bipartisan and independent selection of employees by a commission for covered (or civil service) positions, that is, those over which the commission had jurisdiction. Initially only 10% of federal employees were covered (Van Riper, 1958). The proportion has gradually increased to around 48% in 1900. By 2000, more than 90% were included in civil service positions, broadly construed.

As Merit Expands, So Do Employee Rights and Seniority: 1912–1978

Although a few city and state governments were quick to replicate the new reform model, the increase in civil service systems was slow. To facilitate acceptance of civil service models, the federal government conditioned some financial assistance to other levels of government on the use of merit-based employment systems. Especially effective was the Social Security Act of 1935. Other programs continued this requirement, which led to the institution of at least partial or modified civil service systems in all the states, most municipalities, and many counties. The depoliticization of the personnel process was further enhanced by the Hatch Act of 1939 (amended and relaxed in 1993), strongly prohibiting most political activity by federal workers. Subsequently, "baby" Hatch Acts, modeled on the federal legislation, were enacted by most states.

As civil service systems grew in number and size, so too did employee rights. Although the Pendleton Act prohibited political removals at the federal level, it was frequently circumvented. Through an executive order, President McKinley prohibited removal from the competitive service except for just cause and for reasons given in writing. Further, the person being removed had to have the basic due process right to respond in writing. In 1912, this important principle and process was placed into permanent legislation in the Lloyd-LaFollette Act.

Once in the system and protected from political and arbitrary firing, employee seniority was substantially enhanced. As the legal footing of the seniority principle grew, fewer jobs would be available to those outside the service, and those inside the service would have greater access to promotional selections. With the growth of public sector unions starting in the 1950s, some areas such as public safety frequently eliminated lateral selection from outside the agency.

Expansion of Access: 1964–1990

The era of equal opportunity, which began in the early 1960s, did not replace merit but modified its execution and made hiring more complicated (Chapter 2). The Civil Rights Act of 1964 addressed discrimination based on race, color, religion, gender, or national origin. The Equal Employment Opportunity Act of 1972 expanded these rights to state and local governments and promoted equal employment opportunity through affirmative action. Other major applicant and employee rights that were enhanced during this period were age (1967 and 1974) and disability (1973) discrimination for federal employees. At the federal level, the 1978 Civil Service Reform Act established the "80%" rule to provide selection "floors" for protected classes. That is, selection processes should not result in qualification rates of protected groups that are less than 80% of the highest group.

The burst of attention to representativeness in the 1960s and 70s, symbolized by widespread use of affirmative action programs to correct imbalances, certainly continued into the 1980s as an organizational way of life. Perhaps the final great push for representation was the American With Disabilities Act of 1990 in which reasonable accommodations were required in the selection process for those with allowable disabilities.

The tide turned in the 1990s when bellwether legal cases generally required more tailored and narrowly defined remedies for representational problems. For example, race norming was disallowed in 1991 (see Chapter 2). Quotas have always been illegal except when court-ordered in response to egregious cases. Although equal opportunity continued to be strongly encouraged, it was increasingly through diversity programs rather than affirmative action.

Contemporary Selection Trends: 1978-Present

The potential excesses of the civil service system started to emerge as early as the 1930s when the administration of Franklin Delano Roosevelt toyed with the idea of major civil service reform. Complaints included the following:

- rigidity (e.g., restricting interviews and selection to three top candidates based on technical qualifications)
- proceduralism (e.g., difficulties in hiring rapidly in an applicant's market)
- isolation from the executive branch (e.g., independent centralized testing agencies apart from the hiring agencies)
- inadequate accountability (e.g., difficulties in severing poor performing employees)

Contemporary trends have emphasized flexibility, speed, integration of the selection function with other management responsibilities, and increased employee accountability for productivity. At the federal level, the CSRA of 1978 reintegrated selection functions into the executive branch through the OPM. It also provided for more managerial latitude. Initially personnel responsibilities were tightly held by OPM, but the reinventing government initiative begun in 1992 probably had a greater effect on OPM than any other agency. By 1996, OPM was required to decentralize most of its responsibilities to other agencies ("delegated examination authority"). Civil service commissions today more commonly function as policy and review boards (e.g., the U.S. Merit Systems Protection Board), although in some jurisdictions even these responsibilities have passed to the agencies.

In an important trend, a growing number of agencies or bureaus in agencies were able to opt out of the traditional ("competitive") civil service system. This parallel system (the "excepted service" or noncompetitive service) is still required to follow the broad traditions of merit: notification of open positions, reliance on technical merit through minimum established standards, and due process for employees. It allows, however, far more management flexibility and control over selection and employee appraisal. The largest example of an entirely excepted service agency is the Department of Homeland Security. One third to one half of all federal new hires are through excepted service provisions (U.S. Government Accounting Office [U.S. GAO], 2003).

As expected at the state and local level, the move to more flexible, nimble, integrated, and accountable civil service systems mirrored the federal experience, but this trend was far from uniform. Many progressive cities such as Phoenix and Madison, Wisconsin, never suffered the same degree of rigidity and were quick to enhance managerial rationality. Some cities and counties that had traditionally allowed more managerial and political responsiveness found themselves in vogue. Most states have followed the federal pattern. States such as Maryland, Georgia, and Florida, however, have been more radical in their reform efforts (Condrey & Maranto, 2001), whereas some others have been slow to follow contemporary trends.

The long-time primary values of civil service systems (strict technical merit and seniority seem to have experienced countervailing trends) are managerial accountability and flexibility. States such as Georgia, Florida, and South Carolina have abolished or weakened their civil service systems (see Exhibit 5.3 on Georgia in the next chapter). The use of **temporary employees** (those without contracts, tenure rights, and usually without benefits) rose in significance during the 1990s (Hays & Kearney, 1999), but because the Internal Revenue Service insisted that long-term, temporary employees are de facto regular employees ("permatemps"), a new tendency is the use of **term employees.** For example, the federal government is making widespread use of term appointments for 2 to 4 years, with a contract and benefits but without tenure rights. Although such practices allow public organizations considerable flexibility, they undermine employee security and increase opportunities for politicization of the civil service.

Selection, then, is potentially shared by three areas: a civil service commission, a human resources department, and the hiring department. Up through the 1970s, the most common model was for the civil service commission to "test" and provide formal review, the personnel department to provide technical assistance such as benefits and salary information, and the hiring department to initiate actions for hiring and to make final selections from short lists of **certified** applicants. In the 1980s, the most common model was for personnel departments to provide **certified lists** to hiring units and for the civil service commission to act as administrative judge in disputed cases. By the end of the 1990s, an increasingly common model was for hiring departments to recruit and select applicants directly, following merit principles but having wider discretion in testing practices and interview choices. Human resource departments then provided technical assistance and oversight of legal compliance issues and statistical records, as well as administrative review when necessary. The new model has some definite strengths: greater control and ownership by hiring agencies, greater flexibility, and less perceived red tape by candidates, who often are interested in specific agencies and positions. Inevitably, there are also weaknesses: increased fragmentation of selection practices and less use of economies of scale, less consistency, and more potential for abuse of discretion.

In sum, the eras are defined by their emphasis and deemphasis of values related to selection: social class, patronage (political responsiveness), merit (technical qualifications, performance criteria), seniority (employee protections and expanded privileges), and representativeness. Although all the values (except social class) have been explicit in each of the eras, some values have been emphasized at the expense of others. Below is a rough gauge of the dominant values in each period:

- Administration by gentility: political responsiveness, social class, technical qualifications (fitness of character and education)
- Selection by spoils: political responsiveness, performance (though impressionistically defined and evaluated), representativeness
- Early technical merit: technical qualifications
- Expanded merit: technical qualifications, employee protections, and expanded seniority
- Expansion of access: representativeness via affirmative action (superimposed on technical qualifications and seniority)
- Contemporary trends: performance criteria (flexibility in hiring, employee accountability), representativeness via diversity

SELECTION: FOUR SCREENING PHASES

Selection processes can be divided into four phases of screening, although sometimes these phases are combined for convenience or necessity.

In phase one, the procedure emphasizes discriminating among the qualified and the unqualified. Applicant pools typically have a substantial number of individuals who do not meet basic qualifications and whose applications can be put aside. In order to eliminate candidates, the initial qualifications need to be carefully identified, both from the general job description, as well as those special needs identified for the position in the job posting. Did the applicant provide a complete packet in the required timeline? Does the person have the required education, job-related experience, licensing, test score (for example, of the 25 original applicants for a position, five may have incomplete applications, three may have insufficient educational background, and another half dozen may not have the required experience). Sometimes the screening at this point is done by staff.

In phase two, the most highly qualified candidates are identified. If the initial screening ranked all candidates, it is a simple matter to choose those with the highest scores. In **unassembled tests,** candidates are only ranked on those items that can be submitted by mail—applications, resumes, written work samples, letters of reference, and possibly self-reported assessments. In **assembled tests,** applicants are required to come to a central location or locations to take general aptitude tests or provide live work samples. The idea is to narrow the pool to a number that is practical to interview or test in-depth. In the example, 11 candidates were qualified in phase one, but in phase two, 5 are identified to interview. Until one is chosen and has accepted the position, the others are not barred from later consideration.

In phase three, the finalists are screened in person. Invariably, the interview is the centerpiece of this process. Of course, when the rule of three applies, the finalists are limited to the top three candidates. In some cases, however, the finalists may be numerous, especially when multiple openings exist, or in unusual cases may be limited to one or two clearly exceptional candidates. This is also a good time to require live samples of work and to perform reference checks. This phase results in a single candidate to offer the position to, as well as backup applicants should the individual turn down the offer.

Phase four confirms the qualifications and ability of the candidate after the offer. Many offers are conditional on successful drug tests, medical exams, or even background checks. This phase may also include the first period of employment in which the candidate has probationary status and can be terminated without cause. This is especially apparent in cases where extensive or rigorous schooling is required and new hires "wash out."

The four-phased approach allows for far better review of applicants and less waste of time of unselected candidates and thus represents the selection process ideal. However, it is also more time-consuming for reviewers and may be too slow for the applicant pool or costly for the agency. Therefore, a reduced or consolidated selection process may be appropriate in many cases such as the hiring of term employees or entry-level staff workers, or in the event of an emergency situation.

INITIAL REVIEWING AND TESTING

Critical for all review and test procedures is their relationship to job-related competencies (Arvey & Sackett, 1993). How does the procedure specifically relate to the essential job functions? On one hand, it is important to get good indicators of skills and likely performance. On the other, it is neither appropriate nor legal to pile on job requirements as a screening mechanism. Because of affirmative action cases, courts have insisted that all hiring practices, especially written tests, have verifiable connections to *core* responsibilities and be appropriate predictors of success, that is, that they be "valid" (see Exhibit 4.2 for a discussion of **test validity**). It is not possible to provide high levels of validity without job analysis, a topic that is covered in the next chapter.

✖ EXHIBIT 4.2   Three Types of Test Validity

The *Uniform Guidelines on Employee Selection Procedures* (Equal Employment Opportunity Commission, 1978) established three acceptable validation strategies: content, construct, and criterion. Because of concerns about disparate impact on minorities and women in the 1970s and 1980s, and about applicants with disabilities in the 1990s, test validation has become an important concern in the selection process. For example, the guidelines assert that employers should regularly validate all selection procedures. Where possible, valid selection procedures having less adverse impact on underrepresented groups should be used over those that have more adverse impact. Finally, employers should keep records of all those who applied and were accepted in order to ascertain whether adverse impact occurs, which is generally defined as a selection rate of less than 80% of the group with the highest selection rate.

   Content validity requires demonstrating a direct relationship of the test to actual job duties or responsibilities. It is generally the easiest to verify and is the most common validation procedure (Arvey & Faley, 1988). Validity is documented through conducting a thorough job analysis of the position and connecting those elements to concrete items in the test. Examples are typing tests for clerical positions; written tests that assess specific knowledge needed, such as mathematical skills customarily used by accountants; and actual work samples such as error analysis of social work cases for supervisory positions. A subsequent issue to content validity is proportionality; for example, a typing test is appropriate for a clerical position but is only a portion of the content that is important in the position. Content validity is easiest to conduct on jobs with definable and measurable skills requiring concrete behaviors and knowledge. It is readily customized to individual positions; however, it is relatively difficult to conduct with complex jobs involving extensive discretion, abstraction, and interpersonal skills as well as identifying types of people more innately suited to certain types of work.

   Criterion validity involves correlating high test scores (the predictor) with good job performance (the criterion) by those taking the test. For example, perhaps the applicants need few job skills and knowledge prior to employment because subsequent training will provide that information (and therefore content validation is inappropriate). How does one predict and select those who will be most suitable? This is the case in entry-level public safety and corrections positions. Criterion validity generally examines aptitudes or cognitive skills for learning and performing well in a given job environment—for example, the aptitude to learn language, remember key data, or use logical reasoning.

   The problems with demonstrating this type of predictive ability are twofold. First, how can a sample be obtained with both high and low scorers, given that the agency wants to hire only high scorers? Second, how can it be known that performance ratings are accurate, given that they are often said to be of low reliability and validity (see Chapter 9)? Documenting criterion-related validity that is predictive generally requires experimental designs that are costly and prone to methodological challenges.

   A more common strategy to prove criterion validity is to use a concurrent approach (Barrett, Phillips, & Alexander, 1981). That is, incumbent employees (rather than applicants) are tested to demonstrate a statistical relationship between high scorers and high performers. Again, the quality of performance ratings becomes a significant hurdle to overcome. Because criterion validation is difficult and expensive, it is generally used only for high-volume, entry-level positions or for system-wide generic tests that look at clusters of jobs using related skills such as math, language, spatial ability, and abstract thinking. For example, the federal government formerly used six different general-entry, administrative tests (Administrative Careers With America), such as the health-safety-environment exam, for occupational clusters. It is also used for management tests that employ

(Continued)

(Continued)

generalized assessment centers because concrete skills are difficult to define. The job analysis should determine what general types of skills and aptitudes are necessary for success, and the assessment center should provide opportunities to look for these generalized abilities.

Construct validity documents the relationship of select abstract personal traits and characteristics (such as intelligence, integrity, creativity, aggressiveness, industriousness, and anxiety) to job performance. Tests with high construct validity accurately predict future job performance by examining the characteristics of successful job incumbents and judging whether applicants have those characteristics (Day & Silverman, 1989). Construct validation is used for psychological tests that screen candidates based on trait/attitude profiles. Despite the concerns with construct validity expressed in the Uniform Federal Guidelines and by some researchers (Cortina, Doherty, Schmitt, Kaufman, & Smith, 1992) because of the tenuous connection between personal traits and job performance, tests relying on construct validity are selectively used in some areas such as law enforcement (Johnson & Hogan, 1981; Wiesen, Abrams, & McAttee, 1990) for identifying traits like aggressiveness and hostility. There is also an increase in testing for integrity. Testing for the "big five" personality dimensions (extraversion, emotional stability, agreeableness, conscientiousness, and openness to experience) has been shown to have validity in some occupations (Barrick & Mount, 1991; McCrae & Costa, 1987).

Documenting validity ensures that tests are job related and legally nondiscriminatory. It should not deter organizations from trying to gather as much information as possible about candidates in their efforts in appraising the best qualified and the most likely to succeed. Well-constructed tests can provide an excellent method of identifying and eliminating those without minimum competencies or weak in aptitude or predisposition so that other methods can focus on selecting the best qualified from a smaller pool. It may be a mistake for organizations not to use tests simply because of a disinclination to document test validity. Various types of data help provide different perspectives about job suitability. In fact, when integrated with education and experience evaluations, interviews, and reference checks so that a broad "basket" of indicators is established, content-, criterion-, and construct-based tests can provide a solid base of information on which to make selections.

A wide variety of reviewing and testing mechanisms is available; however, the cost to organizations and the burden to applicants require restraint in the use of these procedures. The most common initial tests (in phases one and two) are education and experience evaluations, letters of recommendation, self-reported assessments, general aptitude and trait tests, and performance tests for specific job qualifications.

Education and Experience Evaluations

Education and experience evaluations include application forms, cover letters, and resumes (Stokes, Mumford, & Owens, 1994). Forms generally run from one to three pages for job- or agency-specific applications to five or six pages for the "general purpose" forms used by many state governments or large agencies. They generally include requests for biographical data, education, job experiences (asking for organization, address, title, supervisor, and duties), the job title(s) for which the applicant is applying, work location preference (in state systems), work limitations (such as availability), and special qualifications. They also normally have additional applicant information about such topics as reasonable accommodation, affirmative action and diversity policies, and veterans' points. Finally, applications invariably have certification and authorization statements to be signed. Such statements notify candidates of the consequences of false information, inform them that applications are available for public inspection, and authorize background checks.

Not all jobs require application forms. Some substitute a cover letter and a resume, especially for management and executive jobs. Although forms have the benefit of uniformity and provide standard pre-employment waivers, they give little insight into the career development, management style, and unique abilities/experiences of candidates. Cover letters require respondents to explain why they feel they are qualified for an advertised position, and the resume generally provides more specific information about job experience than would fit in an application form. Typically, applicants are asked to provide references—addresses and telephone numbers or sometimes completed reference letters (see below). Cover letters and resumes create more work for both the applicant and reviewers, but they generally are more informative. Also, sometimes work samples are requested such as a written work product or visual image of a completed project. Whenever the cover letter and resume is substituted for the application, the selected candidate is generally required to fill out the form later in the process.

A number of jobs require a specific license, certificate, or endorsement. These include many medical positions (such as doctors, nurses, and anesthesiologists), engineering and technician positions, teaching positions, legal positions (such as lawyers), jobs requiring special driver's permits (commercial, chauffeur's), and positions in architecture and hazardous material handling. In such cases, licensure is generally the minimum requirement for consideration. In some cases, certification is required for the position but is provided by the employer as training and therefore is a selection method only to the degree that some candidates drop out or fail the certification process (a prime example is for positions requiring certified peace officer status).

Although licensure is useful for its definitiveness, it does raise the issue of private control over the process in many occupational settings, sometimes leading to excessive selectivity, which in turn creates a market bottleneck and inflates salaries. Some jurisdictions use emergency and temporary certificates to remedy this situation when it becomes acute, such as in teaching.

Letters of Recommendation

Letters take considerable effort on the part of candidates and those nominating them and considerable time to read on the part of the reviewers. Therefore, they should be solicited with forethought. Letters of recommendation are generally most appropriate for those seeking jobs of high potential such as entry-level professional positions or management posts. Although letters are most easily included in the original job posting, increasingly employers are deferring their requests until the finalists have been selected in midlevel and senior positions. Because better jobs require customized letters of recommendation, some highly qualified applicants may choose not to waste a scarce resource on questionable competitions. By deferring this request, the hiring authority often widens its pool. In general, the most useful letters are from former employers. The same is true for references. They can speak to abilities and work effectiveness, as well as work habits, most directly.

Self Assessments

Because past performance is the best predictor of future performance, one effective assessment technique is to ask candidates to provide detailed examples about themselves on the important accomplishment dimensions (i.e., competencies) of the job. The self-reported assessment technique is called the behavioral consistency method (U.S. Office of Personnel Management, 1999). Ideally candidates are asked to report information about 5–10 accomplishment dimensions on which they are rated. Critical competencies for a frontline employee might be mastering new skills, work accuracy, work speed, cooperation with colleagues, innovation, perseverance, and commitment. A supervisory position, in contrast, might include monitoring work, operations planning, delegation, clarifying and informing, developing staff, motivation, team building, managing conflict, and stimulating creativity. Prior to judging the self-reports, the evaluators should have anchored rating scales. If the competencies are valid, and the rating scale is carefully designed, this can be one of the most statistically valid of all selection methods (Schmidt & Hunter, 1998, p. 268). Shortcuts in this method, however, lower the validity significantly, even where the method is encouraged (U.S. MSPB, 2002, p. 28). If this is the only screening device for a particular phase, several of the items can include educational and training background and years of related experience in order to provide a more holistic evaluation.

General Aptitude and Trait Tests

There are at least three types of aptitude and trait tests: psychological, general skills, and general physical qualifications.

Psychological tests examine the personality traits and compare them to the job requirements (Ilgen & Klein, 1988; Kanfer & Ackerman, 1989). For instance, research has shown that, compared with others with equal knowledge and skill, people who have a low sense of efficacy shy away from difficult tasks, have low aspirations and weak commitment to goals, and give up quickly in the face of difficulties (Bandura, 1994). Clearly a test of self-confidence would be a useful piece of information. The challenge is that providing the validity necessary for specific positions is difficult, given the standards of correlation that the courts have demanded (see Exhibit 4.2). Such tests are common only in public safety jobs—law enforcement, corrections, emergency services—where job structure and job stress justify the research and expense. Noncognitive abilities found to be critical are also assessed, such as motivation, attitude toward people, and sense of responsibility. Although not as common, integrity (Ones, Viswesvaran, & Schmidt, 1993) and civil virtue tests (Organ, 1994) are sometimes used (and seem to be on the rise) to screen out those with attitudes poorly suited to public sector ideals and the particularly high ethical standards required.[3] Very broad psychological constructs such as intelligence might be useful (Rae & Earles, 1994) but generally have been considered to fall far short of contemporary validity requirements.

General skills tests provide information about abilities or aptitudes in areas such as reading, mathematics, abstract thinking, spelling, language usage, general problem solving, judgment, proofreading, and memory (Carroll, 1992; Kyllonen, 1994). The measurement of general cognitive skill is used in educational selection extensively in tests such as the SAT, the ACT, and the Graduate Record Examination. In a common case, one 100-item police officer general skills test covers the following abilities: learning and applying police information, remembering details, verbal aptitude, following directions, and using judgment and logic. Although such tests are most often used for broad classification series, they can be developed for single positions that justify the expense and effort, such as air traffic controllers (Ackerman & Kanfer, 1993). For example, for many years the Immigration and Naturalization Service (INS) had a problem with their border patrol training program because over 10% were unable to complete the language component successfully. The INS designed and implemented an artificial language test as a selection screen that assessed ability to learn a new language. Subsequently, the failure rate fell 76% and produced a $6.5 million savings over 5 years (U.S. MSPB, 2002, p. 9).

When physical ability is a major part of the job, as it is for public safety personnel, tests of physical ability (e.g., strength, agility, eyesight) may be part of a battery of tests used to determine initial job qualification (Arvey, Nutting, & Landon, 1992; Hogan, 1991). Generally, however, medical, physical, and eyesight examinations—when incidental but necessary—are done after extending an offer but before employment (see posthiring issues below).

Performance Tests for Specific Jobs

Performance tests directly assess the skills necessary for specific jobs.[4] Although tests based on single-factor performance models are somewhat useful and dominated early personnel research and practice, the multifactor nature of performance is better appreciated today (Campbell, 1994). Some jobs have specific physical skills such as typing (keyboarding) or equipment operation that can be tested. Many job-related knowledge tests use multiple-choice, true-false, and short-answer formats. Sometimes video versions are used as well. Occasionally, an essay or oral format is analyzed in the first screening. Knowledge-based tests are also commonly utilized in promotional hiring in public safety and technical positions.

Job-related skills can be tested through **work samples** or job simulations; that is, those applicants tested are required to produce a sample of the work or demonstrate their skills in a series of simulated activities, generally known as assessment centers. Examples include requiring trainers to conduct a short workshop, operators to demonstrate telephone skills, or management applicants to complete a series of activities requiring them to write memoranda, give directions (in writing), and decide on actions to take. Work samples and assessment centers generally are quite effective but less commonly used as initial screening devices because of the substantial time and cost involved for customized screening. They are more commonly used as a part of the process to review the narrowed pool that goes through an interview process or for promotional purposes.

Other Considerations Regarding Reviewing and Testing

Licensure, general aptitude, and performance tests have proliferated over the years. For example, a civilian detention officer position in an Iowa county sheriff's office in a recent advertisement listed seven tests, excluding the interview: written exam, physical ability test, polygraph exam, psychological test, medical exam, drug test, and residency requirement. Undoubtedly, more and higher-quality testing methods increase the likelihood of successful hires substantially (U.S. MSPB, 2002). Many management critics, however, have called for more selection flexibility and a greater reliance on background education and experience reviews rather than so great a reliance on aptitude and performance tests (Gore, 1993; National Commission on the State and Local Public Service, 1993). The reasons are easy to discern. Lengthy testing protocols are expensive to administer and discourage some qualified job seekers from even applying. Testing often slows the employment process as applicants wait for test dates and organizations wait for test scores. This is particularly true in a low-unemployment economy.

✖ **EXHIBIT 4.3**   Percentage of Supervisors Indicating That Information Predicts Performance "to a Great Extent"

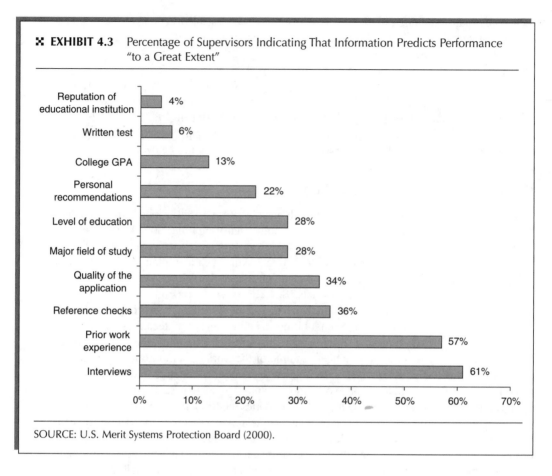

SOURCE: U.S. Merit Systems Protection Board (2000).

Another challenge in using standardized tests is the changing nature of contemporary work (Howard, 1995; Katzenbach & Smith, 1993). Jobs in general tend to be broader, change more frequently, possess more interpersonal and team skills, need more creativity and self-initiative, and have more demanding performance standards, with broader skill sets required (Ilgen, 1994; Van Wart & Berman, 1999). This suggests the increased use of examinations and tests that look for the more abstract characteristics of the job in the applicant. Even with this new need, and although the ability to screen for these skills has increased because of research in affective behavior, general aptitude, and attitude testing (Landy, Laura, & Stacey, 1995), concerns about cost, time, and validity have dampened usage. Thus, there continues to be a strong countervailing trend to reduce the numbers of tests and avoid testing for abstract constructs.

There is no simple rule of thumb for which or how many tests to use (see, for example, Exhibit 4.3, which indicates the selection test preferences of federal supervisors). Factors that lend themselves to larger test batteries include sizable applicant pools and criticality of candidate suitability because of training cost or public safety. Factors that lend themselves to reduced test procedures include difficulties with travel and test administration, the need to move candidates through selection quickly (Sullivan, 1999), and the ability to screen top applicants through interviewing and reference checks (see below).

INTERVIEWING AND REFERENCE CHECKS: REDUCING THE POOL

For candidates, a selection interview means that they have made "the cut." Management interviewees should anticipate one to three other strong candidates, so doing well in the process is key (see Exhibit 4.4).

Interviewing and reference checks are always major responsibilities for the hiring manager and involve discretion. Although this discretion is important for the hiring department and sometimes results in high-quality selections, unstructured interviews and haphazard reference checks frequently result in low validity, wasted resources, frustrated candidates, and illegal practices (U.S. MSPB, 2003). Generally speaking, only structured interviews have high validity (for a general discussion of validity issues related to interviewing, see the meta-analyses by Huffcutt & Arthur, 1994; Schmidt & Hunter, 1998; and Whetzel, Schmitt, & Maurer, 1994). It is especially important to conduct high-quality interviews and reference checks given the trend toward decreasing the number of tests.

The first issue is deciding who will conduct the interviews. The four options are the supervisor, the human resource department or a third party, a panel or committee, or a series of interviewers who may include the immediate supervisor, higher-level supervisors, a committee, a colleague forum, and clients.[5] Nonprofessional entry positions often have a supervisor conduct the interview or professional interviewers in the human resource department in the

EXHIBIT 4.4 How Well Do You Interview?

Management candidates are expected to interview well. Some of the common errors include the following:

Not practicing: To a large degree, interviews are performances, and performances take practice. It is not acceptable answers that get jobs; it is highly articulate responses. Make up a handful of easy questions and another group of difficult ones. Write out the answers and rehearse them. Although these exact questions may not be asked, similar ones will be.

Not knowing the organization and its employees in advance: Read as much about the agency as possible; certainly the Internet has made this easier. Find out about people on the interview committee and in the hiring unit (generally information will be sent in advance of an interview; if not, ask for it).

Not listening: Candidates are "selling" themselves and talking a lot, but as good salespeople know, it is listening that makes the sale. Good listening shows courtesy, makes others feel satisfied with the interaction, and ensures that you do not miss subtle cues. People can tell the difference between active and passive listening, so do not mistake listening for being quiet without paying attention to others' ideas.

Not balancing technical and nontechnical aspects: Reviewing the technical aspects of a job is certainly key, yet just as important are your work philosophy, leadership style, and work-related goals. Do not forget to address the "big picture" while reviewing the details in preparation for an interview.

Not dressing the part: As obvious as it may seem (see Exhibit 2.5), appropriate dress and grooming can make a difference, yet many people "make do" in the critical interview. Clothes should be well fitted and relatively new so that they still have crispness.

case of "no minimum education or experience" requirements in which there is high turnover (laundry workers, aides, receptionists, and drivers). Entry-level professional positions (such as case workers, law enforcement officers, correctional service officers, technicians, engineers, and lawyers) frequently use a selection panel to enhance the diversity of opinions about candidates. It is common for candidates vying for senior or professional positions to have separate interviews with an advisory selection panel and with the hiring supervisor who makes a final selection. High positions may also require more resources by having candidates talk to a variety of parties in addition to the selection committee and hiring supervisor.

A second critical question is that of whom to interview (Biddle, 1993). Public sector employment involves two different approaches. The less common approach is to interview all candidates who meet minimum qualifications. It is time-consuming for the reviewers and may unnecessarily inflate the hopes of candidates. However, where the applicant pool is small, multiple positions are open, or where the time of interviewers is available, such an option may make sense. Or in another case, the candidate pool may lack exceptional candidates so that more extensive interviewing may make sense in trying to discover hidden talent.

By far the most common approach, however, is to interview only the most qualified people. At one time, the **rule of three** was common (promulgated by civil service commissions); it restricted hiring authorities to interviewing the top three candidates. This injunction is still in place in many federal agencies although much criticized (GAO, 2003; U.S. MSPB, 1995). In many civil service systems, the allowable number is often expanded to a rule of four, five, or six. Today, the tendency is to give the hiring authority discretion to interview any number it wishes of those deemed to meet the minimum qualifications (certified or eligible). Nonetheless, there are practical reasons to restrict interviewing. Candidates may be out of state and incur considerable travel expenses. In most cases, the top three or four candidates are obvious, and to interview more is unlikely to be productive.

Where interview discretion exists, hiring authorities can consider alternate models. Online and/or telephone interviews can rapidly provide a good deal of information and answer many preliminary questions. Likewise, two-way videoconferencing can precede on-site interviews and winnow down the applicant field. Reference checks can be done before the interview process to gather information to help select the most desirable candidates to invite.

General Considerations for Those Conducting Interviews

A good procedure takes preparation, knowledge of the position, and awareness of the various interviewer biases that may occur. Ten steps to consider in preparing for an interview are as follows (adapted from Iowa Department of Personnel, 1994):

1. Plan how it should proceed. Who will meet the applicants? Where will applicants wait if they do not proceed directly to the interview? Who will explain the general process to be used, and if there is more than one interviewer, who will ask what questions?

2. Be sure that there is a specific list of written questions asked of all candidates. This should not keep people from asking follow-up questions. Ensure that the questions have a logical sequence. They should always be reviewed in advance and circulated to relevant parties to ensure balance and appropriateness.

3. Use a work sample as a part of the process (Lowry, 1994; Pynes & Bernardin, 1992). For instance, when interviewing for an emergency medical technician, consider having the candidates demonstrate administering CPR with a resuscitation dummy. Other examples, dependent on the position, include map-reading exercises, troubleshooting a mechanical problem, writing a short business letter, and exercises requiring applicants to follow a set of directions. The types of activities that probe candidate abilities include the following:

- Critique or evaluate something (a program, policy, procedure, report's recommendations/conclusions, decision, or viewpoint).
- Define a relevant problem, identify its causes, develop alternative solutions, decide what to do, and outline an implementation plan.
- Apply a set of rules/criteria to a particular case.
- Lay out a plan/steps for conducting a study, researching an issue, or reaching a goal.
- Read and explain, rephrase, or interpret a statement of policy, procedure, law, or other written material.
- Prioritize a number of issues, problems, or activities.
- Solve a supervisory problem concerning planning, organizing, assigning, directing, motivating, evaluating, or facilitating the work of others.
- Persuade or convince a hypothetical client/audience of something.
- Deliver an oral presentation based on information that the candidate is given time to review and prepare.
- Respond orally or in writing to a complaint or hostile person.
- Role-play in a specific work situation.
- Write or edit written material that is specifically job related.

4. Explain basic facts about the position: which department, what division or unit, and the supervisor. Review the job responsibilities.

5. Use the job description and advertisement as guides to ensure that the focus is on essential job functions. In addition, include some of the job challenges and opportunities as part of a realistic preview (Vandenberg & Scarpello, 1990).

6. Set up interviews in a private setting in which distractions are unlikely.

7. Concentrate on listening to an applicant's answers and take notes during the interview. This is important when interviewing several applicants. Also, be sure that the candidate has opportunities to ask questions (if only one such opportunity exists and it is placed at the end of the interview, then the candidate may feel rushed if the interview used up most of the allotted time).

8. Be careful that no oral commitments or suggestions about employment prospects are made. Be prepared to give candidates an estimate of when they will receive feedback.

9. Complete your evaluation notes while impressions are fresh, preferably immediately after the interview. Use a predetermined rating system for the questions.

10. To comply with the Americans With Disabilities Act, be prepared to make accommodations for applicants on request. Even if applicants do not request an accommodation

for the interview, it is best to ask all individuals the following question: "Can you perform the essential functions of this position with or without a reasonable accommodation?" If accommodation is needed, then consult with human resources specialists. Having to provide accommodation is not an acceptable reason for declining to offer employment.

Finally, it is important that interviewers keep questions focused on the job. Appropriate questions include past work experiences (both paid and volunteer), military work experience, education and training, authorization to work in the United States, and personal characteristics related to performing essential functions of the job. Topics to avoid include age, race and ethnicity, disability, national origin, marital status and children, religion, gender (because some jobs are dominated by one gender or the other), arrest record (but not conviction record), credit references, garnishment record, types of military discharges, child care arrangements, height and weight, transportation not explicitly job related, and past workers' compensation claims. Exhibit 4.5 provides a guide for nondiscriminatory interviewing.

✖ **Exhibit 4.5**   Guide to Nondiscriminatory Hiring

Subject	Acceptable	Unacceptable
Name	Whether an applicant has worked under a different name	Asking for a maiden name or what the candidate's name was before it was legally changed
Birthplace, national origin, and residence	Applicant's place of residence, length of applicant's residence in state or city where employer is located	Birthplace of applicant or applicant's parents, ancestry, birth certificate, naturalization or baptismal certificate
Citizenship	Whether an applicant is legally authorized to work in the United States (should be asked in a yes-no format; may be documented after job offer)	Inquiries about whether the applicant intends to become a citizen
Creed or religion	None before hire	Applicant's religious affiliation, church, parish, or religious holidays observed, except in rare cases where religion is a bona fide qualification (e.g., chaplain)
Race or color		All inquiries
Photographs		Photographs with application or after interview but before hiring

Subject	Acceptable	Unacceptable
Language	Languages applicant speaks and/or writes, but only if job related	Applicant's native tongue, language used by applicant at home, or how applicant acquired the ability to read, write, or speak a foreign language
Relatives	Names of relatives already working for the organization	Names of friends working for the organization
Military	Military experience or training	Type or condition of military discharge
Organizations	Applicant's memberships in job-related professional or trade organizations	All clubs, social fraternities, societies, or nonprofessional organizations to which an applicant belongs
Gender and family		None except in rare cases where it is a bona fide job requirement
Arrest and conviction record	Number and kinds of convictions	Questions about arrest records
Height and weight		None except in rare cases when it is a bona fide job requirement
Mental and physical abilities	Applicant's ability to perform essential functions of the position with or without accommodations	Any inquiries into any mental or physical disabilities, preemployment physicals
Marital status, pregnancy, or child care		Inquiries about marital status, family plans, or child care unless inquiry has business necessity and is asked of both males and females and is a bona fide job requirement.

SOURCES: Iowa State University Guide to Non-Discriminatory Hiring (flier); Iowa Department of Personnel (1994, ch. 4).

Reference Checks

References can be verified at different times during the process and in various ways; for example, letters of reference are a type of check. Although perhaps convenient for the search panel, this method can produce dozens of letters that may not be carefully examined, is a nuisance to applicants, and requires candidates to divulge their interest in positions before they may be serious candidates. Telephone reference checking can be done prior to interviews, after interviews and before hiring, or after selection but in advance of the offer. In most cases, it is best to conduct these just prior to or after interviews so that the information may add to the selection decision. Where more thorough—and expensive—background investigations are necessary for reasons of public safety (e.g., education, air traffic control, transportation, law enforcement, corrections, child care, elder care), preliminary checking may be appropriate. Failure to do so could result in **negligent hiring** lawsuits against the agency should the person hired engage in wrongdoing (Walter, 1992).

Telephone reference checks should be planned as carefully as interviews, especially in an environment in which employers are increasingly reluctant to provide detailed reference information. Useful issues to address include (a) verification of employment dates and responsibilities, (b) general assessments of strengths and weaknesses, (c) examples of candidate abilities, and (d) whether the individual was given added responsibilities, was a candidate for advancement, and would be eligible for rehire. Although uncommon, straying beyond documented facts when providing negative information can expose one to defamation suits from the former employee. Despite the more constrained environment for reference checks of former employers, they can be useful, especially if the applicant waives his/her rights to see the letters. Verifying basic information is a requirement of good management. Questions about strengths, successes, and additional responsibilities provide depth in the candidate's abilities. Even muted responses to questions may provide "red flags" to investigate.

CHOOSING AND NEGOTIATION

Who determines who the final candidate will be? What if a clear candidate does not emerge from the interviews? How should the offer be made? What documentation is necessary?

The final candidate is most commonly selected by the supervisor for the position. Often he or she has a ranked list from a search committee for professional or competitive positions. Supervisors should not overturn search committee recommendations lightly. Although these committees (or whole departments) never technically hire candidates, their decisions may be definitive. For some positions requiring minimum or no qualifications, or where competition for qualified staff is particularly fierce, the hiring authority may essentially be delegated to the human resources department so that immediate selection may take place. In some promotional hiring cases with strong seniority systems and an established testing regimen, the decision may be formulaic: the person with the highest score on the required test(s) gets the position.

Sometimes the interview procedure leaves the supervisor or the search committee bewildered about the best candidate; in such cases, a second round of interviewing may be a solution. If the hiring supervisor or committee is confident that the applicant pool is weak, then the search can be continued by readvertising and interviewing a second pool, or the search can be closed entirely, to be opened again at a later date. The situation is different, however, if two or three people look highly qualified but bring different strengths to the position. In such a case, the person doing the hiring should simply make the decision. Delaying decisions with competitive candidates means that they may not be available when needed.

The actual hiring normally begins with an informal phone call. Is the person still interested? Do they understand what the salary is? Do they have any final questions? For entry-level positions, there is usually little ability to negotiate salary or working conditions; senior level and competitive positions may provide flexibility. Both the organization and the candidate should have a clear idea of how long the organization is willing to wait for a decision; at least several days is reasonable. Once the candidate verbally accepts the position, a letter to confirm the offer (**letter of intent**) likely will follow. The person is then generally asked to report to work to complete employment forms. This is also done when the starting date of employment is not immediate because of funds availability or because the applicant must give notice at another job. In very senior positions, the letter of intent dictates the special conditions of employment, including retreat rights (to other positions), special travel or equipment allowances, and so on. Only when the organization is confident that the position has been filled are letters (or calls) made to those interviewed but not selected to inform them that the position has been filled. The aphorism, "Good news travels by phone and bad news travels by letter," describes the hiring procedure.

One significant variation exists when a physical exam or drug test is a part of the hiring process but conducted after the offer; employment is then **contingent**. This must be clearly stipulated. Other contingencies exist such as funding availability, job freezes, or completion of specialized training programs. It is also useful to point out that in the probationary period (which commonly exists), job termination can normally occur without the need to show either cause or reason (Elliott & Peaton, 1994).

The final part of the hiring process is the documentation of the process itself. Generally, the human resource department or affirmative action office will want a form filled out that confirms who the eligible individuals were and the reasons for selection and nonselection. This process is made much easier, and is less subject to challenge, if the hiring authority has done a thorough job of defining essential job functions and then scoring all eligible candidates on the job-related functions.

POSTOFFER AND HIRING ISSUES

Some "tests," as mentioned, occur after the offer, but employment is still contingent on successfully passing them. They are sometimes allowed or required for security purposes or public safety. Although drug testing is generally illegal for most positions, it is legal for those conveying passengers and involved in public safety positions (e.g., peace officers, corrections, emergency services) (Drug-Free Workplace Act, 1988; Omnibus Transportation Employees Testing Act, 1991). Law enforcement and corrections positions also frequently require extensive background checks and sometimes polygraph examinations, although the questions asked must be carefully screened for job relevance (as stipulated in the Employee Polygraph Protection Act of 1988). Generally, these tests are conducted after an offer but before employment is finalized. It is also legal for governments to impose residency requirements for select positions (*McCarthy v. Philadelphia Civil Service Commission,* 1976), a condition that generally has been modified to distance-from-work requirements for appropriate public safety, public works, and other employees with emergency responsibilities.

Even after the person has accepted the position and documentation on the hiring process has been filed, the selection process is not really over (Wanous, 1992). All candidates interviewed or, in some senior level cases, all persons who applied need to be informed that a decision has been made. Just as important, the supervisor needs to review what the new employee will need to be successful and to feel like a valued member of the organization. For example, anticipating any office and equipment needs for the new person helps with a smooth transition.

Next, what are the plans for orientation and training? Orientation includes sessions that inform the new person of general policies and benefits packages and provides familiarization with facilities. Training provides specific instruction on job-related processes and equipment. The workload of new employees should be reduced initially whenever possible, and they should be informed accordingly. Will the training be conducted by a training department/unit and be part of an established program, or will it be conducted by the supervisor or an in-house instructor? Although on-the-job training has the virtues of relevance and immediacy when done properly, it is frequently done in an excessively casual manner that really could be called "you-are-on-your-own" training (Van Wart, Cayer, & Cook, 1993; also see Chapter 8).

A related option to consider is a mentor. Who will make sure that the new employee is introduced to people after the first day, answer questions about the job and culture of the organization, and simply take a special interest in the new employee's well-being? The initial period is the most critical in preventing early turnover as well as in establishing a positive bond between the employee and the agency. Those who realize that the necessary training and support are not provided are wise to ask for it. Lack of training and support is generally a simple oversight; even in resource-poor organizations, additional assistance is likely to go to those who ask for it.

Finally, the probationary period itself, where it exists, can be a key part of the selection function. Most are for 6 months or a year, although the Canadian government allows up to 36 months in some areas. Generally, termination during probation is difficult to challenge as long as it is for nondiscriminatory reasons; mediocre performance is usually grounds for dismissal, and standards of proof may be nonexistent or minimal. That means that supervisors have an exceptional opportunity, although some let probation lapse as the candidate "gets up to speed." Setting tough standards for probationary employees as an extension of a rigorous selection process may avoid future performance problems. Federal data indicate that discharges during probation have increased from 4% to 6% in recent years and that challenges to termination are extraordinarily low (U.S. MSPB, 2002). Overall, the paradox of probation is that it may be the best selection technique but that it may not be taken seriously by some employers for a variety of practical reasons.

SUMMARY AND CONCLUSION

Although almost everyone agrees that the single most important class of management decisions is hiring the "right" people, there is much less consensus on the basis for deciding who is right. In fact, democracies require fundamentally different selection processes for different public sector positions. Presidents, governors, and mayors do not take civil service examinations, and midlevel managers are not elected. Technical merit, the focus of this chapter, may be the heart of the civil service system, but most systems pay attention to seniority and representativeness as well. Even where merit principles apply—hiring technically qualified candidates through an open process that scrutinizes the essential job functions and applicants' special knowledge, skills, and abilities—there are many different models of implementation. Coming out of an era of excessive patronage, civil service systems removed all but the final selection from executive branch agencies to prevent political or managerial tampering. Today, with crass political patronage for nonexecutive jobs relatively uncommon, most public sector systems have moved all selection functions into agency human resource departments or into the hiring units themselves.[6] Line managers have greater responsibilities. Certification lists are being lengthened to give greater discretion, or sometimes are changed to qualified lists.

Test selection includes many possibilities from education and experience evaluations to licensure, to general aptitude and trait examinations, to performance tests for specific job qualifications. The current tendency is for fewer aptitude and performance tests in an environment emphasizing speed and managerial flexibility. Exhibit 4.6 summarizes when various selection tests are most commonly used. Reliance on education and experience can provide flexibility and speed. Interviewing is a complex event with legal pitfalls, yet when it is planned carefully, even candidates who are not selected appreciate the opportunity. With more choices of whom to interview, the process has never been more important. The actual hiring decision also is made much easier by careful planning, which includes contingency planning should the initial round of interviewing not produce a clear choice. Following through on posthiring issues ensures that the candidate is oriented, trained, and supported so that he or she can pass successfully through the probationary period and become productive.

✖ **EXHIBIT 4.6**   When Various Selection Tests Are Most Commonly Used

Type of Selection Test	*Phase One* *Select All Those Eligible*	*Phase Two* *Select the High- Quality Group*	*Phase Three* *Select the Final Candidate for the Job Offer*	*Phase Four* *Confirm Contingency Qualifications and on-the-Job Ability*
Education and experience	X (general review)	X (detailed matching and point system)		
Letters of recommendation	X (part of job application)	X (supplemental request)		
Self-reported assessments	X	X	X	
General aptitude and trait tests	X	X		
Work samples and assessment centers	X (e.g., examples of written work)	X (live samples)	X (live samples)	
Interviews		X	X	
Reference checks		X	X	
Special tests				X
Probationary period				X

Increased demands on organizations to be productive, flexible, and responsive—often while only maintaining staff or even losing employees—make selecting the best people critical. More than ever before, line managers need to be informed about and involved in the selection process.

KEY TERMS

Assembled tests
Certified lists
Civil service commission
Contingent
Disparate impact
Education and experience evaluations
Electoral popularity
General skills tests
Letter of intent
Merit selection
Negligent hiring
Patronage
Pendleton Act

Performance tests
Psychological tests
Representativeness
Rule of three
Seniority
Social class selection
Spoils system
Temporary employees
Term employees
Test validity
Unassembled tests
Veterans' points
Work samples

EXERCISES

Class Discussion

1. The paradox of freedom (Introduction) looms over the selection function, most notably in such areas as drug, lie, and genetic testing. Using dialectic reasoning, stalk this paradox using Einstein's famous dictum: "You cannot solve the problem with the same kind of thinking that created it."

2. What is the "best" balance of selection strategies? Should all civil service jobs be purely merit? Should seniority be a major factor in promotional hiring? Should representativeness (both affirmative action and veterans' points) be phased out? Should the number of patronage appointments be decreased or increased?

3. Has anyone in class taken a civil service examination? What was it like?

4. Who has conducted interviews? What were some of the interviewee "mistakes"? Among the finalists, what was the determining factor: technical competence or interpersonal skills?

Team Activities

5. Discuss what you would do if, in an interview for a merit position, you were asked your party affiliation? What would you do if later you were asked when you graduated from college? If you refused to answer either of these questions and subsequently were not hired, would you do anything about it? How can the selection process be like a chess match?

6. Assume that you are on the search committee for a new management intern program. It has been determined that interns will be paid in the mid 20s, will have 1-year appointments, and may apply for permanent positions if they receive good evaluations. The recruitment is to be announced nationally, but no travel money will be available; therefore, it is expected that the bulk of the candidates will be local. Design the selection process.

7. You are on the search committee for a public information officer (this is a non–civil service, exempt position in the organization). The last incumbent, although a friend of the agency director and a former reporter, was a disaster. Most of the time, people did not know what he did, and when he finally did organize press conferences, he sometimes became more controversial than the issue being discussed. Having learned her lesson, the director has asked you to nominate a slate of three ranked candidates. Design the selection process.

8. If obvious selection techniques did not exist (recall the example of the apple in Exhibit 0.3), then how would you choose employees?

9. Team members should investigate three organizations to determine the virtual nature of their recruitment and selection process. Compare as well as contrast your findings, and report them to the entire class.

Individual Assignment

10. You are the hiring supervisor for a junior management position in the city manager's office that would largely be responsible for special projects—both analysis (requiring strong quantitative skills) and implementation (mandating interpersonal and coordination skills). The three candidates interviewed all have recent MPA degrees. Set up a matrix of no more than five factors, give weights to the factors, and score and rank the candidates.

Jill Owens: Good interpersonal skills, pleasant personality, very talkative and sometimes did not seem to listen very well, mediocre quantitative skills, highly energetic, one internship and one summer job in another city government, the second-best grades of the three, excellent references, and good appearance, manners, and understanding of city government. Former supervisors in the city were quite supportive of her candidacy but admitted that she was not exceptional.

Bruce Hughes: Mediocre interpersonal skills, pleasant personality, quiet but extremely attentive, superb quantitative skills, low energy, one internship in this city, the best grades of the group, below average appearance, acceptable manners, and unsure about his understanding of city government. Has a rave reference from the supervisor about a program evaluation project completed in his internship that resulted in highly successful changes.

Mary Washington: Excellent interpersonal skills, charming personality, very good listener, weak quantitative skills, high energy, no city experience but a year's experience in state government in a clerical function prior to finishing her graduate degree, the third-best grades among the candidates but still high, quite satisfactory references, very good manners, and little understanding of city government. Talked about her project management skills, using examples from church and volunteer work. She is the only "diversity" candidate.

NOTES

1. Patronage certainly has not been wiped out, nor is it ever likely to be. For example, it still exists in Schedule C exceptions (confidential staff for federal executives) and overseas appointments at the federal level. Many state systems have uneven coverage and experience covert intrusion, such as moving political appointees to civil service permanent positions by "persuasion" or executive order. Local systems may be merit systems in name only, and very small jurisdictions may be exempted from state civil service requirements entirely.

2. This description refers to "ideal" merit systems. In reality, most have seniority elements infused in them for promotional opportunities. In other words, many merit systems close promotional hires to agency or governmental personnel, although it is possible that candidates outside the agency might be more meritorious on technical grounds.

3. Ones, Mount, Barrick, and Hunter (1994) have found high degrees of correlation between the integrity factor measured in the new "honesty tests" and one of the "Big Five" personality factors, conscientiousness.

4. Ultimately, there is considerable overlap among performance tests, aptitude tests, and psychological tests, which rely on a continuum ranging from concrete to abstract predictors.

5. An alternative structure today is the self-managed team, which embodies characteristics of both a hiring panel and a hiring supervisor. As in any other group activity, the team has the opportunity to provide a substantially rich experience if the members understand their work and do it well; they can introduce confusion if they do not.

6. Probably more common today than political patronage in the career service is management patronage. That is, managers may manipulate the hiring process to ensure that a favored candidate is selected.

REFERENCES

Ackerman, P. L., & Kanfer, R. (1993). Integrating laboratory and field study for improving selection: Development of a battery to predict air traffic controller success. *Journal of Applied Psychology, 78*(3), 413–432.

Arvey, R. D., & Faley, R. (1988). *Fairness in selecting employees.* Reading, MA: Addison-Wesley Longman.

Arvey, R. D., Nutting, S. M., & Landon, T. E. (1992). Validation strategies for physical ability testing in police and fire settings. *Public Personnel Management, 21*(3), 301–312.

Arvey, R. D., & Sackett, P. R. (1993). Fairness in selection: Current developments and perspectives. In N. Schmitt, W. C. Borman, et al. (Eds.), *Personnel selection in organizations.* San Francisco: Jossey-Bass.

Bandura, A. (1994). Regulative function of perceived self-efficacy. In M. G. Rumsey, C. B. Walker, & J. H. Harris (Eds.), *Personnel selection and classification* (pp. 261–272). Hillsdale, NJ: Lawrence Erlbaum.

Barrett, G., Phillips, J., & Alexander, R. (1981). Concurrent and predictive validity designs: A critical reanalysis. *Journal of Applied Psychology, 14,* 209–219.

Barrick, M. R., & Mount, M. K. (1991). The big five personality dimensions and job performance: A meta-analysis. *Personnel Psychology, 44,* 1–26.

Biddle, R. E. (1993). How to set cutoff scores for knowledge tests used in promotion, training, certification, and licensing. *Public Personnel Management, 22*(1), 63–79.

Branti v. Finkel, 445 U.S. 507 (1980).

Campbell, J. P. (1994). Alternate models of job performance and their implications for selection and classification. In M. G. Rumsey, C. B. Walker, & J. H. Harris (Eds.), *Personnel selection and classification* (pp. 33–52). Hillsdale, NJ: Lawrence Erlbaum.

Carroll, J. B. (1992). Cognitive abilities: The state of the art. *Psychological Science, 3,* 266–271.

Condrey, S. E., & Maranto, R. (2001). *Radical reform of the civil service.* Lanham, MD: Lexington Books.

Cortina, J. M., Doherty, M. L., Schmitt, N., Kaufman, G., & Smith, R. G. (1992). The big five personality factors in IPI and MMPI: Predictors of police performance. *Personnel Psychology, 45,* 119–140.

Day, D., & Silverman, S. (1989). Personality and job performance: Evidence of incremental validity. *Personnel Psychology, 42,* 25–26.

Drug-Free Workplace Act, P.L. 100–6klj90, 102 Stat. 4304 (1988).

Edwards, J. E., & Morrison, R. F. (1994). Selecting and classifying future naval officers: The paradox of greater specialization in broader arenas. In M. G. Rumsey, C. B. Walker, & J. H. Harris (Eds.), *Personnel selection and classification* (pp. 69–84). Hillsdale, NJ: Lawrence Erlbaum.

Elliott, R. H., & Peaton, A. (1994). The probationary period in the selection process: A survey of its use at the state level. *Public Personnel Management, 23*(1), 47–59.

Elrod v. Burns, 427 U.S. 347 (1976).

Equal Employment Opportunity Commission. (1978). Uniform guidelines on employee selection procedures. In *Code of federal regulations* (41 CFR Ch. 60). Washington, DC: Author.

Gore, A. (1993). *Creating a government that works better and costs less: The report of the National Performance Review.* Washington, DC: Government Printing Office.

Hays, S. W., & Kearney, R. C. (1999). *The transformation of public sector human resource management.* Unpublished manuscript.

Hogan, J. (1991). Structure of physical performance in occupational tasks. *Journal of Applied Psychology, 76*(4), 495–507.

Howard, A. (Ed.). (1995). *The changing nature of work.* San Francisco: Jossey-Bass.

Huffcutt, A. I., & Arthur, W., Jr. (1994). Hunter and Hunter (1984) revisited: Interview validity for entry-level jobs. *Journal of Applied Psychology, 79*(2), 184–190.

Ilgen, D. R. (1994). Jobs and roles: Accepting and coping with the changing structure of organizations. In M. G. Rumsey, C. B. Walker, & J. H. Harris (Eds.), *Personnel selection and classification* (pp. 13–32). Hillsdale, NJ: Lawrence Erlbaum.

Ilgen, D. R., & Klein, H. J. (1988). Individual motivation and performance: Cognitive influences on effort and choice. In J. P. Campbell & R. J. Campbell (Eds.), *Productivity in organizations.* San Francisco: Jossey-Bass.

Ingraham, P. W., Selden, S. C., & Moynihan, D. P. (2000). People and performance: Challenges for the future: The report from the Wye River Conference. *Public Administration Review, 60*(1), 54–60.

Iowa Department of Personnel. (1994). *Personnel management for managers and supervisors.* Des Moines: Author.

Johnson, J. A., & Hogan, R. (1981). Vocational interests, personality, and effective police performance. *Personnel Psychology, 34,* 49–53.

Kanfer, R., & Ackerman, P. L. (1989). Motivation and cognitive abilities: An integrative-aptitude-treatment interaction approach to skill acquisition. *Journal of Applied Psychology, 74,* 657–690.

Katzenbach, J. R., & Smith, D. K. (1993). *The wisdom of teams: Creating the high-performance organization.* Boston: Harvard Business School.

Kyllonen, P. C. (1994). Cognitive abilities testing: An agenda for the 1990s. In M. G. Rumsey, C. B. Walker, & J. H. Harris (Eds.), *Personnel selection and classification* (pp. 103–126). Hillsdale, NJ: Lawrence Erlbaum.

Landy, F. J., Laura, S. C., & Stacey, K. M. (1995). Advancing personnel selection and placement methods. In A. Howard (Ed.), *The changing nature of work* (pp. 252–289). San Francisco: Jossey-Bass.

Lane, L. M., & Wolf, J. F. (1990). *The human resource crisis in the public sector.* New York: Quorum.

Lowry, P. E. (1994). The structured interview: An alternative to the assessment center. *Public Personnel Management, 23*(2), 201–215.

McCarthy v. Philadelphia Civil Service Commission, 424 U.S. 645 (1976).

McCrae, R. R., & Costa, P. T., Jr. (1987). Validation of the five-factor model of personality across instruments and observers. *Journal of Personality and Social Psychology, 52,* 81–90.

Mosher, F. C. (1982). *Democracy and the public service* (2nd ed.). New York: Oxford University Press.

National Commission on the State and Local Public Service (Winter Commission). (1993). *Hard truths/tough choices: An agenda for state and local reform.* Albany, NY: Rockefeller Institute of Government.

Omnibus Transportation Employees Testing Act, P.L. 102–143, 105 Stat. 952 (1991).

Ones, D. S., Mount, M. K., Barrick, M. R., & Hunter, J. E. (1994). Personality and job performance: A critique of the Tett, Jackson, & Rothstein (1991) meta-analysis. *Personnel Psychology, 47*(1), 147–156.

Ones, D. S., Viswesvaran, C., & Schmidt, F. (1993). Meta-analysis of integrity test validities: Findings and implications for personnel selection and theories of job performance. *Journal of Applied Psychology, 78*(4), 679–703.

Organ, D. W. (1994). Organizational citizenship behavior and the good soldier. In M. G. Rumsey, C. B. Walker, & J. H. Harris (Eds.), *Personnel selection and classification* (pp. 53–68). Hillsdale, NJ: Lawrence Erlbaum.

Peter, L. J., & Hull, R. (1969). *The Peter principle.* New York: William Morrison.

Pynes, J., & Bernardin, H. J. (1992). Mechanical vs. consensus-derived assessment center ratings: A comparison of job performance validities. *Public Personnel Management, 21*(1), 17–28.

Rae, M. J., & Earles, J. A. (1994). The ubiquitous predictiveness of g. In M. G. Rumsey, C. B. Walker, & J. H. Harris (Eds.), *Personnel selection and classification* (pp. 127–136). Hillsdale, NJ: Lawrence Erlbaum.

Rutan v. Republican Party of Illinois, 497 U.S. 62 (1990).

Schmidt, F. L., & Hunter, J. E. (1998). The validity and utility of selection methods in personnel psychology: Practical and theoretical implications of 85 years of research findings. *Psychological Bulletin, 124*(2), 262–275.

Schuler, H., Farr, J. L., & Smith, M. (Eds.). (1993). *Personnel selection and assessment: Individual and organizational perspectives.* Hillsdale, NJ: Lawrence Erlbaum.

Stokes, G. S., Mumford, M. D., & Owens, W. A. (1994). *The biodata handbook: Theory, research, and application.* Palo Alto, CA: Consulting Psychologists.

Sullivan, J. (1999, June). Gaining a competitive advantage through increasing the speed of hire. *IMPA News,* pp. 14–15.

U.S. Government Accounting Office. (2003). *Human capital: Opportunities to improve executive agencies' hiring processes.* Washington, DC: Author.

U.S. Merit Systems Protection Board. (1995). *The rule of three in federal hiring: Boon or bane?* Washington, DC: Author.

U.S. Merit Systems Protection Board. (1998). *Federal supervisors and strategic human resource management.* Washington, DC: Author.

U.S. Merit Systems Protection Board. (2000). *Merit principles survey.* Washington, DC: Author.

U.S. Merit Systems Protection Board. (2001a). *The federal merit promotion program.* Washington, DC: Author.

U.S. Merit Systems Protection Board. (2001b). *The U.S. Office of Personnel Management in retrospect.* Washington, DC: Author.

U.S. Merit Systems Protection Board. (2002). *Assessing federal job-seekers in a delegated examining environment.* Washington, DC: Author.

U.S. Merit Systems Protection Board. (2003). *The federal selection interview: Unrealized potential.* Washington, DC: Author.

U.S. Office of Personnel Management. (1999). *Delegated examining operations handbook: A guide for federal agency examining offices.* Washington, DC: Author.

Van Riper, P. (1958). *History of the United States civil service.* New York: Harper & Row.

Van Wart, M., & Berman, E. (1999). Contemporary public sector productivity values: Narrower scope, tougher standards, and new rules of the game. *Public Productivity & Management Review, 22*(3), 326–347.

Van Wart, M., Cayer, N. J., & Cook, S. (1993). *Handbook of training and development for the public sector.* San Francisco: Jossey-Bass.

Vandenberg, R. J., & Scarpello, V. (1990). The matching model: An examination of the processes underlying realistic job previews. *Journal of Applied Psychology, 75,* 60–67.

Walter, R. J. (1992). Public employers' potential liability from negligence in employment decisions. *Public Administration Review, 52,* 491–495.

Wanous, J. P. (1992). *Organizational entry: Recruitment, selection, and socialization of newcomers.* Reading, MA: Addison-Wesley.

Whetzel, D. L., Schmitt, F. L., & Maurer, S. D. (1994). The validity of employment interviews: A comprehensive review and meta-analysis. *Journal of Applied Psychology, 79,* 599–616.

Wiesen, J. P., Abrams, N., & McAttee, S. A. (1990). *Employment testing: A public sector viewpoint* (Personnel Assessment Monographs Vol. 2, No. 3). Washington, DC: International Personnel Management Association Assessment Council.

5

POSITION MANAGEMENT
Judicious Plan or Jigsaw Puzzle?

The right people in the right jobs.

—Otto von Bismarck

After studying this chapter, you should be able to

- Identify the profound trends and paradoxical tensions affecting traditional classification strategies that may remake position management systems in the 21st century
- Differentiate among the three overarching types of personnel systems that are found—generally in layers—in almost all public sector organizations
- Understand the two fundamentally different uses of position classification and understand how jobs are grouped together in theory and in practice
- Distinguish between the related concepts of job analysis and job evaluation
- Conduct informal job analyses and job evaluations and understand when and how more formal, rigorous methods are used

Position management is generally thought to be a dry science of little interest to anyone but a few specialists in human resource departments. Such a notion is full of irony and paradoxes, if not outright misconceptions. First, position classification is as much an art as a science, because it is actually composed of different systems, each with distinctly different value biases. Furthermore, the biases of each system shift over time. The art, then, is understanding the different values that exist in various systems at specific times. The science is the rational implementation of that set of values. Unfortunately, when system values become too rigid and when classification and compensation issues are treated as laws based on hard science, an unbalanced characterization of position management exists.[1] This tendency was well expressed in a classic essay by Wallace Sayre (1948) titled, "The Triumph of Techniques Over Purpose."

The second point is related in that the rational order conveyed by classification systems is generally overstated. Most classification systems of large organizations are quite fragmented, and sometimes they are haphazard because competing stresses such as politics, market forces, merit, social equity, and union influence distort them over time. The classification systems of most small organizations (which make up the vast majority of American governments) are actually piecemeal personnel systems rather than true **position management systems**.

Third, although formal methods of job analysis and job evaluation are often preached in management texts and elsewhere, they are not always used in practice. Informal methods are as common, and such skills are equally important for employees and managers. Finally, although classification may seem to be a subject of little utility to non-personnelists, it is actually a critical source of knowledge and, by extension, power in agencies. Understanding the central organizing structures is as important as budgeting or management principles (Condrey, 1998).

Although classification systems generally convey a sense of judiciousness, they are probably more accurately viewed as jigsaw puzzles. One should not be put off by this realization, however. Because of their importance to job aspirants, wage earners, status seekers, career strategists, managers, executives, and legislators, one should consider them fascinating cornerstones in the complex organizational universe. Decisions about position management are very important in all professional lives, as well as in the health of organizations. Mastering general knowledge of the tools used in classification is critical.

THREE TYPES OF PERSONNEL STRATEGIES

The American public sector is composed of three fundamental personnel strategies, each of which is represented in a layered fashion in all government personnel systems. Selection is the core principle in each of these strategies, and it equally affects the subsequent classification and management of positions. The three systems are based on either election, appointment, or rules (composed of merit, seniority, and representativeness factors).[2] Although discussed in the previous chapter, it is important to review it here in the context of position classification.

Election as a strategy for policy making in personnel selection is the foundation of democratic states. The people choose who will make and execute the laws and, to some degree, interpret them as well. Electoral systems emphasize values, debate, political responsiveness, and generalized (rather than expert) knowledge of government. Elected officials are selected as the leaders of most public sector systems but are required to serve terms and be reelected periodically if they want a career in government. Two types of elected officials are common. The most visible is the full-time official who serves in a major office and whose salary is sufficient to provide a living. The more common type, however, is the "citizen-legislator" who serves part-time and whose salary is modest or inconsequential.[3]

A second personnel strategy is appointment made by elected officials. Generally, appointed officials serve at the will of those who select them. The most visible appointed officials are those who run agencies as cabinet level secretaries, directors, and commissioners, and their chief deputies. Appointed employees also typically include policy-related advisers and confidential staff. Ideally, elected officials select individuals for full-time paid jobs who they believe are competent or meritorious and who are generally in agreement about their policy positions. Common practice used to allow elected officials to choose appointees in general government service on the **spoils principle**—either to reward political supporters or to indirectly enhance one's personal situation (such as through the appointment of family members). Gross spoils selection at the career level is rare today, largely because of court action (Hamilton, 1999), although the "thickening" of government (Introduction) with numerous high- and midlevel political appointees should not be overlooked. Some of the most common are those who serve as "citizen-appointees" on innumerable boards and commissions at all levels of government on a part-time basis for little or no remuneration.

The third strategy is rule-based selection, which affects the bulk of those in the public service and is the primary focus of this chapter. This strategy gives precedence to **merit** and is based on technical qualifications and competitive selection as judged by experts. Removal from office is often only for cause (see Chapter 10). Advanced forms of the merit philosophy in organizations evolved only in the 19th century. Two fundamental merit strategies exist (see Exhibit 5.1 for a comparison of the two strategies). **Rank-in-job** personnel strategies are very common in the United States but less common elsewhere.[4] Rank and salary are determined by the job that one holds. Substantial salary increases and higher status are attained only through a better job (promotion or reclassification), but multiple promotions within an organization are uncommon beyond the predetermined job series, such as City Planner I, II, and III. Career development is the responsibility of the incumbent, and promotions are normally open competitions, including **lateral entry** from outside the organization (leading to the term **open personnel system**). Merit selection has relied heavily on systems with many grades or levels.

✖ EXHIBIT 5.1   Job Versus Rank Classification

There are two approaches to merit classification: job and rank. Although neither may be found in pure form (one sees approximations in organizations), there are very real differences in emphasis. The nearest approximation of the job/position (or "open") strategy is the civil service; the best approximation of the rank (or "closed") strategy is the military officer corps. A number of features distinguish the two types.

Job (Open) Merit Strategy	*Rank (Closed) Merit Strategy*
Focus on work: "Job makes the person"	Focus on individual: "person makes the job"
Entry based on technical qualifications only	Entry based on general qualifications and long-term potential
Lateral entry allowed	Lateral entry discouraged or prohibited
Promotion based on open competition in most cases	Promotion based on evaluation by superiors
Grade level maintained as long as performance is satisfactory	Expectation that rank will increase over time; an "up-or-out" philosophy will screen out incumbents
Career development is largely the responsibility of the incumbent	Career development is largely planned by the organization through specified career paths
Tends to focus on/produce specialists	Tends to focus on/produce generalists

✖ **EXHIBIT 5.2**   Three Examples of Rank-in-Person

Army Officer Ranks	Fire Department Ranks	University/Faculty Ranks

Quasi-officers:
  Cadets
  Warrant officers
	Recruit
	
	Firefighter
	
	Engineer
		Unranked/untenured:
		  Teaching assistant
		  Instructor
		  Adjunct faculty

Company officers:
  Second lieutenant
  First lieutenant
  Captain
	Medic
	
	Lieutenant
	
	Captain
		Ranked/untenured:
		  Assistant professor
		
		Ranked/tenured:
		  Associate professor

Field officers:
  Major
  Lieutenant colonel
  Colonel
	District fire chief
	
	Assistant fire chief
	
	Fire marshal
		Full professor
		Professor with special status
		  (distinguished, regent's
		  professor, endowed chair)

General or flag officers:
  Brigadier general
  Major general
  Lieutenant general
  General
  5-star general
    (general of the army)
	Deputy fire chief
	
	Fire chief	

Rank-in-person strategies are less common in the United States; they include the military, paramilitary organizations such as public safety departments, the foreign service, academic departments, some health agencies, and the federal Senior Executive Service. (Exhibit 5.2 provides some typical examples of occupational ranks.) Rank-in-person emphasizes the development of incumbents over time, especially within the organization, and tends to lead to closed systems. **Closed personnel systems** provide few opportunities for lateral entry for those outside the organization. They allow for more position mobility because personnel carry their rank with them no matter what their current assignment. Promotions are prized and are expected over time; these systems typically have a strong **up-or-out philosophy** so that those who are not promoted eventually may be forced to leave the organization. Ranks may number from as few as 3 to as many as 10 for military officers.

Hybrid or mixed strategies are also possible. In selected cases, public servants are appointed but serve for set terms (such as state public safety directors and university regents) like elected officials. Some judges are appointed for life. Today, there is a renewed interest in linking rule-based (merit) selection with termination processes similar to those in appointment strategies, that is, **at-will employment** in which property rights to jobs are limited.[5] Although at-will employment is still the exception rather than the rule in the public sector, this chapter will discuss important contemporary examples of the drive to reform the **civil service**. The conclusion will focus on this and other trends affecting rank-in-position and rank-in-person systems (for an example of this debate, see DeSoto & Castillo, 1995; Somma & Fox, 1997; West & Bowman, 2004).

THE ORIGINS OF POSITION CLASSIFICATION AND MANAGEMENT

In the first century of public sector employment in the United States, from 1789 to 1883, position classification did not really exist as a rational system. Positions tended to be created and salaried in an ad hoc fashion, largely based on a **patronage system**, social class, and regional representativeness, and only coincidentally by merit. The initial period of public service was relatively elitist and staid, but public service evolved over the 19th century into a tumultuous system. Congress enacted legislation in 1853 establishing four major job classes with salary rates for each of the classes; however, this legislation was frequently ignored, and all levels of government struggled with merit, equity, and consistency considerations (Mosher, 1982; Van Riper, 1958).

The civil service reform movement, which had gained steam by the end of the 19th century, changed the landscape of position classification and management over time, but the importance of reform should not overshadow other influences. At the same time that political influence was being reduced in recruitment, selection, promotion, discipline, and other personnel processes, principles of modern management were more generally introduced. By the early 1900s, Frederick Taylor's scientific management, whether really scientific or not, had great sway over the development of position classification processes. Taylor promoted the idea that there was generally "one best way" to accomplish work, which could be found by thorough work analysis. This effectively combated the Jacksonian notion that the government work was "so plain and simple that men of intelligence may readily qualify themselves" (quoted in Van Riper, 1958, p. 36).

Work analysis provided the means to select superior methods of performance, to identify those who could perform better, and to provide superior training. Systematic job descriptions became more commonplace, and work relationships became rationalized. Work analysis highlights differences and breaks work into component parts. Because of this, the scientific management movement then started a long-term trend of "pigeonholing" work, breaking it into hundreds and ultimately thousands of different jobs at dozens of different levels. See, for example, the old *Dictionary of Occupational Titles* or *DOT* (U.S. Department of Labor, 1991), which had 12,741 occupations listed.[6]

The Classification Act of 1923, consolidating the new wisdom of scientific management, provided a national model of a rational position management system. It established that (a) positions and not individuals were to be classified, (b) **job duties** and responsibilities were the distinguishing characteristics of jobs, (c) qualifications were to be a critical factor in determining classification status, and (d) a member of a class would be qualified for all other positions in the class. This act enhanced legislative ability to monitor and control positions in terms of overall employee numbers, grade ceilings, and salary ranges. The Classification Act of 1949 created a separate schedule for white- and blue-collar workers, typical of a trend to divide personnel systems into occupational clusters. The proliferation of rank-in-position systems promoted the idea of fitting people to jobs. During this period, managerial efficiency and legislative control were emphasized on one hand, and employee procedural rights were increasingly enhanced on the other. Jobs tended to become narrower and less flexible.

Equal opportunity substantially changed position management through legislation addressing discrimination based on race, color, religion, gender, national origin, age, and disabilities. Particularly important was the passage of the Equal Pay Act of 1963, which addressed gender discrimination in pay. The notion of equal pay for equal work, regardless of personal characteristics of the job incumbent, was taken to its logical legal extension, as was equal opportunity for employment and advancement. Labor unions in the public sector continued to increase in numbers and power throughout this period, although unions in the private sector began to experience a marked decline by the 1980s.

Although both equal opportunity and strong worker representation had obvious benefits, the excesses of the position management systems initiated after the **Pendleton Act** had also become apparent: classification rigidity, excessive specialization and pigeonholing, weak results-oriented employee accountability, and technical complexity. For example, at the federal level critics complained that promotion from one job classification to another had become positively litigious, the 2,500 different job classifications had become excessive, firing nonperforming employees had become a nightmare, and the technical complexity of nearly three dozen pay systems had become byzantine. State and local government systems tended to demonstrate the same symptoms on a smaller scale. By the mid-1990s, equal opportunity began to recede as the dominant concern in personnel systems (Ewoh & Elliott, 1997).

Although the Civil Service Reform Act of 1978 provided an important initial attempt at reform,[7] the most recent human resources era really starts in the 1990s with an emphasis on broad employee categories, more procedural flexibility, more rigorous employee accountability, and technical simplification. Examples include broadbanding, reinventing government, simplification initiatives in personnel policies and manuals, and revisions in the civil service system. **Broadbanding** occurs when several grades are combined, creating a wide salary range for a position. Formal promotions are not required for pay movement (as is the case with more traditional—and narrow—classification series), although milestone progress is still required and documented. In some versions, people are ranked in a single classification, such as entry level, journeyman, senior, and specialist, but these designations are determined by the unit rather than by a personnel department or **civil service commission**. Reinventing government and simplification initiatives in the early 1990s tended to decentralize many personnel functions to the field and concurrently to streamline procedures so that field staff (such as field offices, individual departments, or units) can implement them. Current civil service reform focuses on enhancing employee accountability to meet moderate and/or definable performance standards (U.S. Merit Systems Protection Board [U.S. MSPB], 1999). The most dramatic examples of this to date are the termination of the civil service system in Georgia in 1996 (see Exhibit 5.3 for a discussion of this case) and the rise of employment contracts as well as posttenure faculty review processes in state universities (Isfahani, 1998). Although the federal classification has yet to undergo major changes with respect to the 1949 act, exemptions from it are increasing (Cipolla, 1999), and recommendations for a moderate (Kettl, Ingraham, Sanders, & Horner, 1996) to radical overhaul (Cipolla, 1999; U.S. General Accounting Office [U.S. GAO], 2003) seem to be increasing.

A final historical issue of note is the effort by human resource experts to try to utilize a single overarching taxonomy of job titles so that they can be compared in and across industries. In practical terms, classification systems will ultimately be customized; however, the ideal is that they all use a common language and framework. That framework is the Standard

---

✄ EXHIBIT 5.3   Reinventing Civil Service in Georgia

On July 1, 1996, the state of Georgia radically changed its personnel system by ceasing to grant civil service protection to incoming employees. After that date, incoming employees are considered "unclassified," which removes them from the jurisdiction of the State Personnel Board and essentially makes them at-will employees. Eventually, no state employees will be covered by the traditional civil service protections afforded under the State Personnel Board. At least four factors seem to have contributed to the ability of Georgia to pass and uphold such radical legislation:

- Georgia being a right-to-work state
- Gubernatorial success in passing a legislative agenda
- Editorial support from the largest newspapers in the state
- Support from bureaucratic leaders in government

Under the new provisions, employees do not have property interest or tenure rights over their jobs, which means that supervisors will have more discretion in termination proceedings. In addition, recruiting and selection will be done on an agency-by-agency basis.

Even before 1996, some agencies had removed themselves from the civil service system so that 18% of state employees were unclassified. By 1998, the proportion had increased significantly to 33%, and the projections are that by 2006, nearly 90% of the state's employees will be unclassified.

To date, the changes have resulted in no prominent abuses such as political intervention, bureaucratic nepotism, or managerial bullying; nor have they resulted in widespread organizational changes. Observers will watch this case carefully because of the ramifications. Of particular interest will be whether examples of spoils appointments become evident and evidence of how a widespread reduction in force (RIF) will affect a system without bumping rights.

SOURCE: Condrey (1998).

Occupational Classification (SOC), maintained by the Office of Personnel Management. It divides jobs into 23 major groups, 96 minor groups, 449 broad occupations, and 821 detailed occupations (Pollack, Simons, Romero, & Hausser, 2002). It is used by federal departments such as the Bureau of Labor Statistics (*Occupational Outlook Handbook*), Employment and Training Administration (the online *Occupational Information Network* or O*NET), Bureau of the Census, and OPM (the federal classification system). Although the hope is that other levels of government—as well as the private sector, which uses the products of these agencies—will eventually gravitate toward the revised SOC, this convergence of systems has yet to occur.

PIECEMEAL PERSONNEL PATTERNS VERSUS POSITION CLASSIFICATION SYSTEMS

Piecemeal personnel systems are those that lack grades or ranks and assign salaries on an ad hoc basis. Job relationships may be reflected in an organization chart and brief job descriptions may exist; however, detailed job analyses, well-articulated job series, and civil service protections are partial or nonexistent. Piecemeal personnel systems are still common in small governments. Obvious drawbacks include inconsistency; lack of integration of the human resource functions such as hiring, appraisal, and promotion; and the possibility of legal challenge for hiring and promotional validity. Piecemeal systems, however, do offer flexibility and a level of informality that may suit small organizations fairly well.

Formal **position classification systems** provide grades or ranks for all merit positions as well for nonmerit positions. This allows for rational position management systems that assign **authorized salary ranges** to each grade or rank. In the ideal, all merit jobs are thoroughly analyzed for content and rigorously evaluated for relative worth. Furthermore, the system should provide *internal equity* among organization members and **external equity** with those in similar positions outside the organization. The system should also furnish an opportunity to reflect seniority, merit, skill, and other specialized **individual equity** concerns (such as locale and shift differences). In reality, position management systems rarely meet such standards, partly because of the expense and effort in maintaining such ideals and partly because of the competing and inconsistent demands placed on these systems.

The Two Primary Uses of Classification Systems

Position classification systems are structures that manage, track, and control employment numbers, costs, and levels of positions. Legislators need to know the number of authorized positions versus the number of filled positions and to anticipate total personnel costs so that they can curb the number of positions in specific areas and control position grades or ranks. Position management systems typically number positions, assign locations, and determine an exact system of compensation. Positions can be tracked by function, such as transportation, and by specialty, such as engineering. Positions also can be tracked and monitored by grade or rank. For example, the state of Iowa has 57 pay grades and six steps in most grades; thus, a legislator can determine how many employees work in what agencies, at what level, and at what cost. A position classification system from this perspective is ultimately a management tool to support compensation systems and control costs.

The second primary function of position classification systems is job support and design. Position classification systems provide the basis for the division and coordination of work, recruitment efforts, selection methods, training programs, appraisal systems, and other human resource functions through analysis and organization of jobs in the organization. Although both the control/management and job support/design functions of position classification examine job content, their different purposes often require different methods in practice.

How Are Positions Grouped Together?

Position systems start with the duties and responsibilities of a single individual, whose job is called a **position**. Clusters of positions with similar characteristics are organized into what is called a **job classification**, job class, classification, or simply job or class (terms are used interchangeably here). Technically, "jobs" refer to identical positions, whereas "classes" refer to similar positions in which there are equivalent responsibilities and training, although the specific duty assignment may vary. For example, "property appraiser" may be the class, but one individual may be assigned to residential properties and another to commercial. For classification purposes, however, both have generic training with easy rotational opportunities, which is why the concept of job classifications is used (so that excessive numbers of categories will not be created). The number of job classifications varies considerably by organization: The federal government has approximately 2,500, states vary from a high of 4,500 (California) to a low of 550 (South Dakota), and very tiny organizations have just a few classifications

(Chi, 1998). Classes that are linked developmentally are grouped into **class series**.[8] For example, the federal government has approximately 450 class series for white-collar workers and another 350 for blue-collar workers. Class series are subsequently grouped into large **occupational families**. Related occupational families, such as all white-collar jobs, are assigned a **pay plan** or schedule in which the grades, steps, and related pay are determined.

As rational as this sounds in theory, practice can produce disorderly systems. The size of the jurisdiction, the number of bargaining units, and the history of the jurisdiction produce very different position classification systems with different sorts of challenges and contradictions. Exhibit 5.4 demonstrates two common problems. First, systems often have an unnecessary number of pay plans, which are often driven by labor-management negotiations rather than by rational planning (Levine & Kleeman, 1986). Blue-collar positions in the example are under three different plans, and public safety is under two different plans. Ideally, they would be grouped together. Second, the example illustrates the change of pay plans by individuals as they move up the chain of command. Firefighters are in Pay Plan G, fire captains are in Pay Plan C (for midlevel managers in the city), and the fire chief is in Pay Plan D (for city executives). The number of pay plans seems to increase as the jurisdiction size increases (see Exhibit 5.5, p. 131, for an example of this problem). Although this may increase responsiveness to market factors and enhance comparability in some cases, it can lead to a system that is complex and unwieldy. Note that the one system with a moderate number of pay plans (the judicial branch of Iowa) was comprehensively reorganized in the 1980s. Other problems are excessively narrow class definitions (sometimes with only a single job incumbent) and positions that have dual classifications (and different compensation patterns) merely because the identical jobs are found in different organizational or bargaining units of the same government.

Rank-in-person systems reduce the number of job classes through the use of a uniform series of ranks for a multitude of operational positions. "Army captain," "district fire chief," and "assistant professor" are generic job titles for numerous positions identified by a specific army unit, fire district, or department. Systems with rank are normally closed to lateral entry (entry from outside the organization without first completing a junior level or entry position), unlike position systems.

In sum, although many small jurisdictions have, and function acceptably with, piecemeal personnel patterns, large jurisdictions need formal position classification systems. Such systems help them track and control positions as well as support those positions by logical groupings called job classes, class series, occupational families, and pay plans. Tools of classification are examined next.

JOB ANALYSIS AND EVALUATION

The two most important tools in position classification and management are job analysis and job evaluation. A **job analysis** is a systematic process of collecting data for determining the knowledge, skills, and abilities (KSAs) required to perform a job successfully and to make numerous judgments about it. In theory, a **job evaluation** is a special type of job analysis, one that attaches a dollar value or worth to the job (Siegel, 1998a, 1998b). In practice, job evaluations are often so specialized that they operate as a completely different function from job analysis; however, no matter what the exact relationship between the two methodologies, they do share similarities. Both can use either a simple "whole job" assessment strategy or a more rigorous "factor system." Both have many formal methodologies (see Appendix A to this

EXHIBIT 5.4 Example of Fragmentation in Classification Systems: The City of Ames, Iowa

The table below presents occupational groupings of employees in the first column (from individual positions to large pay plans), with examples of these in the following columns.

Positions (= 522)	John Doe, unclassified laborer in public works	Jane Doe, fire captain at station[a]	Bob Smith, fire chief	Helen Brown, engineering technician in transportation	Bill West, police officer assigned to patrol	Betty Hernandez, firefighter with paramedic responsibilities	Zed Vandervere, electric line worker on the first shift	Ellen Jordan, power plant fireworker on the second shift
Classes (= 224)	Unclassified laborer	Fire captain	Fire chief (example of single-person class)	Engineering technician	Police officer	Firefighter	Electric line worker	Power plant fireworker
Next class in series	—	Deputy fire chief[a]	—	Engineering technician II	Police corporal	Fire lieutenant	Electric line foreman	Power plant operator
Occupational families (= 8)	Miscellaneous	Nonunion and managers	Department heads and executives	Blue collar unit (IUOE)	Police	Fire service	Blue collar (IBEW)	Electric production (IUOE)
Pay plan or schedule (= 8)	Temporary workers	C Pay Plan[b]	D Pay Plan	E Pay Plan	F Pay Plan	G Pay Plan	H Pay Plan	I Pay Plan

a. Being a small department, Ames does not have a full complement of ranks.

b. Pay plans A and B are no longer in use.

❖ EXHIBIT 5.5   Increase in Number of Pay Plans as Jurisdiction Size Increases (Examples)

	Ames	Iowa Judicial Branch[a]	State of Iowa[b]	United States Federal Government
Number of positions	522	2,200	19,000	5,000,000
Number of classes	224 (average size: 2.3)	132 (average size: 16.7)	850 (average size: 22.4)	2,500 (average size: 2,000)
Number of pay plans or schedules	8	4	15	36

a. This branch of government was rationalized and streamlined in 1986, when the system was converted to a statewide system.

b. The positions do not reflect the 24,000 Regents employees (Iowa State, University of Iowa, and University of Northern Iowa). Regents institutions each have separate classification systems for merit, professional and administrative, faculty, and temporary employees.

chapter) that are relatively complex and expensive but that are important for all organizational members to understand in general terms. Finally, each has common informal methodologies that should be a part of a manager's standard repertoire of skills.

Whole Job Systems Versus Job Factor Systems

Whole job evaluations do not systematically break a job down into its constituent parts; instead, they consider the job in its entirety and make summary judgments based on intuition and past experience. Examples are numerous:

- *Whole job analysis:* A supervisor hires a clerical support person, from another unit in the organization, who clearly has the appropriate skills and already knows the position in general terms. The supervisor needs someone quickly, so no analysis of the position is conducted. Although identified as a "Secretary III" position, the generic job description of the position gives almost no insight into the specific position.

- *Whole job analysis:* A manager hires a special project coordinator for a new position. Although a rough description of the job elements is provided, it is really only suggestive of the types of knowledge, skills, and abilities that might actually be required.

- *Whole job analysis:* An executive appraises a high-performing manager in general terms, without a detailed knowledge of the specific tasks that the person conducts on a daily basis.

- *Whole job evaluation:* A manager in an organization (without a formal position classification system) intuitively selects a salary for a new position that experience indicates will attract competent candidates.

Whole job methods are simple, summary judgments. Their merits include efficiency and a tendency to honor the decision maker's past experience and wisdom. The difficulties are that they can be hasty and based on insufficient or inaccurate information. They also may yield little information for various human resource functions and provide inadequate management or legal defense when the decisions are faulty. For example, in systems with large job classifications and typical job valuations, whole job methods are generally inappropriate.

Job factor systems break jobs down into their component parts. The number and types of factors used vary considerably in job analysis and job evaluation methods. Factors common to both job analyses and job evaluation studies are task requirements, responsibilities, working conditions, physical demands, difficulty of work, and personal relationships (Foster, 1998). Some methods rely on as few as three factors (usually with subfactors), and some use more than a dozen. It is important for the assessor to decide on the exact purposes before selecting the factors and method because formal job factor initiatives are time-consuming and expensive to implement and are scrutinized critically by employees after the fact (for a more complete listing of the limitations of formal job analyses and job evaluations, see Exhibit 5.6). Successful job factor systems bring a degree of coherence to position management systems that can greatly aid morale and operational efficiency.

✖ EXHIBIT 5.6   Limitations of Formal Job Analyses and Job Evaluations

Formal Job Analysis Limitations	*Formal Job Evaluation Limitations*
• First, there is the problem of expense. External consultants are an unusual expense, and internal specialists may lack the expertise or the time.	• First, there is the problem of completeness and integrity. As soon as job evaluations are done, they begin to be compromised by market changes, exceptions, new positions, changes in responsibilities, new technology, and so on.
• Second, there is the problem of obsolescence. The dynamic nature of jobs today means that a formal job analysis soon becomes outdated.	• Second, there is the problem of reward rigidity. Evaluation systems limit the ability of managers to match the abilities and skills of employees with what they are paid. Exceptional and underachieving employees who have "topped out" may receive the same salary.
• Third, there is the problem of organizational rigidity. Today, organizations need employees to be flexible, work in teams, and keep the "big picture" in mind. Formal analyses tend to emphasize narrow job descriptions, individual work, and specialization.	• Third, there are problems of adaptation. Formal evaluation analyses tend to pigeonhole people into categories when those employees need to act in concert with others and may need to fundamentally reformulate their own jobs over time.
• Finally, there is the problem of job definition versus job performance. Although job analyses are good at capturing the outline of the work, they tend to be poor at capturing qualities related to excellence and distinguishing among levels of performance.	

Uses and Methods of Job Analysis

Job analysis typically is used as a key tool for recruitment, classification, selection, training, employee appraisal, and other functions. In terms of recruitment and position classification, job analysis provides up-to-date information for position announcements and a thorough and rigorous basis for the writing of job descriptions and ranking jobs. For selection, job analysis is decisive for determining valid selection criteria that are both practical and legally defensible. For training and development, it can be indispensable in identifying and detailing the competencies needed as well as the specific gaps that typically exist between those competencies and the incumbents' general performance. When considering employee appraisal, job analysis can help define concrete performance standards as well as catalog evaluation criteria. In terms of other human resource functions, it is critical in ascertaining how to make reasonable accommodations for disabled applicants and employees as well as how to redesign or enlarge jobs.

The technique is a powerful instrument because it offers a unique opportunity for learning about fundamental aspects of the organization as well as an opportunity for thoughtful examination of current practices. Executives can encourage comprehensive job analyses to make sure that the organizational structure reflects current management practices, technology, and work distribution requirements. In today's environment, it is likely that job analyses will discover such inefficiencies as excessive middle management, outdated hardware, absence of appropriate software, and areas of under- and overstaffing. Managers can target problem jobs as opportunities for attention and support or clusters of jobs as possibilities for innovation in job design or work flow. Employees can study their colleagues' positions for cross-training in informal job analyses or their own positions for better understanding and to recommend changes in their positions. Even students outside the organization can use job analysis methodology as a part of their internship experiences and as a marketable skill, similar to finance management or policy analysis.

Job analyses rely on a combination of four major methods of collecting information: questionnaires, interviews, observation, and archival data (Foster, 1998). The methods chosen tend to depend on the number of jobs to be analyzed, the kind of work, and the type of information required. For example, a job analysis of a police sergeant's position intended to develop a selection test for a large urban city would require different strategies than would a job analysis of all the positions in an information technology department planning to restructure its operations.

- Use of *archival data* involves a review of job and position descriptions, previous job analyses, performance appraisals, training materials, worker manuals and aids, examples of work products, and other artifacts that help describe and define the position. These data ideally are employed before other analytic steps, but in practice they often become available as the process evolves. An array of archival data provides a potentially invaluable wealth of contextual and detailed information.

- *Questionnaires* can be either open-ended or structured. Open-ended questionnaires ask incumbents to identify the content of their jobs on their own and quantify the functions by percentage of time (Exhibit 5.7 provides an example). Those surveys are then reviewed by supervisors. The strengths of this method are its low cost, standard form, and use of the incumbent's

✖ EXHIBIT 5.7 Position Description Questionnaire

IOWA DEPARTMENT OF PERSONNEL
POSITION DESCRIPTION QUESTIONNAIRE (PDQ)

Read instructions before completing this form.

FOR AGENCY USE ONLY	**FOR IDOP USE ONLY PDQ # _____**
M-5# _____	Class Title _____
☐ New Position	18 Digit Position # _____
☐ Duties have changed:	Personnel Officer _____
_____ Position review requested	Date _____
_____ No position review requested	
☐ Response to IDOP request	

---

1. Name of employee (if none, write VACANT) 2. Current 18-digit positions # and class title

3. Department, Division, Bureau, Section and Work Address

4. Hours worked (shifts, rotations, travel)   5. ☐ Full-time(40 hours per week)
                                                     ☐ Part-time (list number of hours per week)

6. Have the assigned duties changed since this position was last reviewed for a classification decision? ☐ Yes ☐ No
If Yes, place an "X" beside each NEW task written below. Also, describe in detail how those tasks are different from those previously assigned.

7. Name and job classification of the immediate supervisor

8. Description of Work: Describe the work in detail. Make the description so clear that the reader can understand each task exactly. In the TIME /% column, enter the percent of time spent on each task during an average work week. List the most important responsibility first. If this is a reclassification request, the previous PDQ must be attached. This PDQ will be returned if any section is incomplete.

TIME/%	WORK PERFORMED
	(ATTACH ADDITIONAL SHEETS IF NECESSARY)

CFN 552-0094-4   R 4/99

9. Is this position considered to be supervisory? Yes_____ No_____ If Yes, complete a Supervisory Analysis Questionnaire form (CFN 552-0193) and attach it to this form.

10. For what reasons are you requesting that this position be reviewed? Include, if applicable, significant changes or additions to duties, comparison(s) with other positions, etc. Be specific.

I certify that I have read the instructions for the completion of this questionnaire, that the answers are my own, and that they are accurate and complete. I understand that falsification or misrepresentation made in regard to any information submitted may lead to discipline up to and including discharge.

Signed _____   _____
                (Incumbent Employee)   (Date)

If you have not been notified by your department's management of their decision to support or deny this request within 30 days, you may send this request directly to IDOP for review. Address it to: Facilitator, Program Delivery Services, Iowa Department of Personnel, Grimes Building, East 14th & Grand, Des Moines, Iowa 50319-0150.

SUPERVISOR REVIEW OF POSITION DESCRIPTION QUESTIONNAIRE

This section must be completed within 30 days after the PDQ is received from the employee. The employee must be notified of the decision to support or deny the request. Regardless, the request must be forwarded to IDOP. This PDQ will be returned if any section is incomplete.

11. Indicate to what extent, if any, the statements on this form are, in your opinion, not correct or need clarification.

_____

_____

12. Describe the origin of any new duties, i.e., those marked with an "X" in Item 8. If new duties have been added, where were they performed prior to being assigned to this position? Are these duties performed by anyone else? If so, identify the person(s) and the position classification of their positions.

_____

_____

13. What is the basic purpose of this position?

_____

_____

14. Identify the essential functions that must be performed by the incumbent, with or without reasonable accommodation for disabilities. Identify any certifications or licenses that are required. Refer to the instruction sheet and Section 3.15 of the *Managers and Supervisors Manual* for more information on essential functions.

_____

_____

(Continued)

(Continued)

15. Is this position considered to be confidentially or managerially exempt from collective bargaining? Yes____ No____ If Yes, complete the Bargaining Exemption Questionnaire (CFN 552-0631) and attach it to this form.

Signed _____   _____   _____
           (Supervisor)   (Title and Job Classification)   (Date)

APPOINTING AUTHORITY REVIEW OF POSITION DESCRIPTION QUESTIONNAIRE

16. Comments:

_____

_____

Signed _____   _____
           (Appointing Authority)   (Date)

CFN 552-0094-4   R 4/99

SOURCE: Iowa Department of Personnel (1999).

knowledge of the position. Unfortunately, questionnaires generally require significant follow-up to fill in gaps and are susceptible to incumbent embellishment or, in some cases, diffidence. Closed-ended or structured instruments provide task lists (usually lengthy) from which to select. They provide highly detailed information about the job but require computer-based aggregation and trained staff analysis for effective utilization.

- *Interviews* can be conducted with individuals or groups. The content of jobs can be analyzed through semistructured or wholly structured question protocols of either job incumbents or supervisors. This is a particularly useful method for managerial, technical, and professional positions. Group methods are useful when a class of positions has relatively little variation or when a list of unstructured elements is being elicited, such as critical incidents. The major drawback of interviews is their time-consuming nature.

- *Observation* involves watching individuals actually perform their jobs. It is particularly effective for analyzing blue-collar positions for which the activities can be observed and is less useful in analyzing white-collar occupations. It provides the analyst with firsthand experience, which in some cases may be enhanced by the analyst performing the functions.

Formal methods are time-consuming and frequently expensive. In practice, they are employed in a small number of important cases. First, formal job analysis should always be used when there is an employment test that can be challenged easily on the grounds of validity. Validity challenges (see Chapter 4) are most common for large, entry-level classifications, especially for jobs that are highly sought because of their professional potential and that require basic knowledge– or skill-based tests. Examples include firefighter and fire lieutenant, police officer and police detective/corporal, sheriff's deputy, FBI agent, IRS investigator, and auditor. Analysis is also important to determine reasonable accommodations for those with disabilities. These types of analyses are conducted by personnel specialists but are frequently subcontracted to specialized consulting firms. Some jurisdictions, especially small ones, use off-the-shelf tests that have been validated by vendors for positions like firefighter or police officer.

Formal job analysis may be used in reclassifications when there is pressure to upgrade the position. Reclassifications generally are formally requested by the incumbent, must be supported by the supervisor, and are administered and approved by the human resource department. It is highly useful for those requesting, supporting, or discouraging reclassifications to understand formal job analysis methodology (note that Exhibit 5.7 can be used in reclassifications as well as the classification of new positions).

Formal job analysis also may be used as a preliminary step in a job evaluation study in which the positions of a division or entire organization are being recalibrated. Such studies normally are subcontracted to consulting firms, if only for the neutrality that external assessors are perceived to possess. Except for relatively consistent (but highly generic) job descriptions, however, this may supply information of limited value. Finally, formal job analysis is sometimes used for comprehensive training studies (Exhibit 5.8 is an example of such a comprehensive study by the U.S. Coast Guard).

✕ EXHIBIT 5.8   Example of a Comprehensive Job Analysis Leading to a Training Program

The U.S. Coast Guard periodically reviews its jobs in a comprehensive manner to revise job tasks and pay scales, to review staffing levels, to help design career ladders and identify worker satisfaction, to ensure the proficiency of certification programs, to help distinguish training problems from management problems, and to help establish realistic training objectives and standards and refine training content.

When the Coast Guard decided to review the position of machinery technician, the training manager and a line manager spent 3 months preparing for the work of a nine-member panel. The nine panelists were themselves machinery technicians chosen from a range of experiences and sent to Yorktown, Virginia, to the Coast Guard training center. The panel was instructed to use the Lippert Card Approach, which meant that every possible machinery technician task needed to be written down on a different card. The panel broke the job down into categories (e.g., internal combustion engines). Then all possible tasks were identified (e.g., fabricate battery cables). When they were done, the panelists had identified approximately 10,000 different tasks. Next, they had to cluster the tasks to reduce the number to a more manageable quantity. They eventually reduced the task list to 1,503 items.

The next phase was to send a questionnaire to all machinery technicians—more than 3,000 of them. The questionnaire asked for background information about the task inventory and for a work summary. Every machinery technician was asked three questions about every task finally identified: (a) Do you ever do the task? (b) What is the relative time spent on the task? and (c) What should the training emphasis be?

Although the task was long, often tedious, and expensive, the methodological treatment provided a wealth of useful information for decisions to be made by human resource specialists, managers and administrators, and training specialists.

SOURCE: Markowitz (1987).

To summarize, job analysis can be used not only by human resource departments but also by managers and employees. Its formal methods tend to be practiced by internal experts or consultants, but informal usage is now considered a generic management skill.

JOB AND POSITION DESCRIPTIONS

One of the most important uses of job analysis is for job and position descriptions. Although the terms are used nearly interchangeably, with **job description** being the collective reference, they actually represent somewhat different concepts. It is useful to exaggerate the differences for clarity because job and position descriptions are the building blocks of position classification and management systems. Both are written statements about a job that describe or list the duties, but the focus of the two often varies significantly, as do the uses, writers, and level of specificity.

Job descriptions are statements that codify the typical or average duties (sometimes by using work examples), levels of responsibility, and general competencies and requirements of a job class. They are generally prepared by human resource specialists or personnel consultants. Their primary uses are for systems management (placement of positions in specific classes) and compensation decisions; job descriptions tend to be maintained by the human resource department. The language is usually generic so that a description covers many positions, and the examples used may or may not apply to a specific position. Although the format varies tremendously, the underlying structure of job descriptions does not.

Position descriptions are statements that define the exact duties, level of responsibility, and organizational placement of a single position (or essentially identical group of positions). Although they are sometimes written by personnel specialists, they are generally written by job incumbents or their supervisors. Their primary purposes are for recruitment (where they are modified as job announcements), reclassification (where the duties and responsibilities tend to be compared to the job classification requested), and performance appraisal (where work standards and accomplishments tend to be emphasized). Because of the wide variety of objectives, their format varies considerably. Their maintenance is generally dependent on the specific use or the culture of the local unit; true position descriptions are rarely centrally maintained. An example of a comparison of job and position descriptions using the class "equipment operator 2" is located in Appendix A of this chapter. The job description is for a class with more than 1,000 positions; the position description was used as part of a successful effort to reclassify the position from an equipment operator 1 to an equipment operator 2.

In practice, very small organizations may not maintain job descriptions and may use position descriptions only occasionally, such as when they need to recruit. Small and medium-sized organizations that have overhauled their position classification system within a decade or so often find that they are able to maintain job descriptions that have many characteristics of position descriptions because the number of incumbents is small in each class. In bigger organizations with many large classes, job descriptions generally are maintained conscientiously (and used for all purposes even if they prove less than ideal for recruitment and appraisal), whereas position descriptions are created selectively for management and human resource purposes.

Finally, it should be noted that traditional and contemporary job and position descriptions vary in two significant regards. The Americans With Disabilities Act of 1990 (ADA) has had a profound effect on job descriptions, position descriptions, and position announcements. Traditionally, jobs were defined as having 3 to 10 major *duties* (core area of responsibilities), each of which might have two or more **job tasks** (discrete work activities necessary to the performance of a job and that result in an outcome usable to another person).[9] Because the ADA prohibits discrimination against "an individual with a disability, who with or without reasonable accommodation, can perform the **essential functions** of the employment position," the language more commonly used today is adapted to essential and nonessential functions rather than duties and tasks. Furthermore, physical, manual, and special requirements are now routinely spelled out in job and position descriptions.[10] Second, the new management emphasis on accountability and results has led to the incorporation of performance standards in some cases. It remains to be seen whether results-oriented job and position descriptions become a norm in the public sector.

Writing Job Descriptions

Writing job descriptions is a specific skill that takes some study to master. In practice, many templates are used, but the style invariably is terse. The simple format used as an example here is a job summary, essential functions, physical and environmental standards required to perform essential functions, and minimum job requirements and qualifications for a town accounts payable/payroll clerk.

The job summary begins with the level of responsibility and identifies the department and level of supervision, if any, followed by a list of major duties.

> Example: Under general supervision, this position works in the office of the city administrator. This position is responsible for financial support tasks including payroll processing, accounts receivable, accounts payable, bank deposits and reconciliations, and other general clerical support duties for the administrator and council as assigned.

The second category identifies essential functions, generally those that constitute more than 5% of the incumbent's time and are central to the job. These start with a verb followed by an object and sometimes an explanatory phrase. Ideally, 5 to 7 functions are listed, but there may be as few as 3 and as many as 10. Long, unorganized task lists once were typical but now are considered poor form. Tasks should be clustered into duty areas and combined where necessary. It is possible to place a performance standard at the end of each statement.

> Example: Processes biweekly time sheets and enters payroll information into computer; computes used and accrued sick and vacation time and overtime hours; pays required federal and state taxes; deducts insurance and related payroll costs; prints payroll checks and payroll reports. Extreme accuracy and timeliness is required in performing this critical function.

The third category identifies the physical and environmental standards required to perform essential functions. Physical standards should articulate the exact physical abilities required to accomplish job tasks as normally constituted, knowing that reasonable accommodation may be necessary for a qualified applicant or incumbent who is disabled. Environmental standards include such conditions as working outside, dangerous conditions, and nonstandard working hours. Generally, this section uses a format similar to that used for the essential functions.

Example: Requires the ability to handle a variety of documents and use hands in typing, data entry, using a calculator and related equipment; occasionally lift and carry books, ledgers, reports, and other documents weighing less than 25 pounds; use personal automobile in depositing monies at local banks; requires visual and hearing ability sufficiently correctable to see clients, hear phones, and operate in an office environment that has limited auxiliary support.

The fourth category identifies minimum requirements and qualifications. Here, required KSAs are identified, as well as special certifications, degrees, and training. Requirements for excessive credentials should be avoided to ensure consistency with merit principles and equal employment opportunity. Substitutions generally are listed.

Example: Graduation from high school or GED and 3 years of general accounting/bookkeeping experience; substitution of successful completion of a business or accounting curriculum at a recognized college or school may be made for part of the experience requirement. Must also have good interpersonal skills and excellent ability to coordinate and balance numerous, sometimes hectic, activities in a calm fashion without letting technical accuracy suffer.

Job analysis, then, has various functions including the writing of job and position descriptions. It has many levels of rigor (see Appendix A to this chapter). Job evaluation, discussed in the next section, tends to rely exclusively on formal methods.

Using Factors for Job Evaluation

Historically, jobs originally were evaluated using a whole job methodology: What was a particular job thought to be worth in general terms? Despite the flexibility and immediacy of such systems, they are prone to distortions based on personalism, limited information, and excessive focus on the job incumbent. Position classification ushered in an age of factor systems in which job grades or levels were commonly established. Graded systems took into account (often implicitly) such factors as level of responsibility, job requirements, difficulty of work, nature of the relationships, and level of supervision. This led to far more rational and equitable compensation systems; however, the factor methodologies used in most position management systems can use factors quite dissimilarly for different positions. They also allow for considerable subjective judgment in making decisions about the grade of positions.

Today **point factor methods** are considered more rigorous methodologies and are utilized to reevaluate position management and compensation practices. They are generally used when organizations find that their position classification systems have become too inconsistent and outdated. In the majority of cases, an external consultant conducts the underlying pay study to design the new system because of the time and expertise required to accomplish such a large task.

A point factor system starts with the assumption that factors should be broad enough to apply consistently to all jobs in an organization or schedule. In practice, 4 to 12 factors generally are selected. For instance, the Federal Evaluation System (FES) uses 9 for the General Schedule. Each factor is then weighted by determining a maximum number of points that can be assigned to it. In the case of the FES, note the tremendous differences in the weights of the different factors:

Factor	Maximum Points	Evaluation Weight (%)
Knowledge required	1,850	41.3
Supervisory controls	650	14.5
Guidelines	650	14.5
Complexity	450	10.0
Scope and effect	450	10.0
Personal contacts	110	2.5
Purpose of contacts	220	4.9
Physical demands	50	1.1
Work environment	50	1.1

Next, the factors are defined by levels or standards that are used to determine the actual number of points a job classification will receive. Three to five standards interpret the various levels; descriptions are provided of what high, medium, and low levels mean in each factor. Factors may be further subdivided into a number of subfactors. All jobs are then evaluated by individuals, committees, or both. This part of the process should provide internal equity because of the consistency of the process. After all jobs have been evaluated and arranged from lowest to highest, point ranges are selected to determine grade levels.

Point factor systems are excellent for internal equity but by themselves do not ensure external equity. External equity is maintained by linking the entire point factor system to compensation comparisons of select jobs outside the organization. A portion of the classifications are chosen as **benchmark jobs**, anchored to general market salary ranges as indicated by reliable compensation survey information.[11] In large organizations, it may be as few as 5% or 10% of the positions; in small organizations it may be as high as 25%. Benchmark jobs are used for each major class series to ensure external equity and that the entire system is in line with market compensation practices. Today, these relatively complex, hybrid "point factor benchmark" systems are what are most commonly used by consulting firms, although they are usually simply referred to as point factor systems.

As a straightforward example, suppose that an organization finds that its position classification system is outdated, that most job descriptions do not reflect ADA standards, and that there is a good opportunity to modestly increase salaries, which are currently below the market in most cases. An external consulting firm is hired that specializes in government compensation studies. The consultant uses four factors: level of responsibility, complexity of problem solving, degree of accountability, and working conditions.[12] Multiple raters examine 7% of the job classes, using the four factors to ensure reliability. This provides reference points (benchmark jobs) in the evaluation of other jobs.

All classes then are analyzed and evaluated using the four factors. (As a by-product of the evaluation process, new job descriptions are generated that provide essential and nonessential duties as well as physical requirements and environmental conditions for compatibility with the ADA.) The evaluation assigns a specific point value to each job class. After all the classes have been arrayed on a point scale from lowest to highest, intervals are selected that determine the grade levels. Those benchmarked jobs are then matched to salary survey data to ensure comparability to market salaries. Throughout the process, the organization has a task force assigned to work with the external consultant, which includes the human resource specialist for compensation. After completing the study, the results are forwarded to the entire organization, which has an opportunity to review the analysis and to provide further input to the task force. The task force presents the study to the governing body, with its recommendations for adoption (or rejection) and for specific changes. Because such studies usually represent some salary expense increase, the governing board may or may not accept the study or the accompanying organizational recommendations.

Because comprehensive job evaluations (pay studies) are expensive and time-consuming, they occur infrequently.[13] Managers, executives, and legislators need to be aware of how compensation factors were arrived at in the past, how well the compensation system has fared over time, and when a new compensation study and pay plan may be called for, as well as the auxiliary features that such research can produce with planning (see Exhibit 5.9 for a discussion of when to conduct a job evaluation study).

✖ EXHIBIT 5.9   When to Conduct a Job Evaluation Study

Because organizationwide job evaluation studies are expensive, time-consuming, and often controversial, they should not be used as feasibility studies. If the adoption of the final study (with modifications) is not propitious, it is better not to begin at all. Nor should a comprehensive job evaluation analysis be used if only a few job classifications are at issue; in that event, only those cases or class series should be evaluated.

First, preliminary questions must be asked. How and when were jobs last evaluated (using what methodologies) and by whom? How much controversy does the system seem to generate, and what are its major problems (internal equity such as pay inconsistencies; external equity such as widespread below-market salaries; special problems such as hard-to-recruit and hard-to-retain jobs, excessive job plateauing, inadequate financial incentives)?

Second, the purpose of a proposed study needs to be clearly outlined. Is it for an occupational family, a pay plan, or the entire organization? Would the analysis primarily target internal inequities, overall external inequities such as depressed salaries across the board, more flexible salary plans, merit-based pay systems, or a variety of factors? Who would conduct the evaluation, and how would they be commissioned? What would be the role or input of employee unions? Defining the purposes of the initiative ensures that the organizational or legislative leaders and the evaluators do not have two separate notions of what is to be accomplished (which is not uncommon).

Third, feasibility and political reality must be assessed candidly. If the overall problem with the compensation plan is depressed salaries across the board but government revenues are limited because of economic or financial exigencies (such as a recession or an expensive capital building plan), then a job evaluation study will do little but agitate workers, put executives in an uncomfortable position, and annoy elected officials (who will turn down the plan). Practical questions include the following: Will there be money to both pay for the analysis and increase some or all salaries? Do legislators really understand the underlying need (because the study itself is unlikely to convince them) as well as the general plan of implementation? How can the study be used as a means of enhancing labor-management relations rather than become another bone of contention?

Finally, the jurisdiction needs to be clear if it wants more than just a compensation study conducted. A common outcome desired is job descriptions that have wider human resource utility. Such a by-product must not be assumed and should be carefully spelled out before the process.

For their part, it is essential for employees and managers to understand job evaluation factors to maximize the prospects for success in petitions for reclassification. Too frequently, a good employee is performing well but has weak grounds for a reclassification, which is based on the nature of the position and not on the job incumbent's particular skills or assignments. Unless grounds can be established that the position itself has been fundamentally and permanently altered, a reclassification request is likely to be turned down (although a classification specialist might assist with a market adjustment, special step increase, bonus, or other pay modification suggestion). Because of this type of problem, as well as the perceived rigidity of position management systems in general today, alternative systems such as broadbanding (discussed in the next chapter) frequently are recommended.

SUMMARY AND CONCLUSION

Position classification became more of a judicious plan throughout the last century than it ever was before. Outright corruption is uncommon; rational plans for managing jobs in terms of compensation and other human resource functions exist in all large organizations and are tailored to their needs and histories; and specific tools now exist in this area, such as job analysis and job evaluation, which include both highly sophisticated methodologies as well as informal methods commonly used by managers.

Nevertheless, the ability to have greater (but not perfect) control, consistency, precision, and rationality (which position classification and management theory and practice have enabled managers to achieve) should not disguise the underlying truth that it is only partially a science and largely an art. The decisions made in position management systems ultimately are founded on value choices, not universal laws (Van Wart, 1998). Many of the values assumed over the last half century are shifting dramatically because of changed economics, politics, and technology. Furthermore, even at its most rational and ideal, the position classification system of large organizations is a combination of at least three fundamentally different personnel systems based on election, appointment, and rule-based criteria. Indeed, rule-based (i.e., merit) criteria are themselves divided between position-based systems and less common rank-based systems, sometimes occurring in the same organization. Finally, the sheer organizational complexity and level of change in organizations today means that extensive, expensive, difficult-to-maintain position classification systems naturally tend to become less rational, less consistent, and out of date. Paradoxically then, as much as position classification systems are judicious plans, they are also ever-changing jigsaw puzzles of shifting values, of radically different personnel approaches, and of competing human resource needs to control, on one hand, and to support and design jobs, on the other.

The new value changes emanate from elemental transformations in the public sector landscape in terms of what people want public sector organizations to do and how they want them to do it (De Leon & Denhardt, 2000; Yergin & Stanislaw, 1998). Rather than an emphasis on employee rights and internal procedural consistency, there is a far greater interest in employee accountability and concrete achievement translating into an increased reliance on at-will systems (with appointment-based features) and performance standards (Grady & Tax, 1996; Radin, 1998; U.S. MSPB, 2002). This has certainly prompted extensive debate about the advantages and potential liabilities of contemporary civil service reforms (see, for example, the debate between Hays & Kearney, 1999; Kearney & Hays, 1998; and Van Wart, 1999). The emphasis on efficiency and effectiveness is in line with the historic tradition of scientific management and can be seen as a logical progression of the art of position management.

Other trends promise to take position management into new domains and configurations. The demand for agencies that are flexible, flatter, and more entrepreneurial requires not only new organizational structures but also new internal management systems in the United States (Leavitt & Johnson, 1998; Marshall, 1998) and elsewhere in the world (Farnham, 1997). Such trends will propel institutions to reexamine their complex systems and to simplify them. Efforts to use broadbanding (fewer classes and enlarged jobs) and work teams are examples, as are attempts to simplify massive management systems. Contemporary initiatives to decentralize responsibility to local managers who will be more accountable for results, but allowed more flexibility, will also change the landscape. Indeed, some predict the "death of the job" (Crandall & Wallace, 1998) as virtual work designs stretch people beyond narrow, predictable tasks by extending not only their line of sight (understanding outcomes and how their activities relate to them) but also their line of impact (confidence stemming from affecting results).

However, whether one comes to view position management systems more as judicious plans or as jigsaw puzzles, they will remain the core of the human resource function that managers, employees, and job aspirants cannot afford to mystify or underutilize.

APPENDIX A

Comparison of a Job and Position Description

SAMPLE JOB DESCRIPTION

Equipment Operator 2, Class Code: 08111

Definition: Under general supervision, performs specialized and routine roadway and right-of-way maintenance activities including physical laboring activities, the operation of self-propelled mobile equipment, skilled equipment operation, and/or limited direction of work crews; performs related work as required.

Work Examples

(The Work Examples and Competencies listed are for illustrative purposes only and not intended to be the primary basis for position classification decisions.)

- Assists a supervisor by performing limited lead work in accordance with set procedures, policies, and standards, such duties as instructing employees about tasks, answering questions about procedures and policies, distributing and balancing the workload and checking work; makes occasional suggestions on appointments, promotions, and reassignments.
- Works on district paint crew in rotation with other paint crew positions.
- Works on the district bridge crew.
- Acts as a maintenance sign crew leader in maintenance areas where work on signs requires a full-time sign crew.
- Acts as a lighting specialist and may be assigned to the state lighting crew to assist that crew in the maintenance and construction of roadway lights.
- Cleans ditches and culverts, excavates soil, straightens drainage channels, and resets culvert ends using a dragline or hydraulic excavator in a residency or districtwide area.
- Operates a mud pump, grout pump, or high reach in a residency or districtwide area.
- Operates the curb-making machine in a residency.
- Performs herbicide spraying operations in right-of-way areas by using a backpack sprayer, driving truck, and/or operating a pressure sprayer as required.
- Loads and unloads material, demolishes structures, loads debris, etc., using a small bulldozer; and may be required to run a large erosion dozer for erosion control purposes in a district or residencywide area.

Competencies Required

- Knowledge of specialized highway maintenance equipment, its operation, and use.
- Knowledge of highway maintenance procedures and techniques.
- Knowledge of highway maintenance terminology.
- Ability to work outside during inclement weather and to be on call during emergency situations such as snowstorms, pavement blowups, floods, etc.
- Ability to operate a 90 pound jackhammer in the operation of breaking and removing pavement materials.
- Ability to lift and load bagged material weighing up to 95 pounds to a truck that is 55 inches above ground.
- Ability to drive trucks and other vehicles in a safe and conscientious manner.
- Ability to understand and carry out written and oral instructions.
- Ability to direct the work of and train crew members.
- Ability to meet customer needs in a consistently helpful and courteous manner.
- Ability to work cooperatively with others as part of a team.
- Ability to apply personal work attitudes such as honesty, responsibility, and trustworthiness required to be a productive employee.
- Skill in the operation of specialized highway maintenance equipment that requires hand, foot, and eye coordination.

Education, Experience, and Special Requirements

- The equivalency of 1 year full-time experience in the operation of heavy equipment, performing highway or other related maintenance functions, or in subprofessional engineering program areas.
- All positions in this job class require applicants to possess a commercial driver's license, class A, at the time of hire. Endorsements may also be required.
- For designated positions, the appointing authority, with Iowa Department of Personnel prior approval, may request applicants possessing a minimum of 12 semester hours of education, 6 months of experience, or a combination of both, or a specific certificate, license, or endorsement in the following areas: air brakes, doubles/triples endorsement, hazardous materials endorsement, tank vehicles. Applicants wishing to be considered for such designated positions must list applicable course work, experience, certificate, license, or endorsement on the application.

Special Notes

- After accepting an offer of employment, all persons are required to have a physical examination by a doctor of choice verifying the physical ability to perform the duties described.
- Employees must be available to travel and may be required to stay away from home overnight during assignments.
- Certain designated positions require the employee to be certified by the Department of Agriculture and Land Stewardship as a Pesticide Applicator.
- Employees must respond to emergency conditions, which requires them to live within a 15-mile distance or be able to report within a 30-minute period of time to their assigned facility.

SAMPLE POSITION DESCRIPTION
(INTENDED USAGE: RECLASSIFICATION)

Incumbent:	John Doe
Agency:	Iowa Department of Transportation
Division:	Highway Maintenance Division
Unit:	District 2
Place of work:	Waterloo Maintenance Garage, US 63 and West Ridgeway
Position number and class title of existing position:	645 S44 5520 08110 111 Equipment Operator 1
Hours worked:	7:00 A.M. through 3:30 P.M., Monday through Friday
Immediate supervisor:	Robert Fisck, Highway Supervisor 1
Position requested:	Equipment Operator 2

Description of work (List in detail the work you do. List the most important duties first. Indicate the percentage of time or hours in an average work week spent on each duty.)

Time   *Work Performed*

45%   Grout Pump. Operate a grout pump over a districtwide area. Re-establishing pavement support by undersealing, and includes marking and drilling of injection holes and injecting a mixture of cement flash grout under low pressure to completely fill any voids under the pavement. Must understand and be able to locate longitudinal subdrains and any other drains located under the pavement to make sure that the drains are not plugged with grout. Must constantly monitor roadway, shoulder, and under the bridge while pumping to make certain not to damage the bridge, shoulder, or roadway in any way. Train and direct a crew of seven to nine operators on the pump and on proper traffic control. Must understand the mechanics of the grout pump so if any problem occurs can take the pump apart and get the grout out of the machine, so as not to have a flash set before a mechanic can get to the job site.

20%   Routine roadway and right-of-way maintenance activities include the following: (surfaces) patch spalls, seal/fill joints and cracks, remove bumps, fill depressions, remove and replace damaged pavements; (shoulders) fill edge ruts, operate blading equipment to smooth shoulders, patch paved shoulders, etc.; (roadsides) pick up litter, cut brush, repair fences, control weeds by mowing and spraying, erect and dismantle snow fences; (bridges) clean decks, clean and lubricate working members, spot paint; (traffic services) repair guardrails, flag traffic, maintain lighting, erect and maintain signs; (drainage) repair and maintain drainage structures and tile lines, clean ditches. Performance of these tasks includes the use of physical labor and operation of self-propelled mobile equipment such as dump trucks, front end loaders, tractors, motor graders, and an array of support equipment and hand tools such as chain saws, pneumatic hammers, hand drills, weed eaters, lawn mowers, and shovels.

20%   Snow removal. Operate snow removal equipment such as single axle dump truck or a tandem axle dump truck, each of which may be equipped with a tailgate or hopper spreader, a straight blade or V-plow, a wing plow and underbody ice blade. Procedures include the removal of snow, packed snow, and/or ice by plowing and/or spreading abrasives and de-icing chemicals on the roadway surface.

10%   Equipment maintenance. Service and perform preventive maintenance on all assigned equipment traditionally used in the performance of highway and bridge maintenance.

5%   Other duties. Miscellaneous duties are assigned from time to time.

SOURCE: Iowa Department of Personnel, agency documents.

APPENDIX B

Formal Job Analysis Methods

There are many methods of formal job analysis. One researcher describes 18 job analysis methods in detail (Gael, 1988). Because each method involves a good deal of complexity, the purpose here is restricted to providing general familiarization with some of the methods and their strengths and weaknesses.

The strengths of the different methods can be considered on at least three different dimensions. First, what is the purpose of the job analysis? Because the methods' focus varies substantially, this is an important question. Second, how much organizational time can be devoted to the project? This will affect the degree to which inside versus external support is enlisted and the complexity of the design used. Third, to what degree is cost a factor? Consultants and proprietary instruments bring expertise and cut down the time, but they add to the expense.

Another important dimension to consider when reviewing job analysis methods is the degree to which the job tasks will be emphasized versus the job traits. Job traits are defined broadly here as KSAs (knowledge, skills, and abilities) as well as job behaviors. On one hand, it is possible to analyze jobs primarily by task and the complexity of those tasks. The Department of Labor uses a task-oriented method to generate the *Dictionary of Occupational Titles*. The difficulty of the job is evaluated by determining the complexity of worker functions on three dimensions: data, people, and things. Below are the 24 functions used in the DOL method:

Data	*People*	*Things*
0 Synthesizing	0 Mentoring	0 Setting up
1 Coordinating	1 Negotiating	1 Precision working
2 Analysis	2 Instructing	2 Operations-controlling
3 Compiling	3 Supervising	3 Driving-operating
4 Computing	4 Diverting	4 Manipulating
5 Copying	5 Persuading	5 Tending
6 Comparing	6 Speaking-signaling	6 Feeding-offbearing
7 Serving	7 Handling	
	8 Taking instructions-helping	

The DOL method is excellent at job descriptions. The Functional Job Analysis, developed by Sidney Fine and associates, is a variation of the DOL method. Most job evaluation methods (considered in a separate section below) rely heavily on task analysis.

It is possible to focus nearly exclusively on job traits or KSAs in analyzing a job. McCormick and his associates developed the Position Analysis Questionnaire, which primarily evaluates the level of complexity of worker behaviors. Ernest Primoff of the U.S. Office of Personnel Management developed another method for the United States government in the 1970s. In his original method (called the Job Elements Method), a panel of experts first generates a comprehensive list of KSAs (Primoff's job elements) for a job classification. Next, the job elements are rated in four categories. The ratings from the four scales are combined to form a weight for each element. A distinction must be made, however, when using a method for job evaluation or selection. The Job Elements Method was used for selection purposes, but it was later successfully challenged as requiring too great an inferential leap for complex jobs. That is, job elements or KSAs were not sufficient when determining the selection criteria for jobs. Thereafter, nearly all methods relied on combined task-trait methodologies, which does add balance to the analysis but enhances the complexity of the job analysis process.

Some well-known task-trait methodologies include the Threshold Traits Analysis, developed by Lopez in the early 1970s; the Critical Incident Method, developed by Flanagan in the 1950s as an assessment and training tool; the Fleishman Job Analysis Survey, which assumes that the task analysis has already been completed; and the Job Components Inventory, which is useful for lower-level jobs. In all these methods, job task lists are generated, traits are weighted, and the jobs are then assessed.

A second dimension to consider is the use of questionnaires or experts in the generation of task lists, trait lists, and data analysis. Two of the methods mentioned use questionnaires extensively: the Position Analysis Questionnaire (well known in the United States) and the Job Components Inventory (well known in England). Although nearly all the methods supply forms as a guideline, they require extensive expert input relative to each position. Questionnaire-based methodologies provide standardized databases and rapid analysis capacity.

KEY TERMS

At-will employment	Job duties
Authorized salary range	Job evaluation
Benchmark jobs	Job factor systems
Broadbanding	Job tasks
Civil service	Lateral entry
Civil service commission	Merit
Class series	Occupational families
Closed personnel systems	Open personnel system
Essential function	Patronage system
External equity	Pay plan
Individual equity	Pendleton Act
Job analysis	Piecemeal personnel systems
Job classification	Point factor methods
Job description	Position

Position classification systems
Position description
Position management system
Rank-in-job
Rank-in-person

Spoils principle
Up-or-out philosophy
Whole job analysis
Whole job evaluation

EXERCISES

Class Discussion

1. Canvass the class to determine if any members of the class have been a part of a reclassification effort or an organizationwide job evaluation. What happened? Was it successful or not?

2. Ask those in the class who now work or have ever worked in the public sector what position management challenges they have experienced.

3. There is perhaps no better example of the grand paradox of needs (Introduction) than position management. Discuss and seek pathways through the paradox as well as subparadoxes found in various position management techniques.

Team Activities

4. Does the position management function help or hinder in resolving the twin paradoxes introduced at the outset of the book?

5. Analyze a public sector organization's classification system. Determine the number of positions, classes, and pay plans. What are the number of elected, appointed, and merit appointees? Does the system "work" and does the checkerboard make sense to those using the system?

6. A large, growing county decides to place a new service center in another city. None of the current employees is interested in relocating. Furthermore, there is some concern that many of the offices are using outdated technology and old-fashioned methods of customer delivery. For example, services related to building permits, licenses, land records, and tax assessment are scattered throughout a variety of buildings in the county seat. The new model of customer service recommends a single, long service counter for related services, with employees who are cross-trained. Almost all the job descriptions are at least a decade old (some are 25 years old!), and nearly all the "training" is on the job. How might a job analysis study be useful? Specifically, what functions might be supported by such a study, and how?

7. As a class, determine which members are currently employed in the public sector and then select some of them to be interviewed in small groups. The small groups are to write a job description. The person interviewed should not do any of the writing, nor should he or she suggest the format to be used. Compare the results as a class and make friendly suggestions for improvements.

8. You are a manager whose best worker has "topped out"; that is, the employee is at the top step of her pay grade. Furthermore, her job is properly classified. Unfortunately, the government jurisdiction for whom you both work is 20% to 30% below the market in most positions. You know that the person will leave soon if the situation is not altered. You could assign a few people to her to justify a reclassification and pay increase, although it would not make much sense

functionally. Take an imagination break (Exhibit 0.3). What would you do? Teams should compare and justify their recommendations.

Individual Assignments

9. The reform of civil service will be an important discussion and debate for the next several decades. What are the implications of the civil service reform initiative in Georgia? Do you think that the movement to replace independent civil service commissions with executive branch personnel agencies is a good one? Do you think that job property rights should be abolished in all public sector systems? Will the widespread use of at-will systems lead to patronage problems again, as they did in the 19th century?

10. What are the similarities and dissimilarities between broadbanding and rank-in-person systems?

11. If you were the analyst looking at the position reclassification request in Appendix A (for the equipment operator 2), what would the positive and negative points be? Would you grant the request?

NOTES

1.   Position management and position classification are related, but not identical, concepts. Position classification primarily refers to categorization of positions with a rational set of principles. Position management generally refers to the allocation of positions for budgetary purposes. A position classification system is one of the elements of a position management system, but position classification systems can have nonbudgetary purposes as well, such as the fundamental division and coordination of work, selection, training, and performance appraisal. Position management can have aspects not directly related to classification, such as budget authorization, budget "caps," downsizing, privatization, contracting out, loadshedding, and so on.

2.   In the past, hereditary selection was common, and it still exists today, even in some advanced democracies.

3.   This type includes most city council members, school board members, township trustees, boards, and commissions that are locally elected, as well as some county supervisors, among others.

4.   Also known as rank-in-position.

5.   In at-will jobs, the incumbent must prove that he or she was removed from the job for an illegal reason such as discrimination based on race, age, or gender. This puts the burden of proof on the job incumbent and provides a narrow scope of appeal. In most civil service positions, the employer must prove "cause" for termination; that is, the incumbent must be documented to be incompetent, to exhibit inappropriate or illegal behavior, and/or to be unwilling to reform derelict or improper behaviors.

6.   The current version is called the O*NET, standing for the *Occupational Informational Network;* it is an online electronic database compiled by the U.S. Department of Labor. It has consolidated the occupational listing to under 1,200 entries, which are more fully analyzed than those in the old *DOT.* Although the definitive resource is now the online O*NET, some people may elect to use the *O*NET Dictionary of Occupational Titles (O*NET DOT)*, which includes all the occupations but considerably summarizes the information about those jobs.

7.   The Civil Service Reform Act of 1978 provided for (a) the bulk of the Civil Service Commission's routine work to be administered by the Office of Personnel Management (OPM), an executive agency; (b) the creation of a Merit Systems Protection Board (MSPB) to be a watchdog

of merit employees' rights; (c) a reorganized Federal Labor Relations Authority; (d) the creation of a Senior Executive Service (SES), a quasi-rank-based corps that was more flexible and mobile than the former supergrades (grades 16–18); (e) a merit and bonus pay system for GS grades 13–15; and (f) the mandate of performance appraisal systems in the various agencies.

8. *Class series* and *occupational series* are used interchangeably. Both refer to a normal progression pattern that can be followed by employees, sometimes designated by a roman numeral (secretary I, II, III, IV) and sometimes by a traditional management series (lead worker, foreman, supervisor, manager).

9. Usage of the term *task* varies. Here the term *task* means broad activities such as (to use the upcoming example for a payroll clerk) processing time sheets, printing the payroll, and deducting appropriate expenses such as taxes. Another common usage (seen in Exhibit 5.8) for the term *task* is as a synonym for "step performed." For example, paying payroll taxes requires the use of different exemptions, distinguishing between salary and reimbursements, and controlling and paying out from a separate tax account. These subtasks are here referred to as "job elements."

10. Depending on the position and the individual, such physical, manual, or special requirements may require a reasonable accommodation.

11. Because there is a range in the market, the organization must decide whether it wants to be in the middle of the range, at the top, or at the bottom. This is commonly referred to as the "meet, lead, or lag" question (Chapter 6). Because most governments are labor cost–intensive, small differences can be important in terms of budget outlays.

12. These are the general categories for the well-known Hay system.

13. On the other hand, in larger jurisdictions, job evaluation of individual job classes or class series is often constant. This helps with currency but generally leads to inconsistency in the long term in the absence of occasional pay studies to rationalize the overall system.

REFERENCES

Chi, K. S. (1998). State civil service systems. In S. E. Condrey (Ed.), *Handbook of human resource management in government* (pp. 35–55). San Francisco: Jossey-Bass.

Cipolla, F. (1999, July 15). Time for the classification system to go. *Federal Times,* p. 15.

Condrey, S. E. (1998). Toward strategic human resource management. In S. E. Condrey (Ed.), *Handbook of human resource management in government* (pp. 1–14). San Francisco: Jossey-Bass.

Crandall, F. N., & Wallace, M. J. (1998). *Work and rewards in the virtual workplace.* New York: AMACOM.

De Leon, L., & Denhardt, R. B. (2000). The political theory of reinvention. *Public Administration Review, 60*(2), 89–97.

DeSoto, W., & Castillo, R. (1995). Police civil service in Texas. *Review of Public Personnel Administration, 15*(1), 98–104.

Ewoh, A. I. E., & Elliott, E. (1997). End of an era? Affirmative action and reaction in the 1990s. *Review of Public Personnel Administration, 17*(4), 38–51.

Farnham, D. (1997). Employment flexibilities in western European public services. *Review of Public Personnel Administration, 17*(3), 5–17.

Foster, M. R. (1998). Effective job analysis methods. In S. E. Condrey (Ed.), *Handbook of human resource management in government* (pp. 322–348). San Francisco: Jossey-Bass.

Gael, S. (Ed.). (1988). *The job analysis handbook for business, industry, and government.* New York: Wiley.

Grady, D., & Tax, P. C. (1996). Entrepreneurial bureaucrats and democratic accountability: Experience at the state government level. *Review of Public Personnel Administration, 16*(4), 5–14.

Hamilton, D. K. (1999). The continuing judicial assault on patronage. *Public Administration Review,* *59*(1), 54–62.

Hays, S. W., & Kearney, R. C. (1999). Saving the civil service. *Review of Public Personnel Administration, 19*(1), 77–78.

Isfahani, N. (1998). The debate over tenure. *Review of Public Personnel Administration, 18*(1), 80–86.

Kearney, R. C., & Hays, S. W. (1998). Reinventing government, the new public management and civil service systems: A critical assessment of dubious deductions and hidden agendas. *Review of Public Personnel Administration, 18*(4), 38–54.

Kettl, D. F., Ingraham, P. W., Sanders, R. P., & Horner, C. (1996). *Civil service reform: Building a government that works.* Washington, DC: Brookings.

Leavitt, W. M., & Johnson, G. (1998). Employee discipline and the post-bureaucratic public organization: A challenge in the change process. *Review of Public Personnel Administration, 18*(2), 73–81.

Levine, C. H., & Kleeman, R. S. (1986). *The quiet crisis of the civil service: The federal personnel system at the crossroads.* Washington, DC: National Academy of Public Administration.

Markowitz, J. (1987). Managing the job analysis process. *Training and Development Journal, 41*(8), 64–66.

Marshall, G. S. (1998, May/June). Whither (or wither) OPM? *Public Administration Review, 58,* 280–282.

Mosher, F. C. (1982). *Democracy and the public service* (2nd ed.). New York: Oxford University Press.

Pollack, L. J., Simons, C., Romero, H., & Hausser, D. (2002). A common language for classifying and describing occupations: The development, structure, and application of the Standard Occupational Classification. *Human Resource Management, 41*(3), 297–307.

Radin, B. A. (1998). The Government Performance and Results Act (GPRA): Hydra-headed monster or flexible management tool. *Public Administration Review, 58*(4), 307–316.

Sayre, W. (1948, Spring). The triumph of techniques over purpose. *Public Administration Review, 8,* 134–137.

Siegel, G. B. (1998a). Designing and creating an effective compensation plan. In S. E. Condrey (Ed.), *Handbook of human resource management in government* (pp. 608–626). San Francisco: Jossey-Bass.

Siegel, G. B. (1998b). Work management and job evaluation systems in a government environment. In S. E. Condrey (Ed.), *Handbook of human resource management in government* (pp. 586–607). San Francisco: Jossey-Bass.

Somma, M., & Fox, C. J. (1997). It's not civil service, but leadership and communication: Response to DeSoto and Castillo. *Review of Public Personnel Administration, 17*(1), 84–91.

U.S. Department of Labor. (1991). *Dictionary of occupational titles* (4th ed.). Washington, DC: Author. (http://www.oalj.dol.gov/libdot.htm)

U.S. General Accounting Office. (2003). Preliminary observations on DOD's proposed civilian personnel reforms (Testimony # 03–7171). Washington, DC: Author.

U.S. Merit Systems Protection Board. (1999). *Federal supervisors and poor performers.* Washington, DC: Author.

U.S. Merit Systems Protection Board. (2002). *Making the public service work: Recommendations for change.* Washington, DC: Author.

Van Riper, P. P. (1958). *History of the United States civil service.* New York: Harper & Row.

Van Wart, M. (1998). *Changing public sector values.* New York: Garland.

Van Wart, M. (1999). Is making any fundamental change in the civil service dangerous? *Review of Public Personnel Administration, 19*(1), 71–76.

West, J., & Bowman, J. (2004). Stakeholder analysis of civil service reform in Florida: A descriptive, instrumental, normative human resource perspective. *State and Local Government Review, 16*(1), 20–34.

Yergin, D. A., & Stanislaw, J. (1998). *The commanding heights: The battle between government and the marketplace that is remaking the modern world.* New York: Simon & Schuster.

6

COMPENSATION

Vital, Visible, and Vicious

> *I may be unappreciated, but at least I'm overworked and underpaid.*
>
> —A bureaucrat's lament

After studying this chapter, you should be able to

- Recognize that there is no absolute standard used to determine pay—that is, organizations do not pay people what they are worth because they do not *know* what their employees are worth
- Explain why compensation is a key human resource function, but that pay programs, paradoxically, are not a management system
- Understand that a compensation system is the result of law and policy, labor markets, job evaluation, and personal contribution
- Describe key compensation issues such as pay banding, comparable worth, and gain-sharing and their often paradoxical nature
- Design and calculate the essential elements of a salary survey
- Assess and critique criteria for an ideal compensation system in the context of future trends

If position classification defines the individual-organization relationship (Chapter 5), then compensation quite literally quantifies it. Earnings affect a person—not only economically but also socially and psychologically—because they are a concrete indicator of employee value to the institution, purchasing power, social prestige, and, sadly, perhaps even self-worth. Payroll expenses, likewise, represent a substantial investment on the part of the organization; they often constitute the majority of its budget. Labor costs, for example, in the Defense Department and the Postal Service—and most other agencies irrespective of jurisdiction— often amount to more than 80% of outlays.

Accordingly, a compensation system should aim to align individual and organizational objectives, an ideal that may be difficult to achieve when many elected officials—with backgrounds in insurance agencies, real estate offices, law firms, and other small businesses— have little experience in large public organizations.[1] Nevertheless, dilemmas in managing compensation are of paramount importance. Trends in managerial performance accountability and staff reduction suggest that resolution of these issues will be determined by managers and employees with HRM experts serving as consultants, not controllers. It will no longer do to blame controversial decisions on the personnel office.

Organizations have a right to expect employees to be as productive as possible, and individuals have the right to be fairly compensated. Thus, a value-added remuneration system should optimize the balance between institutional constraints and personal expectations by creating value for both the organization and its members. Program goals include attracting new workers, rewarding and retaining existing ones, providing equity, controlling budgets, and supporting the culture that the agency seeks to engender. The design and maintenance of a compensation system is complex and prominent in organizations; other human resource functions are important to some employees, but money is crucial to virtually everyone.

How a jurisdiction handles salaries and benefits, then, is vital (for individual sustenance and organizational credibility) and visible (personnel salaries and agency payrolls are a matter of public record), as well as vicious (real or imagined inequities among workers breed considerable friction in organizations). Competence and performance may be hard to judge (Chapter 9), but pay and benefits are known. For instance, federal bankruptcy judges, excluded from dining and transportation privileges enjoyed by other judges, feel like "second-class citizens."

Despite, or perhaps because of, its importance, the compensation function of HRM is the one that produces the most displeasure among both public and private sector employees ("Many workers dissatisfied," 2001). There are at least three reasons for discontent. One is that people compare themselves with others: those doing the same job in the same agency, performing different jobs in the agency, and holding equivalent positions in other agencies. It is not unusual that perceived discrepancies and real discontent emerge as a result.

A second explanation is that remuneration is driven more by political than economic considerations. "It is completely fallacious," contend Risher and Fay (1997), "to argue that government pay programs represent a management system" (p. 14). Elected officials typically focus on personnel costs, and compensation policies become pawns in a quest for political advantage. Raising taxes, cutting services, or reallocating budget monies to fund a pay increase are not politically popular. Thus, over time, salaries will be affected more by political opportunism than by objective merit—something not likely to engender confidence in compensation policies.

A final, related reason for concern over pay is that many taxpayers believe civil servants are overpaid and underworked—despite arguably noncompetitive salaries and increased workloads from downsizing. As Risher and Fay (1997) also observe, "Some people will always think that public pay levels are too high; but it is safe to say that their views have a life of their own independent of the facts" (p. 323). Stated differently, the effectiveness of any compensation reforms is certainly to be constrained by the culture in which they are created. These three factors—personal comparisons, political expediency, and public beliefs—tend to reinforce one another in a manner that further exacerbates dissatisfaction. At the root of all these explanations is the fact that most organizations want the most work for the least money, whereas many employees want the most money for the least work. Compensation, in short, is considered crucial by employees, decision makers, and taxpayers alike. Indeed, a new model of compensation that emphasizes market data, performance pay, pay banding, and management discretion has emerged in response to claims that the existing approach is antiquated and disintegrating (U.S. Office of Personnel Management, 2002).

The following pages examine factors that affect the determination of pay: policy and law, labor markets, job evaluation, and individual contribution. The analysis is framed by equity theory and illustrated with controversial issues including pay banding and comparable worth, as well as longevity, merit, skill, and gainsharing pay. Having diagnosed problems with compensation programs, the chapter closes with a prescription for an "ideal" program as well as projections of future trends.

EQUITY THEORY

Equity theory—the balance between contributions made by the individual and the rewards received from the organization—provides the basis for most pay programs. Unfortunately, available data suggest that neither "the people who manage the (federal) systems, the managers who use them, [nor] the employee themselves" (Wamsley, 1998, p. 30) hold these programs in high regard. To appreciate the significance of equity theory, the weighing between contributions and rewards, consider the foundations and nature of this balance. Its basis is the presumed link between performance and pay, and its dynamic is how (or whether) this linkage operates. Based on the role of individual perceptions in determining behavior, expectancy theory (Vroom, 1964) offers insights into the choices that people make.

Its tenets are a three-link causal chain:

1. The value ("valence") the employee attaches to a desired result (e.g., higher pay)

2. The person's belief that rewards actually will be provided as a consequence of high performance ("instrumentality")

3. The belief ("expectancy") that the individual can accomplish the task that will lead to reward

Stated differently, the theory assumes that people take action based on their perception of the possible success of that action (expectancy) and the likelihood of achieving outcomes (instrumentality) that they value (valence).

If any of these three links in the chain is weak, then "pay for performance" is called into question. Suppose, for instance, that the parole supervisor in a state department of corrections demonstration project has authority to provide productivity bonuses to caseworkers who increase the number of interviews with their parolees. These parole officers want the bonus (valence) and understand that it would be awarded if they achieve the improvement objective (instrumentality). They are concerned (expectancy), however, that simply adding the contacts they have with their charges, without a reduction in overall caseload, will result in superficial interviews. They are not convinced that the program is desirable (because it minimizes chances of in-depth information gathering) or feasible (overtime work is not available). Accordingly, public safety would be put at risk, and employee burnout is likely. In one such case, few sought the bonuses, and the initiative was discontinued.

Consider a more common scenario. Although most people value money (valence), there are often significant constraints in obtaining more of it. When local, state, or national legislative bodies regularly limit pay raises to inconsequential amounts, for example, the importance attached to those amounts is devalued (repeated raises that are below the rate of inflation in effect constitute a pay cut). Suppose instead that substantial monies are provided. Employees must then have confidence that the performance evaluation system (instrumentality) does, indeed, distribute rewards fairly and accurately. For reasons examined in Chapter 9, such confidence is not often merited. Finally, although many Americans believe that hard work makes a difference (expectation), working smarter also counts. Thus, if training, acceptable working conditions, and/or up-to-date equipment are not provided, then working harder may make little difference.

As these examples demonstrate, expectancy theory can be an effective diagnostic tool to ensure that the HRM system is administered in a manner that coherently establishes linkages between valence, instrumentality, and expectancy. Thus:

- Are available rewards valued by employees?
- Do employees see a link between the reward and their performance?
- Are employees confident, given their background and organizational climate, that tasks can be accomplished?

Equity and expectancy theories mandate, in other words, that policymakers be concerned about more than the absolute amount of money required to fund public service. They must also focus on comparative levels of pay and how these monies are distributed. Reward systems unconnected to productivity indicators motivate poor workers to stay and high performers become discouraged and leave. The irony of such a situation is that overall compensation costs rise because more employees are needed to complete tasks that fewer conscientious ones could readily accomplish.

Determination

With these theoretical—and quite real—considerations in mind, factors affecting pay determination are now explored. An organization confronts two types of decisions in the management of compensation: pay level and pay adjustments. Compensation in any jurisdiction is a product of the following:

- Pay philosophy, as informed by law and policy
- Labor market forces (external competitiveness), as reflected by manipulation of supply and demand
- Job content (internal consistency), as assessed by job evaluation techniques
- Individual contribution, as influenced by longevity, merit, skill, and group pay (Figure 6.1)

Decisions about levels of pay are largely a consequence of philosophy, market, and job evaluation, whereas pay adjustments emphasize an employee's place in the salary structure. Taken together, these decisions should represent the greater good by aligning the interests of the public and its servants.

Philosophy

Organizations can lead, match, or lag behind what other employers offer employees (Exhibit 6.1). In sharp contrast to the strategies of many other advanced democracies, the approach in government has been to limit the pool of job candidates to those prepared to accept noncompetitive pay. Compensation is *not* seen as a strategic tool to achieve organizational objectives but rather as a cost to be managed and contained. At least since the passage of the 1883 Pendleton Act (Chapter 1), public servants have been expected to make financial sacrifices in exchange for an opportunity to serve the citizenry, often in challenging, even unique,

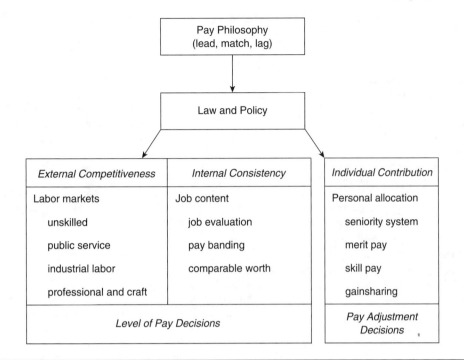

External Competitiveness	Internal Consistency	Individual Contribution
Labor markets	Job content	Personal allocation
unskilled	job evaluation	seniority system
public service	pay banding	merit pay
industrial labor	comparable worth	skill pay
professional and craft		gainsharing
Level of Pay Decisions		*Pay Adjustment Decisions*

Figure 6.1   Determinants of Compensation

✕ EXHIBIT 6.1   Pay Policy: Lead, Match, or Lag?

> *Under the influence either of poverty or of wealth, workmen and their work are equally liable to deteriorate.*
>
> —Plato

The paradox of needs (Introduction) indicates that organizational and individual objectives may not coincide. Ideally, business strategy, human resource philosophy, and compensation goals should be aligned in a manner to meet the needs of both the employer and employee.

A wage-lead approach may reflect a belief that by "working smarter" a high-quality, satisfied workforce is a cost-effective, money-saving strategy. That is, total labor costs are not the same as labor rates. It is possible to achieve high productivity from a relatively small workforce if the cost per unit of output is less with a highly efficient, though highly paid workforce. This plan, however, may be seen as counterintuitive and difficult for many cash-strapped public and nonprofit organizations to adopt in the short run.

A wage-competitive policy, second, in effect neutralizes compensation as a factor in human resource management. It does this by paying fairly and accentuating nonmonetary amenities affecting the overall ability to attract and retain employees. These include such time-honored (and time-worn) techniques as "selling scenery" (or the area's weather), believing that the community is "family-friendly," or claiming to be at the seat of power in a political capitol ("Potomac fever" and

(Continued)

(Continued)

its subnational equivalents). Many of these tactics, though, are available to organizations using above- and below-market pay policies. Still, a match policy does not necessarily place the organization at a disadvantage in the marketplace.

Last, wage-follower plans may be indicative of: unique characteristics of the occupation (military travel, State Department diplomacy), a philosophy that dictates service is not about making money (Salvation Army), high unemployment in the area, short-time horizons, or simply a "lean and mean" approach to human resources by "working harder" to get the most from as few poorly paid workers as possible (despite counterproductive effects such as low morale, turnover, and training costs). A below-market approach might—arguably—be acceptable for low-skill retailing organizations such as Wal-Mart but clearly is a "penny-wise, pound-foolish" strategy for professionally staffed organizations. For example, the Securities and Exchange Commission and the Federal Bureau of Investigation have substantial difficulty in recruiting and retaining top-caliber personnel because the salaries are a fraction of those available elsewhere.

The selection of an appropriate policy involves a complex set of factors including the types of skills required, job market characteristics, ability to pay, desired institutional image, assumptions about employee work attitudes, and employer ideologies. The strategy chosen likely will competitively position the organization within or across sectors of the economy. Thus, in the public sphere, some Florida cities and counties, for instance, use a wage-lead approach at least when compared with state employment. The federal government, however, is generally superior to many subnational pay policies—but inferior to the approach utilized by major corporations. It should also be noted that different policies may exist within one organization. The compensation package available to public service clerical personnel, for instance, may be better than that found in many small businesses. Such a wage-lead approach is reversed, however, for most public and nonprofit executives within the same agency whose remuneration is the result of a wage-lag strategy.

The paradox of needs may be resolved in good measure by employee self-selection provided that basic economic and noneconomic needs are met. Equity theory suggests, however, that if people do not perceive that a balance exists between their contributions and rewards, then they will try to relieve the tension by reducing productivity, misusing organizational resources, or seeking higher rewards either within the agency or outside it.

Expect these trends to continue as agencies seek pay policies designed to reduce the size of the workforce, evidence less concern with competitive compensation and more with what can be afforded, and attempt incentive programs to make payroll costs more variable than fixed expense. Organizations, in the end, usually get what they are willing to pay for.

ways (e.g., environmental protection, criminal justice, teaching, foreign relations, tax collection). Self-enrichment, after all, was and is now the purpose of service. The idea, unlike the spoils system, was to create a corps of career professionals insulated from political intrigue by providing job security, career progression, and reasonable benefits/working conditions. Also important was the fact that they represented but a tiny proportion of the workforce (less than 1% in 1900); they held little political power or ability to organize themselves into unions, and none at all to strike (Chapter 10).

By the 1960s, however, public employees were far more numerous, had fallen substantially behind in compensation, and had won the right to organize. Beginning with the 1962 Federal Salary Reform Act, attempts were made to establish the principle that federal pay would match that found in the private sector. Codified in the Federal Pay Comparability Act of 1970, the law established a mechanism to provide annual comparability adjustments unless the president directed otherwise—which he did virtually every year for two decades.

In 1989, the first National Commission on the Public Service (the Volcker Commission) called for significant salary increases; the passage of the 1990 **Federal Employees Pay Comparability Act** mandated that the 30% public-private sector pay gap[2] be closed gradually by the end of the century. According to the 2003 Volcker Commission II, the gap is wider than ever because administrations repeatedly cited "severe economic conditions," irrespective of the state of the economy, as a reason to deny employees full pay raises. Although the situation is more varied elsewhere, the difficulties experienced by the national government are manifested in many states and localities.

The problems discussed above are mirrored, in different degrees, in the distinct pay systems found in most jurisdictions: an executive schedule for political appointees, a general schedule for career employees, and, in the federal government, a wage grade schedule for blue-collar workers (using, by law, a match philosophy based on local prevailing rates), as well as various rank-in-person systems (Chapter 5). A majority of federal white-collar merit positions are in the General Schedule, which has 15 grades and 10 time-in-grade steps in each; many subnational governments have comparable salary structures. Generalizations are hazardous, but U.S. Comptroller General David Walker believes that government pays below market at entry level, sometimes over market at the middle level, and "way under the market" at the top (Harris, 1999, p. 7; see also www.opm.gov/strategiccomp/whtpaper.txt). It is widely understood that the pay gap is most severe for executive, managerial, and professional positions and less so for managerial and entry-level jobs; one should recognize, however, that in certain jurisdictions or in selected occupations, it may not exist at all, and in some cases it might even be reversed. Overall, though, "the jobs that show the greatest pay disadvantage for federal workers make up an increasing share of the federal workforce" (U.S. Congressional Budget Office, 2002, p. 9).

Paying below-market rates, according to wage efficiency theory, may not be cost-effective. The advantages of low compensation are likely to be outweighed by poor morale, citizen service, and job satisfaction and the resulting high recruitment, training, discipline, and turnover costs. Simply stated, paying more can cost less when productivity, service, and quality are compromised by paying "bottom dollar." It is difficult to see, in any case, how effective organizations, which depend on empowered, high-caliber people, can flourish under these circumstances.

Pay systems, referring again to Figure 6.1, reflect not only law and policy but also (a) comparisons of similar jobs in different organizations using salary surveys (external competition), (b) comparisons among job content within an agency employing job evaluation techniques (internal consistency), and (c) comparisons among employees in the same job category in the same organization using seniority, merit, skill, or group pay (individual contribution). As each of these equity dimensions is explored below, it is important to note that "there are no absolute measures of job value. . . . For things like temperature and weight, . . . instruments are both reliable and valid. Job value is at best a relative or comparative measure" (Risher & Wise, 1997, p. 99). Instead, what exists in many organizations is an inconsistent mix of fair-pay criteria. A common denominator and underlying assumption shared by all forms of equity, however, is that they implicitly hold a time clock model of work; that is, as examined in Exhibit 6.2, labor is commoditized, to be bought and sold in easily measured time units (hours, days, weeks, months, years). Time is money—or is it?

✖ EXHIBIT 6.2   How Much Time Do You Owe the Organization?

Time isn't money; money is money.

—Anonymous

In an attempt to curb exploitative work schedules and thereby create jobs during the Great Depression, the 1938 **Fair Labor Standards Act** (FLSA) instituted the 5-day, 40-hour week—a compromise measure agreed to after the Senate passed a 30-hour workweek bill. Since that time, dramatic changes have occurred in the economy (from industrial to service), the workforce (from white male–dominated to diverse female), and lifestyles (from a husband with a stay-at-home wife with children to singles, single parents, and married as well as unmarried dual-career families). Most organizations, however, still structure work hours as if nothing has happened in the intervening decades, a posture that has exacerbated the paradox of needs (Introduction).

This is not to say that there has been no response to these changes. Many organizations have experimented with **alternative work schedules**—"the joy of flex"—in the last half century.[1] Variations are nearly infinite (e.g., compressed workweeks), but the oldest and most common alternative schedule consists of a specified bandwidth when the office will be open (e.g., 6:00 A.M. to 8:00 P.M. Monday through Friday) and a set of core hours (perhaps 10:00 A.M. to 2:00 P.M.) around which people can arrange their 8-hour workday. Thus, early risers can come in early and leave at 3:00 P.M., and late risers can come in at 9:00 A.M. and leave late. Typically, everyone completes time sheets. Agencies may also benefit by having offices staffed during a longer workday and by having reduced tardiness and absences.

Advantages should be evident: Employees work when they want to work, with all the personal and organizational benefits that may result from that fact. Drawbacks are of two types: inherent and practical. There is some work that is structured so that it cannot be "flexed," and there are organizations that cannot effectively implement flextime—either because record keeping becomes too burdensome or because managers lose a sense of control over subordinates.

Generally, results are varied, but often flextime improves the quality of work life for people more than it enhances productivity of the organization. **Herzberg's theory of motivation** (Herzberg, Mauser, & Snoplerman, 1959) helps explain this finding. Flextime is a "job context" factor (such extrinsic factors focus on policies, supervision, and working conditions) that, when absent, can create job dissatisfaction. When these factors are available in desired forms, however, they normally are taken for granted. Consider university parking: If convenient, it is unlikely that it would create job satisfaction; if it is a continuous hassle, however, it can create substantial on-the-job morale problems. What really matters in explaining productivity, however, are "job content" factors (these intrinsic elements emphasize challenging work, responsibility, achievement, and the like; see Thomas, 2000). Flextime has nothing to do with the substance of work.

This speaks to the fundamental flaw of all forms of flextime—even if perfectly implemented. It assumes, in a functionally rational mode, that work must be a function of time, instead of the actual task to be performed. Indeed, exempt from FLSA, most professionals of yesteryear[2] and today (managers, surgeons, the clergy, military officers) work until the work is done. They are not paid by the clock but rather for their overall contribution to the organization.

It is not necessarily maintained that all jobs could—or should—be reconceptualized in a substantively rational manner. It is suggested, however, that agencies seek a blend of functional and substantive approaches instead of an unquestioning focus on quantity time. A catalytic strategy to accomplish this is an *annual hours program* whereby the number of hours needed during a given year is agreed on and a scheduling format is then designed.

NOTES:

1. Indeed, by most accounts, flexible work hours have steadily increased. Although employers may have these opportunities in parts of their organizations, many employees do not participate because they do not know they could; when they do know, most take advantage of them (www.familiesandwork.org).

2. Samurai warriors, who refused to touch money, simply could not understand how it could be used as a substitute for expertise, discipline, and loyalty. The legacy of that feudal tradition remains, as the contemporary Japanese "salaryman" typically has his wife handle family finances.

Labor Market Forces: External Competition

Classical economic theory holds that the "free market" determines salaries based on the supply and demand for specific jobs. The obvious, if often overlooked, fact is that pay is not a function of a fanciful, pristine, abstract free market—something that has never existed and never will. Rather, occupations exist in different **labor markets,** none of which are free. Supply and demand, instead, is affected by public or private political intervention: unskilled labor (congressionally enacted minimum wage), public service (federal, state, or local legislative enactment), industrial labor (labor-management collective bargaining), and professional and craft occupations (interest group lobbying sometimes resulting in public licensure).

Consequently, pay in most organizations is benchmarked using employer-initiated self-salary surveys and/or those published by the U.S. Bureau of Labor Statistics, state government agencies, industry associations, and consulting firms. The approach taken is to simply ask other organizations what they pay people. For example, universities in the same athletic conference or region of the country may routinely survey one another—a process subject to circumlocution, tautology, and possibly illegal collusion under antitrust laws. Significant technical issues also exist (identifying key jobs and relevant organizations, calculating benefits), but even flawed surveys—in the absence of better data—provide useful information (Exhibit 6.3).[3]

Although salaries form the foundation of most employees' perceptions of pay, accurate estimates of external equity cannot focus solely on salary data. **Benefits**, a trivial "fringe" in most organizations before World War II, now add an average of 41% to the payroll, thus accounting for some 29% of the total employee compensation package. This increase is attributed largely to tax policy (both employers and employees realize tax advantages from certain types of benefits) and the rising costs of health and retirement programs.[4] An interesting paradox nevertheless exists: As the value of benefits increases, employee satisfaction can decrease (see Exhibit 6.4 as well as the next chapter). Further, the utility of benefits in achieving organizational goals is limited because they are available to all members irrespective of employee performance.

Historically, low public salaries have been partially offset by benefits (usually untaxed or tax deferred) because their costs can often be put off by lawmakers and are thereby less visible to voters than salary increases. These programs are reputed to be superior to those found in the private domain, as public employees are sometimes covered under more types of plans. When governments are compared with other large white-collar employers, however,

✂ **EXHIBIT 6.3**   Field Project: Salary Survey

This salary survey exercise is designed to assist a line manager in determining pay levels (a similar process—dramatically enhanced by the Internet using sites such as www.salary.com, www.salary source.com, www.lib.gsu.edu/collections/govdocus.stats.htm—can be utilized by an individual job seeker). The process consists of three steps: (a) identify key or benchmark jobs, (b) select comparable organizations, and (c) collect data. Each is fraught with problems such as (a) vague job categories (especially in team-based units), (b) interpreting competitor information (are the jobs truly comparable, and how do you know?), and (c) how (mail, telephone, and/or interview) and from where (federal or state agencies, professional associations, consulting firms) to gather data.

Knowing what other organizations are paying is necessary but not sufficient in this effort. It is also important to know what those jurisdictions are getting in return for their investment in employees. Even when available, these data are even harder to interpret because they include service quality, workforce quality, citizen satisfaction, and population/employee ratios. Also key are benefits, which are often equally difficult to compare accurately from one jurisdiction to another.

In the light of these problems, and from the perspective of an assistant city manager in a small locality with little HRM expertise, complete the following:

1. Discuss each of the three steps above with the city manager and compensation specialist in a larger nearby city.

2. Visit the Web sites for the World at Work: The Professional Association for Compensation, Benefits, and Total Rewards (www.worldatwork.org), a private firm that collects salary data (www.mnemplassoc.com/surveys/index/html), and/or the International Personnel Management Association (www.ipma-hr.org) to obtain additional information.

3. Outline how you would conduct a salary survey for your jurisdiction based on the information in (1) and (2).

such disparities all but disappear, especially because corporate executive perquisites (e.g., stock options, expense accounts, free insurance, no-cost financial and legal counseling, country club memberships, Christmas bonuses, moving expenses, clothing allowances, first-class travel, company cars, generous severance pay, estate planning) are unusual in other sectors.[5] Indeed, government and nonprofit benefits are often inferior to those in big business. And whatever perceived advantages the public sector has held as a "benefit-rich/salary-poor" employer are being eroded by increasing employee costs and diminishing coverages.

The determination of **external equity**, in summary, should recognize that conventional free market supply and demand theories conceal more than they reveal about labor markets; salary surveys are at once problematic and valuable; and benefit programs, although hard to quantify and compare, constitute a significant, often controversial, part of compensation.

Job Content: Internal Consistency

Pay decisions are made within the framework of the compensation structure: Some form of **job evaluation** method is used to systematically assess the value of jobs and assign jobs to salary grades, which in turn are given a range of salaries. This procedure defines an internal value hierarchy based on comparisons of jobs by their contribution to organizational

> ✖ **EXHIBIT 6.4**   Unbeneficial Benefits?
>
> Organizations have generally decided what benefit coverages were needed and that all its members wanted the same mix of programs. Especially in a diverse workforce, however, individual differences in age, sex, marital status, and number of dependents become manifest.
>
> Rigidity, gaps in coverage, and cost shifting to employees have resulted in discontent with employer benefit programs. Some have
>
> - Standardized packages that require participation whether or not benefits are needed (duplicate insurance for two employees in the family) or even desired (inexpensive—and inadequate—group life and disability insurance)
> - Considerable omissions in coverage that annoy many participants (e.g., eye and dental care, long-term care policies, legal assistance, child and elder care, domestic partner coverage)
> - Cost containment strategies in health care (to the extent that insurance premiums can wipe out pay raises) and retirement plans (changing from employer-paid "defined benefit" programs to employer/employee-paid "defined contribution" programs)
>
> Increasingly popular ways to address such concerns are flexible or "cafeteria" plans, which establish employee accounts or menus equal to the dollar value of benefits. Each person can then choose a combination of appropriate benefits. Administrative barriers may exist in these programs, but they can be overcome (e.g., benefits can be bundled into selected packages to ensure balanced utilization). Such programs can resolve organization-individual conflicts, because employers no longer pay for benefits unwanted by employees—and both can save on taxes. It should be pointed out, however, that flexible programs make it easier for employers to pass cost increases to employees because the individual decides whether to pay more or take less coverage.
>
> More radical than flexible plans would be to simply give employees the cash, and tax, value of their benefits, thus abolishing these programs entirely. Employer-sponsored benefit programs, after all, are largely a result of historical accident; with wage and salary controls during World War II, the only way organizations could keep people from seeking better-paying jobs elsewhere was to add benefits that were not covered by wage and salary restrictions. The logic is straightforward: Even now, desired coverage can be obtained by joining any number of nonemployer group programs that offer rates as low as those provided by employers. Should large organizations terminate their programs, even more, perhaps cheaper, options would be developed by vendors.

objectives. **Internal equity**, then, rewards jobs of equal value with the same amount and pays jobs of different value according to some set of acceptable differentials.

All systems of job evaluation—the most widely used of which is **point factor analysis** (Chapter 5)—are premised on the need to identify criteria relative to job value (e.g., responsibility, working conditions, skill); jobs are then ranked in the hierarchy on these criteria. Despite its facade of objectivity (and resulting drawbacks), job evaluation retains a measure of face validity and thus remains the basis of internal equity in most organizations. This conventionally staid, arcane aspect of salary determination has been the subject of considerable experimentation and controversy that is sure to continue in the years ahead.

Reform projects have focused on a technique called **pay banding** (also known as broad or grade banding), made popular by the downsizing and delayering that characterize many restructured organizations (World at Work, 2002). In this procedure, to make the salary structure more flexible, separate job levels are grouped into broad categories or bands of related jobs. This provides considerable discretion in setting pay within these levels.

In pay banding, (federal) agencies may collapse the 15 General Schedule grades into a smaller number of pay ranges or bands. For example, an agency could establish four bands encompassing GS 1–5, the GS 6–11, the GS 12–13, and the GS 14–15 levels. . . . At today's rates, for instance the second band . . . would allow managers . . . to set pay anywhere from $128,253 to $60,405. The number of bands and the way grades are assigned to bands can be designed to support the organization's mission, values, and culture.

Once the pay bands are defined, the agency determines how employees move within and across pay bands. The GS system uses longevity (time-in-grade) and quality step increases [incentive pay] to move an employee within a grade, and merit promotion to move . . . to a higher grade. Pay under the GS system also is increased through general, governmentwide pay increases. In pay-banding systems, the amount of pay increase within a band is based on the employee's skills or competencies, job performance, contributions, or similar measures. Monies earmarked in the GS system for within-grade, general, and quality step increases may become "at risk" incentive pay in a pay-banding system. . . . A high-performing employee could move to the top of a pay band much more quickly than is possible in the GS system. . . . These flexibilities allow an agency to manage its workforce by rewarding highly valued behaviors. ("Pay banding," 2003, p. 3)

The technique, then, makes it easier to adjust salaries but does nothing to deal with basic pay problems (indeed, when instituted, it is frequently required to be "budget neutral"). In addition, at least at the national level, there is no evidence that it is cost-effective to replace the existing classification system (Blair, 2003). Indeed, pay banding increases payroll costs, reduces promotion opportunities, and it can expose the agency to charges of **Equal Pay Act** (Exhibit 6.5) violations if there are not written plans detailing the method of pay progression within a band.

Whereas pay banding implies that job evaluation may be less important in the future, a subject of considerable debate, **comparable worth** suggests that it will become more significant. That is, job evaluation provides a means not merely to provide equal pay for equal work but also to offer equal pay for jobs of equal worth to the organization (see Exhibit 6.5). Despite these experiments and controversies over job-based compensation plans (and the internal equity they seek to produce), such plans continue to be widely used because few realistic alternatives exist.

Personal Allocation: Individual Contribution

Once job evaluation has established a salary structure and each grade is assigned a range of salaries, attention shifts from internal equity in the agency to **individual equity**, that is, determining the pay level of each employee in the range and, by so doing, the base for subsequent pay adjustments. This requires that rewards be allocated fairly to those doing the same job. Several related approaches are examined here: seniority (including cost-of-living adjustments), merit and skill pay, and gainsharing plans (Figure 6.1).

Seniority Pay

Seniority pay or longevity compensation is furnished on the basis that an employee's value to the organization, as a result of continuous training and development (Chapter 8), increases over time. When this occurs, time-in-grade is compatible with merit and skill pay. If a department does not add value to its career employees, then seniority systems can become stagnant and yearly increments an unearned entitlement. Seniority, in any case, is a major determinant of pay progression, even in business incentive programs.

✖ EXHIBIT 6.5   Job Evaluation and Comparable Worth

It is difficult to get a man to understand something when his salary depends upon his not understanding it.

—Upton Sinclair

Job evaluation systems are designed to build an internal equity hierarchy based on comparisons of jobs; compensation systems assume that in setting pay, an organization should evaluate the contribution of each position to the organization. It follows, then, that equal pay should be offered for equal work; indeed, that is mandated by the 1963 Equal Pay Act (which is not always enforced; see www.aflcio.org/women). Job evaluation also, however, provides a way to equate jobs different in content but equal in value. Comparable worth, or **pay equity**, calls for equal pay for jobs of equal value. In concept, comparable worth is gender neutral; in reality, many of its beneficiaries have been women because jobs often held by them pay less than those held by men.[1]

Although seemingly objective, job evaluation can be undermined by the selection of factors, the way they are defined, and how points are assigned to them (Chapter 5). A compensation system, for example, that pays guards at different base rates in a prison, groundskeepers at a hospital more than nurses, and county dog pound attendants more than child care workers lacks face validity.

Although the Equal Pay Act and Title VII of the 1964 Civil Rights Act deal with issues of pay equality and sex discrimination, comparable worth claims consistently have been rejected by the courts because existing law does not mandate a job evaluation methodology, is not intended to abrogate market principles, and/or is relevant only in cases of deliberate discrimination.

The U.S. Supreme Court has yet to hear a comparable worth case; the concept nonetheless has been implemented in state and local government through legislation, collective bargaining, and the development of more valid and reliable evaluation factors. Nearly half of the states and more than 1,500 local governments either have statutory pay equity requirements or have changed their job evaluation and salary practices to reflect comparable worth principles.

Because few argue against the desirability of pay equity (more than 100 nations, but not the United States, have ratified the United Nations' International Labor Organization convention on comparable worth), most of the controversy focuses on its feasibility. Supporters maintain that job evaluation tools—when properly utilized—advance pay equity; opponents argue that these techniques ignore the free market. Advocates counter that markets seldom operate efficiently (e.g., sex and race discrimination); critics say that job evaluation technology is inherently arbitrary. Although the debates of the 1980s have subsided (job security being a higher priority than pay equity in an era of downsizing), many pay equity issues remain unresolved (not the least of which is a legal definition of the term). Indeed, interest was renewed by President Clinton's 1999 State of the Union Address, legislation proposed in 2001 (Paycheck Fairness Act), and by initiatives in state legislatures—where the percentage of women lawmakers is twice as great as it is in Congress. It is unlikely that comparable worth concerns will disappear in the years ahead.

NOTE:

1. In 2001, the infamous "wage gap" between men and women was 76 cents—for every dollar a male employee earned, a woman worker earned 76 cents, a figure that is approximately 14 cents higher than in 1980 with little change since 1990 (U.S. Census Bureau, 2001). Two explanations—structural factors (e.g., differential experience, education, age, occupational choice) and sex discrimination—contribute about equally to the disparity. Thus, Francine Blau, a Cornell University economist, found that women with the same experience, education, occupation, and union status as men earn 88% of the male wage (it is generally understood that the public service is considerably better than business). The gap is slowly closing, but it is evident that cultural attitudes, even in the face of lawsuits, are embarrassingly difficult to change.

Although conceptually distinct, **cost-of-living adjustments** (COLAs), like seniority pay, are also given annually to maintain external equity. The clear difference between the two is that COLAs are merely a way to maintain the compensation system with no developmental dimension. One should recognize, however, that the failure to provide them is the equivalent of a pay reduction. Thus, many employees today are not earning as much on an inflation-adjusted basis as they did earlier in their careers. The attractiveness of seniority systems and inflation adjustments, in sum, is their simplicity, objectivity, predictability, and perceived fairness, as well as their ability to encourage workforce stability.

Nevertheless many organizations believe that performance should be rewarded and say they use some form of pay-for-performance, incentive, or variable pay plans. Such plans depend on output, personnel, and organizational contingencies (see Exhibit 6.6) and work best in an environment of harmonious labor-management relations characterized by easy-to-understand payouts, high morale, and budgets sufficient enough to provide rewards. For staff personnel to see a link between pay and performance, their work must be evaluated by objective criteria and/or subjective criteria in which they have confidence. Incentive pay also must be clearly distinguished from regular compensation and cost-of-living adjustments.

In contrast, simplistic notions of pay for performance that reject the concept of seniority tend to discount fundamental notions of fairness and loyalty, and managers who condemn seniority . . . may overlook the virtues of a neutral, wholly objective standard of distributing awards and the advantages of accumulated training and experience. Indeed, it could be argued that if a manager's subordinates do not improve their performance with length of service, the manager should be terminated. Used properly, seniority offers a means of avoiding arbitrary action and the appearance of favoritism. (Hogler, 2004, p. 161–162)

Merit Pay

Like seniority programs, **merit pay** is an annual increment to base salary, an annuity that compounds for as long as the employee remains with the department. Unlike time-in-grade approaches, merit programs, which after all are based on achievement, are difficult to argue against because they are supported by leading motivation theories (economic, need, expectancy) as well as conventional wisdom: Incentives lead to improved performance.

It is not surprising that public and private organizations claim to give great deference to merit; the civil service is even named for it. A substantial discontinuity exists, nevertheless, between rhetoric and reality, as "merit pay may not be as desirable, as easy to implement, or as widely used as commonly believed" (Fisher, Schoenfeldt, & Shaw, 1996, p. 573). In the national government, the results at best are disappointing (Kellough & Lu, 1993). The cardinal paradox is that merit pay is a powerful cultural symbol and a source of control for managers over employees, yet they are reluctant to use it.

To understand why this happens, preconditions for merit pay—trust in management, a valid job evaluation system, clear performance factors, meaningful and consistent funding, and accurate personnel appraisal (Chapter 9)—must be present. Even if these exist, merit compensation may perversely (a) focus on the short term at the expense of the long term, (b) encourage mediocrity by setting limits on expectations, (c) destroy teamwork because it increases dependence on individual accomplishment, and (d) generate counterproductive,

✖ **EXHIBIT 6.6** Pay for Performance: Reality or Illusion?

I wish the buck stopped here; I sure could use a few.

—Anonymous

A recent analysis of economic, management, and social psychological research by two Harvard University faculty members demonstrates that what is supposed to occur with pay-for-performance plans in theory seldom occurs in reality. The conditions for success for these programs—(1) the output produced, (2) the people who do the work, and (3) the organization where it is done—"are generally not met in the private sector, and even less so in the public sector" (Bohnet & Eaton, 2003, p. 241).

First, pay for performance runs well if (a) employees have to complete one well-defined task, (b) the output is clearly measurable, and (c) the result can be attributed to one person's efforts. These overlapping and mutually reinforcing factors are difficult to achieve. Most white-collar employees are faced with multitasking problems, hard-to-measure work products, and team-oriented work environments, none of which fit well with individual incentives.

Second, assumptions about human nature and motivation are key to pay-for-performance plans. These programs may be effective if (a) employees work primarily for cash and (b) they care about absolute pay levels. Yet people are interested not only in money but also in job satisfaction and challenge, something not subject to performance pay. Indeed, most research suggests that humans do not want to believe that they work only for money, a finding that is especially true for public servants. Employees can even be offended when treated as if they can be manipulated by transparent monetary incentives.

Further, personnel are less interested in absolute pay than in comparisons relative to some reference point such as others' salaries, the jurisdiction's budget, or the state of the economy, considerations not germane to pay for performance. In fact, although everyone wants to be a winner, incentive plans usually mean that this is not possible. The result is the "silver medal syndrome, based on . . . Olympic champions, [that] shows the most disappointed people are those that come in second" (Bohnet & Eaton, 2003, p. 248). A system that guarantees that most will be losers is not a useful motivational tool.

Third, institutional factors affect performance pay programs. They operate best when employees know what to do and whom to serve. Knowledge of an organization's objectives, however, is not a given for the rank and file; the absence of clear goals is a result of multiple or changing leaders with different goals. This problem, known as "multiagency," is especially evident in government where staff serve many masters: chief executives, legislators, political appointees, judges, and senior career executives.

The university researchers do not claim that incentives are not effective under the right conditions but only that "ideal conditions are rarely met in empirical reality" (Bohnet & Eaton, 2003, p. 251). They endorse the belief that "the rising and falling tides of interest in the various incentive plans have more to do with changing social, political, and economic fashions than with accumulating scientific evidence on how well the plans work" (Blinder, as cited in Bohnet & Eaton, p. 241). Nonetheless, most managers, for motivation and cost control reasons, believe that performance should be an important part of the compensation system: Over 80% of the nearly 1000 private firms surveyed say they "pay for performance," although often for a small part of their workforce (Hewitt Associates, 2003). A meta-study of 39 empirical research projects in the private sector found that financial incentives were not related to performance quality (Jenkins, Mitra, Gupta, & Shaw, 1998).

(Continued)

(Continued)

Performance pay programs, in short, may be good in principle but difficult to do based on past experience with the federal general pay schedule as well as reform attempts in the 1970s, 1980s, 1990s, and the first decade of this century. First, Gage and Kelly (2003) point out that the federal general schedule is, in fact, a performance-based system that has never been correctly implemented. Supervisors do not take advantage of available incentives because there are insufficient funds to do so. When this traditional approach was nonetheless modified to emphasize incentive pay, it had to be repealed as unworkable. Second, as Risher (2002) notes, the performance compensation was tried, "first for managers under the Civil Service Reform Act of 1978 and then under the Performance Management and Recognition Act starting in 1984. Experience was so bad . . . that [the laws] were allowed to sunset . . . and the idea of pay for performance was all but forgotten" (p. 318).

Third, in 1996, the Federal Aviation Administration implemented pay for performance. By 2004, it was dubbed "a failure" that led to inequity and poor morale (Kaufman, 2004). Finally, in a widely touted reform program at the General Accountability Office, it was reported in 2005 that virtually all employees received a pay raise under the new performance-based system, although the top 20% got a one-time $1000 annual bonus before taxes ("GAO Gives Bonuses," 2005, p. 3). Not unexpectedly, comments on proposed Homeland Security Department pay-for-performance regulations were "overwhelmingly negative" prior to their final issuance (Zeller, 2004).

In a triumph of hope over experience, more federal agencies are currently seeking approval for untested pay flexibilities granted to the departments of homeland security and defense. Pay for performance, then, remains as popular in management circles as ever, including state government (Kellough & Selden, 1997). In fact, U.S. Office of Personnel Management director Kay James states that, "there is no need for further demonstration or delay" (Kauffman, 2005, p. 11). At best, it remains to be seen if future initiatives will overcome inherent problems typically found in these incentive plans. Even Howard Risher (2004), in an enthusiastic endorsement of performance pay, believes that the technique "may well prove to be the most difficult change any organization has ever attempted" (p. 46). Hays (2004), however, reports two cases in state and local jurisdictions where the approach apparently works.

"The reality is that pay for performance is likely to be of little benefit to organizations with serious performance problems and may actually be harmful" (Perry, 2003, p. 150). If not well implemented, a demoralized, embittered, unmotivated workforce can result. According to a federal incentive pay expert, reform-minded officials should look at the culture of the agency, the kind of work it does, and the resources needed to deploy a new program. "Instead of saying, 'we want (it) because everyone else has it,' agencies should ask themselves, 'What are we trying to accomplish?'" (Hewitt Associates, 2003, p. 6).

SOURCES: Bohnet and Eaton (2003); GAO gives bonuses (2005); Hays (2004); Hewitt Associates (2003); Jenkins, Mitra, Gupta, and Shaw (1998); Kauffman (2004, 2005); Kellough and Selden (1997); Perry (2003); Risher (2002, 2004); Zeller (2004).

win-lose competition among employees for merit monies. Employees may "eventually come to see merit pay as a kind of punishment" (Gabris & Ihrke, 2004, p. 540).

Merit pay, in theory, has the potential to produce high performance, but in practice it is difficult to administer in a way that personnel perceive as fair, as the example below illustrates.

When a municipal government received political pressure to implement a merit pay plan, the city manager and professional staff contracted a consultant to develop a first-rate, by-the-book, technically sophisticated design. . . . This new system should have worked.

Originally, the total money available from the compensation pool was to be divided, with about 60% going for cost-of-living adjustments and automatic pay increases and 40% reserved for merit pay. When the elected officials heard this, they reversed the formula to 75% reserved for merit pay and 25% for cost-of-living increases. These political officials clearly wanted a strong merit message sent to employees.

The city's employees resisted such intense merit pay strategies, and the police department, to avoid the merit program, unionized that same year. After the efforts of cooler heads and the making of various compromises, the merit distribution went back more or less to the original sixty-forty split. Why was this so important to the rank-and-file employees? Why did they not want more resources put into the merit pool on the premise that if they performed well, they stood to receive considerable pay increases?

By and large, these employees, like others in the public sector, were more concerned with external and internal equity than with individual equity. Merit raises, although helping, usually do not bring public agency base salaries up to market. What happens instead is that employees find their base salaries compressed in relation to what the market would currently pay someone with their level of skills and experience. This **pay compression** happens when people stay in the same jobs for long durations, receiving generally small base salary increases and only periodic merit raises. Ineluctably, these workers find new hires starting with base salaries not much below, and even in some cases above, their salaries. (Gabris, 1998, p. 649; bold added)

Even business admirers like Risher and Fay (1997) conclude that "despite policy statements that make individual merit important, salaries have been managed in a lock step manner. . . . The most aggressive corporate programs rarely give meaningful recognition to outstanding employees. The underlying merit philosophy is solidly entrenched . . . but the typical private sector employee can expect an annual salary increase with almost as much certainty as the typical public sector employee" (pp. 3, 43).

Stated differently, merit plans seldom provide enough funds to reward exceptional employees—without unfairly penalizing valued satisfactory ones. It is a major administrative challenge, in brief, for an organization to continuously reevaluate motivation and productivity, to identify the additional level of performance that warrants special recognition, and to provide those incentives on an equitable and timely basis. Merit pay, in short, should never be oversold as a panacea for organizational problems and, if used, should be merely one part of the compensation system (Gabris & Ihrke, 2004, p. 506). It is understandable why simpler, "set-it-and-forget-it" compensation systems are so widespread.

In spite of—or perhaps because of—such problems, there is no indication that decision makers are ready to abandon merit pay,[6] an idea that has become a kind of management's "fool's gold." Indeed, the U.S. Office of Personnel Management, the second National Commission on Public Service (Volcker II), and the National Academy of Public Administration (http://federaltimes.com/index.php?S=577698) have recently recommended a new federal governmentwide system similar to that found in the Department of Homeland Security.[7] Officials are generally reluctant to admit mistakes, and administrators tend to use merit monies to reward things other than performance (see below and Chapter 9). Merit is simply too titanic a social myth to reject outright; to do so would suggest that individuals do not make a difference. Instead, Gabris (1998) suggests that because merit plans fixate on individual equity, every effort should be made to ensure that the total compensation system strives to align individual, internal, and external equities. This balance must include attention both to how much people receive (distributive justice) and to the processes used to decide how much (procedural justice). Not to do so exacerbates the vicious, visible, and vital aspects of pay, as it is a topic about which few hold neutral feelings.

Skill Pay

Criticisms of merit schemes have triggered a high level of interest in **skill** (knowledge, competency) **pay**. Such plans analyze the job knowledge a competent employee will need to possess, as new skills are (a) learned, (b) used, and (c) show results, employees qualify for salary increments.

Skill compensation is consistent with longevity and merit principles and also is compatible with pay banding because employees are recognized for gaining additional competencies in a broad array of job practices. Note, however, that it is person centered rather than job centered because, unlike job evaluation, it focuses on how well the individual is doing the job, not how well the job is defined.

The technique promises to improve productivity because instead of focusing on minimal qualifications, it emphasizes competencies that a fully performing employee is expected to demonstrate. In so doing, it specifies what organizations need (a competent, flexible workforce) and what people want (control over compensation and job success). As an added benefit, it also helps resolve a nettlesome problem for both employers and employees, that of traditional performance appraisal (Chapter 9), as the individual either does or does not progress in skill level.

Although few studies have validated skill-based pay systems, they are growing in popularity, especially in organizations that focus on participatory management and teamwork. Englewood, Colorado, for example, has developed a skill-based pay system that updated all job descriptions, verified each job position's current salary, and formulated career development plans. The strategy was implemented by developing a new pay line (determining the skill base for jobs and assigning monetary values to each skill category), establishing an individualized career development program for employees, and giving employees a choice as to whether or not they would participate in the plan. The program has resulted in higher individual satisfaction, better defined personal and professional goals, increased employee empowerment, and cost-effectiveness (Leonard, 1995).

The Virginia Department of Transportation program, however, failed because it lacked supervisory or union support, compelled all employees to participate (who then complained to legislators), and neglected to redesign HRM systems needed to support the change (e.g., classification and appraisal). A significant factor was the use of business consultants who did not understand the sensitive political milieu in which the agency operated (Shareef, 2002). Between the experiences of Englewood and the Virginia programs are Veterans Benefits Administration, the Federal Aviation Administration, and the North Carolina State Transportation Department, each of which had to undertake major changes in their skill-based initiatives in order to make them work (Thompson & LeHew, 2002).

These plans are not, then, a panacea, for two reasons. First, intrinsic concerns include both the frustration that occurs either when newly achieved skills go unused or when employees "top out" of the program with no further opportunity to earn raises and the complex bureaucratic processes that likely will develop to monitor and certify employee progress. Second, extrinsic impacts include complementary HRM functions that will be affected (short-term training and long-term payroll costs increase[8]) and the dynamic political atmosphere (electoral cycles, employee-voters, unions, rank-and-file vs. managerial pay). Note also that external equity is far more difficult to determine in this approach to pay.

Gainsharing

In a **gainsharing** type of pay plan, the organization and its employees share greater-than-expected gains in productivity and/or cost reductions; typically, half of the savings revert to the agency general fund, and the balance is distributed equally among the people involved. In several interesting variations, the provision of funds to city personnel in Loveland, Colorado, depends on the results of citizen satisfaction surveys and the amount of funds left over in the budget; and in Blacksburg, Virginia, surplus funds at the end of the year are not shared, but rather public servants decide how the monies will be used to improve operations. Charlotte, North Carolina, has a "competition-based program," which distributes monies either to employees who competitively bid and win projects or when city departments exceed benchmark performance standards (Jurkiewicz & Bowman, 2002).

Gainsharing, in short, is designed to accomplish the same objective as individual incentives: to link rewards with performance. The difference is that performance is measured as a result of group effort, thereby reinforcing team cohesion, promoting a problem-solving culture, and reducing perceived internal inequities. Individual and group incentives are not mutually exclusive but can be blended by concentrating on individual behavior consistent with gainsharing (i.e., contributions to teamwork). The technique requires a high degree of organizational trust as well as widespread information sharing. Focusing on employee empowerment and quality improvement, a number of experiments in the Defense Department since the 1980s experienced varying degrees of success.

The approach, although not widely used in the public sector, carries genuine potential to create a flexible, proactive, problem-solving workforce (Masternak, 2003). This is one—of many—areas, however, where rhetoric and reality collide. Sanders (1998) ruefully observes that lawmakers may argue that "bureaucrats are already paid (perhaps too much) to efficiently use public funds, and that they should not be offered more money to do what they should be doing anyway" (p. 239).

It comes as no surprise, then, that when incentive plans such as gainsharing or bonuses are attempted, an agency's payroll subsequently may be reduced by the amount of savings generated (see Exhibit 6.7). Successful programs require a cultural change to overcome suspicion and cynicism that permeate incentive plans. Yet, should this occur, these approaches, when used as a partial or complete substitute for other plans, can mean less money for most employees than provided under other approaches to individual equity.

Implications

This discussion has examined the similarities and differences among longevity, merit, skill, and gainsharing pay plans. In the end, the similarities engulf the differences. Any reasonable increase becomes a symbolic lightning rod for criticism. As a result, available resources are often so trivial that managers have little choice but to divide the money into small increments to keep everyone from losing ground to inflation.

✖ **EXHIBIT 6.7**   Employee Bonuses

Money costs too much.

—Ralph Waldo Emerson

A growing compensation trend is the use of **bonuses**, one-time payments sometimes made instead of awarding more costly permanent pay increases. To encourage high performance, the payouts must be noticeable, at least 4–5%, because smaller amounts may be demoralizing and counterproductive. For the organization, this technique provides an economical, flexible method to control salary expenditures but nonetheless still reward employees. For the individual, one lump sum may seem like more money than a comparably sized raise spread over an entire year. At least in the short run, then, bonuses appear to resolve the paradox of needs.

Unfortunately, such plans are subject to political processes that often undermine them as the politicization of compensation often results in program underfunding. Administrators, then, are faced with two unattractive options: giving a few employees relatively large amounts and other deserving staff nothing or providing many people with trivial rewards. At the federal level, two thirds of employees received an average bonus of 1.6% of salary, and most believe that their agency's program does not provide incentives to encourage performance (Lee & Straus, 2004). A similar result can be found at the state level as the case below illustrates:

Some politicians are fond of blustering about making government run "like a business" and they often stereotype public employees as do-nothing bureaucrats. So when the government does run "like a business," that, one might think, would make them happy.

The Florida Department of Revenue took state lawmakers up on a challenge issued in 1994 when the legislature passed a law allowing monetary rewards—bonuses—to state employees who go above and beyond the call of duty and save the state money. The department saved state taxpayers $9 million. Not bad.

Having accomplished this, the agency's executive director, Larry Fuchs, asked the legislature to appropriate enough to give half of his deserving staff $100 bonuses. Save $9 million. Spend $250,000. But that's when another stereotype came into play: the stereotype of the conniving, forked-tongue, hypocritical politician. The Senate refused to give Fuchs the bonus money.

Some lawmakers say the state should not pay its employees extra for simply doing their jobs. Others have questioned whether the agency met performance standards, but Fuchs says he was never told why the Senate refused to pay the bonuses. If the Senate does not want to offer financial incentives for meeting higher work standards in state government, it should say so. But government leaders have an obligation to keep their promises. Pay the $100 bonuses.

In the same state more recently, many departments paid identical amounts to eligible staff (e.g., $371, although some payouts ranged from $76 to $2000 for a small number of employees; (Cotterell, 2004). For different reasons, most personnel—those receiving and not receiving the monies—found such bonuses be to demoralizing. In Wyoming, $400 annual performance bonuses were allotted to state agencies for distribution in 12 monthly installments. In some departments, awards were given to a few people who then gave it to others, threw a party, or refused to accept it; in other offices, employees drew straws for the monies (Behn, 2000, p. 4).

SOURCES: Behn (2000); Cotterell, B. (2004, p. 1B); Lee and Straus (2004); "State Should Keep Promise," *Tallahassee Democrat* (December 13, 1996), p. 10A. © Copyright 1996 by *Tallahassee Democrat*. Reprinted with permission.

This is perhaps most clear when cost-of-living allowances not only are used as a substitute for incentive pay but also are adjusted below living costs. With little consistent attempt to "keep employees whole" against inflation, the real issue is not a raise (seniority, merit, skill, or gainshare) but the size of the pay reduction. When the economy improves, many lawmakers paradoxically, if predictably, see even less reason to provide raises—to say nothing of furnishing "catch-up" monies.[9] Indeed, they often argue against raises as a way to keep inflation under control.

This strategy serves as an indicator of elected official "toughness" and responsiveness to taxpayers. Thus, equity—external, internal, individual—is simply replaced by the amount of lost purchasing power as the years go by. Nowhere is the dilemma between organizational and individual goals more evident: Employees wish to be treated fairly at the same time that public compensation systems often act to deny that need. The depth of the problem was illustrated in 1999. Rather than pay soldiers salaries sufficient to keep them off public assistance, recruiting standards were again lowered, and some elected officials advocated reinstating the military draft.[10] The value to the public of this conundrum is limited: Employees in an inequitable situation, according to equity theory, seek to reduce the inequity by decreasing performance, increasing absenteeism and tardiness, or simply quitting.

Although it may be true that relative pay levels will not drive government out of business, it is also true that a noncompetitive salary structure has very real consequences for public service. It serves as an impetus to hire peripheral labor—low-paid, often poorly trained, part-time employees, temporary workers, and even volunteers,[11] many of whom are likely to leave as soon as they find full-time positions. It also acts as an impetus to privatization—the functional equivalent of going out of business—sometimes at a higher cost to the taxpayer.

In this context, then, debates over pay reform plans, although intellectually interesting, are diversionary because they miss the fundamental point: inadequate pay for all employees— women, men, black, brown, yellow, red, and white alike. The actual problem is decidedly not the type of pay technique; rather, the real, substantively rational issue is the amount of pay. It is not unexpected, therefore, that technical initiatives often do not produce expected gains. Congress, for example, is often reluctant to extend successful pay demonstration projects governmentwide; they were set up to fail.

SUMMARY AND CONCLUSION

Pay policies and programs are a significant—and problematic—management tool (Zingheim & Schuster, 2000). Pivotal to the employment relationship, compensation decisions can further fulfillment of individual goals as well as organizational goals. Because compensation represents a powerful symbol of an institution's overall beliefs, employees need to know that the organization is looking out for their interests as well as its own. Without this understanding, pay becomes a target for a wide variety of work-related problems.

This chapter has focused on the elements that influence pay determination. Equity in external competitiveness (labor markets), in internal consistency (job evaluation including pay-banding experiments and comparable-worth debates), and in individual contribution (seniority, merit, skill, and gainsharing compensation) were examined within the context of policy (lead, match, lag) and law (e.g., the 1963 Equal Pay Act and the 1990 Federal Employees Pay Comparability Act). Among the controversies in this important HRM arena are pay dissatisfaction, the public-private sector pay gap, time and money, and benefits. Reading between the lines, key principles characterize this vital, visible, and vicious topic: (a) compensation perhaps more than any other HRM function is a people problem; (b) pay is a nonverbal, but loud and powerful, form of communication; (c) pertinent strategies are contingent on the culture of the jurisdiction and the vision of its organizations—one size does not fit all; (d) pay systems must support and be consistent with all other aspects of the agency; and (e) determination of pay is more art than science (also see Flannery, Hofrichter, & Platten, 2002).

Public and nonprofit, far more than business, employers need to be able to demonstrate that compensation systems are managed effectively and treat people fairly. Failure to honor competitive pay in law and policy in the name of political expediency does little to foster trust in the democratic process or to ensure productivity.

The success or failure of organizations must be supported by the reward system. Fortunately, as this chapter has outlined, there are many compensation techniques available to achieve this end. Unfortunately, none of them is as simple as it may appear. From a technical perspective, the folly is the myth of universal applicability; the ultimate mistake, however, is the failure of political will to provide just salaries so that the public can be faithfully and honorably served.

To put it differently, there is no agreed-upon way to determine compensation; no job has intrinsic economic worth simply because human reality is socially constructed. It is certainly not the free market, if for no other reason than there is no such thing. It is possible, however, to suggest criteria that could define an ideal compensation system. Although such standards are neither mutually exclusive nor exhaustive, they do suggest a starting point from which any plan can be assessed.

The criteria, which strive to align employee and employer goals, include the following:

1. *Stakeholder involvement in system design or reevaluation.* Because equity is often in the eye of the beholder, it is vital that all stakeholders—taxpayers, elected officials, nonprofit contributors, managers, and employees—have a meaningful voice in the policy. For example, Kansas commissioned a state pay study that involved 16 focus groups of randomly selected employees, a survey of 3,000 additional employees, and group meetings with legislators and middle managers. It was, no doubt, a difficult process, but responsible democratic governance demands no less.

2. *Simplicity in base pay and diversity in benefits.* As the basis of most people's perception of the entire compensation system, the structure of base pay, which must be competitive, should be readily comprehensible to all (e.g., Wyoming condensed 37 state pay grades into 11 broad pay bands in 1998). Although the principle of clarity should also obtain for benefits, given the diversity of the 21st-century workforce, there should be a variety and choice among them. The options must be offered in such a manner that no one can gain advantage or suffer disadvantage, something that occurs with uniform benefit packages.

3. *Salary progression tied to continuous improvement.* Whether through seniority or through merit, skill, or gainsharing pay, people need to be rewarded as they become more valuable to the agency. If these systems, singly or in combination, cannot be properly designed, implemented, or funded, then either (a) COLAs, in the name of fairness, should be seen as an automatic cost of doing business, or (b) the number of hours worked should be reduced (e.g., Massachusetts and South Carolina requires 37.5-hour weeks). Employees will then seek promotional opportunities and/or second jobs to increase their pay.

4. *Job security.* Precisely because compensation is vital, visible, and vicious, some form of job security, linked to productivity, is necessary to serve the public effectively in the face of political pressure. People must know, as Winston Churchill stated in a June 18, 1940 speech to the House of Commons, "that they are not threatened men who are here today and gone tomorrow." The more employees are expected to have creative ideas and solve difficult problems, the less we can afford to manage them with the organizational version of capital punishment. To align the goals of the agency and the individual, managers must be developers—not executioners—of human resources.

Ideally, a compensation system should seek to achieve external, internal, and individual equity. In so doing, it should foster self-managed employees, reward innovation, and focus on citizen service. The above standards (some already nominally exist, others are under attack) do not guarantee that every paradoxical problem will be resolved. Their denigration or absence, however, ensures that an equitable system is unlikely.

At the dawn of the new century, a number of compensation trends in base pay, salary progression, and benefits appear evident. To make base pay more attractive, at least in the short run, pay-banding experiments are likely to continue. Automatic increases in salary probably will be minimized gradually in favor of individual or team incentive systems. The doubling of the president's salary in 2000 (to $400,000, a remarkably modest sum compared to the average chief executive salary of over $13,000,000) could make it politically easier to lift salary caps that apply to a variety of federal executive and congressional officials. Finally, although more benefits (especially in the arenas of health and family) may become mandatory in the future, what appears to be evolving is a system in which the employee is increasingly responsible not merely for benefit choices but also for their cost.

Overall, then, low-salary budgets reflect a general trend toward cost containment sparked by global competition for jobs, technological displacement of staff, and increasing use of contingent workers. The traditional social contract at work—hard work justly compensated in exchange for job security and loyalty—has been dramatically eroded as more organizations want less responsibility for their workforces. This portends a turbulent environment for employers, employees, and society in the years ahead.

KEY TERMS

Alternative work schedules
Benefits
Bonuses
Comparable worth
Cost-of-living adjustment
Equal Pay Act
External equity
Fair Labor Standards Act of 1938
Federal Employees Pay Comparability Act of 1990
Gainsharing
Herzberg's theory of motivation

Individual equity
Internal equity
Job evaluation
Labor markets
Merit pay
Pay banding
Pay compression
Pay equity
Point factor analysis
Seniority pay
Skill pay

Class Discussion

1. "We need to pay people based on their value-added contributions to their organization as well as the nation." Discuss, employing da Vinci's "parachute" (Introduction).

2. If teamwork, process improvement, and citizen service are hallmarks of quality management, then discuss the most appropriate pay system for an agency pursuing quality.

3. To what extent do flexible benefit programs resolve individual-organization compensation dilemmas? Would it be better to abolish benefits altogether (Exhibit 6.6)? Identify the conditions necessary for that to occur.

4. At the end of the chapter, it was suggested that the number of work hours be decreased in the name of employee fairness. Actually, European economists have long claimed that organizational productivity increases as hours decrease (see Saltzman, 1997). Discuss how "less can be more."

Team Activities

5. It was claimed that pay is important because it is vital, visible, and vicious in organizations. Divide into groups and analyze, from the perspective of the paradox of needs (Introduction), at least three strategies to ensure (a) external, (b) internal, and (c) individual equity for employees.

6. Resolved: "If recruitment and placement functions of HRM are done well, then incentive pay plans are irrelevant—even harmful." One team should argue the affirmative position, one the negative.

7. Analyze the importance of, and controversies surrounding, benefits from the perspective of the employee (one team) and the employer (another team). If some governments use benefit programs to attract and retain employees, is this ethical?

8. Because managers typically lack flexibility to increase employee pay (except to a limited extent in performance appraisal, Chapter 9), they may resort to finding ways to upgrade jobs (Chapter 5) instead. Discuss the ethics of this tactic and whether or not pay banding is a genuine solution to low pay in government.

Individual Assignments

9. There are many paradoxes in the HRM compensation function. Identify at least three and discuss ways to resolve them. To what extent do they relate to the fundamental paradoxes discussed in the Introduction?

10. Your division has been selected as a demonstration project to establish a pilot program to ensure individual equity. Top management has created an employee advisory committee to recommend how this can best be established. As its chair, which strategy would you recommend for first committee discussion? Why?

11. Discuss the following paradox: American employees work longer hours than they did a generation ago and work longer hours than employees in most other advanced nations, yet they are among the least protected and often the worst paid. The wages earned by the "working poor," in business and in government, in fact, do not lift them out of poverty.

12. Comparable worth is an important issue in rank-in-job classification systems. Why is it irrelevant in rank-in-person systems (Chapter 5)?

13. In the context of the importance of distributive and procedural justice in pay determination, consider this observation: "We apply rigorous discipline to learn how to earn a living, but not how to live."

NOTES

1. Furthermore, their tenure in office, in an era of term limits, may be less than that of many career employees. Decision-making horizons, therefore, are likely to differ, and elected officials may be apt to maximize short-term goals at the expense of long-term effectiveness. Nowhere is this more evident than when it comes to compensation policies. Given the substantial funds devoted to payrolls, it might be anticipated that compensation would be one of the most carefully deliberated aspects of government policy; this is not the case (see Exhibit 6.1).

2. Official pay gap estimates are subject to a variety of technical criticisms. See U.S. General Accounting Office (1995) and Kauffman (2000).

3. It should be noted that many governments, although committed by law to external equity, actually emphasize an internal labor market strategy in recruitment. That is, except for entry-level positions, most career service job opportunities are filled from within; the outside market is resorted to when no internal candidates can be found. For data on selected public service salaries, consult www.govexec.com/careers.

4. The importance of these benefits can be seen in employee recruitment and retention. Some seek employment precisely because comprehensive health insurance and retirement programs are offered. Both discourage turnover and thereby provide the opportunity for the employer to recoup training costs (Chapter 8). The best example of this is U.S. military personnel, who benefit from "socialized medicine" and are able to retire at half pay at age 40. In fact by a margin of nearly two to one, Americans prefer a government system of national health care instead of a private-employer based system (Akst, 2003).

5. Note, however, that legislators, especially at national and state levels, often give themselves very generous benefit programs as well as substantial perquisites and access to campaign funds.

6. It has been said that the definition of insanity is doing the same thing over and over again—while expecting a different result.

7. One federal official, who worked for 5 years under a pay-for-performance demonstration project, claimed that, "The incentives of the new (DHLS) system are a joke, because they are so small. (T)hey constitute a zero-sum game, in that so little money is available for incentive pay that large increases for some translate into small increases for everyone else, regardless of how they performed" (Kauffman & Ziegler, 2004, p. 4). According to a human resources consulting firm, most experts suggest at least a 5% increase in an employee's annual pay is needed for the plan to be consequential (p. 4). Ironically, the typical "employee likely would earn about the same as under the current system" if the DHLS approach was adapted governmentwide (Kaufman & Ziegler, 2004, p. 4).

8. These drawbacks may be moderated by a variation of skill pay where one-time, skill-based bonuses are awarded without permanently increasing the pay base.

9. With the end of the postwar social contract at work, there is no doubt that a full-time job with benefits is a precious commodity in today's America. If the logic in the private sector is "business is great—you're fired," then in the public sector it is "expect nothing—you may be the next to be downsized" (see, for example, Bowman, 2002).

10. Indeed, in 2004, thousands of soldiers were forbidden to return to civilian life when their contracts expired. This was an attempt to stanch the loss of troops from a military stretched thin by the war in Iraq. Some experts found these "stop loss" orders to be inconsistent with the principle of voluntary military service.

11. The Florida Highway Patrol was so strapped for funds in the 1990s that it could not even employ peripheral labor. Instead, one year it purchased department store mannequins, dressed them in uniform, and put them in official vehicles on the roadside. Although this technique may have had some deterrent value, it is not to be mistaken for effective law enforcement in a high-crime state.

REFERENCES

Akst, D. (2003, November 2). Why do employers pay for health insurance anyway? *New York Times,* p. 4BU.

Behn, R. (2000). Performance, people, and pay. *Bob Behn's Public Management Report,* 1–6. Retrieved January 13, 2005, from www.ksg.harvard.edu/TheBehnReport/PerformancePeopleAndPay.pdf

Blair, B. (2003, August 18). Experts debate pay rules for a new personnel system. *Federal Times,* p. 8.

Bohnet, I., & Eaton, S. (2003). Does performance pay perform? Conditions for success in the public sector. In J. Donahue & J. Nye, Jr. (Eds.), *For the people: Can we fix the public service?* (pp. 238–254). Washington, DC: Brookings.

Bowman, J. (2002, Fall). At-Will employment in Florida government: A naked formula to corrupt public service. *WorkingUSA,* pp. 90–102.

Cotterell, B. (2004, July 26). Money talks when handing out bonuses, *Tallahassee Democrat,* p. 1B.

Fisher, C. D., Schoenfeldt, L. F., & Shaw, J. B. (1996). *Human resource management.* Boston: Houghton Mifflin.

Flannery, T. P., Hofrichter, D. A., & Platten, P. E. (2002). *People, performance, and pay: Dynamic compensation for changing organizations.* New York: Free Press.

Gabris, G. T. (1998). Merit pay mania. In S. E. Condrey (Ed.), *Handbook of human resource management in government* (pp. 627–657). San Francisco: Jossey-Bass.

Gabris, G., & Ihrke, D. (2004). Merit pay and employee performance. In M. Holzer & S. Lee (Eds.), *Public productivity handbook* (pp. 499–514). New York: Dekker.

Gage, J., & Kelly, C. (2003, November 10). Unions support smart performance pay for Homeland. *Federal Times,* p. 21.

GAO gives bonuses under merit pay system. (2005, January 3). *Federal Times,* p. 3.

Harris, C. (1999, April 5). Top pay "way under market." *Federal Times,* p. 7.

Hays. S. (2004, September). Trends and best practices in state and local human resource management: Lessons to be learned? *Review of Public Personnel Administration,* 256–275.

Herzberg, F., Mauser, B., & Snoplerman, B. (1959). *Motivation to work.* New York: Wiley.

Hewitt Associates. (2003, September 15). OPM official: Performance pay has staying power. *Federal Times,* p. 6.

Hogler, R. (2004). *Employment relations in the United States: Law, policy and practice.* Thousand Oaks, CA: Sage.

Jenkins, C., Jr., Mitra, A., Gupta, N., & Shaw, J. (1998). Are financial incentives related to performance? A meta-analytical review of empirical research. *Journal of Applied Psychology 83,* 777–787.

Jurkiewicz, C., & Bowman, J. (2002, Fall). Charlotte: A model for market-driven public service management. *State and Local Government Review,* 205–213.

Kauffman, T. (2000, April 3). Studies delay pay locality reform. *Federal Times,* pp. 1, 18.

Kauffman, T. (2004, December 13). Pay reform failure: How FAA's bold experiment led to inequity, poor morale. *Federal Times,* p. 1.

Kauffman, T. (2005, January 3). OMB to push performance pay governmentwide in 05. *Federal Times,* p. 11.

Kauffman, T., & Ziegler, M. (2004, May 2). National Academy of Public Administration: Pay reform for all. *Federal Times,* pp. 1, 4–5.

Kellough, J., & Lu, H. (1993, Spring). The paradox of merit pay. *Review of Public Personnel Administration,* 45–63.

Kellough, J., & Selden, S. (1997, Winter). Pay for performance systems in state government: Perceptions of state agency personnel managers. *Review of Public Personnel Administration,* 5–21.

Lee, C., & Straus, H. (2004, May 17). Two thirds of federal workers get bonus. *Washington Post,* p. A1

Leonard, B. (1995, February). Creating opportunities to excel. *HRMagazine,* 47–51.

Many workers dissatisfied with pay. (2001, June 30). *HRMazazine,* 37.

Masternak, R. (2003). *Gainsharing: A team-based approach to driving organizational change.* Phoenix, AZ: World at Work.

Pay banding in the federal government. (2003, February). *Issues of Merit.* U.S. Merit Systems Protection Board, Office of Policy and Evaluation. Retrieved December 20, 2004, from http://www.mspb.gov/studies/newsletters/03febnws.html

Perry, P. (2003). Compensation, merit pay, and motivation. In S. Hays & R. Kearney (Eds.), *Public personnel administration: Problems and prospects* (pp. 143–153). Englewood Cliffs, NJ: Prentice Hall.

Risher, H. (2002, Fall). Pay for performance: The key to making it work. *Public Personnel Management,* 317–332.

Risher, H. (2004). *Pay for performance: A guide for federal managers.* Washington, DC: IBM Center for the Business of Government.

Risher, H., & Fay, C. (Eds.). (1997). *New strategies for public pay.* San Francisco: Jossey-Bass.

Risher, H., & Wise, L. R. (1997). Job evaluation: The search for internal equity. In H. Risher & C. Fay (Eds.), *New strategies for public pay* (pp. 98–124). San Francisco: Jossey-Bass.

Saltzman, A. (1997, October 25). When less is more. *U.S. News,* 78–84.

Sanders, R. P. (1998). Gainsharing in government. In S. E. Condrey (Ed.), *Handbook of human resource management in government* (pp. 231–252). San Francisco: Jossey-Bass.

Shareef, R. (2002). The sad demise of skill-based pay in the Virginia Department Of Transportation. *Review of Public Personnel Administration, 22*(3), 233–240.

State should keep promise. (1996, December 12). *Tallahassee Democrat,* p. 10A.

Thomas, K. W. (2000). *Intrinsic motivation at work.* Williston, UT: Berrett-Kohler.

Thompson, J. R., & LeHew, C. W. (2002). Skill-based pay as an organizational innovation. *Review of Public Personnel Administration, 20*(1), 20–40.

U.S. Census Bureau. (2001). *Statistical abstract of the United States* (121st ed.). Washington, DC: U.S. Government Printing Office.

U.S. Congressional Budget Office. (2002, November). *Measuring differences between federal and private pay* (CBO Paper). Washington, DC: Author.

U.S. General Accounting Office. (1995). *Federal/private pay comparisons* (OCE-95-1, pp. 231–252). Washington, DC: U.S. Government Printing Office.

U.S. Office of Personnel Management. (2002). *A white paper: A fresh start for federal pay: The case for modernization.* Washington, DC: Author.

Vroom, V. H. (1964). *Work motivation.* New York: Wiley.

Wamsley, B. S. (1998). Are current programs working? In S. E. Condrey (Ed.), *Handbook of human resource management in government* (pp. 25–39). San Francisco: Jossey-Bass.

World at work. (2002). *Best of broadbanding.* Phoenix, AZ: Author.

Zeller, S. (2004, September 8). Union's opposition to pay-for-performance systems unrelenting. Retrieved January 12, 2005, from www.govexec.com/dailyfed/0904/090804sz1.htm

Zingheim, P. K., & Shuster, J. R. (2000). *Pay people right!* San Francisco: Jossey-Bass.

7

EMPLOYEE-FRIENDLY POLICIES

Fashionable, Flexible, and Fickle

People are assets whose value can be enhanced through investment.

—David Walker

After studying this chapter, you should be able to

- Understand the composition of the workforce and trends that drive employee-responsive programs
- Identify different employee-friendly initiatives and their applications
- Determine the relative merits of proposals for resolving work/home conflict
- Develop a telecommuter agreement for use in a public organization
- Assess the impact of employee-friendly policies on agencies and their staff
- Recognize relevant paradoxes

Robert B. Reich, former secretary of labor, discusses work/family stresses in his memoir, *Locked in the Cabinet* (1998). Four brief quotations help frame the topic of this chapter:

- On deciding whether to accept the president's call to serve in the cabinet in 1992, he muses: "Is it possible to play in the major leagues—in the rough and tumble high stakes world of putting ideas into practice—and still be a good father and husband?" (p. 10).

- On how his job affected his wife's home life and how working women shoulder dual responsibilities: "She ended up with most of the home responsibilities, we used to share. Millions of women across America are trying to parent their children alone while at the same time managing a full time job. . . . The stresses are enormous and the children inevitably feel them too" (p. 275).

- On missed time with family: "How can I do this job *and* be with them? I'm lonely for them. But, I am obsessed by the job" (p. 276).

- Ultimately, on leaving the administration: "The decision to leave the cabinet . . . was painful, because it meant giving up this part of my life's work. But my children were young teenagers who would be home only a few more years, and I couldn't bear the thought of forfeiting this precious time with them" ("Note to the Reader").

Another cabinet officer—Paul O'Neill, in the Bush administration—acknowledged similar concerns about the difficulty of juggling work and personal demands (Suskind, 2004). Most can identify with Reich's and O'Neill's dilemma, one shared by many in the public service (see Dobel, 2003): We want to do our jobs, *and* be good spouses/parents, *and* avoid giving up our life's work, *and* spend precious time with our family. Employers can help, but too few provide pro-employee policies, and when they do, employees may be reluctant to use them.

Like Reich, people seek to fairly balance work and home life. This is not easy. Career demands often conflict with personal pressures, and juggling the two poses problems in both settings.[1] Work/life balance is a top career priority for many: 73% of 3,278 U.S. workers "strongly agree" that "I am willing to take a back seat in my career in order to make time for my family," according to results of a Spherion Corporation survey (Kleiman, 2003, p. 3E). Some employers, responding to employee expectations, have introduced employee-friendly policies to reduce home/work conflict and help people achieve a better balance between work and home. They also expect a return on this investment in the form of improved productivity at work. Critics maintain that such organizational initiatives are unjustified, uneven, and extravagant in a period of declining resources.

Pro-employee policies are fashionable (stylish and responsive to trends), flexible (adaptable to the unique needs of a diverse workforce), and fickle (unstable and subject to the fluctuating fortunes of the economy). For example, paternity leave is currently offered to employees at Fannie Mae (Federal National Mortgage Association), a government-sponsored enterprise. This policy allows fathers to take up to 4 weeks of paid leave spread out over an extended time period to care for their newborns. The availability of such policies might change with downturns in the economy.

Worker-responsive policies include a variety of initiatives to address employee needs and advance organizational interests. Individuals' needs are addressed when agencies introduce work schedules and benefit plans tailored to their age and stage of life. Organizational interests are served if staff performance improves as a result, or if recruitment is enhanced. Experience suggests, however, that "win-win" outcomes are not easy to achieve. Reflecting the paradox of needs (Introduction), institutional goals of efficiency and productivity (Chapter 11) may conflict with employees' goals of a supportive workplace. For instance, flextime might be a boon to some, enabling them to care for young children or ailing parents, but in practice may create problems such as office coverage and on-time project completion.

This and other paradoxes help explain why employers may hesitate before they undertake large-scale programs of this type and why employee-friendly policies might exist on paper but lack top-management support when people seek to use them. Organizations may not trust employees who are working in remote locations, or they might resist change that reduces on-site staff and redefines managerial roles. Paradoxes also help explain why personnel may lobby for specific worker-responsive programs but then underutilize them once they are available. This might result from management that does not "walk the talk" of employee-friendly policies. Alternatively, people may like to know the policies exist (e.g., child care, elder care, wellness programs, telecommuting), whether or not they use them at the moment. Employees often fear that taking advantage of flexible work options signals to their supervisors that they do not take their careers seriously.

Consistent with the distinction between personnel administration and human resource management, this chapter focuses on the person as a whole by considering the characteristics and use of employee-friendly programs. The social trends that may make such programs popular are summarized. Organizational responses to these trends and the challenges they pose are explored. A range of family/work initiatives, health/wellness programs, flexible benefit plans, and relocation assistance efforts is considered. The impacts of such programs on employee and organizational performance are discussed together with selected implementation issues. Finally, the chapter highlights paradoxes that may be encountered when implementing specific programs.

WORKFORCE AND WORKPLACE TRENDS

Characteristics of the changing American workforce have been widely discussed (Families and Work Institute, 1997; Wooldridge & Maddox, 1995). Projections suggest that coming decades will bring more women, older workers, temporary employees, minorities, and immigrants into positions in both the public and private sectors[2] (Guy & Newman, 1998; West, 2005). For example, 63.7% of women with children under 6 years old participate in the labor force, and 78% of women with children between 6 and 17 years old are working (Bureau of Labor Statistics, 2002; Ezra & Deckman, 1996). This feminization of the workforce has had numerous ripple effects on life at home and at work. Workforce composition has changed in other ways as well:

- Seven in 10 working husbands are now married to women in the labor force
- More than one eighth of American full- or part-time employees have elder care responsibilities
- According to a National Alliance for Caregiving (1997) study, about two of every three caregivers are employed (64%; 52% are full-time and 12% are part-time).
- Women are five times as likely as men to be in charge of single-parent families, but the number of fathers responsible for their children is increasing more rapidly than the numbers of mothers with this responsibility (Leonard, 1996; Levine, 1997; Peterson, 1998)

The rise in dual-career couples and in nontraditional families, along with the need to consider work and caregiving for dependent children and elderly, adds to the stress of home and career.

As the workforce diversifies, pressures will intensify for policies that address the special needs of these employees. Thus, employer assistance in meeting day care and elder care responsibilities will be priority concerns for the **sandwich generation** (those with responsibilities for both children and elderly parents), as will flextime and parental leave programs. Telecommuting might have particular appeal for the more technologically sophisticated members of **Generation X** (those born between 1960 and 1980). Those in **nontraditional families** (including gay and lesbian couples, unmarried couples in committed relationships, single-parent families, and reconstituted families) will be especially interested in domestic partner benefits.

Alternative work arrangements and cafeteria-style benefit plans (which allow workers to choose among benefits to best suit their needs) will appeal to employees who seek a better balance between job and home life and whose benefit preferences may change over the life cycle of their employment. One survey reports that two thirds of state and local governments offer flexible benefit plans (Hunt, 1997). Workers who are **downshifting** (scaling back their career ambitions and giving more time/attention to their family and personal needs) may find part-time work or job-sharing options appealing. Those losing their positions because of **downsizing** (e.g., caused by government reductions in force, outsourcing, base closure) will press employers for employee relocation assistance.

These trends will come up against countervailing pressures in the workplace. With the declining size of the workforce (relative to those who are retired or not yet working), there is a need for organizations to consider adopting employee-friendly policies to attract and retain staff. This will help public employers remain competitive with businesses that may offer a variety of workplace alternatives. To the extent that jurisdictions continue to face resource scarcity, competition, and taxpayer demands that they be lean, mean, and productive, they will avoid expenditures on all but the most essential programs. Indeed, as public organizations are becoming flatter, more nimble, and more automated, they are simultaneously downsizing as well as increasing use of temporary workers and contractors. These trends will lead to lower investments in human capital.[3] Worker-responsive policy proposals, especially absent hard evidence of pending benefits, will be a hard sell in such an atmosphere.

Public officials and managers need to respond to these competing, often contradictory, demands of the workforce and workplace in crafting policies. The menu of options available to promote supportive employee relations is broad, tempting, and rich with possibilities; the options, however, can be costly, and there is a risk that personnel may not come away satisfied. The three sections that follow discuss this array of possibilities: family/work programs, health and wellness programs, and flexible work arrangements.

FAMILY/WORK PROGRAMS

For employees, it is important to know what work/family conflicts might exist and how they can be resolved. For employers, the issues are what programs, if any, to provide and how to implement them. This section briefly examines these questions from both perspectives.

Employees with dependent children or elderly parents are concerned about their home/family responsibilities. They want to know about the support and benefits the organizations might provide to reduce conflicts. Employers will need to decide how best to respond to work/family conflicts and whether such responses require institution-sponsored services or modifications in benefit packages.

Five programs address these dual employee and employer concerns:

- Child care
- Elder care
- Parental and military leave
- Adoption assistance
- Domestic partners coverage

These program types, plus those discussed subsequently, illustrate that one activity (e.g., child care service) represents a small part of a much broader approach to "holistically" managing employee-responsive policies. Each of these initiatives is discussed in turn below.

Child Care

Former U.S. Representative Pat Schroeder reports a conversation with a colleague early in her career in Congress. She was asked how she would juggle her responsibilities as a mother and a legislator: "I have a brain and a uterus," she answered, "and they both work" (Schroeder, 1998, p. 128). Many women (and men) want what Ms. Schroeder wanted—to use their mental and physical endowments to be both parents *and* employees. This raises the thorny and much-discussed question of what to do about dependent children while parents are working.

The issue touches most people in one way or another. Consider two facts:

- Of the 21.8 million children under 6 years of age in the United States, more than half (12.8 million) need day care because both parents work
- 18,000 preschoolers and 38,000 grade-schoolers need day care according to the 2000 census (U.S. Bureau of the Census [U.S. Census], 2003).

Most parents at one time or another have experienced problems with child care arrangements that interfered with work. Tardiness, absenteeism, and productivity are all affected. Even if employees arrive on time and work throughout the day, parents may be subject to the **three o'clock syndrome**—attention to work-related tasks wanes as they begin thinking about children ready to leave school and return home. Employers can minimize these disruptions and distractions by providing child care benefits.

The types of benefits employers make available to working parents vary. A small percentage of organizations furnish on-site or near-site day care centers. A far larger proportion offer financial assistance for off-site child care, and many more provide information and referral services. Paradoxically, a majority of federal agencies offer on-site, near-site, or referral services for child care, but a very small percentage of eligible employees use these facilities. By contrast, only 9% of middle and large companies surveyed by the Family and Work Institute provide on- or near-site child care facilities (Daniel, 1999). Specifically, Exhibit 7.1 reports family benefits for full-time employees in private industry as well as state and local government.

✖ **EXHIBIT 7.1**   Eligibility for Specific Family Benefits by Full-Time Employees

Specific Benefits	Private Sector 2000	State Government 1998	Local Government 1998
Employer assistance for child care	5%	20%	3%
Employer provided funds	2	4	1
On-site child care	2	9	2
Off-site child care	1	10	1
Long-term care insurance	8	20	8
Paid family leave	N/A	10	2
Unpaid family leave	N/A	97	94
Adoption assistance	6	5	.5
Wellness programs	21	57	23
Fitness center	10	27	12
Employee assistance program	N/A	86	64

SOURCE: Bureau of Labor Statistics (2000).

Eligibility for such benefits is greater in state government than either private industry or local government. President George W. Bush signed a law (P.L. 197–67) in 2001 authorizing the use of appropriated funds by executive agencies to provide child care services for federal civilian employees. (Exhibit 7.2 identifies several types of employer-sponsored child care options.)

Two examples from local governments suggest creative approaches to child care. The city of Westminster, Colorado, formed a public-private partnership with other area employers to provide child care for employees. The local school district and private businesses are members of the partnership consortium. It provides in-home backup care for ill children, subsidizes school vacation programs, and has a resource/referral program for child care. The South Florida Water Management District provides child care for personnel at no cost to the agency as a result of negotiations with a developer who agreed to build a day care facility on property owned by the agency. The developer is leasing the land from the district for a nominal fee ($1/year for 25 years) and rents the building to a child care operator. The facility will be turned over to the district after 25 years, and it will be paid for using the rent paid by the day care operator.

⊁ EXHIBIT 7.2 Employer-Sponsored Child Care Options

1. Child care facility
   - On- or near-site center
   - Consortium center
   - Family day care home or network
   - Expansion of local centers

2. Financial assistance
   - Child care subsidies
   - Dependent-care assistance plans

3. Resource and referral service
   - Referrals for parents
   - Quality improvements

4. Mildly ill/emergency/special-needs child care
   - "Get well" rooms in child care program
   - Satellite family day care homes
   - Home visitor program
   - Special program just for mildly ill children
   - Backup care when school is not in session

5. Flexible benefits
   - Flextime, part-time work
   - Flexplace
   - Job sharing
   - Voluntary reduced time

6. Parental leave

7. Investing in community resources
   - Creating new supply
   - Funding provider training programs

Elder Care

Caring for elderly relatives is an increasingly common, time-consuming, expensive, and stress-inducing problem. The U.S. Office of Personnel Management's (U.S. OPM, 2002) survey of 1,472 employees found that 21.7% had elder care responsibilities and 42.9% expected to have such responsibilities within the next 3 years. According to OPM, 25.8 million Americans spend an average of 18 hours a week caring for a relative. A 1997 study conducted by MetLife, Inc. found that productivity associated with caregiving was $11.4 billion a year nationally (U.S. OPM, 2002). Caregivers face additional concerns that take a personal toll. They have reduced time for leisure activities (hobbies, vacations) and are more likely to report physical or mental health problems.

This issue is pervasive and costly to the workplace as well. Two thirds of caregivers are full- or part-time workers. One in 10 caregivers quit their jobs, a similar proportion take leaves of absence, and 6 in 10 display sporadic attendance at work. Increased absenteeism, abbreviated workdays, diminished productivity, and excessive turnover linked to caregiving for dependent elderly persons add to costs employers must bear (Levine, 1997). Exhibit 7.1 reports the percentage of full-time employees in private, state, and local government who are eligible for long-term care insurance. Once again, state government personnel are more likely to be eligible than those in local government or the private sector.

Elder care programs address both employee and employer needs to reduce work/family conflict by providing staff with some combination of the following: social work counseling, financial assistance, subsidies to service providers, leave policies, information and referral sources, support groups, and/or other forms of aid. Programs with some of these services/ benefits are found in more than half of America's cities and one third of private corporations (Mercer, 1996; West & Berman, 1996). The demand for such programs is bound to increase with the continued graying of America's workforce (West, 2005). Among the proposals is one suggesting a wage replacement for family caregivers of the elderly. Giving parents time off is another way to address their needs. Resource and referral services for elder care and child care, offered by 8 in 10 federal agencies, actually have been used by a paltry 0.1% of workers (Daniel, 1999).

Parental and Military Leave

The **Family and Medical Leave Act** (FMLA) of 1993 provides eligible workers with up to 12 weeks, during any 12-month period, of *unpaid* leave for childbirth or adoption; for caregiving to a child, elderly parent, or spouse with a serious health problem; or for a personal illness. Two thirds of the U.S. labor force, including private and public sector employees, work for employers covered by FMLA (U.S. Department of Labor [U.S. DOL], 2003). Thus, it is not surprising that **parental leave** policies are among the most prevalent of the five items discussed in this section for subnational governments and private sector organizations. Estimates from the Employment Policy Foundation (2000) are that 24 million Americans have taken advantage of the program since 1993. Exhibit 7.1 shows that paid and unpaid leave for full-time employees is more available in state than local government. Paid leave (maternity and paternity) is much less common. International City/County Management Association (ICMA) surveys indicate that 19% of cities offer paid maternity leave, whereas less than 9% offer paid paternity leave. Where paid maternity or paternity leave is available, cities typically make it available to all staff.

Managing parental and family leave programs involves costs of various types at different stages:

- Before leave (absenteeism and productivity impacts)
- During planning (securing and training potential replacements)
- During leave (disability pay and stakeholder impacts)
- While staffing (temps/replacement costs, overtime)
- After leave (retraining, possible turnover costs)

Estimates of the costs associated with parental/family leave, according to five surveys analyzed by Martinez (1993), most frequently ranged between 11% and 20% of annual salary. Employee gains in flexibility and support must be weighed against employer costs in subsidizing parental leave programs.

Those who serve in the military are also protected by federal and state laws. The Uniformed Services Employment and Reemployment Rights Act of 1994 prohibits discrimination against those in the military or the reserves. Negative job actions against employees because they are in the armed forces or reserves are prohibited. Furthermore, employers are required to reinstate any person who leaves his job to serve in the armed forces so long as certain conditions are met (e.g., advance notice, time limitations, honorable release). Furthermore, most state laws provide additional protections against discrimination against those in the state's militia or National Guard (NOLO, 2003a).

Adoption Assistance

Adoption assistance includes benefits ranging from time off to reimbursement of expenses following adoption of a child. Although employees who give birth to a child typically enjoy paid leave and medical coverage, this may or may not be the case for those adopting a child. Expenses can be substantial, ranging from zero to $30,000 (e.g., medical costs, legal fees, travel expenses) (http://costs.adoption.com/). Employers are beginning to recognize that adoptive parents need assistance. Three key issues need to be considered: eligibility, leave time, and reimbursement. Factors related to eligibility are length of employment, age of the child, and whether coverage includes step- or foster-care children. Regarding leave, considerations are the length of time available for unpaid leave; the permissibility of using of sick leave, annual leave, or personal leave; and whether those who take leave are guaranteed job reinstatement. Reimbursement issues concern the coverage of legal or medical expenses.

The percentage of private organizations offering adoption assistance ranges from 15% to 32% depending on the survey (e.g., Mercer, 1996). For example, Dow Chemicals USA, Wendy's International, and Campbell Soups provide adoption benefit programs. The city of Philadelphia is a public sector pioneer in making such coverage available. According to the National Adoption Center, the average reimbursement in the private sector for adoption expenses is $4,000 (Price & Price, 1997). Local government employees are less likely than either private sector or state government employees to be eligible for assistance (see Exhibit 7.1). The rationale for employers to provide such benefits is linked to equity: If parents giving birth are entitled to benefits, why not adoptive parents? Two other reasons are important: cost factors (adoption benefits are low cost because few use them) and stakeholder loyalty (support for adoptive parents can increase loyalty, morale, and retention). Similar equity, cost, and loyalty issues surround questions of domestic partner benefits.

Domestic Partnership Coverage

Domestic partnership coverage refers to benefits such as health insurance and sick/bereavement leave that may be made available to a person designated as a domestic partner of an employee. Less encompassing policies might involve little more than public recognition of cohabiting couples; more encompassing plans include dental/vision benefits, employee assistance programs, and posttermination benefits for domestic partners. The need for such coverage has increased in recent years because of changes in the American family and workforce, the importance of benefits as a key component in an employee's total compensation package, and efforts to avoid discrimination against gays and lesbians. According to the 2000 census, 5.5 million couples are living together but not married, 4.9 million were households with partners of the opposite sex. One in 9 (594,000) had partners of the same sex (U.S. Census, 2003).

Many public and private sector benefit plans have been restructured to add flexibility and take into account these changes. From 2002 to 2003, there was a 16% increase in the number of U.S. employers offering health insurance to same-sex domestic partners ("Study: Gays, Lesbians Gain," 2003). According to the Human Rights Campaign Foundation (2003), the 5,805 employers that offer domestic partner health benefits include the following:

- State governments   ($n = 10$)
- Local governments   162
- Fortune 500 companies   198
- Private companies, nonprofits, and unions   5,247
- Colleges and universities   187

New York City provides benefits for domestic partners of employees, and San Francisco goes even further, requiring private organizations that contract with the city to provide such benefits. In response, the House of Representatives denied federal housing dollars to cities that require organizations doing business with them to provide same-sex domestic partner benefits to the organization's employees. The experience at Disney and the Salvation Army (see Exhibit 7.3) suggest that granting domestic partner coverage is controversial in the private and nonprofit sector as well: It pleases some stakeholders and angers others. Additional obstacles to domestic partner benefits are rising costs of health care benefits and reluctance by insurance companies to cover unknown risks. As workforce diversity continues, pressures for such benefits will mount. Vermont's experience with civil unions and the Massachusetts court decision finding gay marriage constitutional in 2004 illustrate the increased salience of this issue.

Each of the five work/family programs discussed in this section is likely to appeal to a different group of employees. Jurisdictions that provide a smorgasbord of offerings will be most responsive to a diverse workforce. Some policies have broad appeal; others are important to a narrower clientele. Potential gains in loyalty and productivity may warrant investments in these areas. Health and wellness programs, covered in the next section, promise similar returns on human capital investments.

Family Friendly or Single Hostile?

There are some single employees who harbor resentment against policies designed for their married coworkers. They may feel shortchanged or overburdened when employers expect them to "take up the slack" for their absent coworkers who are given "special help" in dealing with spousal or child-related problems. An example of this sentiment appeared in a published letter to Randy Cohen, author of the popular "The Ethicist" column in the *New York Times Magazine,* with the writer questioning whether his employer's paid "family days" discriminated against single people (Cohen, 2002). If single or childless workers receive fewer benefits, subsidize benefits for which they are ineligible, and are expected to assume more responsibilities than others, friction will likely intensify. In seeking to achieve work and life balance, it is important for employers to design "lifestyle-friendly" policies that are inclusive, flexible, and offer choices to workers (Gannon, 1998; Kirkpatrick, 1997; Lynem, 2001).

✖ **EXHIBIT 7.3** Flip-Flops at the Salvation Army
___

In November of 2001, the Western Branch of the Salvation Army announced it would extend health benefits to same-sex partners of employees. This new policy would affect employees in 13 western states plus Guam, Micronesia, and the Marshall Islands. They said they were acting in compliance with San Francisco's landmark 1998 Equal Benefits Ordinance. Previously the Salvation Army had forfeited $3.5 million in contracts for noncompliance. According to Colonel Phillip Needham, chief secretary for the Salvation Army's Western Corporation, the action "reflects our concern for the health of our employees and those closest to them, and is made on the basis of strong ethical and moral reasoning that reflects the dramatic changes in family structure in recent years" (quoted in People for the American Way [PFAW], 2001).

In response to this action, the national offices of the Salvation Army received 10,000 e-mails and 1,500 phone calls in protest. Groups such as the American Family Association, Focus on the Family, Concerned Women for America, the Traditional Values Coalition, and the Family Research Council loudly decried the act and began protesting. Vociferous negative reactions were also voiced on Christian radio and television and from the evangelical Salvation Army denomination.

Two weeks following the announcement, the policy was rescinded by the national Salvation Army's Commissioners Conference, stating, "We will not sign any government contract or any other funding contracts that contain domestic partner benefit requirements" (quoted in Gordon, 2001).

In response, Parents, Families and Friends of Lesbians and Gays (PFLAG) organized a protest supporting reversal. Opponents to rescinding the policy placed fake money (phony $5 bills), printed from an Internet site, in the Salvation Army collection kettles. They claimed this was more about sending a message than doing harm. The Salvation Army maintains the protest did not hurt their collection efforts.

This issue shows that implementation of domestic partner plans raises complex and contentious political and social issues. National support or opposition is linked to broader gay rights issues.
___

SOURCE: Gordon (2001); Heredia (2001a, 2001b); King (2001); PFAW (2001); Price (2001).

HEALTH, SAFETY, AND WELLNESS PROGRAMS

As society has become more health conscious, employees have taken greater interest in the health-promoting activities of their employers. Typical personal concerns are accessibility of wellness programs, the range of activities offered, cost-sharing arrangements, convenience, and privacy. Employers are inclined to focus on issues of program demand and productivity returns on whatever funds are invested. Four relevant initiatives are stress reduction, wellness programs, safety initiatives, and employee assistance programs.

Stress Reduction

The causes and consequences of stress at work have been widely discussed, and the human resource management implications are important. Too much stress impedes individual and organizational performance, but too little stress also can be counterproductive. The challenge to managers is to create optimal levels of stress and promote employee well-being while avoiding chronic mental or physical problems that reduce performance. Such "negative stress" is often characterized by high levels of absenteeism and turnover. Because it has been estimated that more than 10 million people in the nation's workforce experience stress-related problems, it is not surprising that some organizations have responded with stress reduction programs.

The prevention, detection, and management of negative stress are beneficial for both employees and employers. Below are ways of reducing stress, linked to human resource management functions:

- Using effective screening devices in recruitment to ensure a good person-environment fit
- Avoiding individual-organization "misfits" in selection by matching the right person with the right job
- Orienting employees in ways to reduce the gap between job expectations and reality
- Providing assessment, observation, feedback, counseling, and coaching in career planning and development
- Offering worker support systems that foster attachments among employees
- Furnishing crisis intervention counseling (including emotional support and problem-solving strategies) to employees who experience difficult moments
- Tracking organizational indicators of stress to identify problem areas
- Training employees with behavioral self-control skills to increase relaxation on the job
- Equipping staff with cognitive problem-solving skills to improve problem solving
- Offering workshops and short courses on time management to reduce stress

Stress reduction programs incorporating some or most of these strategies are found in a majority of local governments (64%) and private sector settings (52%) (Mercer, 1996; West & Berman, 1996). Exhibit 7.4 suggests further stress reduction strategies for managers and employees.

Wellness Programs

The goals of **wellness programs** are to alter unhealthy personal habits and lifestyles and to promote behaviors conducive to health and well-being. Employers offer such services as health assessment (first aid and emergency), risk appraisals, screenings (blood pressure checks, blood sugar and cholesterol tests), injections (allergy, immunizations), and health and nutrition education/counseling. They may provide exercise equipment and facilities or negotiate health club discounts and reimburse employees for participation. Health promotion activities often focus on physical fitness, weight control, smoking cessation, and health awareness. These activities can be emphasized at brown-bag lunches or wellness fairs. Psychological and physiological benefits, and resulting reductions in insurance premiums, have been reported for participating employees; improved morale, organizational commitment, sense of belonging, recruitment/retention, and productivity are potential benefits to organizations that emphasize wellness.

Program availability is greater in state government (92% of states) than in either local governments (65%) or the private sector (46%) (Council of State Governments [CSG], 1997; Mercer, 1996; West & Berman, 1996), yet benefit eligibility figures for full-time employers are lower than these figures suggest (see Exhibit 7.1). The city of Loveland, Colorado, has an innovative wellness program called Healthsteps. It offers bonus points to those with positive medical history and healthy lifestyle choices. Based on the number of bonus points employees

---

✖ EXHIBIT 7.4   Tips for Managers and Employees on Ways to Reduce Work-Related Stress

---

What can managers do?

- Follow a consistent management style.
- Avoid actions that erode the competence or confidence of employees.
- Treat all employees fairly.
- Give positive feedback whenever appropriate.
- Support flexible work schedules and job sharing.
- Clarify objectives and communicate them to employees.
- Establish performance targets that are challenging but realistic.
- Make sure tasks are well defined and responsibilities are clear.
- Introduce some variety if jobs are extremely monotonous or boring.
- Establish good two-way communication.
- Increase decision latitude.
- Avoid work overload or underload.
- Decrease role conflict and ambiguity.
- Promote career development and career security.
- Develop job content that avoids narrow, fragmented tasks with little extrinsic meaning.
- Promote participation and control.
- Avoid under- and overpromotion.

What can employees do at work?

- Schedule time realistically.
- Avoid unrealistic expectations for yourself.
- Do one thing at a time.
- Do not depend on your memory to keep track of all tasks.
- Ignore situations you cannot control.
- Get away from your desk at lunchtime.
- Identify sources of stress.
- Mentally rehearse stressful situations.
- Allow extra time when you travel.
- Review your priorities and lifestyle.

What can employees do at home?

- Exercise regularly.
- Explore ways to reduce caregiving and work conflicts.
- Take advantage of community support networks.
- Build fun into your schedule.
- Express your feelings openly.
- Be prepared to wait.
- Begin to rid your life of clutter.
- Spend time each day in relaxing activity.
- Set aside time to eat leisurely, well-balanced meals.

earn, they are eligible for distributions of up to 50% of any annual health plan savings. Attending the annual health fair and undergoing tests there can earn lifestyle points. Lifestyle points also can be earned if employees' test results meet targets for blood pressure, weight, and cholesterol and/or if they participate in various fitness activities (walking, jogging, running). Medical points can be awarded for all premium dollars paid for employees and their families (with points subtracted based on the dollar value of claims paid). They are never penalized for heavy use of medical care because point totals do not fall below zero. Some other cities have similar creative, incentive-based initiatives.

Stress reduction and wellness plans promote healthy lifestyles and reduce the likelihood of serious illnesses. Such preventive activities may be buttressed by employee assistance programs designed to address health-related problems when they appear.

Safety Programs

Employees are protected from an unsafe workplace by federal and state laws. Provisions of the Occupational Safety and Health Act provide staff with several rights if they are concerned about unsafe conditions or practices in the workplace (see Exhibit 7.5). State laws typically conform closely to the federal legislation.

Employee Assistance Programs

Organizations with **employee assistance programs** (EAPs) use them to improve employee health and help employees cope with personal problems such as the difficulties resulting from work/family conflict. Such plans usually offer counseling or referral services for people having problems with alcohol, drug abuse, personal debt, domestic abuse, or other problems that impede job-related performance. The objective of EAPs is to improve employees' competence, performance, and well-being. Eligibility for EAP in state and local governments is reported in Exhibit 7.1.

✖ EXHIBIT 7.5 Worker Rights to a Safe Workplace Under the Occupational Safety and Health Act

---

Workers have the right to the following:

- Receive training from employers on the health and safety standards that the law mandates
- Receive training from employers on any dangerous chemicals workers are exposed to and on ways employees can protect themselves from harm
- Receive training from employers on any other health and safety hazards (e.g., construction hazards, blood-borne pathogens) in the workplace
- Receive information from employers regarding OSHA standards, worker injuries and illnesses, job hazards, and workers' rights
- Make direct requests to employers to cure any hazards or OSHA violations
- File complaints with OSHA
- Make a request that OSHA inspect the workplace
- Find out the results of an OSHA inspection
- File a complaint with OSHA if the employer retaliates for asserting employee rights under the act
- Request the federal government to research possible workplace hazards

---

SOURCE: NOLO (2003b).

The profile of a comprehensive program includes the following:

- Counseling and referral for employees and their families
- Staff with solid clinical background and knowledge of providers for referral
- Broad health coverage (including mental health) in the benefit package
- Staff familiarity with the health package to ensure that provider services are covered
- Confidential services
- A training component for employees, supervisors, and managers
- Reference checks on all service providers

Many local governments like Ventura County, California; Chesterfield, Missouri; and Middletown, Rhode Island, have EAP programs reflecting several of these "ideal" characteristics. One legal caution: Employees and managers need to be aware that information gathered during EAP sessions may belong to the employer, not the employee.

Institutional sponsorship of health and wellness programs signals to individuals that the organization is concerned about their well-being. Another way that agencies can communicate that concern as well as address workforce diversity is by offering more flexible work arrangements, the subject of the next section.

FLEXIBLE WORK ARRANGEMENTS

Flexible policies go a long way in reducing work/family conflict. Worker surveys indicate that overwhelming majorities support practices like flextime, job sharing, and telecommuting (Goodman, 2003). Employees are interested in the range of options available to them at work that might minimize problems at home: Will they have any control over the hours and location of work? Are there options to leaving home at 8 and returning at 6, Monday through Friday, year-round? Can they work at home? Can they choose their benefits? Can alternatives to full-time work be negotiated? Are job- or leave-sharing arrangements permissible? These are important issues in management. Employers are interested in getting the work done. They have to weigh the pros and cons of flexible arrangements before making such options available to large numbers of employees. This section briefly considers seven alternative work arrangements:

- Flex options
- Telecommuting
- Part-time work
- Voluntary reduced work time
- Temporary work
- Leave sharing and pooling
- Job sharing

Flex Options

Flextime refers to work schedules that allow differential starting and quitting times but specify a required number of hours within a particular time period. According to the Bureau of Labor Statistics (2001), about 29 million full-time wage and salary workers (28.8%) had flexible schedules; one third of these (11.1% of total) worked flexible hours as part of a formal employer-sponsored flextime program. In the private sector, 33.3% of those working in service-producing industries and 23.1% of those in goods-producing industries have flextime. Comparable public sector figures are 34% in federal, 29.7% in state, and 14% in local government. Formal flextime programs are more prevalent in the public sector than in private industry: Over half the workers in the public service with flexible schedules had a formal program. Nearly three fourths of federal employees with flextime participated in a formal program, whereas only about one third of private sector workers with flextime participated in such a program.

Another flex option is the **compressed workweek**, in which the number of hours worked per week is condensed into fewer days. For example, employees work a set 160-hour schedule per month but do it in less than 20 workdays by working more than 8 hours a day and fewer than 5 days a week. According to OPM (2003a), 357,326 federal personnel use compressed schedules. Compressed workweeks enable employers to extend hours of operation and enable employees to reduce commuting costs and gain leisure time. They may, however, introduce problems of employer supervision and employee fatigue. These two flex options are discussed in Chapter 6 (see Exhibit 6.4), so treatment here is limited.

Organizations are more likely to offer flextime than compressed workweek options.

Ninety-two percent of federal agencies implement flexible work schedules; compressed and flexible work schedules have more than one third of the federal workforce participating. Only 14% of states (California, Illinois, Maine, Massachusetts, Minnesota, Missouri, and Tennessee), 79% of federal agencies, and 60% of firms offer compressed workweek options. Eight in 10 employees in the U.S. Department of Labor work flexible schedules (Daniel, 1999). In California, air quality regulations provided the impetus for many governments to try alternative schedules as a way to decrease pollution and traffic congestion. A bare majority of cities (52%) nationwide offer flextime to some employees. It may take various forms:

- Core hours (required presence at work)
- Band of flexible hours (typically at the end or beginning of the day)
- Variable lunch hour
- Sliding schedule (variation in the start/stop times daily, weekly, or monthly)
- Bank time (variable length of workday; hours from long days can be banked for short days later on)

Clearly, the greatest flexibility is present when a combination of options is available.

Implementation problems can result when employees are expected to work as a team, when unions or supervisors resist the move to flextime, and when laws (e.g., maximum hours and overtime requirements) introduce complications. Care needs to be taken to ensure that there is adequate staffing during noncore hours. Compressed schedules may be less successful in smaller governments where staff coverage for leave-taking employees may be inadequate. Research on flex options in state government shows that flextime leads to reductions in absenteeism, tardiness, and turnover and increases in employee morale (Lord & King, 1991). Telecommuting is another type of flexible benefit.

Telecommuting

Telecommuters are people who work away from the traditional work locale (e.g., at home, at satellite locations, or on the road). It is estimated that anywhere from 13 to 19.6 million employees in America telecommute, and their numbers are increasing. An OPM survey (2003b) found over 90,000 federal employees in 77 agencies were teleworking: 35% of the workforce was eligible and 14.4% of eligible employees teleworked. Legislation (P.L. 106–346) requires each executive agency to establish a policy under which eligible employees may participate in telecommuting to the maximum extent possible without impeding employee performance. Four cabinet level departments reported in 2002 that 100% of workers were eligible to telecommute, but the percentage of eligible workers actually telecommuting for each agency was Education 31%, Labor 18%, Energy 8%, and State 1% (Dembeck, 2003). Some members of Congress have considered sponsoring legislation to financially penalize agencies that are not moving aggressively to implement meaningful telecommuting programs, but the Bush administration believes such action is unnecessary at this time (Barr, 2004).

According to an International City/County Management Association (1995) survey, approximately 128 cities reported telecommuting arrangements for their employees. Palo Alto, California, has approximately 25 employees telecommuting in a variety of positions. Lombard, Illinois, restricts telecommuting to exempt employees with a personal injury or illness or a workers' compensation injury. Experience with telecommuting in the city of Richmond, Washington, suggests that the tasks most suitable for work at home include writing, reading, telephoning, data analysis/entry, computer programming, and word processing.

A majority of states (56%) allow some of their employees to telecommute, and nearly half of corporate firms (49%) offer the same option. Kemp's (1995) 50-state survey indicates that most states have no formal telecommuting program, but informal arrangements often exist in selected agencies. Arizona, California, Hawaii, Colorado, Florida, Iowa, Minnesota, and Utah all have telecommuting mentioned on their Web sites. In Arizona, every agency is mandated to implement the state's program with the goal of having 20% of state employees in Maricopa County actively participating; 3,300 (or 15.5%) of the state workforce in Maricopa County are currently teleworking (ADOA, 2003). Advantages of telecommuting programs include productivity, flexibility, economy, and satisfaction. Disadvantages or impediments are loss of management control, inadequate technology, absence of policy guidance, stakeholder resistance, concerns about customer complaints, office coverage, problems scheduling meetings, and insufficient funds (see Appendix A at the end of this chapter). Subsequent sections of this chapter discuss implementation of telecommuting in greater detail.

Part-Time Work

Some employees might prefer working a specific number of hours fewer than the traditional workweek on a recurring basis. Part-time employment is defined by the federal government as involving fewer than 35 hours per week. The part-time employment rate in the United States is 13%; in Japan it is 24%. By law (5 U.S.C. 3402), nearly every federal agency is required to have a program for part-time employment. According to OPM (2003a), 92% of federal agencies implement part-time work, yet Daniel (1999) reports only 3% of workers pursue this option. In Florida, one fifth of the state government workforce consists of part-time employees. This might be a very attractive option for new parents who want to convert to part-time work temporarily as a transition between family leave and full-time work.

Voluntary Reduced Work Time

Selected full-time employees want to reduce their work hours and their pay, and some employers prefer this option as a way to reduce labor costs. Such reductions often range from a few hours a week up to 20 hours. Typically, health benefits are prorated. Voluntary reduced time (**V-time**) enables parents to meet caregiving responsibilities, provides an alternative to layoffs or use of part-time replacements, and helps phase workers into retirement. These arrangements are often negotiated.

Temporary Work

The rise of the contingent workforce is tied to employers' need for flexibility and to employees' desires for variable work schedules and employment. For individuals, temporary employment enables them to meet family responsibilities, complete education or training, master new skills, or compete for full-time positions. For organizations, temporary staffing provides a source of specific skills for only the time they are needed, allows for development of a core workforce while supplementing it as budgets fluctuate, and controls labor costs by moving labor from a fixed to a variable expense. The number of temporary workers employed nationwide on an average day in the first quarter of 2002 was 2.1 million ("Staffing Stabilized," 2003).

The hiring of "temps" has been a common accompaniment of downsizing in business, and it is becoming more evident in government as belt tightening occurs. For example, the state of Texas has put a legal employment cap on full-time positions to restrain personnel costs. The cap does not cover temporary employees or outside workers. In 1997, Texas had more than 20,000 consultants, contractors, and temps working in state government, a 300% increase from just a decade earlier. This "hidden workforce" in 1997 cost $41 million; of that amount, $24 million was spent on temporary workers (Gamino, 1997). The movement from full-time permanent workers to the "contingent" workforce is likely to continue in both the public and private sectors, and it may raise performance quality, legal, and work alienation issues. Gains in flexibility should be weighed carefully against potential losses in effectiveness before proceeding with new workplace initiatives.

Leave Sharing and Pooling

Leave sharing and pooling are types of employee-to-employee job benefits whereby healthy workers donate sick time or other benefits to coworkers in crisis. Unlike some employee-friendly policies common in the private sector, leave sharing and pooling are found more often in government. For example, although only 8% of companies nationwide offer such sharing benefits, the federal government, two thirds of state governments, and many municipal jurisdictions and public school districts allow leave sharing and pooling (CSG, 1997; Suttle, 1998). Despite its availability, only 1% of federal employees use it (Daniel, 1999).

Washington State allows employees to pool and share leave days. More than five dozen different agencies, employing 99% of state workers, offer shared-leave programs. Over 800 employees used time donated to them by their coworkers in 1997. The cost of shared leave in that year was about $3 million. Eligibility to use shared leave is contingent on health status: A serious or life-threatening illness is necessary to qualify. The Tacoma School District, for example, further requires that a worker cannot donate more than 6 days in a 12-month period and cannot reduce his or her own sick leave account below 60 days. For the donor of sick leave, such programs are a way to give support and express concern for coworkers. For the recipient, it is a way to fill in the gaps not covered by insurance, cope with medical emergencies, and reduce financial hardship (Suttle, 1998). Overall, when organizations offer leave sharing, like V-time, it is an example of addressing the paradox of needs.

Job Sharing

Job sharing enables two employees to split the responsibilities, hours, salary, and (usually) benefits of a full-time position. A 1997 status report to the president on the federal workplace family-friendly initiatives found that 63% of federal agencies offer job sharing. A study conducted by the Human Resources Division (HRD) of the Massachusetts government in 1999, found that 29 states have job-sharing programs. HRD determined in a survey of 88 state agencies that 344 out of 3000 total part-time positions were job shares. Earlier studies report favorable experiences in some states (Michigan and Massachusetts), others found limited use (Colorado, Minnesota, and Tennessee), and still others do not allow job sharing (Lord & King, 1991). Colorado's Web site says that it has had job sharing since 1977. Successes are partially attributable to careful planning, supervisory training, and highly motivated workers; problematic results are linked to supervisory resistance and state-imposed restrictions on participation. Examples of positions where job sharing is used include nursing, social work, law, and mental health workers. Job sharing offers employees the advantages of balancing home/work responsibilities, earning professional wages, and maintaining a career while cutting back on hours (Lord & King, 1991).

Job sharing is less frequently reported as a benefit in local government (11%), although nonreporting governments may be willing to approve such arrangements in response to specific proposals. The city of Redmond, Washington, uses it to jointly fill secretarial, street maintenance, financial analyst, and recreation coordinator positions. Agencies see potential advantages in job sharing, especially when facing severe financial constraints, possible layoffs, or needs of working mothers. Employers may also see it as a way to reduce absenteeism and turnover and to heighten productivity. However, benefit levels, promotion implications, and seniority issues remain problematic under this arrangement.

To summarize, two factors regarding the employee-friendly and flexible policies discussed so far—employers' attitudes and "the power of peers"—are important determinants of work/family conflict and of whether employees use benefits. The importance of employer attitudes is apparent from research that shows that work/family conflict is greater for employees whose supervisors put work first, regardless of the worker-friendly or flexible benefits provided. The "power of peers" is stressed by research showing that employees more frequently use alternative work schedules when those in their work groups are already using them (Clay, 1998). Contrary to critics' claims that encouraging individuals to use employee-friendly policies will erode employee commitment and loyalty, research by the Families and Work Institute, drawing on a national sample of 2,877 employees, found that support from employers, as demonstrated by flexibility and family-friendly policies, was the most important factor in job satisfaction (Clay, 1998). Clearly, the employment context is crucial.

In addition to employers' attitudes and peer pressures, it is important to consider costs. Although costs may be offset by employee gains in flexibility and support, they can be substantial. This leads to two key problems. First, unlike the private sector, public organizations cannot pass the costs through to the marketplace. Second, managers are, with some exceptions, usually not in a position to authorize these programs; appropriate governing bodies must approve them. That usually means that they become part of negotiations of overall compensation, fringe benefits, and work rules. The complexity of adopting, financing, and implementing such programs requires careful consideration. Furthermore, initiatives can become politically volatile (e.g., domestic partner benefits), suggesting the need to consider intangible costs in addition to tangible ones.

The preceding sections have highlighted different strategies managers can use to minimize family/work conflict and promote employee well-being. Experimentation to discover the appropriate mix of such plans is necessary as employers search for the best "fit" between employee needs and organizational requirements (see Exhibit 7.6). The U.S. Office of Personnel Management opened a new Family-Friendly Workplace Advocacy Office in 1999 to encourage these programs. Resource scarcity might limit the range of options available for some jurisdictions and agencies, but workforce diversity will provide a counterweight pushing for reform. Jurisdictions will be more likely to respond if the proposed changes meet pressing needs and if payoffs are evident. These issues are considered in the next section.

IMPLEMENTATION, ASSESSMENT, AND EVALUATION

Organizations seeking to help workers become more effective and employees seeking supportive workplace relations have a convergence of goals. The trick is to design a program that meets the objectives of both employers and employees while avoiding the paradoxes described previously. Before embarking on flexible work options or deciding on the mix of employee-responsive policies to pursue, agencies should conduct a needs assessment. Appendix B at the end of this chapter lists some of the questions employers should consider as they assess the needs of their agency. At a minimum, data should be gathered on workforce demographics, the range and utilization of existing programs, employee-identified problem areas, satisfaction levels and program preferences, and so forth (data sources include employee personnel records, surveys, interviews, and focus groups). Exhibit 7.7 is a tool for helping to select appropriate programs to meet specific needs; Exhibit 7.8 provides relevant Web sites. Once the needs, resources, values, and issues have been clarified, the benefits and risks of acting or not acting need to be assessed. Exhibit 7.9 provides an aid for making assessments. Professionals in the human resource office are the most likely candidates to collect, analyze, and interpret relevant data and to present recommendations to officials.

The activities and stages involved in implementing employee-responsive policies (Collins & Magid, 1990; Hall, 1990; Mikalachki & Mikalachki, 1991; Stanger, 1993) can be grouped as follows:

- Set policies and values for the program (task force/advisory committee, values clarification, issue framing, needs and resource assessment, policy formulation and adoption, program management)
- Identify options or models (personnel policies, benefit plans, work restructuring, information and referral, parent education and counseling, direct service, career paths, dependent care)
- Articulate program objectives (goals, expectations, eligibility, benefits, participation levels, advantages, external factors, planning estimates)
- Plan for implementation (involvement of key stakeholders, pilot or phased projects, breadth and depth of change, modified work environments, costs, timetables, communication system, building support, overcoming resistance, training)

✖ EXHIBIT 7.6   Local Government Examples of Employee-Friendly Policies

---

DuPage County, Illinois: Flexible Scheduling. No formal policy of flexible scheduling is in place; each decision to change a schedule is decided by the department head on a case-by-case basis. In some instances, however, a schedule change may affect an entire department. For the computer operations division, employees work three 12.5-hour days. Because it was often difficult to get weekend coverage, the county's convalescence center implemented a similar schedule for nurse's aides. Any employee can adjust his or her schedule with the approval of the department head (the schedule change must not negatively affect service delivery).

    Dane County, Wisconsin: Telecommuting. About a dozen employees are allowed to telecommute a few days a week. Telecommuting is not a systemwide policy; it tends to be limited to management staff whose positions do not involve a great deal of public interaction. Telecommuting is also allowed under special circumstances. For instance, one critically ill department head's chemotherapy treatments make her susceptible to illness. To limit her exposure to germs, she is allowed to work at home.

    Most employees supply their own equipment (computers, modems) for their home offices, but in the case of an information systems staff person, the county supplies a special computer that allows him to service the county's 911 system. A portable computer is also available to staff members who do not have their own computer equipment. Supervision of these employees generally is not an issue because most are professional or managerial employees and their performance is judged on the end result of their work.

    Birmingham, Alabama: Job Sharing and Subsidized Child Care. There is limited job sharing that tends to be used primarily by library employees because library hours are different from and longer than other city departments' hours. To qualify for benefits, job-sharing employees must work at least three-quarters time; otherwise, they are not eligible for health insurance, sick leave, or vacation. They earn holiday leave based on the percentage of time they work (if they work 75% of the time, they earn 75% of the holiday pay). They can purchase medical insurance, but the locality does not contribute to the payment of premiums.

    The city also subsidizes child care costs for employees with sick children. It is not unusual for an employee to miss a day or several days of work caring for a sick child. Rather than lose an employee, the city encourages employees to take the child to a day care center that has trained medical staff on hand. The city then reimburses the employee for all child care costs incurred. Program costs are estimated at about $10,000 annually, but the city gains in productivity.

    Kalamazoo, Michigan: Incentive Program. The city offers employees an opportunity to earn extra cash. If a city employee has a spouse who works for another organization and the city employee can be covered under his or her spouse's health insurance policy, the city will offer the employee a yearly $1,500 bonus for dropping city coverage. This provides the employee with extra cash and reduces the city's health insurance expenditures.

SOURCE: Adapted from International City/County Management Association, *Employee Benefits in Local Government* (special data issue), pp. 5, 7. © Copyright 1995 by International City/County Management Association. Adapted with permission of the International City/County Management Association, 777 North Capitol Street NE, Suite 500, Washington, DC 20002. All rights reserved.

- Specify outcomes and benefits (benefit/cost projections, impact on key indicators, negative side effects)
- Measurement and evaluation (data sources, tracking outcomes, employee surveys, focus groups, cost accounting, program evaluation, data analysis and use)

※ EXHIBIT 7.7 Selecting Work/Life Programs Based on Agency Needs

Results	Alternative Work Schedules	Wellness Programs	Telecommuting	Caregiver Programs
Improve productivity	Can double productivity	Significantly improved	Particularly for work requiring intensive blocks of time	Reduce stress that interferes with productivity
Improve recruitment	Most sought-after work/life program	Not applicable	Particularly for information technology jobs	For those needing elder/child care
Reduce attrition	Can cut attrition in half	Fewer employee terminations	Positive impact on retention	For those needing elder/child care
Reduce absenteeism	Can cut absenteeism in half	Significant reductions	Can cut absenteeism in half	Lower rates of unexpected absenteeism
Reduce facility costs	Not applicable	Not applicable	Can cut costs 30–50%	Not applicable
Reduce costs for overtime, recruitment, workers' compensation, travel, relocation	Reduces costs for overtime, recruitment, workers' compensation, travel	Not applicable	Reduces costs for travel, recruitment, relocation	Reduces recruitment costs to replace those with elder/child care needs
Improve customer service	Expands office hours	Not applicable	Permits use of cost-saving technology	Not applicable

SOURCE: Adapted from National Academy of Public Administration, *Work/Life Programs: Helping Managers, Helping Employees*, p. 4. © Copyright 1998 by the National Academy of Public Administration. Evidence for generalizations made in cell entries is summarized in this NAPA publication.

✂ **EXHIBIT 7.8** Web Sites

Bureau of Labor Statistics	www.bls.gov
Bureau of National Affairs	www.bna.com
Families and Work Institute	www.familiesandwork.org
HR World	www.hrworld.com
Jobs in Government	www.jobsingovernment.com
Local Government Institute	lgi.org
National Civic League	www.ncl.org
National League of Cities	www.nlc.org
U.S. Department of Labor	www.dol.gov
U.S. Equal Employment Opportunity Commission	www.eeoc.gov
U.S. government	www.fedworld.gov
Work Index	www.workindex.com

Research by McCurdy, Newman, and Lovrich (2002) on worker-friendly policies in Washington State's local governments notes the paucity of measurement and evaluation efforts. Roberts's (2001) findings from local governments in New Jersey reiterate this concern regarding the need for better documentation. Becerra, Gooden, Dong, Henderson, and Whitfield (2002, p. 315) also stress the need to assess the "intergroup variations in the work-life needs of their employees."

AVOIDING AND COPING WITH HOSTILITY AT WORK

Another challenge facing managers is developing and implementing a program dealing with hostility in the workplace. In seeking to create a pro-employee environment, it is necessary to remove threats to worker well-being. This includes reducing the likelihood of intimidation, harassment, or violence. Chapter 2 discusses sexual harassment (in the context of legal requirements prohibiting it), and Chapter 9, Exhibit 9.1, examines workplace violence (especially its causes and some prevention strategies). Here it is important to emphasize that managers and officials committed to employee-friendly policies need to consider ways to avoid or cope with hostility. Not to do so is to invite disruption, damage to the lives and health of workers, and loss of productivity. Braverman (1999) offers a seven-step approach to violence prevention; six of these steps can be adapted as a guide to sexual harassment prevention as well.

- *Obtain and demonstrate top-level support.* Demonstrate that a cadre of leaders (management and union) at the highest levels is committed to culture change and willing to craft a policy and work together to implement it.

✖ **EXHIBIT 7.9**   Factors in Decision Making

Benefits	Risks
Acting	
• Improved employee morale • Improved productivity • Reduced absenteeism • Reduced attrition • Improved recruitment • Reduced costs • Improved customer service	• Startup costs • Ongoing costs • Possible negative effect on quality or quantity of work • Potential for unfavorable media or legislative attention • Employee perception of programs as entitlements, creating problems if circumstances later change • Poor program management, leading to reduced productivity
Not Acting	
• Saving funds for other initiatives • Saving staff time needed to set up the program • Keeping options open when the future is uncertain	• Negative effect on employee morale when programs are not available to meet their needs • Continuing decline in productivity resulting from low morale • Increase in attrition when employees leave for employers who offer the programs • Continuing high levels of absenteeism resulting from lack of programs that can help employees meet personal needs

SOURCE: Adapted from National Academy of Public Administration, *Work/Life Programs: Helping Managers, Helping Employees,* p. 46. © Copyright 1998 by the National Academy of Public Administration.

- *Appoint a team.* Key stakeholders should be represented (human resources, labor relations, employee assistance program, union, management) and participate in training sessions.
- *Conduct a violence/harassment risk audit.* The risk profile that results will contain information on employee attitudes, prior experience with harassment/violence/disruption, and existing policies and procedures
- *Design policies and procedures.* Specify what is meant by the hostility in question (workplace violence/sexual harassment), create a "zero tolerance" standard and specific sanctions for violations, outline reporting channels, and provide protection for those who report violations.
- *Train in the policies and procedures.* Help managers and employees to detect early warning signs of hostile, harassing, conflictual, and threatening behavior and to report these to the appropriate parties.
- *Provide access to medical/mental health experts.* Have professionals on tap, ensure that employees are comfortable accessing the assessment process, and provide the organization with immediate, lawful access to information about conflictual, harassing, and threatening behaviors.

The seventh step, although sensible for any organization, is primarily targeted at workplace violence:

- *Develop sensible layoff/termination policies and procedures.* Many of the widely reported instances of violence are linked to job loss or "to the way they [employees] were made to feel in the process of losing their job" (Braverman, 1999, p. 130).

There is a paradox in implementing both workplace violence and sexual harassment policies: Many organizations have policies on these subjects; there is widespread agreement about what constitutes harassing and threatening/violent behavior; and there are numerous instances of such behaviors at work—yet the number of reported violations is low (Braverman, 1999; Reese & Lindenberg, 1997). Implementing the seven steps above, with special attention to protecting those who report violators, will help resolve this paradox. Clear policies regarding threats, harassment, and disruptive and dangerous behavior—and specific procedures to follow in case of a critical incident—will reduce the risk of hostility and help to cope with it when it occurs (ICMA, 1994).[4] Preventing workplace violence, sexual harassment, and other forms of hostility is consistent with creating a pro-employee environment.

BEST PLACES TO WORK

Recently there has been an attempt to identify exemplary workplaces in the federal government. The OPM's 2002 Human Capital Survey collected data from over 100,000 federal employees in 2002 (www.bestplacestowork.org). Staff ranked agencies according to 10 categories. Two of these categories are work/life balance and family-friendly culture and benefits. Exhibit 7.10 reports these rankings. Four agencies are among the top five in both rankings: NASA (rank 1, 1), General Services Administration (2, 3), Department of Energy (3, 5), and the Office of Personnel Management (5, 2).

SUMMARY AND CONCLUSION

Management fads come and go. Are family- or employee-friendly policies just another passing and politically correct fad? This is not an easy question to answer. The subtitle of this chapter refers to pro-employee policies as fashionable, flexible, and fickle. The reader may have the impression that most jurisdictions are responding to changes in the workforce with "fashionable" policies that will reduce work/family conflict, promote employee health and wellness, build flexibility into the workplace, and assist in employee relocation. This is not the case. Some public sector environments are more accurately described as family- and employee-unfriendly, in that they do not offer the type and range of programs discussed here to all or most employees. Instead, the experiences highlighted are those of progressive jurisdictions. Many of these experiments are informal, are restricted to a limited number of areas, involve a small number of employees, and may come and go as budgets rise and fall.

Evidence is mounting (although incomplete) that employee-friendly policies can lead to important positive outcomes that "ideally" would catch the attention of public employers—improvements in job satisfaction, absenteeism, productivity, morale, recruitment and retention, and loyalty. On the other hand, some studies show negligible to no effects from such policies because of underutilization or effects that do not benefit the intended groups (Bruce

✖ **EXHIBIT 7.10**   Best Places to Work in the Federal Government in 2004

Agency	Work/Life Balance Ranking	Family-Friendly Culture and Benefits Ranking
National Aeronautics and Space Administration	1	1
General Services Administration	2	3
Department of Energy	3	5
National Science Foundation	4	16
Office of Personnel Management	5	2
Department of Health and Human Services	6	9
Environmental Protection Agency	7 (tie)	6
U.S. Air Force	7 (tie)	17
Department of Commerce	9	11 (tie)
Department of the Army	10	21 (tie)
Department of Education	11	4
Department of Labor	12	10
Department of the Navy	13	18 (tie)
Department of Agriculture	14	7
Department of the Interior	15	15
Department of State	16	27
Defense Agencies	17	11 (tie)
Department of Treasury	18 (tie)	8
U.S. Marine Corps	18 (tie)	24
Department of Transportation	20	18 (tie)
Office of Management and Budget	21	28
Small Business Administration	22	14
Department of Housing and Urban Development	23	13
Department of Veterans Affairs	24	21 (tie)
Agency for International Development	25	25
Federal Emergency Management Agency	26	23
Department of Justice	27	26
Social Security Administration	28	18 (tie)

SOURCE: Adapted from www.bestplacestowork.org

NOTE: Rankings based on survey data collected by the U.S. Office of Personnel Management in 2002. Best Places to Work in the Federal Government rankings were released in 2004.

& Reed, 1994; Shuey, 1998). Paradoxes abound and should not be overlooked by employers tempted to undertake such policies or by employees who push for them. Key among the paradoxes is that once adopted, programs may not be used. When funding for new programs is limited, as is often the situation, a persuasive case must be made to skeptical budget guardians that the returns on investments will be substantial.

It is important to keep in mind, however, that employee-friendly policies refer to a broad range of initiatives, and a holistic view is needed when assessing their value and effectiveness. Failure or underutilization of one should not diminish the value of others. Some plans may appeal or be relevant to a relatively small segment of the workforce (telecommuting, domestic partner coverage, adoption assistance, leave sharing, job sharing, spousal employment assistance, outplacement services). Others have much broader appeal and relevance (child/elder care; parental leave; wellness, stress reduction, and EAP programs; flex options; cafeteria plans; and other than full-time work options). Some plans are provided in-house, but many (such as EAP services) are often purchased from private and third-sector providers. Furthermore, the use of selected programs (e.g., flextime) differs based on the size of the organization and its service demands. Large organizations that need not address widely varying walk-in service requests have more management flexibility than small ones in this regard. They can handle leaves of absence better and accommodate flextime more easily than other jurisdictions.

Large, innovative, and resource-rich organizations are more able to provide both the broad and narrow range of worker-responsive programs. Unfortunately, this does not characterize most governmental jurisdictions in the United States, which are small or medium-sized, traditional, and strapped for funds. They may be able to offer a few, but not a complete set, of these programs. Nevertheless, personnel want help in reducing work/family conflict and in meeting both individual and organizational obligations, and employers need to explore ways to help them do so.

APPENDIX A

Questions for Employees and
Employers Regarding Telecommuting Arrangements

- Has a pilot program been conducted?
- What are the results of the pilot program?
- Who is eligible to telecommute?
- If telecommuting is not to their liking, can employees return to their office work location?
- If the program is terminated, can employees return to their office work location?
- If an employee's performance deteriorates, will he or she be asked to return to the office work location?
- Will salary, job responsibilities, or benefits be changed because of employee participation in the program?
- Will the total number of work hours change during the program?
- How will employees account for time worked?
- Can employees vary their hours to suit their preferences?
- How can employers be assured that employees are accessible during working hours?
- Will employees divide their time between days at the office location and at home?
- Will employees be expected to come into the office as requested when the workload requires it?
- Will employers provide the equipment required for the job?
- Does the employer retain ownership of property provided to telecommuters?
- Who absorbs costs (installation, monthly service) of telephone lines installed for use during the program?
- Who is responsible for home-related expenses (e.g., air conditioning, renovation)?
- Who is responsible for travel expenses to and from work on days when employees come into the office?
- Who provides needed office supplies?
- Who absorbs costs of insurance to protect equipment from theft, damage, or misuse?
- How will confidential or proprietary materials be protected?
- Does the employer have the right to visit the home to see if it meets health and safety standards?
- Will the employer provide assistance to ensure the adequacy/safety of the home work area?
- Will the employer be liable for injuries resulting directly from home work activities?

- Is telecommuting viewed as a substitute for dependent care?
- Will the employer provide income tax guidance to employees who maintain a home office area?

SOURCE: Adapted from "Generic Telecommuter Agreement" from Gil Gordon Associates, Telecommuting/Teleworking Site (www.gilgordon.com). © Copyright 1998 by Gil Gordon Associates.

NOTE: These are suggested items to include; the actual agreement must be tailored to the needs of each employer and its employees.

Appendix B

Some Questions to Answer When Considering Implementation of Employee-Friendly Policies

- What is the percentage of females employed?
- What is the size of the organization?
- What is the age profile of the employees?
- To what extent are resources available to recruit and train employees?
- What are the education levels required of qualified employees?
- What are current dependent care arrangements, costs, and satisfaction levels?
- What special work/family problems are employees facing?
- How many employees have young children, and how many days have those employees missed work to care for an ill child?
- How many employees care for elderly dependents, and how many days have those employees missed work to provide elder care?
- What is the percentage of employees who currently engage in a variety of wellness-related activities?
- Which employees are more likely to prefer flextime?
- Which employees are more likely to prefer telecommuting?
- What is the percentage of employees who indicate that they experience high levels of work-related stress?
- What are the main sources of work-related stress?
- What is the percentage of employees who have adopted children?
- What is the percentage of employees who are unmarried with domestic partners?
- What is the percentage of employees who are dissatisfied with the current range of employee benefits?
- What is the percentage of employees who are being displaced as a result of downsizing?

KEY TERMS

Compressed workweek
Domestic partnership coverage
Downshifting
Downsizing
Employee assistance programs (EAPs)
Family and Medical Leave Act
Flextime
Generation X
Job sharing

Leave sharing
Nontraditional families
Parental leave
Sandwich generation
Telecommuters
Three o'clock (3:00) syndrome
V-time
Wellness programs

EXERCISES

Class Discussion

1. On an overhead projector or chalkboard, observe two columns: "Buzzwords of Government Success" and "Ideal Friendship and Family Life." Brainstorm words for each topic, one column at a time. Compare and discuss the words in each column. Discuss the reasons that none or only a few words are on both the left and right lists.

2. Form groups and let each group select one of the family-friendly policies discussed in this chapter. Discuss the following: (a) the advantages, (b) the disadvantages, (c) the outcome indicators you would use to judge program success, (d) the obstacles that you expect to encounter in implementing this program, and (e) the types of employees most likely to benefit from the program. Present a group report on your results to the class.

3. Review examples of employee-friendly policies discussed in this chapter. Identify as many paradoxes related to those policies as you can, and be prepared to discuss ways to resolve them.

Team Activities

4. Separate into four or five different groups. Each group should select three to five of the worker-friendly programs covered in this chapter. Each group member should interview someone who is currently using one of these programs regarding its pros and cons from the user's perspective. Write up the individual interviews in no more than two typed pages and then compile them into an integrated group report for submission to the instructor.

5. Each team member should create a hypothetical employee profile by identifying that individual's personal characteristics on each of the following dimensions: age, gender, dependent children, marital status, sexual preference, distance from work, health status, emotional health, stress level, and job security. The student should then choose three employee-friendly policies that would be most helpful to the hypothetical employee and justify the choices. As a team, compile the personal profile analyses from the individual student papers and add a group analysis section making some generalizations about which policies appeal most to particular types of employees.

Individual Assignments

6. Choose any one of the employee-friendly policies mentioned in this chapter and outline the implementation steps that are most important at each of the six stages, from the point of view of the individual public manager or supervisor. Develop your response in a four-page paper and submit it to your instructor.

7. Identify each of the paradoxes mentioned in this chapter and consider various ways to resolve each paradox. Can you identify additional paradoxes related to these topics?

8. Select one of the programs discussed in this chapter and visit one of the Web sites listed in Exhibit 7.10 in search of additional information on this subject. Share the information you find with the class.

9. Review the questions for telecommuters in Appendix A and answer either a or b.

   a. Develop a written telecommuter agreement for a particular public organization to be signed by both the employer and the employee. Make sure the agreement adequately addresses each of the questions listed in Appendix A.

   b. Obtain a written telecommuter agreement used by a specific organization and write a brief paper showing how the agreement you have obtained responds to each of the questions in Appendix A. Attach a copy of the agreement to your paper.

NOTES

1. This chapter is titled "Employee-Friendly Policies" instead of "Family-Friendly Policies" because it addresses the needs of single persons as well as those in both traditional and nontraditional families (see Hoyman & Duer, 2004).

2. Although this chapter focuses primarily on the changing workforce in terms of gender, it is important to note that cultural diversity introduces a range of different issues in addition to those covered here. For example, gender stereotypes and familial relationships vary from culture to culture and have important significance for the workforce. The existence of extended families may have changed dramatically over the past four decades for white families of European heritage in the middle class, but the situation is quite different for other cultural groups and socioeconomic status categories.

3. Human capital refers to the knowledge, skills, and abilities (KSAs) characterizing a workforce. Investments in human capital (e.g., training, development) are expected to bring improvements in performance and thus to provide a competitive advantage to individual workers and employing organizations. In contrast, human resources traditionally have been viewed primarily as costs to be minimized rather than as assets worthy of investments. Investments were made in other assets such as land, capital, and raw materials (see Carnevale, 1996; West & Berman, 1996).

4. Some examples of local governments with innovative workplace violence programs include Phoenix, Arizona; Broward County, Florida; Evanston, Illinois; Ventura County, California; and Cary, North Carolina (ICMA, 1994).

REFERENCES

ADOA. (2003). *Partnering to make a difference.* Retrieved January 10, 2005, from www.teleworkari
zona.com/telefiles/program.htm

Barr, S. (2004, July 9). Congressmen plan to rev up telecommuting. *Washington Post,* p. B2.

Becerra, R., Gooden, S., Dong, W., Henderson, T., & Whitfield, C. (2002). Child care needs and work-
life implications. *Review of Public Personnel Administration, 22*(4), 295–319.

Braverman, M. (1999). *Preventing workplace violence.* Thousand Oaks, CA: Sage.

Bruce, W., & Reed, C. (1994). Preparing supervisors for the future work force: The dual-income couple and the work-family dichotomy. *Public Administration Review, 54*(1), 36–43.

Bureau of Labor Statistics. (2000). *National compensation survey.* Retrieved January 10, 2005, from
http://www.bls.gov/ncs/home.htm

Bureau of Labor Statistics. (2001). *Workers on flexible and shift schedules in 2001.* Retrieved January
10, 2005, from http://www.bls.gov/news.release/flex.nr0.htm

Bureau of Labor Statistics. (2002). *Workforce and workplace trends.* Retrieved January 10, 2005, from
http://www.bls.gov/bls/newsrels.htm

Carnevale, D. (1996). The human capital challenge in government. *Review of Public Personnel Administration, 16*(3), 5–13.

Clay, R. (1998, July). Many managers frown on use of flexible work options. *APA Monitor,* p. 29.

Cohen, R. (2002, September 8). The ethicist. *New York Times Magazine,* pp. 29–30.

Collins, R., & Magid, R. (1990). Work and family: How managers can make a difference. *Personnel,
67*(7), 14–19.

Council of State Governments. (1997). *The book of the states.* Lexington, KY: Author.

Daniel, L. (1999, April). Feds and families. *Government Executive,* 41–46.

Dembeck, C. (2003, March 24). Managers accept telecommuting—slowly. *Federal Times,* pp. 16–17.

Dobel, P. (2003). The odyssey of senior public service: What memoirs can teach us. *Public
Administration Review, 63*(1), 16–29.

Employment Policy Foundation. (2000). *Should the U.S. follow Europe's work-family policies?*
Retrieved April 18, 2000, from http://www.hr.com/

Ezra, M., & Deckman, M. (1996). Balancing work and family responsibilities: Flextime and child care
in the federal government. *Public Administration Review, 56*(2), 174–179.

Families and Work Institute. (1997). *National study of the changing workforce.* New York: Author.

Gamino, D. (1997, December 28). State makes use of "temps" despite job cap. *Austin American-Statesman.*
Retrieved January 10, 2005, from http://www.austin360.com/news/12dec/28/temps28.html

Gannon, J. (1998, June 19). Single and childless workers say they're not getting fair share of benefits.
Pittsburgh Post-Gazette. Retrieved January 10, 2005, from http://www.post-gazette.com/business
news/19980619bbenefits1.asp

Gil Gordon Associates. (1998). Telecommuting/teleworking site. *Generic telecommuter agreement.*
Retrieved January 10, 2005, from www.golgordon.com/downloads/agreement.txt

Goodman, C. (2003, July 30). New work priority: Flex time. *Miami Herald,* pp. 1C, 8C.

Gordon, R. (2001, November 2). Salvation Army OKs partner benefits: Charity's reversal to allow ties
with S.F. *San Francisco Chronicle.* Retrieved January 10, 2005, from http://sfgate.com/cgi-bin/
article.cgi?file=/chronicle/archive/2001/11/02/MN128788.DTL

Guy, M. E., & Newman, M. (1998). Toward diversity in the workplace. In S. Condrey (Ed.), *Handbook
of human resource management in government* (pp. 75–92). San Francisco: Jossey-Bass.

Hall, D. (1990). Promoting work/family balance: An organization change approach. *Organizational
Dynamics, 18*(3), 5–18.

Heredia, C. (2001a, November 14). Salvation Army says no benefits for partners: National panel overturns regional OK. *San Francisco Chronicle.* Retrieved January 10, 2005, from http://sfgate.com/cgi-bin/article.cgi?file=/chronicle/archive/2001/11/14/MN143620.DTL

Heredia, C. (2001b, December 22). Gays spurning Salvation Army: Rights groups protesting benefits policy. *San Francisco Chronicle.* Retrieved January 10, 2005, from http://sfgate.com/cgi-bin/article.cgi?file=/chronicle/archive/2001/12/22/MN200149.DTL

Hoyman, M., & Duer, H. (2004). A typology of workplace policies: Worker friendly vs. family friendly? *Review of Public Personnel Administration, 24*(2), 113–132.

Human Resources Division. (1999). *Job sharing information packet.* Alternative Work Options Program, Commonwealth of Massachusetts.

Human Rights Campaign Foundation. (2003). Retrieved January 10, 2005, from http://www.hrc.org/content/contentgroups/publications1/state.of.the.family/SoTF.pdf

Hunt, K. (1997). Survey finds flexible benefits on the rise, particularly among public employers. *Government Finance Review, 13*(4), 54–55.

International City/County Management Association. (1994). Focus on violence. *HR Report, 2*(8), 3–6.

International City/County Management Association. (1995). *Employee benefits in local government* (Special Data Issue). Washington, DC: Author.

Kemp, D. R. (1995). Telecommuting in the public sector: An overview and a survey of the states. *Review of Public Personnel Administration, 15*(3), 5–14.

King, M. (2001, November 3). Salvation Army allows health-care access for domestic partners. *Seattle Times.* Retrieved January 10, 2005, from http://archives.seattletimes.nwsource.com/cgi-bin/texis.cgi/web/vortex/display?slug=salvation03m&date=20011103&query=%22Salvation+Army%22

Kirkpatrick, D. (1997, April 2). Child-free employees see another side of equation. *Wall Street Journal Interactive Edition.* Retrieved January 10, 2005, from http://lexisnexis.com/

Kleiman, C. (2003, October 8). Workers willing to put family ahead of career advancement. *Tallahassee Democrat,* p. 3E.

Leonard, B. (1996). Dual-income families fast becoming the norm. *HRMagazine, 41*(8), 8.

Levine, S. (1997, March 24). One in four U.S. families cares for aging relatives. *Washington Post,* p. A13.

Lord, M., & King, M. (1991). *The state reference guide to work-family programs for state employees.* New York: Family and Work Institute.

Lynem, J. (2001, May 13). Family-friendly or single-hostile? Unwed employees feel shortchanged by policies aimed at helping parents. *San Francisco Chronicle.* Retrieved January 10, 2005, from http://sfgate.com/cgi-bin/article.cgi?file=/chronicle/archive/2001/05/13/AW152151.DTL

Martinez, M. (1993). Family support makes business sense. *HRMagazine, 38*(1), 38.

McCurdy, A., Newman, M., & Lovrich, N. (2002). Family-friendly workplace policy adoption in general and special purpose local governments. *Review of Public Personnel Administration, 22*(1), 27–51.

Mercer, W. M. (1996). *Mercer work/life and diversity initiatives.* Retrieved July 30, 2001, from www.dcclifecare.com/mercer/mercer-1.html

Mikalachki, A., & Mikalachki, D. (1991). Work-family issues: You had better address them! *Business Quarterly, 55*(4), 49–52.

National Academy of Public Administration. (1998). *Work/life programs: Helping managers, helping employees.* Washington, DC: Author.

National Alliance for Caregiving. (1997). *Family caregiving in the United States: Findings from a national survey.* Retrieved January 10, 2005, from www.caregiving.org/finalreport.pdf

NOLO. (2003a). *Military Leave.* Retrieved January 10, 2005, from www.nolo.com/lawcenter/ency/article.cfm/ObjectID/8077364D-A7D1-4E44-8E88F9B97B187DFB/catID/40338C48-92FD-49FA-93CB1BF16195D519

NOLO. (2003b). *Health and Safety FAQ.* Retrieved January 10, 2005, from www.nolo.com/lawcenter/ency/article.cfm/ObjectID/1710112D-A8C2-4DBC-97A3E271E3C8A169/catID/0A323459-4B09-4D32-BB8CD8E6058BE1CF

People for the American Way. (2001). Salvation Army rescinds domestic partner benefits after right-wing backlash. *Civil Rights and Equal Rights.* Retrieved January 10, 2005, from www.pfaw.org/pfaw/general/default.aspx?oid=4162

Peterson, M. (1998, July 18). The short end of long hours. *New York Times,* pp. B1–B2.

Price, J. (2001, December 10). P-FLAG targets Salvation Army: Drops fake money in kettles over repeal of 'partner' perks. *Washington Times,* p. A6.

Price, S., & Price, T. (1997, July 27). Working parents: Raising issues surrounding adoption could get good results with employer. *Orange County Register,* p. E3.

Reese, L., & Lindenberg, K. (1997). "Victimhood" and the implementation of sexual harassment policy. *Review of Public Personnel Administration, 17*(1), 37–57.

Reich, R. (1998). *Locked in the cabinet.* New York: Vintage.

Roberts, G. (2001). New Jersey local government benefits practices survey. *Review of Public Personnel Administration, 21*(4), 284–307.

Schroeder, P. (1998). *24 years of housework and the place is still a mess.* Kansas City, MO: Andrews & McMeel.

Shuey, P. (1998, October 19). Few use flexible benefits. *Federal Times,* pp. 1, 4.

Staffing stabilized in 2002. (2003, March 10). *staffing today.net.* Retrieved January 10, 2005, from www.staffingtoday.net/staffstats/release03–10–03.htm

Stanger, J. (1993). How to do a work/family needs assessment. *Employment Relations Today, 20*(2), 197.

Study: Gays, lesbians gain in workplace. (2003, May 17). *Tallahassee Democrat,* p. 5B

Suskind, R. (2004). *The price of loyalty.* New York: Simon & Schuster.

Suttle, G. (1998, March 8). Solidarity in sickness. *News Tribune,* p. F1.

U.S. Bureau of the Census. (2003, February). *Married-couple and unmarried-partner households: 2000.* Washington, DC: U.S. Department of Commerce.

U.S. Department of Labor. (2003). *Families and employers in a changing economy.* Retrieved January 10, 2005, from http://www.dol.gov/esa/whd/fmla/index.htm

U.S. Office of Personnel Management. (2002, March). *Elder care responsibilities of federal employees and agency programs.* Washington, DC: Author.

U.S. Office of Personnel Management. (2003a). *Part-time employment and job-sharing guide.* Retrieved January 10, 2005, from http://www.opm.gov/pt.employ/pt09.htm

U.S. Office of Personnel Management. (2003b). *The status of telework in the federal government.* Retrieved January 10, 2005, from http://www.opm.gov/telework/documents/tw_rpt04/rpt.pdf

West, J. P. (2005). Managing an aging workforce: Trends, issues, and strategies. In S. Condrey (Ed.), *Handbook of human resource management in government* (2nd ed., pp. 164–188). San Francisco: Jossey-Bass.

West, J. P., & Berman, E. M. (1996). Managerial responses to an aging municipal workforce: A national survey. *Review of Public Personnel Administration, 16*(3), 38–58.

Wooldridge, B., & Maddox, B. (1995). Demographic changes and diversity in personnel: Implications for public administrators. In J. Rabin, T. Vocino, W. Hildreth, & G. Miller (Eds.), *Handbook of public personnel administration* (pp. 183–215). New York: Dekker.

8

TRAINING AND DEVELOPMENT

Creating Learning Organizations

Excellence is an act won by training and habit.

—Aristotle

After studying this chapter, you should be able to

- Understand recent trends in training and development
- Be familiar with the role of this HRM function in organizations
- Use adult learning theories to improve training and development activities
- Identify seven relevant strategies and their applications
- Develop methods for evaluating the effectiveness of this management process

Employees often begin new jobs with the expectation that they will receive sufficient training and information to learn the ropes and quickly become productive, successful members of their new organizations. If they are fortunate, as many are, they are assisted by newfound colleagues. And employers do furnish training. Yet some new employees may feel that they do not receive adequate formal instruction or assistance and are left to learn their jobs through trial and error and frustration. Why do institutions invest so little in their new members?

This chapter examines training and development, not only for new recruits but also for existing staff, who also must adapt to change because the need for learning and skill development is continuous.

Training is defined as the effort to increase the knowledge, skills, and abilities (KSAs) of employees and managers so that they can better do their jobs. New employees frequently need training to help them understand their tasks, technologies, and procedures unique to the organization and to correctly implement key rules and regulations. Existing personnel periodically need to acquire new abilities, giving real meaning to "lifelong learning." For example, they need to learn new information technology applications, regulations that affect job performance, criteria of performance appraisal, and patterns of organizational communication.

Whereas training focuses on improving performance in present jobs, **development** is defined as efforts to improve future performance by providing skills used in a subsequent assignment. Development increases staff potential, assists in succession planning, and is tied to the strategic organizational development, ensuring that agencies have the employees with relevant skills. The distinction between training and development is somewhat inexact because many developmental activities have immediate uses. To illustrate, leadership training for employees can be regarded as a developmental activity, but such skills are likely to also improve employee teams as such personnel gain new knowledge and insights of group dynamics and processes.

The environment for training and development reveals key paradoxes. The first is that almost everyone from presidents and management gurus to shop stewards and department heads emphasizes the importance of training and development—and agree that it is inadequately provided. Ensuring that people have adequate technical skills has never been more important, and as employees are more empowered and cross-trained to do multiple jobs, it is obvious that concerns about their job skills increase. But most observers believe that organizations perennially underinvest in training. To illustrate, the Winter Commission (National Commission on the State and Local Government Public Service, 1993) recommended some years ago that state and local government expenditures for training and development activities be about 3–5% of salaries. Following this report, one estimate placed these federal expenditures at just 1.3% (Kettl & DiIulio, 1995). An estimate of the FY2005 budget suggests a similar percentage (about 1.4%). In short, training and development remains the oft-forgotten budget item.

It is interesting to speculate about some of the reasons for this. One is that although training and development are important, they are less urgent than other budget necessities (salaries must be paid, programs must be implemented). A second reason is that it is very difficult to measure the return on investment of any specific training and development activity. The training function may be necessary, but if the impact cannot be measured, then organizations are apt to limit training expenditures to those instances in which it is seen as absolutely necessary (such as ensuring new repair procedures for jet fighters or ensuring that legal rights and responsibilities are met in prison inmate management). A third explanation is that organizations may be reluctant to invest in employees who are viewed as mobile, switching between employers. Some answers to these questions are explored below (Selden & Moynihan, 2000).

The second paradox is that as training and development become more important to the organization, responsibility for fulfilling these needs is shifted downward to individual employees, supervisors, and units. That is, **decentralization of training** has occurred. The days of the large training departments are over. Now, departments and employees must identify, assess, and meet their own needs. One size does not fit all. Many organizations have cut back or even eliminated training staff in HR departments to reduce costs and take advantage of consultants with specialized knowledge. Training often is outsourced. In this environment, HR departments no longer provide such leadership.

The third paradox is that as responsibilities increase, employees may have less time to focus on training. They may recognize their need for increased knowledge, skills, or abilities (KSAs) and complain about not getting enough training and development, but that does not mean that employees have the time or energy to pursue them. Many people work extra hours, and most have substantial outside obligations. There is only so much that can be done. Still, not all feel this way. Dedicated employees and managers do make the time to pursue career development and strive for high levels of professionalism, and although many organizations do not reward them for doing so, others do take notice. Some invite or even require employees and managers to work with higher administrators to formulate a "professional development plan" in which such activities are identified.

These paradoxes reveal the underlying cross-currents that affect training and development: tight budgets, increased technology, cross-training, employee mobility, and overworked staff. Organizations vary in how they respond to these paradoxes. Some recognize the challenges and ensure that training and development are part of the strategic plan that articulates how the organization will meet its new and emergency needs. But for others, the lack of training and development—often because of the crush of immediate demands—means that these requirements go unmet. Exhibit 8.1 provides one manager's perspective on training.

✖ EXHIBIT 8.1   Perspective on Training and Development

It is not sufficient for people to do their assigned jobs.

—Al Pietrasanta, manager

The following is from an interview with Hal Worrall, PhD, former executive director of the Orlando-Orange County Expressway Authority (Florida), an award-winning regional transportation toll road authority. The OOCEA operates 80 miles of roads, generates more than $100 million in annual revenues, and has $1 billion in outstanding bonds.

I believe that there are two aspects that determine the success of people on the job: their desire to do the job and their ability to do the job. First, there are possibilities for redefining a job to make it more interesting, such as expansion, enrichment, or sharing; but in the end the desire rests heavily with the employee. You can only provide an environment in which they can motivate themselves. Second, training and development has much more to do with ensuring that employees have the ability to do their job. This concerns technical expertise, job knowledge, agency knowledge, and the ability to work with colleagues in teams.

Managers need to consider different approaches. On-the-job training is perhaps most important for gaining knowledge to accomplish specific tasks for the agency. There is no substitute for learning from someone who has been around awhile. We also use in-house seminars to help employees with subjects concerning the "technology" of the organization, such as computer technology, task procedures, and the like. Formal training is also important in understanding governmental regulations such as EEO, civil rights, sexual harassment, and so forth. These subjects require a formal approach. Perhaps one of the most productive uses of training is in the area of people skills, team building, and helping people getting to know one another.

I am a big fan of using universities in such broader areas as mathematics, economics, principles of management, and the like. You just can't get the broader perspective from in-house seminars and training. Universities also confer more status on employees ("I have completed three credit hours" sounds better than "I just received a certificate"), and it motivates employees to know that they can succeed in a university setting.

I also believe that training and development is most successful when it is voluntary for employees, although not all training can be voluntary. Employees who are motivated will take advantage of training opportunities, and those who are not motivated will not. Some of my best managers are those who were motivated to take advantage of the opportunities we provided them. I monitor who participates in training. Our agency has a very liberal tuition reimbursement policy, requiring only that employees dedicate the time to attend. When training is mandatory, people participate in a spirit of compliance, and the effectiveness of such training is often minimal. A lot of money is wasted through mandatory training.

I do not spend much time worrying about measuring the effectiveness of our training dollars. I require that our managers examine how training and development can benefit each employee, and participation in training activities is tied to employees' annual performance appraisal. It is very difficult to determine what the right amount of training is for any department, and the right amount must be argued on a case-by-case basis in terms of staff development needs. In this regard, I do think we need to do a better job in needs assessment. It is important that managers and supervisors talk with each employee about their training and development needs.

This chapter begins by examining the strategic role of training. Then specific training and development activities as well as theories of adult learning are discussed. Finally, analytical techniques are presented related to needs assessment and to training justification and evaluation.

THE STRATEGIC ROLE OF TRAINING AND DEVELOPMENT

Why do organizations provide training and development? Most agencies and managers are apt to vary in their assessment, but acknowledge that this HRM function is important. Training and development contributes to:

1. assisting new employees to get up to date on the unique procedures, equipment, or standards of the organization;

2. helping existing staff to adapt to new tasks as a result of promotion, restructuring, or other reassignments;

3. confirming that employees are abreast of new laws, procedures, or knowledge pertinent to the organization, the environment, or their jobs;

4. ensuring that personnel in jobs critical to the organization's performance—and which have high costs of failure—perform in satisfactory ways (risk management);

5. using training and development as a tool to ensure that desirable employees and managers stay current and committed to the organization (retention); and

6. ensuring that everyone has the KSAs that are consistent with what is needed to help the organization move forward (planning).

The importance of these responsibilities is readily seen. For example, many law enforcement agencies have increased their concern with terrorism. Training and development is a cost-efficient and effective way to help personnel acquire these new KSAs. Consultants may be brought in, and such training also allows staff of different agencies to work together and exchange information. Training can be focused on the critical needs of communities (risk management). Indeed, embracing these new law enforcement tasks has resulted in myriad, multimillion-dollar training programs.

How do agencies organize themselves to implement this key HRM function? Note that items 1, 2, and 3 above reflect broad organizational needs (all employees have some training requirements, especially recent hires, the newly promoted, or those dealing with new technology or procedures). Given the breadth and diversity of these needs and trends toward empowerment, it is increasingly the employees and their immediate supervisors who are best positioned to assess their own deficits. Different jobs require different KSAs, and those doing or overseeing the work are more likely to know what is required. For example, who knows more about the needs of computer maintenance personnel than the personnel themselves and possibly their supervisors? Certainly not the HR specialist, city manager, mayor or Congressman, solid waste director, or health director, unless any of these persons happen to have current training and experience.

✂ EXHIBIT 8.2   Does Training Bring Excellence?

Can training turn mediocre employees and managers into excellent ones? Probably not by itself, but it can be part of a strategy that does. Berman and West (2003b) in their article, "Solutions to the Problem of Managerial Mediocrity: Moving Up to Excellence," show that training can be used to establish higher expectations and ensure that managers have necessary skills. But excellence requires more than knowledge, skills, and ability; it also requires that top managers commit the organization to higher standards, are willing to support people in achieving those standards, and provide consequences for performance.

Training appears to be an essential component in achieving excellence. In their study, Berman and West find that 81.5% of organizations in which perceived managerial commitment to excellence is strong also require staff to pursue their continuing professional development. By contrast, this percentage is only 26.6% among organizations in which such managerial commitment is considered to be "mediocre." And in organizations with robust managerial commitment to standards of excellence, 57.4% provide training to managers in program evaluation and accountability, compared with only 20.0% of organizations with mediocre commitment. These results tease the reader to consider that training is indeed part of a transformational strategy of managers and their organizations to achieve higher levels of excellence.

Organizations, through upper management, can do much to ensure that these lower-level assessments of training needs are indeed undertaken. First, they can require, for example, that supervisors develop a training plan with each employee, perhaps as part of the annual appraisal process. Such a plan identifies employee skill shortfalls and includes a plan to address these areas. Berman and West (2003a) report that among staff and supervisors who have established informal, mutual understandings about each others' expectations and contributions, training and development expectations are present in about 39% of such understandings. Of course, even without such a requirement, supervisors are usually free to engage in a discussion with their employees, but having an agency directive obviously broadens use. Exhibit 8.2 examines the relationship between management training and organizational excellence.

Second, organizations can set aside monies or require that lower units spend a certain amount of their expenditures on training and development. Percentages of 1–2% are sometimes reported, and such expenditures are typically coupled to some form of heightened accountability that shows how these expenditures support the various strategic aims of the organization. Employees may be required to pay for part of these expenditures or develop a work plan showing how training will be used.

Third, upper management can arrange for training that cuts across different units, such as (a) generic management training for new supervisors, (b) legal and workplace matters affecting employees (e.g., sexual harassment and discrimination seminars), (c) benefit seminars (e.g., retirement planning, health care expenses), and so on. Often the HR department is responsible for ensuring that these cross-cutting training efforts are in fact carried out (International City/County Management Association [ICMA], 2002; Reese & Lindenburg, 2003; Ugori, 1997).

Items 4, 5, and 6 (p. 220) above reflect needs that, in practice, often are less routine special needs. These frequently reflect areas important to senior managers, such as risk management, key personnel, and organizational development. As previously noted, terrorism emerged as a new or expanded management concern in the wake of the September 11, 2001, attacks. Many local communities greatly increased their management of threats to safe drinking water. Building protection against bomb threats gained increased importance. These new risk management challenges led many top managers to send their staff to seminars designed to address these topics. Initially, this was clearly a nonroutine matter, but the possibility of new and unforeseen threats has made it an ongoing salient issue.

Line managers are increasingly responsible for knowing where and when they and their staff can acquire new KSAs necessary to address emerging, strategic, or special issues. Training and development often are important parts of implementation strategies, and sometimes of assessment and awareness strategies as well. Administrators cannot depend on others to tell them where they can get such KSAs. One of many reasons managers often attend professional conferences is to become better informed and learn where they can find support. About 75% of top local government managers report that they attend annual meetings of professional organizations (Berman, 1999), and such attendance assists in their own development as well.

Finally, the broad range of purposes for training and development, coupled with increased demand and tight budgets, is causing agencies to search for cost-effective delivery approaches and to find better ways of assessing training effectiveness. But the search for such cost-effectiveness is nothing new, and managers should not expect simple answers. For example, there exists no optimal percentage of spending for training and development, and more spending does not necessarily make for more productive organizations. Rather, it is important that training and development efforts reflect the organization's strategic needs and priorities and incorporate "best practices," discussed in the next section (Bjornberg, 2002).

GENERAL PRINCIPLES OF LEARNING

Learning theories provide a foundation for successful training and development and are based on principles gleaned from cognitive psychology, behavioralism, and social learning, which focus respectively on the roles of information and understanding, feedback and incentives, and role modeling and tasks (Van Wart, Cayer, & Cook, 1993). The fundamental **principles of learning** are discussed below with an eye to **adult learning theory.** The theory emphasizes the extensive experiences of adults, interest in self-improvement and problem solving, and preferences for active participation and exercise of some control in learning. Consistent with these principles, motivation, relevance and transference, repetition, underlying tasks, as well as feedback and positive reinforcement, are discussed here.

Motivation

A key principle in successful training and development is that people learn better when they are eager to acquire new KSAs, seek out application opportunities, and are not readily discouraged by obstacles. For this reason, training efforts should ensure **motivation in training**. At a minimum, managers should explain the reasons for training, such as the need to meet changed requirements, to master new technology, or to adapt to a more efficient approach to service delivery (ICMA, 2003).

Employees often have concerns about how new approaches will be put into practice, whether they will have the opportunity to use or adjust any training to specific conditions or concerns, and how training might affect their jobs or job security. Will the new procedures interfere with their flextime arrangement or opportunities for career advancement? Because people have such varied concerns and interests, trainers and managers often encourage open discussion prior to training in which these issues are voiced. Some administrators also initiate one-on-one discussions in which employees can privately voice their concerns. The point, of course, is to provide an opportunity for aligning the needs of the organization for training with those of employees, thereby ensuring that they are well motivated to put the training into practice and work through whatever adjustments occur.

Relevance and Transference

Training relevance and effectiveness are increased when training addresses specific work problems. Trainers must explain how information and skills relate to tasks and how they can be completed. For this reason, it is important that trainers solicit the input of employees and their supervisors in program design. Effectiveness is further increased when new knowledge and skills are readily transferred into the workplace. The problem of **transference** may occur when training is conducted in a setting other than the work environment. For example, classroom lectures for customer- and employee-relations training may not match the real-life situations. Training requires illustrative cases. Often the transference of learning is facilitated by breaking complex objectives into smaller modules. Employment law is, for example, best understood by allowing time for addressing problems such as recruitment, discrimination, appraisal, and termination. Each should include multiple examples that help staff relate the material to their workplace issues.

Repetition and Active Participation

Most people do not immediately retain complex information and use new skills. The **rule of three** states that people hear things only after they have been said three times, and the **rule of seven** states that people must practice something seven times to master it. The problem is, in part, that adults learn at different speeds. Repetition facilitates the learning process by allowing individuals to process information at their own pace. People also experience **learning plateaus**, or periods during which they must first fully absorb and assimilate material before they learn more. Individuals also vary with regard to the type of material that they find easy to comprehend. Repetition helps address this and allows those who readily grasp subject areas to benefit from further honing their knowledge.

Most adults are active learners, who prefer to learn through participation in learning processes. Adults prefer to participate in discussions about the meaning of concepts and how they might be correctly applied rather than sit passively in a classroom. Repetition and multiple examples increase opportunities for active involvement, especially when applications occur out of class and training is scheduled over multiple sessions, allowing reflection on what was learned.

Overlearning refers to assimilation of material so that it becomes second nature, that is, so that new KSAs are completely integrated into one's repertoire. Overlearning is an important aspect of training when high levels of performance mastery are needed. Practice makes perfect, and it takes repeated applications before new skills and knowledge become ingrained. Overlearning is particularly important where mistakes are expensive or dangerous, and it aids performance later when there are time constraints or substantial psychological pressures.

Underlying Principles

Underlying principles help employees deal with situations that they have not previously encountered. Although in some situations immediate goals are straightforward (perhaps how to replace a cartridge in a piece of office machinery), more substantial learning situations call for a review of general principles such as basic assumptions, physical laws, and legal theories. Matters of computer security, customer relations, and ethical conduct usually require a clear understanding of the principles that give rise to specific protocols and procedures. Such principles not only help employees comprehend the reasons for specific operations, but they also provide a context from which new applications can later be developed.

Feedback and Positive Reinforcement

Training impact is enhanced by immediate, direct feedback, which helps reduce errors, enhance motivation, and increase attention to standards. Generally, positive feedback is used to reinforce activities, whereas negative feedback is designed to arrest it. Although negative feedback is important (for example, pointing out an incorrect application or faulty outcome), it must be constructive in nature to be successful. For many employees, negative feedback must be balanced with **positive reinforcement** lest critical comments decrease motivation and willingness to succeed. Positive reinforcement is key to ensuring staff acceptance and can involve verbal acknowledgment, certificates of appreciation, or new assignments.

As the saying goes, "What gets measured gets done." Some employees use the extent and nature of feedback as a measure of their organization's commitment. Not surprisingly, effective training outcomes often require that employers demonstrate commitment to follow-through and practical results. This is reflected by the frequency of feedback as well as in other ways such as making applications part of management objectives. Trainees may also be asked to report how the training has benefited their areas of operation.

In sum, the above principles provide important points for ensuring the effectiveness of training and development. Participants need to be motivated to learn and apply that which is taught, and concerns they have must be addressed. The material should be relevant to their work and illustrated through multiple examples and opportunities for practice and application. Participants must understand both the specific applications and the underlying principles that may be relevant to future uses. Finally, employers need to follow though by providing feedback and encouragement about the importance and appropriateness of workplace applications.

TRAINING STRATEGIES

This section discusses training strategies: on-the-job approaches, mentoring, in-house seminars, simulation and role playing, Web-based learning, cross-training, and formal education.

On-the-Job Training

On-the-job training (OJT) is perhaps the most common technique and is used most often for new hires. It is customized job instruction, either intermittent or continuous, involving detailed monitoring and feedback for rapid improvements in basic skills. The approach involves learning the application of formal knowledge, regulations, and other general principles to actual tasks, as well as the acquisition of often idiosyncratic information linked to specific jobs, such as evolving technology systems, regulations, or agency procedures. Quality OJT involves the assignment of one or more coaches to the trainee. OJT is not "sink or swim," for example giving an employee a manual and the name of a supervisor to contact if there is a problem. Rather, bona fide OJT involves a thoughtful and guided approach to learning the job as it is performed, and it is often supplemented by additional formal instruction. Although associated with employees assuming new positions, it also can be used when employees face changes in job responsibilities or new technology (Barron, Black, & Berger, 1997; Wu & Rocheleau, 2001).

Because this training concerns knowledge tied to specific positions, it follows that OJT is often best delivered by those currently or recently in positions that new employees are asked to fill. **Coaching** involves assigning an experienced employee to help other employees to master their job situations. OJT involves one-on-one student-teacher interaction that focuses on helping workers apply material in practice, often by working through specific job situations. In this technique, it is important that teachers identify all relevant job situations or problems that may require new skills or knowledge, provide opportunity for application, and provide positive feedback when material is learned. The approach is usually regarded as a cost-effective way of transferring essential job skills and knowledge, although part of the appeal lies in the fact that it seldom requires a separate budget. Existing staff are simply asked to supply it as a temporary, additional duty.

OJT has the potential to meet many of the requirements for effective learning: New employees are often highly motivated, the knowledge is relevant and transference is usually not an issue, there are ample examples that can be repeated as necessary, and employees have opportunities to receive feedback. But there are also threats to the success of OJT. It depends heavily on the credibility of the "manager-as-teacher" as well as the ability to transfer his or her job-specific KSAs to the "employee-as-student." OJT is best provided by employees who are respected for their abilities in the organization, including the ability to teach. In addition, "students" must be motivated and able to learn, and OJT is no substitute for formal training. When students lack formal knowledge such as essential accounting or information technology skills, OJT will not be successful because teachers cannot build on critical foundations. Also, employees sometimes are not motivated to learn their jobs under conditions such as having been involuntarily transferred to new assignments.

Although it may seem obvious that managers can improve the effectiveness of OJT by carefully selecting and training experienced employees to fulfill the instructor role, this is not always done. Expert employees do not always make for expert OJT coaches, and it may be useful to send some employees/OJT coaches to "train-the-trainer" workshops in which instruction methods are taught. Trainees may request more examples that facilitate their learning, and managers need to ensure that their "teachers" have sufficient time to properly train employees. Administrators must develop a realistic time schedule for acquisition of job skills and develop realistic expectations about the abilities of employees to complete tasks correctly. The success of OJT ultimately is judged by the ability of employees to perform new duties with minimal supervision.

Mentoring

Mentoring is a developmental approach through which inexperienced employees learn and develop their career potential through ongoing, periodic dialogue and coaching from senior managers (Olivero & Bane, 1997). Whereas the issues that are dealt with in OJT are usually fairly technical and immediate, mentors often assist in dealing with long-term goals, complex skill development, and professional socialization. Typically, the mentor-employee relationship evolves into one that is both personal and professional. Many officials report having mentors who were key to their career success; employees and beginning managers, accordingly, are encouraged to reach out and identify mentors. Mentors help shape one's career, avoid pitfalls, and expand networks by opening doors and opportunity. Women and minorities report that they find it useful to select mentors who themselves are women or minorities because such people are able to address their needs. Many personnel prefer to choose their mentors or at least influence the selection of their mentors.

Similar to OJT, mentoring reflects the principles of adult learning. Mentors and coaches provide employees with examples (e.g., making the right career moves or tailoring one's job interview), and discussion usually focuses on their application and relevance. Feedback on performance is often used to reinforce important principles, and mentoring and coaching assume that employees are motivated to advance their careers and job skills. But the issues of career development and professional development also include those that are somewhat more abstract than the KSAs imparted through OJT and thus require more opportunity for reflection, clarification, and feedback through trial and error.

A principal barrier in using mentors is the failure of employees to cultivate relationships with more experienced managers. Individuals need to identify prospective mentors rather than wait for mentors to appear. Recognizing this, some organizations take a proactive approach by asking senior administrators to volunteer as mentors. For instance, in some health care agencies, nurses are mentored by senior managers as they transition to supervisory positions. But few organizations are proactive in this area, and employees do well to seek their own mentors. Exhibit 8.3 discusses supervisory training, in which good mentoring is important.

In-House Seminars

In-house **seminars and presentations** are widely used to communicate to groups of employees information such as new developments, expectations, or rules and policies. When limited to small groups, they often include opportunities for clarification, application, and feedback. Indeed, an important trend is seminars tailored to the needs of small work units rather than auditorium-sized groups.

But seminars, though information-based, may lack important elements of effective learning. When seminars are mandatory, staff may not be motivated. Information obtained is often general, not job specific, and employees may struggle to see its relevance. Because seminars

> ## ✄ **EXHIBIT 8.3** Supervisory Training
>
> Employees frequently are promoted to supervisory positions on the basis of their technical accomplishments, time in service, and perceived ability to get along with others. None of these qualifications, however, offers much of the know-how and skills that are necessary to succeed as a supervisor. Few employers provide their managers and supervisors with training prior to promotion, and there usually are few persons who are able and willing to help new supervisors learn the ropes of supervision. Promotion to the rank of supervisor is often an exercise in "hitting the ground running."
>
> The main challenges of supervision concern (a) the ability to get work done through staff, in a productive way; (b) dealing with employee discipline, conflict management, and other personnel matters; (c) implementing various policies (e.g., promoting workforce diversity); (d) nuturing a unitwide perspective and efforts to move the unit forward; (e) learning how to develop and administer budgets; (f) ensuring the safety and cleanliness of offices; (g) ensuring adequate information and other technology; (h) ensuring adequate employee training and development; and (i) developing administrative and legal expertise in dealing with employee discipline. Finally, they must continue to develop their interpersonal competencies.
>
> Organizations may assist new supervisors by providing an orientation guide. The problem is that, despite good intentions, such manuals may go unread or be forgotten in the heat of everyday managing. Supervisors need to learn how to learn from employee feedback. Some agencies also provide 1- or 2-day seminars on supervision and leadership. Although these seminars do provide and reinforce important information, "trainees" may be hesitant to share their ignorance with those at similar rank. Selected departments send new supervisors to off-site workshops and seminars. Although the presence of strangers from other organizations ensures some anonymity, such off-site training efforts may lack follow-through.
>
> Perhaps a more effective strategy is the use of mentors. In this approach, new supervisors are asked to identify a mentor, either inside or outside the organization, with whom the supervisor meets on a regular basis. These confidential conversations allow feedback and advice from those who have held similar jobs in the past. Mentors can help deal with a variety of challenges. They also help supervisors respond to employee feedback and prepare themselves for higher functions. Through mentoring, new supervisors get real-time feedback that helps them to quickly progress on the learning curve.

are often short, there is little repetition or hands-on application. For these reasons, seminars are sometimes regarded as inadequate except for strictly one-way communication by management to staff. Their impact is even more problematic when supervisors fail to follow up and ensure that the information is used.

Effectiveness can be increased, however. To illustrate, managers might gauge employee interest and concern beforehand and address it during seminars. Lecturing can be kept to a minimum, and opportunities thereby exist for participants to discuss training materials. Increasingly, training techniques emphasize the development of insight, understanding of principles, and creativity in seeking new applications (Lucas, 2003; Newstrom, Scannell, & Nilson, 1998). Perhaps most important is that trainers and managers provide follow-up and implementation. Trainers might offer to work with groups of employees to assist in application, and

---

⚫ EXHIBIT 8.4   Effective Presentations

Effective oral presentation is key in the delivery of in-house seminars, and managers frequently make presentations in professional settings as well. The following guidelines can help ensure the success of an oral presentation:

- State why the topic is important and how it benefits employees.
- Provide a brief outline of what they will be covering.
- Discuss the topic in "bite-size," manageable pieces.
- Use notes to remind them of what material must be covered (not verbatim reading!).
- Provide multiple, relevant examples and applications of new concepts or procedures.
- Invite comments at appropriate intervals and provide clarifications as needed.
- Defer tangential comments to the end of the seminar.
- Consider the use of small groups to discuss problems or generate solutions.
- Practice keeping the presentation as short as possible.
- Summarize main points, and discuss implementation or follow-through as appropriate.

Seminars increasingly use overhead slides (for example, in PowerPoint) and printed materials that have a professional appearance and that facilitate the communication and dissemination of information. Handouts should help participants focus on the presentation and minimize the need to take notes. It is also useful to defer information that is not covered during the presentation to separate handouts that are provided at the end of presentations. Printed materials also help employees to draw on the information provided by seminars long after they have been completed (Van Kavelaar, 1998).

---

managers can ensure that application is sufficient. Exhibits 8.4 and 8.5 provide suggestions on making presentations and developing writing skills.

Simulation and Role Playing

Simulation allows managers and employees to replicate on-the-job experiences without disruption of ongoing work processes. It is appropriate when employee learning through OJT could result in unacceptable outcomes. For example, pilots use flight simulators to hone their skills and practice difficult maneuvers. NASA's astronauts simulate entire missions, and firefighters practice blaze control in simulated settings because they cannot risk on-the-job learning. Antiterrorism units practice in mock settings. Simulation is also used to help technicians learn new tools and procedures. Vestibule training is the use of separate areas on which workers practice skills or processes without disrupting ongoing work activities. Budget analysts simulate alternative fiscal scenarios to predict revenue shortfalls, and computer simulation is also used in solving a variety of operations and inventory control problems. Finally, managers test staff by simulating real-life examples. The military, for example, simulates attacks without informing personnel that the event is actually a simulation. Such exercises help managers to assess staff performance under real-life conditions (Gillespie, 2002).

Simulation helps employees acquire and perfect skills in ways unavailable through OJT or seminar training; however, it is moderately to very costly. Although it is obvious that flight simulators are expensive, so too is role playing. The rule of seven suggests that trainees must

---

⚙ EXHIBIT 8.5   Basic Skills Workshops

Training and development is primarily for employees and organizations to upgrade their skills, but this does not always involve advanced skills. Many organizations are concerned about basic skills, too, and in recent years widespread concern has developed about the writing abilities of employees and managers. Writing is part art, part science, and essential for many purposes, including grant and proposal writing, for example. Here are some tips that can improve anyone's writing:

- Have a clear picture in mind of the audience.
- Know the audience's preferred writing style, and adopt it.
- Make an outline of the main points.
- Identify the audience's concerns and address them.
- Use third person and active voice whenever possible.
- Write clearly, concisely, and make it easy for people to follow.
- State key points in a professional way.
- Refresh familiarity with the rules of grammar.
- Make each paragraph count.
- Quote, don't plagiarize.

Workshops are useful settings for reintroducing employees and managers to these basic points. But practice makes perfect. The learning principles of relevance, adequate examples, repetition, and opportunities for reflection and feedback are valid here. Effective training suggests that personnel should also be encouraged to write real-life letters and memos. These samples, then, are to be shared so that participants can get new ideas and suggested improvements. Training also requires follow-up to ensure that improvements occur and are reinforced in practice. Writing is clearly an important skill and, for some employers, a competitive advantage that prospective employees bring to the table.

---

have ample opportunity to practice, and they must receive competent feedback if they are to make forward progress. Thus, simulation often requires employees to be absent from their work for considerable periods of time. The usefulness of simulation is further affected by transferability, that is, the extent to which simulation reflects actual work conditions. In sum, simulation requires imitation of real-life conditions, ample time for trainees to acquire new skills, and follow-up in the workplace.

Some widely used applications are customer service and employee relations. During customer orientation training, staff are advised of new expectations and are provided an opportunity to discuss how they can best handle service challenges. Role playing and simulation are part of these efforts. Typical exercises include dealing with irate customers and contingency situations that upset client expectations. Prison personnel, for example, may have to explain to family members of inmates why they will not be able to visit relatives during visiting hours. Role playing is useful when it closely matches or exceeds the intensity of emotions and behaviors that occur. Experienced trainers often fulfill these roles rather than coworkers, who may hesitate to be as aggressive to their colleagues as they are to clients. Video recordings are also used so that trainees can watch and learn from their own reactions. Through repeated interactions, until they "get it right," employees increase their skills without risking the adverse consequences of the workplace.

Web-Based Learning

Web-based education (or "distributed learning") is increasingly popular in employee training. Generally, it is information-rich, involving various techniques of information dissemination and sharing. Web-based learning typically involves employees and managers working through content modules, with links to other sources and Web sites, often with video clips and downloadable documents. This form of learning may include online chat sessions with the instructor or other students, asynchronous postings to bulletin boards and replies, and "private" e-mail to individual students and instructors. These latter efforts further information, information exchange, and personal reflection.

The technique has important advantages such as remote access and the ability to participate in training at convenient times. But it also has inherent limitations, which suggest that it might best be used in combination with other strategies. Web learning does not provide much hands-on learning and experience, other than through simulation. Feedback follows from communications rather than direct observation. Discussions are often delayed rather than occurring in real time or in groups. And, currently, the development and delivery is still quite costly. Still, it is rapidly becoming a significant means of information dissemination, and its use is expected to expand. According to one study, about 40% of local governments used computer- or Internet-based training (Berman & West, 2001). Another report suggests that the military forces could improve their foreign language training by using distributed learning (U.S. General Accounting Office, 2003).

Cross-Training

Cross-training involves training employees for fulfilling multiple jobs, thereby allowing them to better serve customers. It is used to assist staff to learn new KSAs in ways that are directly relevant to the organization. Cross-training is at the heart of "one-stop shopping" and decreases the number of times that work is handed off to others, a common source of delays, miscommunication, and errors. The technique also allows organizations to better adjust to reorganizations, vacations, and peak demands. It also helps make people aware of how they fit into the organization, and it improves teamwork by increasing understanding of the needs and challenges associated with different jobs. For all these reasons, cross-training has become more common and accepted in recent years as a tool of productivity improvement (Berman, 1998).

Cross-training usually is achieved through a combination of job rotation, seminars, and on-the-job training. Job rotation is the practice of moving employees through different positions, thereby helping them to acquire various skills. For instance, computer analysts might be asked to serve at a computer help desk to better understand and appreciate user problems. Prior to assuming this new task, analysts receive an overview of the responsibilities and procedures of service representatives at the help desk. This is provided through seminars and, to lesser extent, written manuals. Once in the position, they receive OJT and coaching from an experienced employee in service. Whereas some units require all personnel to be equally proficient at different jobs (especially when new, integrated jobs are created), other units require only a minimal proficiency so that everyone can pitch in when necessary.

Cross-training is sometimes used in conjunction with reorganization. One example concerns the merging of lifeguard operations and beach patrols in a medium-size coastal city. Beach patrol personnel were required to learn rescue operations, and lifeguards were required to learn public safety techniques. The cross-training was complicated by the fact that some beach patrol personnel had to greatly increase their fitness to meet water rescue standards. In addition, the lifeguard "culture" was markedly different from the paramilitary backgrounds of the beach patrol personnel. Some lifeguards refused to carry arms or weapons. Although cross-training was implemented, selected personnel sought transfers, which were granted, and the overall impression was that productivity slumped as morale of both groups deteriorated, although the remaining staff gained skills in both areas.

In other cases, cross-training has been used with considerable success. Usually, these instances build on employee involvement in processes of work redesign and training. Personnel like the increased autonomy that comes from being able to assume new responsibilities and often see it as an opportunity for advancement. Employees (and their unions), however, sometimes see it as the organization trying to get "something for nothing." Keys to success are that employees and their unions are assured of the organization's commitment and proper intentions, and that training and development are perceived as important. Managers must also provide adequate OJT as well as positive feedback and rewards to those who are successfully cross-trained in multiple tasks.

Education: Beyond Training

Advanced academic degrees are increasingly a prerequisite for management positions, so many employees return to universities. **Education** prepares people for the future. It differs from training in that it is concerned with broad principles of knowledge and practice rather than the technical details of work. Training makes people more alike, because they learn the same skills. Education, because it involves self-discovery, makes them more different; it emphasizes not merely information but also formation. This includes better understanding of the context of personal choices, a perspective on human affairs, and ideas about what is important—a passion for living well. The master's in public administration (MPA) is the degree of choice because it provides students with telling viewpoints on the role of agencies as democratic institutions, the structure of public budgeting and personnel systems, the role of leadership, and many other vital topics. Employees who receive the MPA are assumed to have the appropriate background to quickly apply such. Education has become accessible through distance learning and outreach efforts (branch campuses, off-site education) as well as the growing trend toward certificate programs that involve just a set of courses from graduate or undergraduate curricula.

At least two contrasting views exist about the use of education as a training and development strategy. Some organizations view education benefits as excessively expensive and uncertain in their returns. Current graduate fees range from several hundred to more than $1,200 per credit hour at private universities, and employees who receive tuition benefits usually pay only a share of the bills. Organizations cannot be wholly certain how education will benefit their agencies, as some employees may fail to be promoted and others may leave. To avoid the latter, some agencies require staff to continue working with the agency for up to 3 years on program completion. Some other agencies view education as a useful instrument to attract and retain highly qualified personnel. Motivated employees are likely to stay for the duration of their education (often pursued on a part-time basis over many years), and it gives employers a first crack at retaining them on graduation, even if competitive, market-based salary increases are required. It also motivates employees to know that their agencies offer education benefits, thereby contributing to creating a favorable work climate. Exhibit 8.6 discusses some advanced forms of learning.

❎ EXHIBIT 8.6   Advanced Forms of Learning

Although many of the training techniques discussed in this chapter focus on basic and intermediate knowledge, skills, and abilities, **advanced forms of learning** are especially useful for solving new or complex problems, restructuring whole processes or systems, reanalyzing a job from a completely different perspective, or reengineering an organization to adapt to major environmental changes. These forms of learning include learning by sharing, comparing, systems thinking, competing, and suspending disbelief.

Learning by comparing is based on the scientific method. It can result from systematic examination of past experience (individual or organizational), careful analysis of others' experience (commonly called benchmarking), and experimenting. Rigorous examination of past experience helps employees pay close attention to what they do well and poorly, to maintain and improve standards, and to use their experience as a laboratory of invention. Benchmarking can include looking at a range of programs to examine a diversity of models or looking only at the best performers.

Learning by systems thinking is an antidote to tunnel vision, turf-ism, stove-piping, and other "bureau-pathologies" that accrue from overspecialization of function and responsibility. Ultimately, learning by systems thinking is at the base of most contemporary management initiatives such as total quality management (TQM) and reengineering. By examining processes as a complete system, from the perspective of many stakeholders, managers can better understand the needs of these various actors.

Learning by competition can lead individuals to learn by requiring them to determine what they want to achieve, by driving them toward that achievement or level of excellence, and by creating both incentives for succeeding and disincentives for floundering. Aspects of learning by competition include goal setting, risk taking, and failing. Competition tends to create tougher—but realistic—goals, the assumption of appropriate risks based on experience and small-scale experiments, and the willingness to "fail small" in order to "succeed big" eventually.

Learning by suspending disbelief, the most difficult and ethereal technique, requires the ability to suspend disbelief that things new to us can work—or to put it the other way around, to suspend current beliefs and assumptions about the correct way to do something, the proper way to value things, or the nature of truth. It is critical for creativity, an element that many people believe had been squeezed out of the public sector because of decades of excessive emphasis on due process, hierarchical structures, and past practices.

Ultimately, advanced forms of learning do not replace basic forms; they complement them. The transmission of standard information and knowledge is primarily accomplished through standard instructional methodologies, yet the sharpening of professionals and the creation of new knowledge cannot occur through basic methods alone. Contemporary organizations need to learn how to accomplish both well. Some methods of assessing the learning needs and evaluating how well they are doing are provided in the next section.

ASSESSMENT AND EVALUATION

Needs assessments are systematic efforts used to identify organizational and personnel strengths and weakness. Although some assessments are little more than impromptu managerial assertions ("we need to get more employees who can do X"), systematic approaches are discussed below. Many managers acknowledge the importance of conducting a formal assessment, but, paradoxically, few actually utilize them. Just 27% of state agencies, for instance, use needs assessments for 60% or more of their training efforts (Gray, Hall, Miller, & Shasky, 1997). Other methods of gathering data are employee **surveys** (used by 39% of state agencies), followed by upper management discussions (31%) and interviews with supervisors (13%). Whereas assessments are prospective, **evaluation** is largely retrospective. It is used to ensure that training activities have achieved their aims. Evaluation is used not only to justify current training but also to obtain user input in designing future programs.

Needs Assessment

Needs assessments are undertaken to determine training requirements that are (a) organization and unitwide, (b) related to improving specific work processes, and (c) concerned with the training needs of individual employees (Brown, 2002; Clardy, 1997; Jacobson, Rubin, & Selden, 2002). At the organizational level, assessments can reflect a variety of different purposes from which training and development needs are inferred. Van Wart (2004) discusses seven types: (a) ethics assessments; (b) mission, values, vision, and planning reviews; (c) customer and citizen assessments; (d) employee assessments; (e) performance reviews; (f) benchmarking; and (g) quality assessments. Each of these areas may suggest different needs for employee training. Organizations vary in the extent they perform these assessments, if they do them at all. In some, such assessments are little more than discussion items in top management leadership meetings ("I have heard several complaints that involve our employees. Does anyone think that training might help?"). Other organizations conduct discussions in a more systematic way (such as by conducting focus groups at different levels of the organization).

Many organizations now also conduct employee surveys in a systematic and valid way. Such surveys can be quite comprehensive, involving 50–100 items that address areas such as working conditions; supervisory relations and collegiality; access to technology, policies, and procedures; salary and benefits; availability of training and development; and many other areas, too. To ensure that employees complete the survey, they can be instructed to complete it during work hours. To ensure confidentiality, names are not included on the surveys, analysis is typically done by outside consultants, and where legally allowed, completed questionnaires are destroyed upon analysis. Exhibit 8.7 shows a sample of a survey. Low ratings in any area, is an obvious reason for concern, may prompt further inquiry and future training. Although local governments do not always use surveys, state and federal agencies often conduct them on a (bi) annual basis. The development and implementation often is led by the HR staff, and results are disseminated to managers and employees through a succession of meetings.

In addition, assessments are employed to identify needs that span multiple units or even the entire organization (e.g., initiatives on sexual harassment, information security, or workforce diversity). Periodically, HR supervisors ask units and their managers about their needs or their requirements for services such as recruitment, advertising, screening, and testing. Many HR departments now organize a broad range of mandatory training activities that involve employee relations, legal rights and responsibilities, updates on budgeting and accounting procedures, and new technology.

Second, needs assessments are conducted prior to undertaking work process improvements. In recent years, many organizations have reengineered their service delivery processes to make them more citizen oriented and to take advantage of new information technology capabilities. Top managers sometimes require lower units to rigorously assess their performance by collecting performance data and by evaluating their delivery processes to detect shortfalls or bottlenecks. In addition, they may also require units to increase performance. Such improvement processes may require skills that employees currently do not have.

✖ **EXHIBIT 8.7**   Selected Survey Questions for Needs Assessment

Please note your level of agreement with the following statements, using the following letter codes:

SA   = Strongly Agree
A   = Agree
DK/CS = Don't Know, Can't Say
D   = Disagree
SD   = Strongly Disagree

A. Rules and Regulations

I am familiar with the laws and policies concerning workplace discrimination.
I am familiar with the laws and policies concerning workplace harassment.
I am familiar with workplace leave policies.
I am familiar with my benefit options.
I am familiar with the workplace safety rules of my unit.
I am familiar with ethics requirements and expectations

B. Workplace Relations

My unit needs to improve its teamwork.
My supervisor is considerate and supportive.
I can approach my supervisor to discuss almost any work-related issue.
In our unit, we conduct ourselves in ethical ways.
Colleagues support one another in carrying out their duties.

C. Training Needs

I would like to learn more about conflict management skills.
I would like to improve my spreadsheet skills.
I would like to learn how to better use PowerPoint for presentations.
I would like to improve my report-writing skills.
I would like to improve my public speaking skills.
I would like to improve my time management skills.
I would like to improve my basic computer skills.
I would like to learn how to use the following equipment: please identify _____.
I would like to learn new skills so that I can contribute to a broader range of tasks.

D. Performance Management

I know the vision and mission of my department.
We maintain high standards of customer satisfaction.
We regularly survey our customers about their needs.
We regularly compare our performance to that of similar organizations.
We regularly measure and discuss our performance.
My supervisor tells me what is expected from me.
My supervisor provides adequate, ongoing feedback about my performance.
Colleagues discuss new or better approaches for improving operations.
My coworkers are solid professionals.

Third, some managers ask employees regularly about their training needs. This demonstrates commitment to employees, and the resulting training and development activities are likely to increase staff contribution to unit objectives. Of course, some do not seek opportunities to upgrade their skills, and others may ask for training that is only marginally related to the agency's mission. So, managers relate a development plan to present or future agency needs. This approach is especially useful in dealing with employees that an organization wants to retain—it is a clear signal that their supervisors and employers care about them. It is increasingly common to require some cost sharing, which increases individual accountability; and a few (though not all!) public organizations have very liberal training and development budgets that offer employees many education opportunities.

As this discussion shows, justification for training and development almost always follows from the context in which the assessment is made: a widespread employee or management concern, a rise in complaints or other problems, the need to implement new delivery procedures, or the desire to help employees develop new skills. These justifications can be augmented by the following efficiency-focused, analytical techniques: comparing the cost of training and follow-up to that of recruiting new employees or using consultants, the cost of continuing to use outdated technology, and the cost of dealing with resulting errors. Managers can also compare the cost of different training methods to further justify a preferred training approach. Such analyses can help to further bolster the case for using training (Fitz-Enz & Davison, 2001).

Evaluation

Different evaluation approaches can be distinguished based on the nature of the process and the type of information collected. These are (a) controlled pre- and postevaluations, (b) subjective assessments of training seminars (obtained immediately after completion), and (c) subsequent assessments about on-the-job improvements (obtained some period after completion, usually 1 to 3 months).

Discussion of evaluation frequently conjures up images of carefully controlled, scientific approaches. Ideally, managers should assess employee skill levels before and after training and then compare these pre- and posttraining scores against a "control group" of workers who did not receive training. The reality of organizations necessitates some deviations from standard experimental design models; it is seldom feasible to ensure that these two groups are equivalent through random assignment. It also may not be possible to deny some employees the benefits of training. Even when such control groups are not used, measurement of pre- and posttraining capabilities cannot conclusively prove that skill increases are caused by training—they could be affected by other learning not part of formal training. Nevertheless, pre- and posttest measurement supports arguments about training effectiveness; statistical control techniques take common variations into account, despite the absence of randomly assigned control groups.

It is quite common to obtain employees' perceptions about training immediately after it has been received. Exhibit 8.8 shows a sample evaluation instrument that can readily be adapted for organizational use. Such forms are sometimes also used by HR departments for soliciting input about their service from other departments. The advantages of student perceptions are that they are easy to obtain. Although low levels of satisfaction indicate that training has not met needs of employees, high satisfaction levels do not necessarily imply that the training will be beneficial. Management may fail to follow up, and there may be problems of transference that obstruct application. Furthermore, in some settings employees generally

✖ **EXHIBIT 8.8**   Questions for Evaluating Training Seminars

Please note your level of agreement with the following statements, using the following 5-point scale:

5 = Strongly Agree
4 = Agree
3 = Don't Know, Can't Say
2 = Disagree
1 = Strongly Disagree

The training accomplished the stated objectives.   [ ]
The training was useful.   [ ]
The level of difficulty was about right.   [ ]
The material was presented in a way that facilitated learning.   [ ]
The training included practical examples.   [ ]
The training material was up to date.   [ ]
The trainer tried to address our needs.   [ ]
The trainer was approachable.   [ ]
The supplemental materials were relevant and useful.   [ ]
Overall, I am satisfied with the training I received.   [ ]

. . . and please answer the following questions, too:

What was the most helpful thing that you learned today?

Would you like a follow-up session? If so, when?

What suggestions do you have for improving this session?

give positive ratings to trainers, reducing the effectiveness of this approach. A final problem is that some evaluations focus on delivery style rather than the content and usefulness of the material, information that is useful to trainers rather than managers.

Evaluation is also performed after employees have had an opportunity to apply the training material. Such evaluations emphasize changes in on-the-job behaviors as well as results obtained through training (Kirkpatrick, 1998). For example, training on hazardous materials should include behaviors associated with safe handling, such as the use of protective devices or consulting handbooks to better familiarize oneself with properties of chemicals. Evaluations might also include implementation efforts. Results evaluation might focus on the number of accidents or near accidents. The main variations on this type of evaluation are, first, whether they solicit employee as well as management assessments and, second, the extent to which they combine subjective perceptions about usefulness with objective, administrative data that indicate productivity improvement (Paddock, 1997). A broad, balanced perspective is obtained by surveying stakeholder perceptions affected by training outcomes.

Modern trends support user input in survey design and evaluation. Staff input also enhances commitment to evaluation results, which in turn can be used to suggest future training and development. This may also increase the relevance of evaluation items. The process of conducting an employee-based evaluation process is as follows:

- Determine what training activity should be evaluated.
- Identify past and present participants in programs.
- Distribute a draft survey instrument and obtain employee input (to ensure that it meets relevant concerns and interests).
- Discuss the evaluation process (e.g., data collection, analysis) and identify a date for discussing the evaluation findings.
- Invite input and interpretation of the findings.

The outcomes of such evaluations are likely to increase employee commitment to effective training and suggest new training needs.

Many examples show how evaluation can be used to improve training initiatives and program performance. In one instance, a county jail faced numerous complaints from families about inmate visitation and release procedures. The jail director suspected that part of the problem was inadequate client orientation. A client satisfaction survey was conducted among inmates' family members before a customer service training improvement effort, and a second survey was conducted shortly thereafter. By comparing the scores, the effect of training on satisfaction could be determined. A second illustration concerns the use of job coaches in a state social services organization. New caseworkers were assigned senior employees as coaches. After several months, the new workers were surveyed about the job coaches program, and management was able to discern its effectiveness. These cases show how training evaluation is used for program decision making and improving future training (Fitz-Enz & Davison, 2001; Green, 2000; Phillips, 1997).

SUMMARY AND CONCLUSION

Training and development assist personnel to acquire and maintain up-to-date skills as well as knowledge about procedures of the organization. Training and development activities have become increasingly decentralized, and managers are encouraged to develop a **strategic focus**, one that relates training and development to the objectives and strategies of their units. Although managers can often count on central HR to provide general training (such as for word processing or ADA compliance), they must develop their own training resources to provide for their unit's needs.

As the new century unfolds, several contemporary trends become evident. First, the need to ensure basic skills remains important, such as those relating to writing, public speaking, working with others, and information technology. Second, as the workforce becomes increasingly diverse, organizations managing diversity classes deserve attention. Third, the tenets of productivity and quality—customer service, process improvement, employee empowerment—must be present in any training program as these continue to be organizational priorities. Fourth, the enthusiasm for distance learning, virtual training, and computer-mediated technology (Schreiber & Berge, 1999) likely will affect employee training and development in the years ahead. Finally, as the legal environment continues to evolve, and sometimes becomes more complex (Chapter 2), training for managers and staff about legal matters, regulations, standards, and procedures remains important.

Effective training and development builds on the principles of adult learning, ensuring that participants are motivated, that material is relevant and transferable to the specific problems and settings at hand, that training includes numerous examples and opportunities for practice and application, that training addresses the underlying principles of whatever material is being taught, and finally that participants get sufficient feedback to encourage correct application and use of the material. Application of these principles should guide how different training approaches are used, such as on-the-job training, seminars, cross-training, simulation, mentoring and coaching, Web-based learning, and education.

Managers must assess the need for training and development. Such assessments emphasize the needs of organizations or units, specific delivery processes or procedures, or the developmental needs of employees and managers. Assessments can be systematic, such as by using surveys or in-depth analysis of the skills required by specific delivery processes, or more informal, relying on the hunches and assessments of leaders or employees. Similarly, the evaluation of training and development often relies on the perceptions of training participants and administrators.

Ultimately, employees and managers are expected to take an active role in ensuring their own needs for training and development. Organizations can help by providing processes that invite such participation and the resources and environment that promote continuous professional development. Public service increasingly is based on knowledge residing in employees. The traditional tendency to roll along needs to be replaced by training and development that extends and stretches human resources to better serve citizens.

KEY TERMS

Adult learning theory	Overlearning
Advanced forms of learning	Positive reinforcement
Coaching	Principles of learning
Cross-training	Rule of seven
Decentralization of training	Rule of three
Development	Seminars and presentations
Education	Simulation
Evaluation	Strategic focus
Learning plateau	Surveys
Mentoring	Training
Motivation in training	Training relevance
Needs assessment	Transference
On-the-job training	

EXERCISES

Class Discussion

1. Discuss how the principles of learning apply to a training program to improve the effectiveness of (a) agency trainers, (b) frontline customer service personnel, (c) supervisors.

2. How many agencies require supervisors to develop a skills development plan for individual employees? How can agencies go about doing that, and what should be some elements of such a plan?

3. Examine how the paradoxes and trends discussed in the Introduction to this book are present in the agencies where students in the class are employed.

4. "You will always find some Eskimos ready to instruct the Congolese on how to cope with heat waves" (Stanislaw Lec, Polish writer). Discuss.

Team Activities

5. Identify three objectives of a training program for new police officers. Focus on what participants should be able to do on completion. What should be the relative emphasis of OJT, in-house seminars, cross-training, simulation, and formal education? Why?

6. Analyze a training program for first-time supervisors. Identify some competencies for which overlearning is relevant. Develop a needs assessment.

7. Many employees complain about a lack of positive reinforcement. Design a training program to increase its use. Why don't managers use positive reinforcement, and how does the program address this problem?

8. "We don't want to invest money in training because it is lost when employees leave." Explore the paradoxes in this statement.

9. Consider this statement in the context of the paradox of needs: "Never let your professional development be governed by our organization."

Individual Assignments

10. Identify job-related skills and knowledge that your employer should provide. How likely is it that your employer will actually help you acquire these skills? How will not acquiring these skills or knowledge affect your job performance and career? What can you do to acquire these KSAs?

11. Consider how small organizations might differ in their training approaches from large organizations. Consider how training might differ between different types of employees, for example old versus young, technical versus managerial, supervisory versus senior management.

12. You have been appointed the training director in a large state agency university to develop and implement programs for staff personnel. Paradoxically, no monies are budgeted for this. Can this dilemma be resolved? How?

13. Develop a skills acquisition plan for yourself. Identify specific skills that you would like to acquire and when you will be acquiring them over the next 24 months. Try to identify at least one additional skill every 6 months.

REFERENCES

Barron, J., Black, D., & Berger, M. (1997). *On-the job training.* Kalamazoo, MI: Upjohn.
Berman, E. (1998). *Productivity in public and nonprofit organizations: Strategies and techniques.* Thousand Oaks, CA: Sage.

Berman, E. (1999). Professionalism among public and nonprofit managers. *American Review of Public Administration, 29*(2), 149–166.

Berman, E., & West, J. (2001). From traditional to virtual HR. *Review of Public Personnel Administration, 21*(1), 38–64.

Berman, E., & West, J. (2003a). Psychological contracts in local government. *Review of Public Personnel Administration, 24*(4), 267–285.

Berman, E., & West, J. (2003b). Solutions to the problem of managerial mediocrity: Moving up to excellence. *Public Performance & Management Review, 27*(2), 28–50.

Bjornberg, L. (2002). Training and development: Best practices. *Public Personnel Management, 31*(4), 507–516

Brown, J. (2002). Training needs assessment: A must for developing an effective training program. *Public Personnel Management, 31*(4), 569–578.

Clardy, A. (1997). *Studying your workforce: Applied research methods and tools for the training and development practitioner.* Thousand Oaks, CA: Sage.

Fitz-Enz, J., & Davison, B. (2001). *How to measure human resource management* (3rd ed.). New York: McGraw-Hill.

Gillespie, G. (2002). High tech training for military air traffic control. *Summit 5*(4), 25.

Gray, G., Hall, M., Miller, M., & Shasky, C. (1997). Training practices in state governments. *Public Personnel Management, 26*(2), 187–203.

Green, P. (2000). *Building robust competencies.* San Francisco: Jossey-Bass.

International City/County Management Association. (2002). *Supervisory skills for improving employee performance* (training package). Washington, DC: Author.

International City/County Management Association. (2003). *So, now you're a trainer!* Washington, DC: Author. Complete text available at http://bookstore.icma.org/freedocs/NowYoureATrainer.pdf

Jacobson, W., Rubin, E., & Selden, S. (2002). Examining training in large municipalities: Linking individual and organizational training needs. *Public Personnel Management, 31*(4), 485–506.

Kettl, D., & DiIulio, J. (1995). *Inside the reinvention machine: Appraising governmental reform.* Washington, DC: Brookings.

Kirkpatrick, D. (1998). *Evaluating training programs: The four levels.* San Francisco: Berrett-Koehler.

Lucas, R. (2003). *The creative training idea book: Inspired tips and techniques for engaging and effective learning.* New York: AMACOM.

National Commission on the State and Local Government Public Service (Winter Commission). (1993). *Hard truths/tough choices: An agenda for state and local reform.* Albany, NY: Rockefeller Institute of Government.

Newstrom, J., Scannell, E., & Nilson, C. (1998). *The complete games trainers play: Vol. 1.* New York: McGraw-Hill.

Olivero, G., & Bane, D. (1997). Executive coaching as a transfer of training tool. *Public Personnel Management, 26*(4), 461–470.

Paddock, S. (1997). Administrative benchmarks in management training. *Public Productivity & Management Review, 21*(2), 192–202.

Phillips, J. (1997). *Handbook of training evaluation and measurement methods.* Houston: Gulf.

Reese, L., & Lindenburg, K. (2003). The importance of training on sexual harassment policy outcomes. *Review of Public Personnel Administration, 24*(3), 175–191.

Schreiber, D. A., & Berge, Z. L. (Eds.). (1999). *Distance training.* San Francisco: Jossey-Bass.

Selden, S., & Moynihan, D. (2000). A model of voluntary turnover in state government. *Review of Public Personnel Administration, 20*(2), 63–74.

Ugori, U. (1997). Career-impending supervisory behaviors. *Public Administration Review, 57*(3), 250–255.

U.S. General Accounting Office. (2003). *Strategic planning and distributive learning could benefit the special operations forces foreign language program.* Washington, DC: Author.

Van Kavelaar, E. (1998). *Conducting training workshops: A crash course for beginners.* San Francisco: Jossey-Bass.

Van Wart, M. (2004). Organizational investment in employee development. In S. Condrey (Ed.), *Handbook of human resource management in government* (2nd ed.). San Francisco: Jossey-Bass.

Van Wart, M., Cayer, N., & Cook, S. (1993). *Handbook of training and development for the public sector.* San Francisco: Jossey-Bass.

Wu, L., & Rocheleau, B. (2001). Formal versus informal end user training in public and private organizations. *Public Performance & Management Review, 24*(4), 312–321.

9

APPRAISAL

A Process in Search of a Technique

If anyone can solve the performance evaluation problem, he should be entitled to the Nobel, the Pulitzer, and the Heisman in the same year.

—Federal personnel official

After studying this chapter,[1] you should be able to

- Learn why personnel appraisal is at once important and paradoxical
- Weigh the advantages and drawbacks of typical types of appraisal
- Value why the root problem is not technical in nature
- Demonstrate and apply appraisal interview skills in a self-study exercise
- Consider ways to improve the process
- Assess alternative approaches to employee discipline
- Evaluate an appraisal system, through fieldwork, in the light of the characteristics of a "litigation-proof" process
- Explore future trends in this area

After having been hired, classified, paid, and trained, an employee will have his or her work reviewed to assess the extent to which individual and collective needs coincide—or conflict. The process may be valued by employees for both intrinsic reasons (as a validation of one's efficacy) and extrinsic factors (recognition and rewards). Because many decisions can hinge on these ratings, the process is central to human resource management. Playing key functions in employee compliance, performance improvement, and system validation, reviews are mechanisms to reinforce organizational values; they provide data on the effectiveness of recruitment, position management, training, and compensation (where such information is most frequently used). In the absence of this feedback, supervisors may have difficulty in understanding how well other management systems are working. Likewise, judgments about individual conduct may be needed if performance-contingent decisions in such areas are to have a rational basis.

Clearly, then, employee evaluation is a chief function of management. It is also a complex topic that includes administrative decisions (e.g., pay), developmental recommendations (e.g., training), technical issues (system design), and interpersonal skills (superior-subordinate appraisal interviews). Although a well-designed process can benefit an agency, creating, implementing, and maintaining it is not easy. Programs serving multiple purposes may, in fact, serve none of them particularly well.

An emotional, inexact, human process, it is a complex task that is difficult to do—one that is not done well by most organizations. In business, for instance, a 2004 survey found that just a third of employees believed that performance appraisal accomplished its goals (http://www.watsonwyatt.com); further, less than 10% of organizations judge their appraisal systems to be effective (Grensing-Pophal, 2001). There is no reason to believe, as discussed below, that the situation is any different in government. Indeed, only 20% of federal employees indicate that the appraisal system motivates them to do a better job (U.S. Merit Systems Protection Board [U.S. MSPB], 2003). Donna D. Beecher, a founding member of the federal Senior Executive Service, writes that "performance management systems are rarely effective in communicating specific expectations, providing helpful feedback, engaging and energizing the workforce and raising levels of employee satisfaction" (2003, pp. 463–464).

Personnel appraisal, in short, is one of an administrator's most difficult issues, precisely because it is both important and problematic. Few managerial functions have attracted more attention and so successfully resisted solution than employee evaluation (Halachmi, 1995, p. 322). Personnel systems predicated on rewarding merit are undermined when questionable appraisal practices take place. What these widely used and intensely disliked systems reveal is that instead of being a solution, they are often part of the problem; in point of fact, many authorities agree that personnel appraisal contributes to Enron-style corruption (Meisler, 2003; Spector, 2003) and/or workplace violence (see Exhibit 9.1).

EXHIBIT 9.1   Preventing the "Ultimate" Evaluation Solution

The work site definitely has become leaner and meaner in the last generation. The traditional social contract between employers and their minions has been broken: Organizations downsize, management turns over, employees wonder if they are "next," pay stagnates, benefits become more expensive, and computers monitor humans (see discussion later in this chapter). Beginning in the 1970s (with blue-collar employees) and continuing in the 1980s and 1990s (with white-collar workers), organizations have regarded employees not as valuable assets but rather as a flexible cost to be excreted as necessary. It is perhaps no coincidence that violence at work has become an important issue in recent years.[1]

About half of workplace violence is employee on employee (the balance is citizens or family members entering offices), and one in four employees have been harassed, threatened, or assaulted. Homicide is the leading cause of occupational death for women, the second for men. The costs of abuse to personal well-being, organizational productivity, and American society as a whole are substantial in terms of counseling, turnover, litigation, security measures, insurance premiums, and the social fabric of the nation.

Although many employees—incorrectly—feel safe at work, offices, courts, schools, and hospitals are no longer safe havens; occupational violence is a serious and underreported public health problem. Indeed, defense mechanisms such as denial ("it can't happen here") actually put employees at risk and impede preventive measures.

Management policies, including personnel practices, can both provoke and help prevent violence in organizations. Factors such as poor job design, inadequate space and outdated equipment, demanding schedules and workload, and weak interpersonal skills can lead to aggressive behavior. A key critical incident provoking danger, for instance, is performance appraisal and its consequences: close supervision, layoffs, and terminations.

In an already tense workplace, the evaluation method used, how it is employed, and the way people learn about its results can produce paroxysms of shock and sorrow, anger and rage. For example, not long ago a newly elected speaker of a southern state house of representatives distributed Christmas cards to all house employees on December 24. If the card came in a green envelope, then the employee still had a job; if it was in a red envelope, the person was told to clear out his or her desk by 5:00 P.M. Similarly (albeit without the Christmas cheer), a private corporation called the police to secure the premises, then asked 200 employees to go to the auditorium. They were told to turn in their building keys and were escorted from the company property. Neither case, luckily, resulted in further violence, but abandoned employees sometimes return to the workplace months or years later to exact retribution.

Although it is not possible to prevent violence entirely in American culture, its probability in organizations can be lowered by the following:

- Establishing a violence prevention team to conduct a needs assessment that includes a review of HRM recruitment, training, and appraisal practices, as well as employee assistance programs (see Chapter 7)
- Developing a plan comprising a clear agency policy on workplace violence, a penalty schedule for violations, a mechanism to report incidents, and employee training (on topics such as stress management, problem solving, negotiation)
- Forming a crisis management team, to be mobilized when needed, with defined procedures and role definitions in key areas such as employee communication (e.g., rumor hotlines), media relations, and counseling (see, e.g., Minor, 1995)

As an official in a security firm observed, "A written plan may not work but an unwritten plan never works."

A carefully designed approach, then, can mean the difference between acting decisively to cope with and defuse incidents and reacting haphazardly in a manner that may exacerbate a difficult situation. Yet prevention is a low priority in many organizations, as "most employers remain unprepared to deal with violent episodes in the workplace" (Grossman, 2002, p. 36).

Likely to increase in the years ahead, trauma at work is related to management practices as well as all experiences employees bring to the organization. Yet effective HRM makes it easier to contain than violence in the streets. It is the agency's responsibility to provide a safe working environment—and the Americans With Disabilities Act (Chapter 2) specifies that reasonable accommodations be made for those who exhibit stress-related symptoms that may lead to aggressive conduct. Is this duty being fulfilled in your jurisdiction? To help answer this question, see Chappell and DiMartino (2000) and U.S. Office of Personnel Management (1998).

NOTE:

1. Contrary to popular perceptions, the U.S. Postal Service—a very large, visible, hierarchical, and high-pressure organization—does not have a greater rate of incidents than other workplaces. Indeed, it has an effective prevention program that has reduced the amount of violence in recent years (Trimble, 1998, p. 12).

Not surprisingly, paradoxes abound: People are often less certain about "where they stand" after the appraisal than before it; the higher one rises in a department, the lower the likelihood that quality feedback will be received; and most employees perceive little connection between performance and pay (Daley, 1992). Despite—or perhaps because of—the vexing, intractable nature of personnel appraisal, political pressures to "just do it" are substantial. Although members of the general public know appraisal problems from their own work experiences, they nevertheless make an odd assumption: Because evaluations are done successfully (somewhere) in business bureaucracies, they should especially be used in government agencies. For this HRM function, myth is not merely more important than reality; instead, it often seems to be reality.

The chapter begins with the evolution, as eerie as it is, of the appraisal function. Common types of appraisal, who does them, and typical—if robust—rating errors are then examined. That section climaxes with a discussion of the fundamental and beguiling reason for these problems. Diagnosis completed, attention then shifts to ways to design and improve evaluation programs. This leads to a specification of the characteristics of a system that could withstand legal scrutiny. The chapter closes by sketching future trends in personnel appraisal. The overall objective is to describe the processes, problems, and paradoxes, as well as to critique the premises on which many appraisal systems are built.

EVOLUTION

The paradoxical nature of service ratings—rarely do they deliver in practice what is promised in theory—stems from the legacy of the spoils system (Chapter 1). Aghast at widespread looting, plunder, and corruption during the spoils system era, good-government groups, armed with scientific management techniques such as job analysis (Chapter 5), sought to guarantee competence by insulating employees from political influence. Reformers established merit systems, closely monitored by nonpartisan civil service commissions. As these systems evolved, the emphasis was on recruiting meritorious people (Chapter 3) and protecting them from partisan entanglements. Less attention was devoted to divining ways to evaluate their work; after all, the system was designed to select competent workers in the first place.

It should not be surprising, then, that although concern for appraisal has existed for a long time (Congress mandated evaluations as early as 1842), the topic for decades was a stepchild slighted by both academicians and managers. The dramatic growth of government during the Great Depression and World War II, however, culminated in considerable interest in appraisal programs so that by the 1950s many jurisdictions had adopted them.

Characteristic of the times, an underlying faith in science to control, direct, and measure human performance resulted in the continuing search for, if not the perfect evaluative scheme, then at least ways to improve existing technology. Thus, many of the early systems, based on personal traits (discussed in the next section), were widely criticized for failing to differentiate between employees: Virtually everyone received a "satisfactory" rating.

Aiming to correct this problem, the 1978 Civil Service Reform Act sought to evaluate employees, not on subjective characteristics but on objective, job-related performance standards. This effort, in turn, produced its own set of problems so that in 1993 the National Performance Review (NPR, 1993, p. 36) declared it to be dysfunctional and detrimental to the success of governmental programs. For its part, in calling for simplified, decentralized, team-based evaluation, the NPR deemphasized the need for results-oriented appraisals; this approach, as discussed below, has not been any more successful than it has been in business.

Today, service ratings remain as certainly the most criticized area of HRM and seem to be endured only because realistic alternatives are not currently in wide use. Abandoning the function altogether may not be a solution, however, because human beings have always made informal or formal evaluations of others. The challenge is to decide what to appraise in a manner that meets the needs of the organization and the individual. Ironically, "the primary problem supervisors encounter is not *knowing* who are the best performers, but rather *measuring* and *documenting* performance differentials" (Perry, 2003, p. 147; italics original).

COMMON TYPES OF APPRAISAL

Because there are few jobs with clear, comprehensive, objective output measures that eliminate the need for judgment, the most widely used evaluation methods are judgmental in nature.[2] What differentiates them is the degree of subjectivity that is likely in the judgments made. The approaches can be readily grouped as trait-, behavior-, and results-based systems. Recognize, however, that there is considerable variety in available techniques. Not only are they frequently combined with one another, but different systems may be used for various types of employees.[3] Only the most familiar are examined here, and even these, albeit it in differing degrees, produce evaluations that are either **deficient** (not all pertinent factors are considered) or **contaminated** (irrelevant considerations are included).

Trait-Based Systems

Trait-based systems require judgments on the degree to which someone possesses certain desired personal characteristics deemed important for the job (Exhibit 9.2). Despite the inherent subjectivity of this format, it continues to be practiced because human beings often make trait judgments about others in daily life. The approach, although often inscrutable, seems intuitively sensible as a result.

There are colorful iterations of such graphic rating scales based on the characteristics chosen, their definitions (if any), and the number of categories (adjective or numeric) used. None, however, overcomes serious validity and reliability questions. Thus, because it is difficult to define personality characteristics (much less the extent to which someone has them), subordinates may become suspicious, if not resentful, especially because this technique has little value for the purpose of performance improvement. Human traits, after all, are relatively stable aspects of individuals.

This is not to suggest that vivid personal characteristics are unimportant in job performance; individuals can hardly perform without them. And people routinely make trait judgments about one another because they can be a powerful way to describe someone, so powerful that recalling something about a person usually elicits a personal trait. Indeed, the use of flexible, subjective criteria seems inevitable, especially for ambiguous managerial jobs. The problem is that of valid measurement. When used with accurate job descriptions and trained evaluators, such ratings may become more credible. Even when the traits measured are job related (e.g., job knowledge, dependability), however, a landmark court opinion (*Brito v. Zia*, 1973) criticized their subjective nature because the results were not anchored in or related to actual work behavior.[4]

> ✪ **EXHIBIT 9.2**   Examples of Trait Appraisal, a Behaviorally Anchored Rating Scale, and
> Management by Objectives
>
> **Trait Appraisal**
>
> | | Excellent | Good | Fair | Poor | Failure |
> |---|---|---|---|---|---|
> | Loyalty | | | | | |
> | Manner | | | | | |
> | Attitude | | | | | |
> | Drive | | | | | |
> | Adaptability | | | | | |
> | Knowledge | | | | | |
> | Decisiveness | | | | | |
>
> **Behaviorally Anchored Rating Scale**
>
> Dimension: Communication Skills
>
> | | |
> |---|---|
> | Far exceeds requirements | Talks with God |
> | Exceeds requirements | Talks with angels |
> | Meets requirements | Talks with himself |
> | Needs improvement | Argues with himself |
> | Lacks minimum requirements | Loses those arguments |
>
> **Management by Objectives***
>
> | Objectives for This Evaluation Period | Percent/ of Job | Present Status | Types of Measures (how objectives will be measured) | Results Achieved | Rating* |
> |---|---|---|---|---|---|
> | Objective One | | | | | |
> | Objective Two | | | | | |
> | Objective Three | | | | | |
>
> Employee Signature   Supervisor Signature
>
> NOTE: *Exceeds, met, or not met objectives.

Just as trait rating is no longer likely to be used alone, neither is the narrative essay technique; in fact, in one form or another written descriptions often supplement most appraisal formats. Because individuals are unique, a thoughtful commentary can provide personal, intimate, and detailed information. Done well, such an essay includes an employee's strengths and weaknesses, developmental needs, and potential for advancement. The premise of the approach is that a candid statement is at least as useful as more complicated techniques. Or maybe not.

The "anything goes" nature of these essays lends them to rater idiosyncrasies, subjectivity, and pop psychology. Their interesting, sometimes ambiguous, statements (e.g., "When it comes to self-improvement, Van Westman has great potential") make comparisons virtually impossible. Subject to a wide variety of rater errors (see discussion in a later section), essay-type appraisals are often deficient and contaminated, thereby unreliable and invalid. Although they may be of value to the employee, such reviews are of limited use to anyone else. In their pure, stand-alone form, then, narratives are rarely used (for the writing impaired, ready-to-copy samples can be found in Arthur, 1997).

Behavior-Based Systems

Unlike trait-focused methods, which emphasize who a person is, **behavior-based evaluation systems** attempt to discern what someone actually does. The relatively tangible, objective nature of these systems makes them more legally defensible than personality scales. In point of fact, civil rights legislation of the 1960s and 1970s led to the development of a number of tools that concentrate on behavioral data, two of which are considered here.

The **critical incident technique** (CIT) is used to record behaviors that are unusually superior or inferior. It can be implemented in a responsive and flexible manner; supervisors can be trained to pay more attention to incidents of an exceptional behavior in some performance areas at certain times and in other areas in different periods (Halachmi, 1995, p. 326). A critical incident log may be helpful in supporting other appraisal methods.

Important drawbacks, however, include its "micro management" feature: Supervisors keep a "book" on people, and mistakes, rather than achievements, may be more likely to be recorded because employees are supposed to be competent. Another concern is that subordinates may engage in easily documented activities while hiding errors and neglecting tasks not readily observed. In addition, valuable, steady performers, not generally involved in spectacular events, may be overlooked. Halachmi also notes that the record could be incomplete or unreliable because of the rater's knowledge or the nature of the appraisee's job—either one of which makes comparisons between individuals problematic. The anecdotal nature of the method, in short, is both its strength and its weakness.

The **behaviorally anchored rating system** (BARS) builds on the incident method as well as the graphic rating scales discussed in the previous section. It defines the dimensions to be evaluated in behavioral terms and uses critical events to anchor or describe different performance levels (Exhibit 9.2). When introduced in the 1960s, BARS was claimed to be a breakthrough technology because raters could match observed activity on a scale instead of judging it as desired or undesired (Halachmi, 1995, p. 330). Because the scales are developed from the experience of employees, it was also thought that user acceptance was likely. As a job-related system, it remains relatively invulnerable to legal challenge.

Yet the method is often not practical because each job category requires its own BARS; either for economic reasons or the lack of employees in a specific job, the approach is often infeasible. Second, Gomez-Mejia, Balkin, and Cardy (2004, p. 230) argue that if personal attributes are a more natural way to think about other people, then requiring supervisors to use BARS (or for that matter, any nontrait technique) is merely a sleight of hand that introduces psychometric errors (discussed below). Indeed, they cite research finding that both employers and employees prefer trait systems. Other studies demonstrate that managers and staff personnel do not make much of a distinction between BARS and trait scales (e.g., Wiersma & Latham, 1986). Not surprisingly, there is little evidence to support the superiority of this technique over other approaches (Borman, 1991).

Finally, most experts do not find that the potential gains in using BARS warrant the substantial investment required in time and resources. Thus, where this technique is used, it often plays a residual role, limited to either a small number of selected job categories or to the developmental function of personnel appraisal. Overall, then, whatever else trait- and behavior-based systems may do, they are largely silent on the question of what an employee is to accomplish.

Results-Based Systems

As measures of neither personal characteristics nor employee behaviors, **results-based systems** or outcome-oriented approaches attempt to calibrate one's contribution to the success of the organization. Although "results" have always been of keen interest to administrators, **management by objectives** (MBO)[5] promises to achieve substantial organization-individual goal congruence. Introduced in the 1950s, this most common results-focused approach establishes agency objectives, followed in cascading fashion by derivative objectives for every department, all managers, and each employee. These systems require specific, realistic objectives, mutually agreed-upon goals, interim progress reviews, and comparison between actual and expected accomplishments at the end of the rating period (Exhibit 9.2).

Despite its rationality and evidence of effectiveness (Rogers & Hunter, 1991), MBO, like other appraisal techniques, has serious drawbacks:

- Although development of objectives may not be as technically demanding as BARS, the process nevertheless is quite time-consuming; an effective program takes 3–5 years to implement (accordingly, few agencies adopt the formal hierarchical process to ensure organization-department-manager-employee linkage).

- There likely will be conflicting objectives, differing views on the appropriateness of the objectives, and disagreements about the extent to which objectives are mutually agreed-upon—and fulfilled.

- Because it focuses on short-term goals, a compulsive "results-no-matter-what" mentality can produce predictable quality and ethical problems, as anything that gets in the way of the objective gets shunted aside (in a public or private service organization, how a job is done often is as critical as its output).

- Not only is establishing equally challenging objectives for all people difficult, but expectations that they will invariably improve (an MBO-induced "treadmill") also can lead to user acceptance problems.

- The technique can stifle creativity because employees may define their job narrowly (as they "work to quota"), leaving some problems undetected and unresolved.

- Teamwork is likely to suffer if employees become preoccupied with personal objectives at the expense of collegiality (they may fulfill their goals but not be good all-around performers).

- The method may not assist in the employee development function because performance outcomes do not indicate how to change.

In short, results-oriented approaches are susceptible to contamination errors (when results are affected by factors beyond employee control) and deficiency problems (when results are emphasized, important "organizational citizenship" behaviors may be discouraged). And supervisors must devote considerable effort to such result-based performance schemes, which provokes comments like this one from a federal manager: "I don't have time to do evaluations, now, so how would I have the time to do this?" (Ziegler, 2004, p. 6). Nevertheless, MBO, in particular, remains a popular technique to appraise managers because their roles are often ambiguous, and it does provide a measure of accomplishment against predetermined objectives.

Commentary: "Man plans, God laughs" (Jewish Proverb)

To summarize, Exhibit 9.3 specifies the promise, problems, and prospects of the three categories of appraisal. Although the intuitive appeal of trait rating is considerable, it is highly susceptible to both contamination and deficiency errors; its future potential, accordingly, is limited to a supplemental role in the review process because of subjectivity and vulnerability to court challenge. Systems based on employee behavior also hold substantial promise because they are job related—something most judges expect. They too are likely to play a modest role in the years ahead, however, largely because of their susceptibility to deficiency errors and, in the case of BARS, high technical demands coupled with limited applicability. Results-derived approaches, like the others, have face validity but often suffer from a host of deficiency and implementation problems. Still, they do emphasize actual accomplishments, as opposed to personalities or behaviors, and therefore may survive litigation.

Although combined techniques may offer advantages, available research does not support a clear choice among methods (e.g., Wanguri, 1995). Because each has its own strengths and weaknesses, selecting one to cure a problem likely will cause a new problem; there is no foolproof approach. Notice too that all three systems are backward looking; because there is no systematic continuous improvement process, they may be self-defeating as they perpetuate the organizational status quo. The better traditional appraisals are done, paradoxically, the more likely it is that the organization will remain the same. Hauser and Fay (1997, p. 193) wistfully

✖ EXHIBIT 9.3 Promise, Problems, and Prospects of Person-Centered Appraisal Systems

System	Promise	Characteristic Problems	Prospects
Trait based	high (intuitive appeal)	high (contamination and efficiency errors)	low (supplemental role)
Behavior based	high (job related)	average (susceptible to deficiency errors)	average (high technical demands)
Results based	high (face validity)	average (deficiency problems)	average (emphasizes accomplishments)

argue that the search for the perfect instrument—a goal that has eluded industrial psychologists for more than 50 years—is now largely regarded as futile. Instead, they suggest, efforts to improve the overall appraisal process likely will provide much larger returns than developing (and redeveloping) seemingly better rating forms every time a new high official takes office.

Paradoxically, then, the technique used is decidedly not the central issue in personnel appraisal because the type of tool does not seem to make much difference (Cardy & Dobbins, 1994). A National Research Council study report found no conclusive evidence to support claims that distinguishing between behaviors and traits has much effect on rating. Psychologically, supervisors form broad opinions that affect evaluation of actual work behaviors. There is little available data that rating systems based on job-specific factors produce results much different from those using general dimensions (Milkovich & Wigdor, 1991).

That is, available evidence indicates that judgments about performance are not necessarily correlated with results (Murphy & Cleveland, 1995) precisely because these decisions rely on cognitive abilities that are notoriously prone to error (see below). Not surprisingly, the choice of a tool is less important than the fact the employees often have little confidence in the abilities of managers to implement them effectively. The National Performance Review (1993, p. 32) found, for instance, that "performance ratings are unevenly distributed by grade, gender, occupation, geographic location, ethnic group, and agency" (shoe size was not mentioned). That is, technically sophisticated and well-designed systems do not operate in a vacuum; organizational culture, leadership credibility (Gabris & Ihrke, 2000), employer-employee relations, and levels of trust affect the efficacy of appraisal processes. Stated differently, it is important to ensure that there is an alignment between organizational performance and individual performance (Riccucci & Lurie, 2001). The exact evaluation method used to assess performance is less important than building a goal-oriented organization where people have productive attitudes toward work and each other (Palguta, 2001).

Appraisal software programs nonetheless promise to (a) enable managers to select predigested forms (or to design their own), (b) walk them through form completion (including tips and hints, provision of preprogrammed phrases and prompts for examples, and even reminders when appraisals are due), and (c) verify their work with arithmetical, logical consistency and legal checks before printing out a professional-looking report. Prospective customers are assured that "it's a snap" by one enthusiastic vendor. In a balanced review of these programs, however, Grote (1996) notes that they run on algorithms with no knowledge of the organizational culture, job standards, or individual performance—problems likely to intensify in a virtual workplace. Indeed, they make the process too easy; managers should devote real thought to appraisals, not merely point and click. The software contributes nothing to the most important part of service ratings: the manager-employee interview (discussed in a subsequent section).

RATERS

Given that common appraisal methods are judgmental in character, an important question is, "Who makes this judgment?" Traditionally, there was one answer: the subordinate's immediate supervisor. Other knowledgeable information sources include the ratee, peers, computers, and outsiders.

Self-appraisals, based on the belief that the employee has important insights about how the job should be done, can provide valuable data, particularly when the supervisor and employee engage in joint goal setting. These evaluations are, however, subject to distortions including self-congratulation or, less likely, self-incrimination. It is well established, for instance, that many people attribute good performance to their own efforts and blame poor performance on other factors. These biases can be moderated if objective standards exist and the ratee is regularly provided genuine feedback. Still, because these evaluations tend to focus on personal growth and motivation, they are best used for developmental rather than administrative purposes.

As work in some organizations has changed from a stable set of tasks done by one person to a more fluid ensemble of changing requirements done by groups of employees, **peer** or team **evaluation** becomes appropriate. In an agency culture high in trust where coworkers develop rating scales and have access to relevant information, such assessments can be accurate. When these conditions do not exist, supervisors likely will be reluctant to give up control, and subordinates will often see these techniques as a disruptive competition that can easily be sabotaged by lenient ratings or converted into "popularity contests." Thus, these reviews are often most useful when done anonymously and for developmental reasons.

The objective of **electronic monitoring** is to increase productivity, improve quality, and reduce costs; it does so by continuously collecting performance data, pinpointing problems, and providing immediate feedback. When such monitoring provides objective performance appraisals, employee satisfaction and improved morale may result. Today, computer-generated statistics are the basis for evaluations of millions of office workers engaged in clerical, repetitive tasks, and the virtual work site of the future is almost certainly going to expand the collection and use of such information. Indeed, as software becomes more sophisticated, a wide variety of occupations (e.g., medicine, engineering, accounting) are likely to undergo electronic scrutiny. When implemented without reasonable safeguards (e.g., employee access to data, rights to challenge erroneous records, rating decisions made on the basis of nonelectronic as well as electronic information), these programs can create an "electronic sweatshop" environment damaging creativity, morale, and health. If employees feel helpless, manipulated, and exploited, then most techniques eventually will be circumvented.[6]

Finally, **multirater** or **360° evaluation systems**—those that gather information from subordinates, peers, and citizens—by definition provide more data than other approaches. More data may produce more reliable, but not necessarily more valid, information. The administratively complex and time-consuming nature of these systems is compounded by a lack of convergence among the different sources. That is, managers may be confronted with a host of seemingly conflicting opinions—all of which may be accurate from their respective viewpoints. Still, systems that assure respondent anonymity and encourage participant responsibility no doubt supply some useful feedback for improving both management processes and employee development. There is growing acknowledgment of the value of the technique. In short, although one's immediate supervisor is apt to play an important role in the rating process, feedback from other sources is increasingly seen as a way to obtain a more holistic understanding of performance (Society for Human Resource Management, 2000) as a third of American organizations use multirater systems. An effective program is one that is developed in a participatory manner, is pilot tested, and provides adequate training to both managers and employees. There has been little critical evaluation of 360° appraisal systems (DeNisi & Kluger, 2001).

RATING ERRORS

The use of ratings assumes, rather naively, that the definition of job performance is clear and direct measures are available to assess the employee—and that evaluators are reasonably objective and precise. Regardless of the appraisal instrument used, though, a large number of well-known errors occur in the process. These result from (a) cognitive limitations, (b) intentional manipulation, and (c) organization influences. When they happen—and they are difficult to prevent—not only is the rater's judgment called into question, but the resulting evaluation also may leave the ratee unable to accurately judge his or her own performance.

When confronted with large amounts of information, people generally seek ways to simplify it. **Cognitive information processing theory** maintains that appraisal is a complex memory task involving data acquisition, storage, retrieval, and analysis. To process data, subjective categories are employed that in turn produce no less than five problems. Thus, **compatibility** ("similarity" or liking) **error** is potent because both compatibility and ratings are person focused. Indeed, most employees believe their supervisor's liking of them influences evaluations (Cardy & Dobbins, 1994).[7] This error may be tempered, however, to the extent that managers like good performers (i.e., flaws in rating can, paradoxically, represent "true" performance levels, and removing such errors may not improve accuracy!) (Hauenstein, 1998).

The next mental shortcut is the **spillover** (halo or **black mark**) **effect**—that is, if the ratee does one thing exceptionally well (halo) or poorly (black mark), then that unfairly reflects on everything else. The **recency effect**, third, takes place when a major event occurs just prior to the time of the evaluation and overshadows all other incidents. **Contrast error** exists when people are rated relative to other people instead of against performance standards. Finally, **actor/observer bias** (partially alluded to earlier) occurs when subordinates, as actors, often point to external factors, whereas supervisors, as observers, attribute weak performance to employees.

The second general source of rating problems is that appraisals in many organizations are adroitly seen as a political, not necessarily a rational, exercise: Results are intentionally manipulated, higher or lower, than the employee deserves. The goal is not measurement accuracy but rather management discretion and organizational effectiveness. As stated by one expert, "It would be naïve to think of performance appraisal as anything other than a political process. Rating accurately is not always the goal of appraisers and there are many situations when providing inaccurate appraisal data is sound management" (Hauenstein, 1998, p. 428).

Accordingly, **leniency** or friendliness **error** (the "Santa Claus" effect) is the consequence of a desire to maintain good working relationships, maximize the size of a merit raise, encourage a marginal employee, show empathy for someone with personal problems, or avoid confrontations (and appeals) with an aggressive worker.[8] Conversely, **severity error** (the "horns" effect) may be emphasized as a way either to send a message to a good performer that some aspect of his or her work needs improvement or to shock an average employee into higher performance. More than 70% of managers in one survey (Longenecker & Ludwig, 1990) reported that they deliberately inflated or deflated evaluations for such reasons.

Note that the inherent conflict of interest present in supervisory evaluations is a powerful political reason likely to make the leniency effect prevail over other psychometric errors. That is, if all (or most) subordinate evaluations are inflated, then the supervisor may look like an effective manager; if the appraisals are not so inflated, then his or her management abilities may be called into question.[9] The employer, however, has an obligation to conduct appraisals with due care. This duty may be violated (as a result of the Santa Claus effect) when a poor performer receives satisfactory ratings and subsequently is subjected to attempts at termination.

This leads to examination of a set of organizational influences that cause at least four problems. The first is insufficient management commitment to performance appraisal. In the light of the difficulties with various evaluation schemes, much skepticism, a sense of futility, and even doubts about the possibility of performance appraisal exist (Nigro & Nigro, 2000, pp. 124–126). Investing heavily in these systems, then, does not make a lot of sense for some administrators. The daily press of business makes it a peripheral, not central, responsibility; it is often isolated not only from getting the job done but also from organizational planning and budget strategies. There are few incentives—and sometimes genuine disincentives— to use appraisal as a management tool. Employee reviews, then, are done for the sake of evaluation: an irrelevant, once-a-year formality to complain about, complete, and forget in the service of administrative rules. Such programs quickly become "organizational wallpaper" that exist in the background, but are not expected to add value.

Such an attitude leads to the **error of central tendency** (if not leniency), where nearly all employees are rated satisfactorily—if for no other reason than higher or lower scores may require time-consuming documentation. This "error" is, in turn, reinforced by the **no money effect**—that is, there frequently are insufficient funds to distribute and/or they are awarded on an across-the-board basis (see also Chapter 6).

Overall, cognitive, political, and organizational limitations help explain the reasons for rater error. Although some of these constraints can be addressed in training (see below), something more fundamental lies at the root of personnel appraisal difficulties: human nature. Its pertinent aspects are revealed by risk aversion, implicit personality theory, conflicting role expectations, and personal reluctance.

Because defending one's judgment in open court is not something most relish, it is natural that supervisors reduce risk by being aware of all possible pitfalls in the appraisal process. A paradox arises, however, when playing safe through leniency may invite a legal challenge on the grounds that appraisals did not differentiate employees by performance (Halachmi, 1995, p. 325).

Second, **implicit personality theory** suggests that people generally judge the "whole person" based on limited data (stereotyping based on first impressions or the spillover effect); ratings then tend to justify these global opinions rather than accurately gauge performance. Conflicting role expectations, third, are inherent in the appraisal process because evaluators must reconcile being a helpful coach with acting as a critical judge. In playing these roles, administrators (as noted earlier) also, in effect, evaluate themselves. Human nature suggests that better-than-deserved ratings will occur because one's own managerial skills may be called into question should employees receive poor evaluations.

Last, appraisal systems are complicated by the understandable distaste that people have for formally evaluating others. Because there is no such thing as infallible judgment, when administrators must take responsibility for judging the worth of others, "it is dangerously close to a violation of the integrity of the person" (McGregor, 1957, p. 90). Most people, especially in the light of all the other questions about the reliability and validity of personnel appraisal, are as reluctant to judge others as they are to be judged themselves. It is onerous, in other words, to "play God."

It is little wonder, then, that the sentiment expressed in this aphorism is shared by many: "Appraisal is given by someone who does not want to give it to someone who does not want to get it." More formally, "Employees and supervisors alike dread the end-of-the-year annual performance appraisal cycle, when productivity plummets for several weeks and hard feelings translate into grievances. The paperwork, damage to self-esteem, and drops in productivity are simply not worth [it]" (Beecher, 2003, p. 464). Lest one think that human nature in its various forms inevitably makes personnel appraisal a hopeless task, one veteran county manager provides a balanced defense of this HRM function (see Exhibit 9.4 and McElveen, 2000).

EXHIBIT 9.4   A Manager's View of Performance Appraisal: Theory in Practice

Mary L. Maguire
Administrative Manager/Public Information Officer
Department of Fire and Rescue Services
Loudoun County, Virginia

Having nearly 25 years' experience with city and county government agencies, I have been on the giving and receiving ends of a wide array of evaluation methods. From early forms where we were judged on appearance to the more modern ones where we are judged on contributions to the organization, each has had its merits. The one that seems to be the most promising is our current performance management system. It is a multifaceted tool aimed at improving individual employee job performance. It is anticipated that through the effective use of this system, managers and supervisors will be better equipped to help with the enhancement, motivation, and retention of employees (the county's most valuable resource), while achieving the goals of the organization.

From the minute a new employee sets foot through the door, they are provided instructions on the finer points of the system. Through classes and written guidelines, managers and subordinates are told that emphasis on the following skill sets is essential to be successful:

- Performance planning
- Coaching
- Counseling
- Documenting
- Recognizing/motivating employees
- Handling unsatisfactory employee performance
- Assessing performance

Although each piece is equally important, the attention focuses heavily on the beginning and end components: planning and assessment. This so to speak, is where the "rubber meets the road," or in other words, where the employees believe they will be rewarded for their efforts. As one of many tools in the managerial toolbox, the planning and assessment components provide opportunities for the organization to show its commitment to its employees, while recognizing them for their contributions. The system is designed to ensure that all parties involved know up front what is expected. Through the other components—coaching, counseling, documenting, recognizing and motivating employees, and addressing unsatisfactory performance—supervisors are provided with additional tools for guiding and evaluating their employees. By effectively outlining expectations, maintaining open dialogues between manager and subordinate, keeping employees apprised of their progress, and redirecting them when improvement is needed, everyone knows what to expect when it comes time for the year-end evaluation.

All this looks good on paper, but how does it really work? Annually, employees outline their goals as they relate to the department's mission and that of the county. The goals are then weighted based on relative importance. Both the employee and the supervisor develop and sign this plan; it can be modified as the person's duties evolve. This way, by the end of the evaluation cycle, there will be no surprises.

As the year draws to a close, the subordinate is asked to prepare a self-evaluation, while the manager develops his or her assessment. When they meet, an open dialogue helps clarify areas where the supervisor may have some concern. If consensus is reached and the employee has met the goals and objectives, he or she may receive a merit increase. If expectations were exceeded, then he or she may be nominated for a performance bonus (if not in agreement with the evaluation, then an appeal can be made; it is interesting to note that employees are also afforded the opportunity to anonymously evaluate their supervisor).

During the meeting, a development of the upcoming year's plan will begin. Although this process can be quite time-consuming and cumbersome, it is effective. I was a bit dismayed, however, when I actually began comparing this process with a list of common appraisal defects. For every effort made to fight these defects, I can find example after example where the defects still exist. For instance, the system was designed so that we wouldn't be evaluating for evaluation's sake. Although great pains were taken to eliminate this defect, many agencies find themselves scrambling at the end of the year to get the paperwork done. In addition, although the system was set up so that it can be modified at any time, this does not really occur. Employees continually find themselves being evaluated with respect to the goals found in outdated plans. Managers also continue to pit people against one another and have a tendency to grade everyone the same, whether positively or negatively. And employees, not only supervisors, become victims of the halo effect. Employees might do a bang-up job on one little project, and because they were recognized for their work on this assignment, the employee believes that they have exceeded the expectations on every other aspect of their evaluation, which can lead to great disappointment during the evaluation phase.

Furthermore, during economic downturns, there is often little to nothing left to reward employees. Bonuses for exceptional performance are thrown out the window in an effort to cut taxes. Employees are given miniscule or no increases in salary for cost of living and even less for performance. Therefore, the exceptional employee who strives to do his or her best may receive the same increase as the average employee who is just meeting expectations. There is no incentive for doing well. Even more devastating is the fact that one of the organization's core values of recognizing its employees as the primary resource for service delivery is compromised. The entire process, as a result, becomes suspect.

Despite its faults, there are benefits to this process. It provides guidance for future performance and is used to help further develop our staff. People at all levels have been involved in its design. Furthermore, they play an active role in the actual development of individual plans. The approach tries to use valid and reliable standards that are usually based on past performance. In addition, the standards are often measured against criteria established in the county. For instance, there are specific criteria for processing purchase orders. If met, then the employee would be rated fully successful. If able to complete the purchase order accurately in less time than allocated, thereby reducing costs, then the employee may be seen as exceeding the criteria. Supervisors are also provided ample opportunity to conduct the evaluation, and they are trained so that they would be capable of doing it. Finally, the process provides for continual feedback and when properly documented this would, I believe, stand up in court. Although far from perfect, the performance management system still exceeds many of the subjective alternatives based on perception not performance. In light of the problems, why even bother with appraisal systems? We take the time because, when done correctly, they will provide an effective mechanism that can recognize and reward employees while providing the necessary documentation that shows the organization is successfully meeting its goals.

To summarize, because many jobs are not amenable to objective assessment and quantification, ratings typically incorporate nonperformance factors—for all the reasons discussed above. When this occurs, of course, it leads to a violation of the most revered principle of this field of HRM: Appraisals evaluate performance, not the person.[10] Verisimilitude trumps veracity. When this happens, issues of law and liability arise (see key legal principles and their relationship to appraisals identified in Exhibit 9.5). Suggestions for limiting liability in the personnel evaluation process based on selected problems include the following:

Harassment or constructive discharge	Require employees to notify employer of any conditions related to job, job performance, or appraisals (for example, supervisor bias or improper conduct) that allegedly are so severe as to require quitting; establish and consistently follow procedures to promptly investigate and eliminate any such offending conditions or conduct by supervisors or other employees to avoid claim that employer tacitly accepted or approved of harassment
Age discrimination	Train supervisors to avoid age-loaded comments in verbal or written appraisals; update performance criteria as technology changes to avoid pretext claims when older workers are laid off for lack of newer skills
Disability discrimination	Review recommendations and appraisal results for evidence of perceived ("regarded as") discrimination; ensure that only essential functions are evaluated; train supervisors to identify reasonable accommodations in performance criteria and appraisal procedures on an interactive basis in a discrete and confidential manner
Defamation or misrepresentation	Establish procedures to control or avoid providing false performance information (favorable or unfavorable)
Negligence	Keep employees advised if performance is poor so they cannot contest discharge by claiming performance would have improved but for faulty evaluation process

SOURCE: Adapted from Smither (1998, p. 78).

If these are successfully confronted, and the evaluation and discipline process improved as discussed below, then it may be more realistic to take such steps to reduce potential problems rather than to abolish personnel reviews entirely.

IMPROVING THE PROCESS

Designing an appraisal system requires not only establishing policies and procedures but also obtaining the support of the entire workforce and its union(s). Top officials must publicly commit to the program by devoting sufficient resources to it and by modeling appropriate behavior. Managers, in turn, need to be convinced that the system is relevant and operational. Employees likewise should see it as in their interest to take it seriously. A profile (or "slice") task force, representing all these groups from different parts of the department, can then conduct a needs assessment by collecting agency archival and employee attitudinal data. It should then revise an existing system (or create a new one) based on the findings and test it on a trial basis. This could be done in jurisdictions that allow customization to agency needs (more than

✖ EXHIBIT 9.5   Selected Legal Principles and Laws Relating to Performance Appraisal

Legal Principle or Law	Summary	Relationship to Appraisals and the Employment Relationship
Employment at will	Status under which the employer or employee may end an employment relationship at any time	Allows the employer considerable latitude in determining whether and how to appraise
Implied contract	Nonexplicit agreement that affects some aspect of the employment relationship	May restrict manner in which employer can use results (for example, may prevent termination unless for cause)
Violation of public policy	Determination that given action is adverse to the public welfare and is therefore prohibited	May restrict manner in which employer can use appraisal results (for example, may prevent retaliation for reporting illegal conduct by employer)
Negligence	Breach of duty to conduct performance appraisals with due care	Potential liability may require employer to inform employee of poor performance and provide opportunity to improve
Defamation	Disclosure of untrue information that damages an employee's reputation	Potential liability may restrict manner in which negative performance information can be communicated to others
Misrepresentation	Disclosure of untrue favorable performance information that causes risk of harm to others	Potential liability may restrict willingness of employer to provide references altogether, even for good former employees
Fair Labor Standards Act (FLSA)	Imposes (among other things) obligation to pay overtime to non-exempt (nonmanagerial) employees	Fact that employee appraisals may influence determination that employee functions as supervisor or manager and is therefore exempt
Family and Medical Leave Act (FMLA)	Imposes (among other things) obligation to reinstate employee returning from leave to similar position	Subjecting employee to new or tougher appraisal procedures upon return may suggest that employee has not been given similar position of employment

SOURCE: Adapted from J. W. Smither (Ed.), *Performance Appraisal: State of the Art in Practice* (San Francisco: Jossey-Bass, 1998), p. 52. © Copyright 1998 by Jossey-Bass. Adapted with permission.

half of state governments, for example) or as part of a government-sponsored pilot program. It is, of course, possible to marginalize formal requirements entirely.

> In one major unit of a large hospital, a charismatic department manager decided that whatever the administration of the hospital did, he was going to run his facilities department on the basis of total quality management (TQM). Well in advance of the hospital's annual tedious performance appraisal drill, he gathered his troops together, reviewed the hospital's sorry form, and then told them that what it represented was the starting point for them to practice their kaizen—continuous improvement—skills.
>
> "What do we need to do, given the fact that this basic form is mandated, in order to complete it well enough to keep the personnel monkeys off our backs but also get some good out of the process for ourselves?" he asked his team. He funded a series of weekly pizza meetings for a task force of facilities employees who were charged with developing an answer to his question that everyone supported enthusiastically. (Grote, 1996, p. 351)

Finessing the system may be faster, more flexible, and just as effective as formally reforming it.

The design chosen involves numerous key technical questions, many of which were discussed earlier. These include selection of the most useful tool(s), as well as raters, based on system objective, practicality, and cost. Training is needed in an effort to minimize the various kinds of errors previously examined. Yet, it is generally acknowledged that mere awareness of these problems is unlikely to affect behavior; instead, raters must engage in and receive feedback from role plays, simulations, and videotaped exercises. Evaluators also need training in interpersonal skills to conduct appraisal interviews effectively.

Monitoring performance in the period between plan approval and formal appraisal includes frequent positive or corrective feedback based on performance, not personality. When performance is monitored conscientiously throughout the year, the actual evaluation will then simply confirm what has already been discussed.[11] Stated differently, the process of performance management is a continuous one involving coaching, development, accountability, and—last and least—assessment.

Finally, the evaluation process culminates in the appraisal interview. In preparing for the meeting, the employee may do a self-assessment, and managers should collect necessary information and complete, in draft form, the rating instrument. Although a collaborative problem-solving approach is effective, most managers use a one-way "tell-and-sell" technique in which they inform subordinates how they were rated and then justify the decision (Wexley, 1986). No matter the approach, supervisors should use the event to support the policies and practices of the entire system and be trained in goal setting, communication skills, and positive reinforcement.

Thus, before the interview, communicate frequently with subordinates, get training in appraisal interviewing, and use a problem-solving approach. During the session, judge specific performance (not personality), be an active listener and avoid destructive criticism, and set mutually agreeable future objectives. Afterward, periodically assess progress toward goals, and make rewards contingent on performance (Cascio, 2003, p. 358). Although conducting a good interview requires a great deal of skill and effort, many managers say that having an honest exchange is the hardest part of the entire process. Most do not do it (Pickett, 2001), and those who do see little or no value in doing such interviews (London, 1995).

Like appraisal, employee discipline and termination (the next discussion topic) can be awkward and difficult. The goal, accordingly, should be to reduce the need for adverse action, and when it is necessary, make it as easy as possible to use.

DISCIPLINARY SYSTEMS

For the most part, employees discipline themselves by conforming to what is considered acceptable behavior simply because it is the sensible thing to do. Yet mistakes are made that require attention, and the test of a well-managed agency "is not how many personnel problems arise, but how effectively" they are addressed (Wise, Clemow, Murray, Boston, & Bingham, 2005, p. 181). The need for managers to use best professional practices in the disciplinary process is illustrated by the availability of employment practices liability insurance to safeguard one's livelihood and career.

The term "discipline" is best understood as orderly conduct at work achieved by self-control and respect for agency rules. When performance problems (failure to satisfactorily complete assignments) or behavioral issues (insubordination, document falsification, loafing, carelessness, fighting, drug use) occur, the personnel appraisal and/or discipline systems may be utilized to improve performance. Factors to consider when using these systems include problem severity, duration, frequency, extenuating circumstances, organizational policies and employee training, agency past practice, and management support.

Given the nature of the issues involved, taking action is indispensable to ensure a productive workforce. Yet, paradoxically, officials may tolerate poor performers because they lack an understanding of agency rules, documentation, and top management support—to say nothing of fearing onerous employee grievances and/or false accusations of discriminatory behavior (U.S. MSPB, 1995). Indeed, managers may avoid discipline procedures and write acceptable personnel reviews for marginal employees to avoid unpleasantness, something that may haunt them if there is a subsequent attempt to discharge someone for sustained inadequate performance.

Simply demanding that managers "get tough" is not an efficacious approach because, "a supervisor who is very effective at removing someone can nevertheless be ineffective at selecting good employees in the first place or at motivating superior performance from that majority of employees who are capable of doing good work" ("Firing Poor Performers," 2003). Critics also ignore that poor performance needs to be addressed in a larger context comprising societal and organizational culture, compensation levels, and training. Those who focus on the difficulty of terminating workers overlook the utility of existing procedures that result in more than 10,000 separations per year in federal service—not counting those who resign first or those removed through layoffs ("Firing Poor Performers," 2003).

To protect both the individual and the institution, the use of appraisal and discipline must be for justifiable reasons. To ensure fair treatment, actions must be derived from written guidelines; be corrective not punitive; be based on the act, not personality; and be timely, consistent with previous cases, and proportionate to the problem. Documentation is the cornerstone, and it commences with a prompt and thorough investigation. Records should include the date, location, and nature of the incident(s); the effects on the organization; prior actions by the person and agency; the decisions made and improvement anticipated; and the employee's reaction.

Progressive punishment (aka discipline) and **positive discipline** are two approaches used by organizations. For either to be productive, workers must know what the problem is, what change is expected, and the consequences of inaction. Progressive punishment, the most common policy, is the application of coercive measures by increasing degrees of severity: informal counseling, verbal warning/reprimand, written warning/reprimand, minor suspension, major suspension, and discharge.

Because this can be autocratic, adversarial, and intimidating, some jurisdictions have replaced it with positive, nonpunishment discipline based on the premise that adults must assume responsibility for their conduct. Rather than treating people "worse and worse and expecting them to get better and better," affirmative discipline uses reminders instead of reprimands. More participative than punitive, the technique utilizes these steps:

- A conference to find a solution to the problem, with an oral agreement to improve
- A subsequent meeting, if reform is not accomplished, to determine why the agreed-upon solution did not work, with a written reminder that the solution is the responsibility of the individual as a condition of employment
- Paid leave time (a "day of decision"), if change is not forthcoming, wherein the employee is expected to return the next day either with a written commitment or a decision to leave the agency
- In brief, the employee, not the employer, is the decision maker.

The principle underlying both approaches is a "just cause" standard: Was the investigation done properly? Was the employee aware of the rule violation? Was the standard reasonable? Was the rule in question violated? What mitigating circumstances merit consideration? And have comparable cases occurred and how were they addressed? The premise is that a just procedure should help ensure a fair outcome.

The purpose of the system is not to win battles but to provide feedback and training to foster responsible employees. Many of the problems that managers experience during the discipline process can be reduced through training, establishing clear work rules, following procedures, and documenting actions taken (DelPo & Guerin, 2003; Guffey & Helms, 2001). The key is to understand the scope of one's administrative authority, focus on behavior—not the person, avoid decisions based on hearsay, use appropriate penalties, and follow through on the judgments made.

Although the objective of personnel appraisal and disciplinary systems is to ensure employee development and rehabilitation, the documentation they provide can be used to support termination decisions. Unlike much of the private sector, where employees can be arbitrarily discharged for no reason or any reason not contrary to law, public servants have constitutional rights as citizens to due process. Although there may be good grounds for action (deficient performance or egregious misconduct such as theft), managers nonetheless can create serious problems if the process is not handled well (Wise et al., 2005). Indeed, approximately two thirds of former private sector workers who contest their firing prevail in court (Bowman, 2002). It is imperative, therefore, that administrators, in consultation with the human resources department, follow established procedures—to avoid mistakes that could lead to organizational liability as well as to assist employees whose rights might have been violated.

Because discharge is a painful event for both the individual and the organization, it is critical that it be done with care and deliberation. This means that it must be approached in a humane, confidential, professional, nonaccusatory, factual way, and that it be based on substantiated, legitimate business reasons consistent with similar cases. Specifically, the termination interview should present the situation to the employee in a concise, considerate, final manner that avoids arguments about past behavior; explains outplacement services and how references will be handled; and includes delivery of a paycheck (Coleman, 2001). When people are treated fairly, wrongful discharge suits are unlikely to withstand legal scrutiny.[12] Employee termination is part of a manager's job: Doing it well is an opportunity to learn how to improve other HRM functions such as recruitment and training.

SUMMARY AND CONCLUSION

To distill this chapter, the characteristics a personnel appraisal system should contain to satisfy both employers and employees—and to survive a court challenge—are specified below. As discussed, however, implementing this HRM function is fraught with paradoxes. Indeed, readers are invited to evaluate the extent to which the following standards are met by agencies in their jurisdictions:

1. The rating instruments, which should strive for simplicity rather than complexity, are derived from job analysis (Chapter 5).

2. Training is provided to all employees about the systems and to managers in their use.

3. The appraisal is grounded in accurate job descriptions, and the actual ratings are based on observable performance.

4. Evaluations are completed under standardized conditions and are free of adverse impact (Chapter 2).

5. Preliminary results are shared with the ratee.

6. Some form of upper level review, including an appeal process, exists that prevents a single manager from controlling an employee's career.

7. Performance counseling and corrective guidance services exist.

Although many systems may not compare favorably to such standards, recall that the crux of the appraisal problem is not system design. Instead, because evaluation is a matter of human judgment, the conundrum is how the plan and the information it generates are used. Typical barriers to effective appraisal include the absence of trust in the organization, supervisory training and top management support, rater accountability, and overall evaluation of the system itself (Roberts, 2003). Ways to overcome such barriers are providing constructive, nonthreatening feedback and coaching; avoiding numeric rating scales that pigeonhole employees and pit them against each other; ensuring multiple sources of data through use of peer reviews; and utilizing group evaluations.

The perennial, melancholy search for the best "genuine fake" technique, nevertheless, relentlessly (sometimes shamelessly) continues. Peering into the century ahead, personnel appraisal will become—either more or less—complex. Should the long-standing preference for person-centered evaluations persist, then both organizational downsizing and workforce changes will likely complicate appraisals. The virtual workplace—unbound by time and space—is likely to exacerbate this situation.

Downsizing has been a one-two punch. Personnel offices have shrunk, placing more responsibilities on line managers; at the same time, the numbers of supervisors have been reduced, requiring the remaining ones to evaluate more subordinates (U.S. MSPB, 1998). The potential for both system design and implementation problems, as a result, has increased.

Several changes in the composition of the workforce also imply a more challenging climate for appraisals. Employees are becoming increasingly diverse, and evaluating people of all colors and cultures is surely more arduous than assessing a homogenous staff. Also, the fastest growing part of the working population is contingent employees—temporaries, short-term contract workers, volunteers—who, by definition, present evaluation challenges.

EXHIBIT 9.6 Evaluating Organizations, Not Individuals

Body swayed to the music, O brightening glance, How can we know the dancer from the dance?

—William Butler Yeats, *Among School Children*

As this chapter shows, individual appraisal is a complex issue. Even when done with great care, it can be devastating to people and destructive to organizations. Although it may be true that management practices are seldom discarded merely because they are dysfunctional, it is also true that the reinventing government movement (Chapter 1) provides an opportunity to reexamine orthodox approaches to appraisal.

The premise of organization-centered evaluation is that quality services are a function of the system in which they are produced. Systems consist of people, policies, technology, supplies, and a sociopolitical environment within which all operate. Note that these parameters are beyond appraisee control; indeed, the employees themselves are hired, tasked, and trained by the organization. A person-only assessment, stated differently, is deficient if the goal is to comprehend all factors affecting performance. In a well-designed management system, virtually all employees will perform properly; a weak system will frustrate even the finest people.

Traditional, person-centered appraisal methods are based on a faulty, unrealistic assumption: that individual employees are responsible for outcomes derived from a complex system. Because an organization is a group of people working to achieve a common goal, the managerial role is to foster that collaboration. If the result is inadequate, then it is management's responsibility—and no one else's.

From a systems perspective, the causes of good or bad performance are spread throughout the organization and its processes. Many results in the workplace are outside the power of employees traditionally made responsible for those outcomes. When more than 90% of performance problems are the consequence of the management system (Deming, 1992), holding low-level minions accountable is a way of evading responsibility; the cause of most performance problems lies not within the individual employee but within the organization divined by its leaders.

Because employees have little authority over organizational systems, relevant appraisals should provide two kinds of feedback:

- System performance data automatically generated from statistical process controls (i.e., evaluation is built into the work process itself)
- Individual performance data—used primarily for developmental purposes—derived from anonymous multirater 360° evaluations (focusing on attributes such as teamwork, customer satisfaction, timeliness, communication skills, and attendance)

The key is to listen to customers of the process and emphasize continuous improvement. By making the system as transparent as possible, the focus can be kept on nonthreatening analyses of work processes and people's contributions to those processes. Such an approach would be organizationally valid, socially acceptable, and administratively convenient—key criteria for any appraisal method. Importantly, it would change the process from an often adversarial one to a more constructive collaborative effort.

Reflecting American individualism,[1] the field of HRM has focused on people rather than systems. It is politically unlikely, therefore, that organizational appraisals will supplant individual ratings (indeed, when performance appraisals were abolished at one well-known federal government demonstration project in California, the project was terminated, partly because productivity improved). A number of public agencies (National Oceanic and Atmospheric Administration, Internal Revenue Service, Social Security Administration) and private companies (Motorola, Merrill Lynch, Procter & Gamble) have modified their approach to appraisals. To better reflect a systems perspective, they have incorporated teamwork (in addition to individual achievements), citizen/customer feedback (in addition to supervisory opinions), and process improvement (in addition to results) dimensions into their evaluations.

A more complete reform would be to clearly state a performance standard and then assume that most employees will do the job for which they were hired. Greg Boudreaux (1994), a manager at the National Rural Electric Cooperative, continues by saying that for the small number who do not do their jobs, "Investigate why. Some will need further training or management counseling. Some may be an actual problem. But deal with those problems on a case-by-case, and not through a generic, faculty performance appraisal system" (p. 24; also see Eckes, 1994).

Indeed, the approach described here is partly consistent with the most recent appraisal fad: performance management (Cedarblom & Permerl, 2002). This strategy emphasizes that managing performance (not merely appraisal but also planning, accountability, compensation, training) is key to institutional goal setting. Thus, performance management is a continuing cycle of goal setting, coaching, development, and assessment. From a systems perspective, however, it exemplifies the "wrong-problem problem." Yet it tries to solve the wrong problem precisely by emphasizing the individual, not the organization. The same criticism can be levied at multirater 360° evaluation systems, discussed earlier in this chapter.

NOTE:

1. This is an area where our myths may be more dangerous than our lies. The lone frontiersman and the outlaw gunslinger—largely products of Hollywood—were far less important in the American West than farmers raising barns together and shopkeepers settling in small towns. The myth also does not explain the wild popularity of team sports in contemporary life.

Alternatively, should institutions begin to shift away from person-centered appraisal and toward **organization-centered** or process-centered appraisals, individual evaluations may be less complex in the years ahead—or perhaps abolished altogether (see Exhibit 9.6; Coens & Jenkins, 2000). For example, one organization stopped doing the orthodox top-down appraisals and instituted APOP—the Annual Piece of Paper. The one-page, bottom-up review form simply summarizes ongoing daily feedback (there are no scores or future goals) by focusing on what the manager can do to make employee tasks easier and what gets in the way of accomplishing the job. Whether the appraisal function becomes more or less difficult in the 21st century, it is worth doing only if it is an integral part of the management system and if it helps both the institution and the individual develop to full potential.

KEY TERMS

Actor/observer bias
Behaviorally anchored rating system
Behavior-based evaluation systems
Black mark effect

Cognitive information processing theory
Compatibility or liking error
Contaminated (evaluations)
Contrast error

Critical incident technique
Deficient (evaluations)
Electronic monitoring
Error of central tendency
Implicit personality theory
Leniency error (Santa Claus effect)
Management by objectives
No money effect
Organization-centered evaluations
Peer evaluations

Positive discipline
Progressive punishment
Recency effect
Results-based systems
Self-appraisals
Severity error
Spillover (halo) effect
Three hundred sixty–degree (360°)
or multirater systems
Trait-based systems

EXERCISES

Class Discussion

1. What would be the most appropriate rating instrument for a middle manager? Staff assistant? Telecommuter? Intern? Why?

2. Visit a local agency to determine why, how, and by whom appraisals are done there. Analyze the rating form used. Is it legally defensible? Report the findings to the class.

3. In theory, personnel appraisal can provide feedback on management processes such as selection, position management, training, compensation. Given the many problems with appraisal, however, it often does not supply this information. Accordingly, appraisal has been called the "missing link" in HRM. Comment.

Team Activities

4. "Performance appraisal seldom improves performance." Debate, with one team taking the affirmative and one the negative position.

5. Using the "25 in 10" technique (Exhibit 0.3), discuss this statement: "The root problem in performance rating is not technical in nature."

6. David is a star performer who frequently irritates his coworkers and managers. The city's appraisal includes an interpersonal relations category, and his supervisor rates him low in this category and in other categories as well. Discuss in the context of the paradoxes of freedom and needs (Introduction).

7. Does traditional performance appraisal help or hinder other HRM functions and their paradoxes?

Individual Assignments

8. Identify three of the most difficult rater errors. How can they be dealt with?

9. Use the last examination you took in any class to discuss the reasons for using performance appraisals—and their limitations.

10. Consider the tips for conducting a performance appraisal interview. Would they have helped you—either as a manager or employee—the last time you were involved in this situation?

11. Take an "imagination break" (Exhibit 0.3) and speculate about alternative futures for personnel appraisal.

NOTES

1. The chapter subtitle is purloined from Tyer (1983).

2. Whether or not such decisions should be relative (based on comparisons between employees) or absolute (based on performance standards) is largely settled because ranking is not the equivalent of rating employees. That is, relative judgments do not reveal how well someone actually performed; thus, they are not job related. The 1978 Civil Service Reform Act, as a result, does not permit ranking methods (e.g., simple rankings from best to worst or forced-distribution techniques such as the bell-shaped curve) for evaluation of federal employees. Relative approaches, however, may be used for other, related administrative matters such as promotions, pay, and layoffs. Most jurisdictions traditionally make these judgments annually to coincide with the fiscal year, although more frequent informal assessments tied to project completion are valuable.

3. It is neither feasible nor desirable, therefore, to discuss all these instruments; to do so would be to encourage the notion that the problem of performance measurement is merely one of technique.

4. Despite all these problems, the technique has obvious intuitive appeal because traits may simply be a shorthand way of describing a person's behavior. This may explain why some psychologists contend not only that personality rating scales are reasonably valid and reliable but also that they are more acceptable to evaluators (Cascio, 1998).

5. Fondly known in the trade as "massive bowel obstruction," precisely because such a bureaucratic hyper rationalism system could, in the view of critics, never work with human beings.

6. Early examples include (a) data entry personnel who, when evaluated by the number of keystrokes, pressed the space bar while making personal calls and (b) telephone operators who, when expected to fulfill a quota in a given time period, would hang up on people with complex problems. The National Institute of Occupational Safety and Health estimates that two thirds of all video display terminals are electronically monitored (Ambrose, Alder, & Noel, 1998, p. 70). The American Management Association recently found that over three fourths of private firms use routine monitoring of their employees' activities, a figure that doubled since 1997.

7. Several comprehensive studies have found that racial and sex discrimination, once common in evaluations, are no longer pervasive (Pulakos, Oppler, White, Borman, 1989; Waldman & Avolio, 1991).

8. According to Bernardin, Cooke, and Villanova (2000), raters who score high on "agreeableness" (trust, sympathy, cooperation, politeness) are more lenient than those characterized as "conscientious" (excellence, high performance, difficult goals).

Leniency (also known as "grade inflation") in academe is "the refusal by faculty members to behave like adults, that is, like people with enough integrity to disappoint other people. It is as though some professors want to believe that everybody deserves to be first. Everybody doesn't" (Carter, 1996, p. 79).

9. The saying. "When you point your finger at me, remember that your other fingers are pointing back at you," is appropriate here.

10. The pervasiveness of this problem accounts for the use of the term "personnel appraisal," not "performance appraisal," in this chapter.

11. In the private sector, those companies that emphasized frequent feedback outperformed those that did not in all financial and productivity measures (Campbell & Garfinkel, 1996).

12. Treating employees fairly includes avoiding attempts at (a) constructive discharge (deliberately creating intolerable working conditions that compel employees to resign) and (b) retaliatory discharge (actions taken against personnel, such as demotions or denial of pay raises, when they exercise their rights under employment laws like the Civil Rights Act of 1964).

REFERENCES

Ambrose, M. L., Alder, G. S., & Noel, T. W. (1998). Electronic performance monitoring: A consideration of rights. In M. Schminke (Ed.), *Managerial ethics: Moral management of people and processes* (pp. 61–80). Mahwah, NJ: Lawrence Erlbaum.

Arthur, D. (1997). *The complete human resources writing grade.* New York: AMACOM.

Beecher, D. (2003, Winter). The next wave of civil service reform. *Public Personnel Management,* 457–474.

Bernardin, L., Cooke, M., & Villanova, P. (2000). Conscientiousness and agreeableness as predictors of rater leniency. *Journal of Applied Psychology, 85,* 232–234.

Borman, W. C. (1991). Job behavior, performance, and effectiveness. In M. D. Dennette & L. M. Hough (Eds.), *Handbook of industrial and organizational psychology* (Vol. 2, pp. 271–326). Palo Alto, CA: Consulting Psychologists.

Boudreaux, G. (1994, May/June). What TQM says about performance appraisal. *Compensation and Benefits Review,* 20–24.

Bowman, J. (2002, Fall). At-will employment in Florida government: A naked formula to corrupt public service. *WorkingUSA,* 90–102.

Campbell, R. B., & Garfinkel, L. M. (1996, June). Strategies for success in measuring performance. *HRMagazine,* 98–104.

Cardy, R. L., & Dobbins, G. H. (1994). *Performance appraisal: Alternative perspectives.* Cincinnati, OH: South-Western.

Carter, S. (1996). *Integrity.* New York: Basic Books.

Cascio, W. F. (1998). *Applied psychology in human resource management* (5th ed.). Upper Saddle River, NJ: Prentice Hall.

Cascio, W. F. (2003). *Managing human resources* (6th ed.). Boston: Irwin.

Cederblom, D., & Permerl, D. (2002). From performance appraisal to performance management: One agency's experience. *Public Personnel Management, 31*(2), 131–140.

Chappell, D., & DiMartino, V. (2000). Violence at work (2nd ed.). Washington, DC: Brookings.

Coens, T., & Jenkins, M. (2000). *Abolishing performance appraisals: Why they backfire and what to do instead.* San Francisco: Berrett-Koehler.

Coleman, F. (2001). *Ending the employment relationship without ending up in court.* Alexandria, VA: Society for Human Resource Management.

Daley, D. (1992). *Performance appraisal in the public sector: Techniques and applications.* Westport, CT: Quorum/Greenwood.

DelPo, A., & Guerin, L. (2003). *Dealing with problem employees: A legal guide.* Berkeley, CA: Nolo Press.

Deming, W. E. (1992). *The new economics.* Cambridge: MIT/CAES.

DeNisi, A., & Kluger, A. (2001). Feedback effectiveness: Can 360 appraisals be improved? *Academy of Management Executive, 14,* 14–150.

Eckes, G. (1994, November). Practical alternatives to performance appraisal. *Quality Progress,* 57–60.

Fernandez, L. (1999, May 10). Pass-fail appraisal system deserves another look. *Federal Times,* p. 15.

Firing poor performers. (2003, June). *Issues of Merit,* p. 4.

Gabris, G., & Ihrke, D. (2000). Improving employee acceptance toward performance appraisal and pay systems. *Review of Public Personnel Administration, 20*(1), 41–53.

Gomez-Mejia, L. R., Balkin, D. B., & Cardy, R. L. (2004). *Managing human resources* (4th ed.). Upper Saddle River, NJ: Prentice Hall.

Grensing-Pophal, L. (2001, March). Motivate managers to review performance. *HRMagazine,* 44–48.

Grossman, R. (2002, November). Bulletproof practices. *HRMagazine,* 34–42.

Grote, R. C. (1996). *The complete guide to performance appraisal.* New York: AMACOM.

Guffey, C., & Helms, M. (2001). Effective employees: A case of the Internal Revenue Service. *Public Personnel Management, 30*(1), 111–127.

Halachmi, A. (1995). The practice of performance appraisal. In J. Rabin, T. Vocino, W. Hildreth, & G. Miller (Eds.), *Handbook of public personnel administration* (pp. 321–355). New York: Marcel Dekker.

Hauenstein, N. (1998). Training raters to increase accuracy and usefulness of appraisals. In J. Smithers (Ed.), *Performance appraisal: State of the art in practice* (pp. 404–442). San Francisco: Jossey-Bass.

Hauser, D., & Fay, C. H. (1997). Managing and assessing employee performance. In H. Risher & C. H. Fay (Eds.), *New strategies for public pay* (pp. 185–206). San Francisco: Jossey-Bass.

London, D. (1995). Giving feedback: Source-centered antecedents and consequences of constructive and destructive feedback. *Human Resource Management Review, 5,* 159–188.

Longenecker, C. O., & Ludwig, D. (1990). Ethical dilemmas in performance appraisals revisited. *Journal of Business Ethics, 9,* 961–969.

McElveen, R. (2000, March 6). Rewards for employees reap reward for agency. *Federal Times,* pp. 1, 10.

McGregor, D. (1957, May/June). An uneasy look at performance appraisal. *Harvard Business Review,* 89–94.

Meisler, A. (2003, July). Dead man's curve. *Workforce Management,* 44–49.

Milkovich, C. T., & Wigdor, A. K. (1991). *Pay for performance: Evaluating performance appraisal and merit pay.* Washington, DC: National Academy Press.

Minor, M. (1995). *Preventing workplace violence.* Menlo Park, CA: Crisp.

Murphy, K. R., & Cleveland, J. N. (1995). *Understanding performance appraisal: Social, organizational and goal-based perspectives.* Thousand Oaks, CA: Sage.

National Performance Review. (1993). *From red tape to results: Creating a government that works better and costs less.* Washington, DC: Government Printing Office.

Nigro, L. G., & Nigro, F. A. (2000). *The new public personnel administration.* Itasca, IL: F. E. Peacock.

Palguta, J. (2001, October 1). Go beyond performance appraisal for good performance. *Federal Times,* p. 15.

Perry, J. (2003). Compensation, merit pay, and motivation. In S. Hays & R. Kearney (Eds.), *Public personnel administration: Problems and prospects* (pp. 143–153). Englewood Cliffs, NJ: Prentice Hall.

Pickett, L. (2001, January 1). *Annual fiasco.* ARDTO (Melbourne, Australia: Asia-Pacific HRD Center).

Pulakos, E. D., Oppler, S. H., White, L. A., & Borman, W. C. (1989). Examination of race and sex effects on performance ratings. *Journal of Applied Psychology, 74,* 770–780.

Riccucci, N., & Lurie, I. (2001, Spring). Employee performance evaluation in social welfare offices. *Review of Public Personnel Administration,* 27–37.

Roberts, G. (2003). Employee performance appraisal system participation: A technique that works, *Public Personnel Management, 32*(2), 89–97.

Rogers, R., & Hunter, J. (1991). Impact of management by objectives on organizational productivity. *Journal of Applied Psychology, 76,* 322–326.

Smither, J. W. (Ed.). (1998). *Performance appraisal: State of the art in practice.* San Francisco: Jossey-Bass.

Society for Human Resource Management. (2000). *Performance management survey.* Alexandria, VA: Author.

Spector, B. (2003). Human resource management at Enron: The unindicted co-conspirator. *Organizational Dynamics, 32*(2), 207–219.

Trimble, S. (1998, June 8). The postal scene: Workplace violence hits a five-year low. *Federal Times,* p. 12.

Tyer, C. B. (1983). Employee performance appraisal: A process in search of a technique. In S. W. Hays & R. C. Kearney (Eds.), *Public personnel administration* (pp. 118–136). Englewood Cliffs, NJ: Prentice Hall.

U.S. Merit Systems Protection Board. (1995). *Removing poor performers in the federal service.* Washington, DC: Author.

U.S. Merit Systems Protection Board. (1998). *Federal supervisors and strategic human resources management.* Washington, DC: Author.

U.S. Merit Systems Protection Board. (2003). *Federal workforce for the 21st century: Results from the merit principles survey 2000.* Washington, DC: Author.

U.S. Office of Personnel Management. (1998). *Dealing with workplace violence.* Washington, DC: Government Printing Office.

Waldman, D. A., & Avolio, B. J. (1991). Race effects in performance evaluations: Controlling for ability, education, and experience. *Journal of Applied Psychology, 76,* 897–911.

Wanguri, D. M. (1995). A review, an integration, and a critique of cross-disciplinary research on performance appraisals, evaluations, and feedback. *Journal of Business Communications, 32*(3), 267–293.

Wexley, K. (1986). Appraisal interview. In R. A. Berk (Ed.), *Performance assessment* (pp. 167–185). Baltimore: Johns Hopkins University Press.

Wiersma, U., & Latham, G. (1986). Practicality of behavioral observation scales, behavioral expectation scales, and trait scales. *Personnel Psychology, 39,* 619–628.

Wise, C., Clemow, B., Murray, S., Boston, S., & Bingham, L. (2005). When things go wrong. In S. Freyss (Ed.), *Human resource management in local government.* Washington, DC. International City/County Management Association.

Ziegler, M. (2004, March 1). Merit pay anxiety. *Federal Times,* pp. 1, 6.

Part III

Designing the Future

10

UNIONS AND THE GOVERNMENT

Protectors, Partners, and Punishers

The best union organizer? Bad management.

—Anonymous

After studying this chapter, you should be able to

- Appreciate the mixed views of unions held by employees and managers
- Identify differences in orientation and behavior between unions and management
- Understand paradoxes, contradictions, trends, and variations in labor-management relations
- Determine key bargaining issues that require resolution before, during, and after negotiations
- Distinguish between positive and negative behaviors at the bargaining table
- Recognize differences between the doctrine of hostility and the doctrine of harmony, as well as between traditional bargaining and cooperative problem solving

Organized labor flexed its political muscle to help defeat a controversial California ballot initiative in 1998. The proposal, Proposition 226, would have required public and private unions to get annual written permission from each worker in advance of spending dues for political purposes. Defeat of the proposal (53% to 47%) was a come-from-behind victory for labor. Their vigorous $20 million campaign helped to overcome the 2-to-1 margin of support for the proposal that existed several months prior to the election. Union staffing helped as well: 25,000 union members made phone calls and knocked on doors. Dubbed a "political buzzer beater" by the media (Bailey, 1998), the unions' successful efforts illustrate the political power of organized labor to mobilize members and leverage public policy.

Visible opposition came from the AFL-CIO, California Democratic Party, California public employee associations, and other unions. Union leaders, concerned about the declining economic power of unions in recent years, were anxious about preserving their political clout; this depended in large measure on their ability to obtain dues from their members. They detected a not-so-hidden agenda on the part of business to silence the political voice of working families. Supporters of Prop. 226 called the measure a "paycheck protection" plan (Crampton, Hodge, & Mishra, 2002). They argued that it would be fair to workers who disagreed with their union's stance on political issues and candidate endorsements. Prominent supporters then included Governor Pete Wilson, House Speaker Newt Gingrich, the California Republican Party, the National Federation of Independent Business, and others (Berke, 1998; "Union Foes," 1998).

Union leaders were concerned that a victory for anti-labor forces in California would propel "paycheck protection" onto the national agenda. According to a policy brief by the Americans for Tax Reform (1998), five states now have some form of paycheck protection— Idaho, Michigan, Ohio, Washington, and Wyoming. Ohio's law, however, is inoperative due to conflicting federal and state rulings. In 1998, paycheck protection legislation was introduced in 26 states and placed before voters in statewide initiatives in Oregon as well as California. At the national level, Congress has been unable to pass a paycheck protection bill, despite repeated attempts to do so (Crampton et al., 2002).

Protecting the political clout of unions was deemed essential in California if labor was to be able to protect members' interests in the future. To succeed in defeating the 226 proposal, unions had to "partner" with other concerned parties (public employee groups including teachers, firefighters, nurses, and police). The defeat of Prop. 226 highlights another role of unions: They are "punishers" of those whose interests run counter to those of labor. Business typically outspends unions by an 11-to-1 margin on politics, so unions battled valiantly to avoid restrictions on union political spending (Green, 1998). They succeeded in punishing the "enemies of labor" who supported the proposal by engineering a public and embarrassing defeat of the proposition.

As this case shows, unions are adept at hardball politics: They act as protectors (defending employees' rights and interests), partners (with pro-labor stakeholders), and punishers (against stakeholders perceived to be anti-labor). These three roles help explain union behavior both internally (within the employees' workplace) and externally (outside the employees' workplace).

The defeat of Proposition 226, along with some union victories in the private sector, may signal a resurgence of union strength. Improved union prospects may be linked to the national trend toward an "hourglass" economy with high-wage, high-skill jobs on one end, low-wage service jobs on the other, and a shrinking middle class in between. The Proposition 226 case also may give the mistaken impression that public sector unions are currently very strong. Although some unions in selected locales exercise considerable clout, the trend in recent years has been in the opposite direction, notwithstanding the numbers of employees who belong to unions. This chapter examines union roles in governmental labor-management relations (LMRs). It explores the mixed perspectives of employees and managers toward unions. Key paradoxes, contradictions, trends, and variations in LMRs are highlighted. Issues linked to representation and collective bargaining in government are discussed. The doctrines of hostility and harmony are contrasted, as are the practices of **traditional bargaining** and cooperative **problem solving**. In short, labor-management relations are critical to both the foundations and functions of HRM now and in the future.

DIFFERING VIEWS OF UNIONS

Most public employees and managers have definite opinions about unions, some favorable, some unfavorable. On the positive side, employees dissatisfied with their job or working conditions might see unions as a way to salve their smoldering discontent by championing workplace reforms. Unions might protect vulnerable workers and enable them to seek redress against arbitrary or capricious actions by employers. Workers may also think union membership would amplify their voice in the workplace and increase their influence with management. Vigilant unions can help keep management honest and ensure fair dealings with personnel. Collective action, especially in the labor-intensive public sector, sometimes yields results unattainable through concerted individual efforts. For example, unions have assumed leadership in supporting employee-friendly initiatives (Chapter 7) and in helping workers' stagnant salaries (Chapter 6) become more competitive. Indeed, a recent public sector survey finds that professional employees in collective bargaining states have weighted mean salaries nearly 20% higher than those in states without collective bargaining (American Federation of Teachers [AFT], 2004). Employees might also enjoy the feelings of solidarity as well as the perks (discounts, legal aid, loans, credit cards, insurance) that accompany union membership.

Negative views might dwell on union dues, unresponsive labor leaders, unflattering stereotypes associated with unions, and questionable benefits. Additional objections could include distaste at the defense unions may give to nonproductive workers, their tendency to support "one-size-fits-all" solutions, and a belief that unions are unnecessary to accomplish worker aims. Furthermore, some staff might prefer to be represented by a professional association rather than a union.

Administrators might have negative or positive views toward unions as well. Some see unions as spiking up costs, pushing down productivity, impeding organizational change, and concentrating more on advancing employee interests than on serving citizen interests. Others oppose union organizing efforts fearing that rigid, binding labor contracts alter or erode managerial rights and decrease administrative discretion and flexibility. Managers may view unions as introducing conflict, distraction, and disruption into the workplace, thus inhibiting more cooperative working relationships. Unions may be viewed as reflexively pro-employee and anti-management. Also, unions may be seen to complicate or delay policy implementation. Some managers, especially those in **right-to-work states** (where mandatory union membership is outlawed), believe that current organizational policies and procedures are fair to employees. Such managers may believe that there is no need for **meet-and-confer rights** (i.e., laws requiring agency heads to discuss, but not to settle, grievances) or bargaining rights with unions on employment matters. Those opposed to unions often combine their criticisms with proposals to privatize public services. Managers may try to inoculate employees against union appeals by quickly responding to morale concerns, establishing grievance procedures, and empowering workers. Some officials think that union organizing efforts result from management's unfair treatment of employees. Actually, proper treatment could be the best impediment to union organizing. This is the view taken by the AFL-CIO, which has identified six factors that reduce the chances for union organizing (Exhibit 10.1). Appendix A at the end of the chapter provides a list of tips to managers for dealing with unions.

Employers with positive attitudes see unions as contributing to a form of workplace democracy, enabling labor and management to join in improving conditions of employment. Such managers may want to tap employee preferences, prefer one-stop bargaining, and see unions as a way to ensure a level playing field for workers. They prefer to work with member-supported union representatives rather than disparate groups purporting to reflect worker sentiments but lacking the legitimacy of a **representation election**.

Managers and employees can have either positive or negative perceptions about each other. In some cases, this is most evident in relations between the chief executive officer and his or

✕ EXHIBIT 10.1   AFL-CIO: Factors That Reduce the Chances for Union Organizing

- A conviction by employees that the boss is not taking advantage of them
- Employees who have pride in their work
- Good performance records kept by the agency (employees feel more secure on their jobs when they know their efforts are recognized and appreciated)
- No claims of high-handed treatment (employees respect firm but fair discipline)
- No claim of favoritism that's not earned through work performance
- Supervisors who have good relationships with subordinates (the AFL-CIO maintains that this relationship of supervisors with people under them—above all—stifles organizing attempts)

SOURCE: Reprinted from "What to Do When the Union Knocks," *Nation's Business* (November, 1966), p. 107. © Copyright 1966 by *Nation's Business*.

her union leader counterpart. When stereotypes threaten to poison such relationships, it is often based on negative perceptions each participant has of the other party (see Benest & Grijalva, 2002). Exhibit 10.2 shows some of the stereotypes that might get in the way of effective relations between labor union leaders and city managers, as well as some steps that might be taken by each to enhance the relationship.

City managers and union leaders often have negative perceptions of each other:

✕ EXHIBIT 10.2   Overcoming Stereotypes and Enhancing the Chief Executive Officer-Union Leader Relationship

Union Leaders' Perceptions of Managers	Managers' Perception of Union Leaders
Managers "don't get it."	Leadership is not management oriented.
They are "political" animals.	They are insulated, isolated.
They have no backbone in the face of political controversy.	Leaders have a high need to be liked by their members.
Managers have no ethics.	They "don't do much."
Administrators have a short attention span and are "frenetic."	Union leaders are not politically savvy.
	They lack a big picture perspective.
They are shortsighted regarding labor relations.	Leaders are change resistant.
They are too concerned about quantity, not quality.	They do not promote diversity.
They are "cheap."	Leadership knows more about their service than managing people.
	They are poor collaborators.

Fifteen Ideas to Enhance the Relationship:

Ideas for both partners:

- Acknowledge difference in roles
- Put aside negative perceptions
- Get to know each other
- Look at the relationship as a partnership

Suggestions for chief executive officers:

- Acknowledge the benefit of improved public services
- Support the advocacy of union leaders
- Do not demonize the union
- Appreciate the union leader's relationship to an active union
- Reach out to public employees
- Insist that union leaders develop wider perspectives

Suggestions for the union leader:

- Educate the manager
- Pick your battles
- Distinguish between facts and perception
- Proactively become an asset to the larger organization
- Broaden the perspective of union members

SOURCE: Adapted from Benest and Grijalva (2002).

It is not surprising, then, that employees and managers react differently to unions. Working in a unionized environment prods both parties to consider how their jobs are affected by the presence of organized labor. Exhibit 10.3 lists some questions that public employees and administrators are likely to ask as they sort out their thoughts on unions, labor relations, and collective bargaining. Answers to these questions will change from one work environment to another because of the complicated nature of public sector labor-management relations and existing trends. These complications are discussed below.

PARADOXES AND CONTRADICTIONS

Like other areas of human resource management, paradoxes are plentiful and contradictions are unavoidable in labor-management relations. Some examples include the following:

- High-performance work organizations require high levels of trust and cooperative activity, but zero-sum bargaining where one side's gain is another side's loss makes this difficult
- Collective bargaining arrangements are crucial but may be incompatible with efficient merit system operations
- Union and management might profess support for productivity improvement efforts, but that support might drop off when job security is threatened

- Dispute resolution mechanisms add stability to labor-management relations, but such provisions in collective bargaining laws empower unelected arbitrators, which may diminish democratic accountability to citizens
- Unions claim to compete on a level playing field with other interest groups (e.g., taxpayer associations, privatization advocates) seeking to influence government; however, they have a distinct advantage over these groups given the union's right to bargain on wages, hours, and working conditions, as well as to lobby the legislative body for special benefits
- Managers are held accountable for making decisions and taking actions in the public interest, but the extent of public employee unionization and the provisions of a management-approved labor contract may limit their discretion
- Administrators frequently profess support for employee participation in program design and implementation, but they often prefer that such participation be conducted through nonunion channels
- Adoption of cutting-edge managerial initiatives may be impeded in unionized workplaces because of restrictive work rules codified in approved labor contracts

Three other paradoxes and problems deserve mention. First, labor-management relations in government are based on old-style, private sector conflict resolution where both sides stake

---

✂ EXHIBIT 10.3   Questions for Employees and Employers Regarding Unions, Labor-Management Relations, and Collective Bargaining

Employee

- Should I join a union?
- What do unions do?
- Will I have a voice in a union?
- Will unions act on my complaints?
- Will unions protect my rights?
- Will unions affect my relationship with management?
- What is the downside of a union?
- Does collective bargaining affect me?
- Will unions effectively represent my interests?
- What should unions push for in negotiations?
- Should I participate in a work stoppage?

Employer

- How will a union affect my organization?
- How do unions affect the way employees work?
- Should I support or resist unionization?
- Will relationships with unions be cooperative or adversarial?
- Can I work effectively with union leaders?
- Do I have confidence in management's negotiating team?
- What should management seek to have in a contract?
- Will management prerogatives be protected in negotiations?
- Will contract provisions limit my managerial discretion?
- How will employee grievances be handled?
- How will contract or grievance disputes be resolved?

✕ EXHIBIT 10.4   Government Union Membership and Representation, 2001, 2002 (in thousands)

In Thousands	Total Employed	Members of Unions		Represented by Unions	
		Total	Percentage	Total	Percentage
2002 gov workers	19,587	7,351	37.5	8,223	42.0
Federal	3,296	1,063	32.3	1,244	37.7
State	5,706	1,758	30.8	2,005	35.1
Local	10,585	4,530	42.8	4,974	47.0
2001 gov workers	19,340	7,186	37.2	8,086	41.8
Federal	3,324	1,046	31.5	1,221	36.8
State	5,729	1,737	30.3	1,980	34.6
Local	10,287	4,403	42.8	4,885	47.5
2002 private	102,419	8,756	8.5	9,548	9.3
2001 private	103,142	9,201	8.9	10,028	9.7

SOURCE: Data are from http://www.bls.gov/bls/newsrels.htm (accessed in March 2003).

out adversarial positions before negotiations commence. The traditional framework underlying the labor-management relationship actually undermines it. A new style for managing conflict would turn this old process on its head and put greater emphasis on cooperation, with labor and management representatives talking first and drafting specific policies last. Experiments in labor-management relations using this newer approach show promising results (Fretz & Walsh, 1998; Parsons, Belcher, & Jackson, 1998).

Second is the **free rider** problem that is based on the distinction between union membership and union representation: Employees may benefit from unions without being members. Membership figures are often much smaller than representation figures (i.e., employees belong to bargaining units but fail to join the union). For example, in 2003 the American Federation of Government Employees (AFGE) had 222,000 dues-paying members, but it represented approximately 600,000 employees. This represents a free-rider rate of 64%. Thus, in many **open shop** governmental settings, workers may be the beneficiaries of union-sponsored initiatives without joining the union or paying dues.[1] Free riders avoid the pain but receive the gain from union efforts.[2] Overall trends in union membership and representation in the federal, state, and local government sectors are shown in Exhibit 10.4. The two columns represent membership versus the number of employees represented by the unions. (These data reflect a less pronounced free rider problem than the AFGE example above).

Third is the paradox relating to the inherent value differences between unions and management. Although there was some movement toward greater cooperation, a number of incompatibilities still existed between organized labor and management in the 1990s (see Exhibit 10.5).

✖ EXHIBIT 10.5   Union-Management Value Differences

Union	Management
Egalitarian—few distinctions between members, all are treated the same	Hierarchical—more distinctions between people, levels of control, chain of command
Democratic decision making by members	Decision making by few
Security through mutual protection, "an injury to one is an injury to all"	Security based on competition, each gets what each deserves, individualism
Seniority is basis for deciding among members	Performance is basis for deciding among members
Goals: job security, quality of work life, safety, better wages and benefits	Goals: productivity, approval from voters, low tax rates, customer satisfaction
Past practice and precedent control actions and decisions	Pragmatic—what works best now

As noted in this exhibit, unions and management differ in the distinctions between organization members, involvement in decision making, the basis for security, allocation of rewards, goals, and the basis for action (these differences will become more apparent below). The next section fleshes out the context of public sector labor relations and highlights some of the trends and variations that distinguish it from the private sector—patterns in labor-management relations that evolved in the business sphere were later adapted to the government arena.

Trends and Variations

Union membership has been steadily declining since the 1950s in business and industry, despite fluctuating growth spurts in public sector union membership. Overall, organized labor's share of the workforce dropped from 14.5% in 1996 to 12.9% in 2003, down considerably from 1954 when unions represented 35% of the nation's workers. From 2002 to 2003, the number of workers belonging to a union dropped by 369,000. Exhibit 10.6 reports the percentage of union membership in the private and public sectors for the period from 1990 to 2003; total union membership was 15.8 million in 2003. Note that in 2003, 37.2% of public sector employees belonged to unions, contrasted with only 8.2% of private employees (Bureau of Labor Statistics [BLS], 2004). Thus, nearly 4 in 10 government workers are union members compared with less than 1 in 10 private sector workers. The unionization rate among government workers has varied little since 1983. Currently, government workers account for 45.6% of union membership in the United States. Exhibit 10.7 reports membership in selected public sector unions in 1997 and 2003 and provides their Web sites.

There are several reasons for the drop in private sector union membership. Among the most frequently mentioned is the growth of high-tech industries (where unions are harder to organize), geographic shifts (from Frostbelt to Sunbelt), and changes in the workforce (from blue collar to pink collar, Hispanics, Asians, and African Americans) and the workplace (downsizing, outsourcing). Other factors include management opposition in representation elections, replacement of striking workers, and reluctance by unions to push organizing drives in an era

⊠ EXHIBIT 10.6 Union Memebership in Public and Private Sectors, 1990–2003

Year	Public (all levels)	Private
1990	36.5	11.9
1991	36.9	11.7
1992	36.6	11.4
1993	37.7	11.1
1994	38.7	10.8
1995	37.7	10.3
1996	37.6	10.0
1997	37.2	9.8
1998	37.5	9.5
1999	37.3	9.4
2000	37.5	9.0
2001	37.2	8.9
2002	37.5	8.5
2003	37.2	8.2

SOURCES: Bureau of Labor Statistics (1998, 2003); Council of State Governments (1998); U.S. Bureau of the Census (2002).

when gains in union jobs can be erased by losses. Stanley Aronowitz (1998) attributes declining membership to the tendency of unions to cater to the least needy (steel and auto workers) rather than the neediest (farm and hotel workers), the self-interested parochialism of union leaders, and misplaced attention on bargaining and grievance processing rather than organizing. Thomas J. Donahue, president of the U.S. Chamber of Commerce, puts a different spin on the reasons for declining membership: "Improved employer-employee relationships, the fading appeal of labor's 'big government' politics, and persistent tales of union corruption" ("U.S. Labor," 1998, p. 7A). Whatever the explanation, public sector unions have done a better job of **maintaining membership** than their private sector counterparts.

The rise in public sector union membership has occurred in the last four decades with the largest growth spurt in the 1960s and 1970s, moderate growth in the 1980s, and flat growth in the 1990s and early 2000s. In 1960, there were 900,000 public sector union members (penetration of 10.8%). By 1980, government unions were the largest department in the AFL-CIO, and two out of five public employees had union representation. The overwhelming majority of all public sector union members are currently at the state and local level (85.5%), not at the federal level (14.5%) (BLS, 2003). This represents a remarkable "flip-flop" from 1950 when more members were federal (69%) as opposed to state and local government employees (Orzechowski & Marlow, 1995). The following are some of the reasons for growth:

- Changes in public policy (executive orders, statutory laws)
- Vigorous union organizing efforts
- The rise of social movements (civil rights, antiwar, feminism)
- The success of various job actions (slowdowns, strikes)
- Lagging wages

✖ EXHIBIT 10.7   U.S. Membership in Selected Public Sector Unions: 1997 to 2003 (in thousands)

Labor Organizations	1997	2003	Web Site
American Federation of Government Employees	210	222	www.afge.org
American Federation of State, County & Municipal Employees	1,300	1,400	www.afscme.org
American Federation of Teachers	940	1,200	www.aft.org
American Postal Workers Union	350	366	www.apwu.org
International Association of Firefighters	225	260	www.iaff.org
International Union of Police Officers	80	NA	www.iupa.org
National Association of Letter Carriers	315	304.7	www.nalc.org
National Association of Postal Supervisors	36	36	www.naps.org
National Education Association	2,300	2,700	www.nea.org
National Federation of Federal Employees	150	NA	www.nffe.org
National Fraternal Order of Police	270	308	www.grandlodgefop.org
National Rural Letter Carriers Association	NA	96	www.nrlca.org
National Treasury Employees Union	150	155	www.nteu.org
Service Employees' International Union	1,110	1,500	www.seiu.org

SOURCES: Bureau of Labor Statistics, AFL-CIO, and individual unions (personal communication).

- Rising public sector employment
- Inexperience of government employers in resisting early union organizing campaigns
- Increasing threats to employee job security

An example of efforts to organize and represent younger public workers is found in Exhibit 10.8.

✖ EXHIBIT 10.8   Organizing Younger Workers: Teaching Assistants

---

The Lion Tamer School of Management: Keep them well fed and never let them know that all you've got is a chair and a whip.

—Anonymous

Organized labor has targeted younger workers in recent membership drives. Labor-sponsored surveys of young workers' concerns reveal that they focus on wage rates, health care, and retirement security (Brackey, 1999). They worry about the cost of living, high debt levels, job discrimination, and availability of affordable housing. The difficulty involved in gaining union victories with these workers is illustrated in the efforts to win union recognition and bargaining rights for graduate students who work as teaching assistants (TAs) in public universities. The 16-year battle on behalf of TAs in California is the most recent example.

In March 1999, the University of California reluctantly recognized the results of graduate student union elections. This occurred only after a 4-day strike on all eight teaching campuses simultaneously. Representation elections were held on UC campuses such as UCLA and Berkeley, resulting in local affiliates of the United Auto Workers representing TAs. The Coalition of Graduate Employee Unions estimates that 20,000 of the nation's 100,000 graduate assistants are part of a union.

Opposition to union representation is based on contentions that teaching assistants are more like apprentices than employees, that unionization drives would raise the cost of higher education, and that graduate students aren't eligible to organize. Opponents further argue that unionization would replace a flexible/collegial system with an industrial/adversarial one and that TAs have no legal rights to bargain. Others opposed to unionization fear that it would result in pay stagnation, rigid working hours, corruption of the faculty-student mentoring relationship, and strikes. The California Public Employees Relations Board (PERB) rejected these claims and concerns. Supporters of bargaining rights for teaching assistants argue that they carry a heavy portion of the teaching load (an estimated 60% of undergraduate instruction in the UC system) as a result of university downsizing and cost cutting and that they are like unprotected corporate "temp" workers. They maintain that unions will help them achieve reduced workloads/fees; increased salary/stipends; improved health benefits, working conditions, and job security; and more effective grievance procedures.

Although some successes have been achieved in organizing younger workers such as teaching assistants, union victories are matched by union losses; and when victories do occur, they are hard fought and follow prolonged struggles. It took 16 years, numerous work stoppages, intervention by influential state legislators, and considerable agitation to achieve labor peace, recognition, and bargaining rights for UC's teaching assistants. Nevertheless, it is easier for public university teaching assistents to unionize because state labor laws govern public universities, whereas private universities fall under the jurisdiction of the National Labor Relations Board. The NLRB has ruled in the past that students who work as part of their education do not meet the definition of "employees" under prevailing law and therefore lack the right to organize. Graduate students at several private universities have waged a bitter, decade-long battle challenging this interpretation, but it was upheld in a 2004 NLRB decision.

SOURCES: Bacon (1999); Bernstein (1998); Brackey (1999); Folmar (1999); Greenhouse and Arenson (2004); Palmaffy (1999); Sanchez (1996).

✖ **EXHIBIT 10.9**   Five Major Pieces of Private Sector Labor Legislation From 1926 to 1959

1926: Railway Labor Act—grants rail workers unionization and bargaining rights. Also covers resolution of disputes with, and interpretations of, any negotiated contract.

1932: Norris-LaGuardia Act—restricts injunctions and repudiates "yellow-dog" contracts.

1935: Wagner Act—also known as National Labor Relations Act, or NLRA, gives all workers the right to unionize and collectively bargain, lists unfair labor practices, describes union certification elections, and creates the National Labor Relations Board to watch over it all.

1947: Taft-Hartley Act—amended the NLRA and created the Federal Mediation and Conciliation Service to aid in dispute resolution; provides emergency procedures, lists unfair union labor practices, and gives states the right to pass right-to-work laws.

1959: Landrum-Griffin Act—also known as the Labor-Management Reporting and Disclosure Act; requires unions to file financial and trusteeship reports and to set employee rights, including the ability of union members to attend meetings and nominate/vote for candidates.

Not only do membership trends vary between the two sectors, but labor law does as well. Public sector labor law has lagged behind developments in the private sector, but it draws on several concepts first codified in private sector legislation, so some familiarity with the earlier legislation (summarized in Exhibit 10.9) is important as a foundation. Although public sector labor relations are an adaptation from the private model, there are significant differences that need clarification (see Exhibit 10.10) before introducing public sector policy developments in labor-management relations.

Turning to policy, at the local government level, New York City Mayor Robert F. Wagner Jr. issued Executive Order 49 in 1958 recognizing collective bargaining with unions, establishing grievance procedures, and setting procedures for bargaining unit determination and exclusive representation (see Aronowitz, 1998). The evolution of public policy dealing with federal public sector legislation began 4 years later with a series of executive orders in the Kennedy (EO 10988), Nixon (EO 11491), and Ford (EO 11838) administrations. These were then brought together and amplified with the passage of Title VII in the **Civil Service Reform Act (CSRA) of 1978** during the Carter administration.

This provision gives federal employees (general schedule and wage grade) the right to form unions and bargain collectively. It created the **Federal Labor Relations Authority (FLRA)** to oversee federal labor-management relations, disallowed union security arrangements, restricted the scope of bargaining (e.g., excludes wages and benefits), and banned strikes. The Office of Personnel Management's Office of Labor-Management Relations assists federal agencies with contract administration and technical advice.

President Bill Clinton issued an executive order in 1993 establishing a National Partnership Council to further empower federal employee unions to work cooperatively with management in identifying problems and designing solutions to improve service delivery. President George W. Bush revoked the executive order and dissolved the council in early 2001, reflecting his administration's more pro-management, pro-agency philosophy.

Bush's action together with civil service reforms in the Departments of Defense and Homeland Security (see Exhibit 10.11), outsourcing initiatives, cutbacks, pay-for-performance plans, and concern about reducing the scope of bargaining and employee appeal rights, had at least one

---

⚡ EXHIBIT 10.10   Public and Private Sector Differences

---

1. Benefits
   - *Public sector.* Many nonbargained benefits are provided via civil service statutes (e.g., employee grievance procedures, health/life insurance, sick leave, holidays), and the scope of negotiations is narrow (e.g., pay and benefits for federal employees are excluded as bargaining topics).
   - *Private sector.* The scope of negotiations is broad, with most terms and conditions of employment open for negotiation.

2. Multilateral Bargaining
   - *Public sector.* Dispersed authority means bargaining involves more players (e.g., negotiators, public/taxpayers/media, elected officials, courts, other third parties) and more complex approval processes.
   - *Private sector.* Bargaining is a two-party process resulting in agreements that each party's policy body ratifies.

3. Monopoly Versus Competition
   - *Public sector.* Government is a monopoly and generally not subject to market forces, making product/service (e.g., police, fire) substitution difficult.
   - *Private sector.* Businesses are subject to market forces, and consumers can shop for price/availability of desired goods/services.

4. The Strike
   - *Public sector.* Strikes occur, but they are often illegal and strikers/unions can be punished.
   - *Private sector.* Strikes are legal and a legitimate tool when negotiations reach impasse.

5. Sovereign Versus Free Contract
   - *Public sector.* The **doctrine of sovereignty** maintains that government has responsibility to protect all societal interests; therefore, it is inappropriate to require it to share power with interest groups (e.g., unions in negotiations) or dilute managerial rights. Similarly, the **special responsibility theory** maintains that public employees hold critical positions in society and therefore should not be permitted to strike.
   - *Private sector.* The sovereignty doctrine does not apply.

6. Political Versus Economic
   - *Public sector.* Decisions have economic impacts but are based on political criteria.
   - *Private sector.* Decisions can have political impacts, but they are economic decisions.

SOURCES: Adapted from Coleman (1990, pp. 8–12); Denholm (1997, pp. 32–33).

---

federal union leader claiming, "This administration is attacking the civil service, period" ("AFGE's 'Fighting Spirit,'" 2003). As the quote from a Department of Defense logistician indicates (see Exhibit 10.12), some employees sense that they are losing their leverage on this and other issues and that they are increasingly vulnerable. George Nesterczuk, vice president of Global USA, a consulting firm, supports the Bush initiative claiming that under Clinton's

---

✖ EXHIBIT 10.11   Civil Service Reform and Unions in the Defense Department

---

A 30-union coalition is mobilizing to oppose new Defense Department personnel rules that will affect hundreds of thousands of civilian defense workers, reduce union influence, and modify the structure of labor-management relations in existence for 45 years. Congress passed the 2004 National Defense Authorization Act, which enabled DOD to rewrite personnel policies and labor-management rules. The proposed changes included the following:

- Reducing the number of workers eligible to be in a bargaining unit
- Creating a pay-for-performance system
- Removing seniority and veterans preference in layoff decisions
- Removing prohibitions against unfair labor practices
- Allowing unions to "consult" on personnel changes, but absent agreement, authorizing management to act unilaterally
- Substituting in-house review of employee appeals and union grievances in place of third-party reviews
- Barring from collective bargaining all employees who must be certified to work (i.e., those in professional occupations)
- Changing the criteria for employees to join or leave unions
- Instituting national collective bargaining in place of local bargaining

Supporters of the changes argue that management currently negotiates with an unwieldy number of recognized bargaining units (1,300), that it is difficult to achieve its objective of converting tens of thousands of jobs from military to civilian status, that the intent is not to rescind collective bargaining rights, and that a more agile, flexible, and responsive system is needed. Union leaders view the proposed changes as union busting that would reduce workplace protections for employees, harbor mistrust, replace bilateralism with top-down decision making, and set the precedent for dismantling collective bargaining rights in other agencies. Indeed, 2 weeks after DOD proposed its rules, the Department of Homeland Security announced a similar set of proposals.

SOURCE: Adapted from International Brotherhood of Electrical Workers (2004), Kaufman (2004), and Losey (2004).

---

partnership policy: "Unions had the power to run around management to get what they wanted" (Young, 2001, p. 17). Management and labor have had to seek a new footing in their relationship following the dissolution of the National Partnership Council and have had to recognize the new leeway given to agencies in establishing their own labor relations philosophies.

A bewildering array of federal, state, and local laws, regulations, court decisions, ordinances, and attorneys' general opinions shape government labor-management relations. The federal system for labor-management relations is different from the state or local system, and the local arrangements are different, in many instances, from the state. Local level developments reflect considerable variation; however, the vast majority of serious labor issues arise in a relatively narrow range of local government unions associated with police, fire, sanitation, and education. At the state and local levels, public policy dealing with public employee labor relations is difficult to summarize; nevertheless, Exhibit 10.13 provides a brief sketch of some key features of state public employee labor relations laws.

✖ EXHIBIT 10.12   Ruminations of a Department of Defense Logistician

As a Department of Defense logistician, I was affected by the 2002 port closures on the west coast because several suppliers shipping directly to U.S. troops could not move their material through the ports. As we dismantle government capability and outsource, these are the type of strategic concerns that must be addressed. Material going to a war zone sat idle due to a compensation and automation issue. When material was shipped from government locations on government-leased vessels, federal employees were always there, although they made nowhere near the $117,000 annual salary these commercial dock workers make.

In the federal sector, we have no leverage. We abandoned the right to collectively bargain and strike. We surrender first amendment rights to criticize (whistleblowers are still scorned). We postpone current remuneration (33% less than commercial), betting on a retirement system that is constantly under assault as "too generous." Our health insurance contribution went up this year an average of 13% and the raise will be 4.1%. Our deputy commander is an SES making about $120,000 per year. The organization has almost 3000 employees and has revenue of $6 billion per year. This places it in the Fortune 500. Are there any CEOs out there making $120,000?

Government employees have had a bull's eye painted on their backs for the past several decades. We are political footballs and the closest thing to indentured servitude going.

SOURCE: Private communication to author.

✖ EXHIBIT 10.13   Key Features of Public Sector Bargaining Laws

Responsibility to bargain: bargaining in good faith, the public's role and right to know

The bargaining team: selection of representatives for the team, and the qualification, certification, representation, and obligations of the team

Collective bargaining relationship/agreement: union, employer, and individual rights under the agreement; unfair labor practices; legal status of the agreement; and grievance procedures

Union rights: focused on the right to strike, picket, protest, or, where striking is prohibited, a right to impasse resolution, mediation, fact finding, or arbitration

Civil rights: legal processes, employer-employee discrimination, and regulation of partisan political activities

Government obligations: creation of administrative instruments to administer labor laws and manage/oversee labor relations in public sector employment

---

Another trend deals with labor-management relations themselves. The legal right of public employees to strike is hotly debated (see Exhibit 10.15). In recent years, there has been a decrease in *work stoppages* (strikes) and an increase in the use of third-party mediators. There were 19 major work stoppages in 2002: 16 in the private sector and 3 in the public sector (BLS, 2003).[3] The decline in government work stoppages may be attributable to growing anti-tax, anti-union, and anti-government public sentiments, the discharge of air traffic controllers by President Reagan in 1981 (see Exhibit 10.16), employer practice of hiring permanent replacements for striking workers, and increased use of alternative dispute resolution mechanisms. Nonetheless, strike rights for some state employees have been established in 10 states, and in four other states judicial rulings have upheld strike rights for pubic workers (Kearney, 2003). Use of alternative dispute resolution mechanisms has occurred at all levels of government (e.g., Dibble, 1997).

✕ EXHIBIT 10.14   Arguments Opposing and Supporting Public Sector Strikes

Opponents to public sector strikes argue the following:

- Sovereignty rests with the American people, and public workers should not be entitled to strike because it would violate the public's will and undercut governmental authority.
- Strikes pervert the policy process by bestowing special privileges on unions that other interest groups do not have.
- Public services are monopolistic, and labor market constraints to hold down labor costs are absent where strikes are allowed.
- Essential services are curtailed in strikes, posing a threat to public health and safety.

Supporters of the legal right of public employees to strike contend the following:

- Not all public services are essential, and the disruption of government services seldom seriously threatens public health and safety.
- Alternatives to government services are frequently available from the private sector.
- Denying the right to strike to public employees but allowing it for private sector workers performing identical work is inequitable.
- Work stoppages will occur regardless of legal strike bans.
- The incidence of strikes is no greater in states that permit work stoppages than it is in those that prohibit them.

SOURCES: Adapted from Kearney (1998a, 1998b).

✕ EXHIBIT 10.15   PATCO Strike: Misguided and Overreaching Strategy

The Professional Air Traffic Controllers Organization (PATCO) strike was a watershed development in federal labor-management relations in the 1980s. The strike resulted in 11,400 air traffic controllers losing their jobs, PATCO's decertification and eventual dissolution, and Ronald Reagan's signaling to public employers that they should stand firm and take a hard line against unions.

The union had been involved in rocky, bitter bargaining with the Federal Aviation Administration (FAA) from the late 1960s to the early 1980s. These negotiations took place on a range of issues despite restrictions on the scope of negotiations under Executive Order 10988. PATCO demands included substantial salary hikes, improved overtime pay rates, better night shift differentials, and more generous severance pay. Other demands were for greater union involvement in determining operational/safety policies, a shorter workweek, and lucrative early retirement plans. The FAA resisted union proposals. After unsuccessful haggling with the FAA, union members voted overwhelmingly in favor of an illegal strike in 1981.

President Reagan gave strikers an ultimatum: Return to work within 48 hours or lose your jobs. PATCO did not comply. The president then delivered on his threat, dismissing and ultimately establishing a process for replacing strikers. In the end, union leadership and strategy was faulted for failing to garner public sympathy, framing the issues too narrowly, discounting the public interest, overreaching, and making insufficient effort to shore up support for the strike from AFL-CIO affiliates.

SOURCES: Coleman (1990, pp. 52–53); Devinatz (1997, pp. 105–106); Northrup (1984).

✂ EXHIBIT 10.16   Selected Legal or Contextual Factors Regarding Unions

Relationship Between the Parties

Meet-and-Confer—characterized by inequality between partners (labor and management); employer selects agenda items and is not obligated to bargain; management retains virtually all rights and exercises ultimate authority; and outcomes are nonbinding and typically skewed to management's perspective.

Collective Bargaining—the rights of employees to form and join unions for bargaining purposes are recognized; an administrative agency oversees bargaining unit determination and establishes administrative procedures; unions with majority support become exclusive bargaining agents; employers are obligated to bargain; selected management rights are protected; and provisions provide for union security, impasse procedures, and unfair labor practices.

Union Security Provisions

Union Shop—Employee must join the representing union after a certain number of days (e.g., 30–90 days) specified in the collective bargaining agreement. This is rare in government.

Agency Shop—Employee is not required to join the union, but most contribute a service charge to cover collective bargaining, the grievance process, and arbitration costs. Nonpayment can result in job loss. Such arrangements are infrequent in the public sector.

Maintenance of Membership—Employee is obligated to maintain union membership in the representing union once affiliated during the life of the contract. Withdrawal may lead to forfeiture of job.

Dues Check-off—Employee may select payroll deduction option to pay union dues to representing union.

Administrative Arrangements

Public Employee Relations Boards (PERBs)—state administrative agencies typically charged with determining appropriate bargaining units, overseeing certification elections, and resolving unfair labor practices. At the federal level, the three-member Federal Labor Relations Authority (FLRA) performs PERB functions. In the private sector, administrative responsibilities rest with the National Labor Relations Board (NLRB).

Unfair Labor Practices (ULPs)

Unfair Employer Practices—interfering with a public employee's right to form or join a union, discriminating against public employees because of union membership, dominating a labor organization, or violating a collective bargaining agreement.

Unfair Union Practices (UUPs)—denying union membership because of race, color, creed, and so forth; interfering with, restraining, or coercing (a) employees in exercising their statutory rights or (b) employers regarding the exercise of employee rights; refusing to meet with the public employer and to bargain in good faith; or interfering with the work performance or productivity of a public employee.

Impasse Procedures

Mediation—a dispute resolution procedure that relies on a neutral third party who attempts to facilitate communication and bring the parties together to reach an agreement.

(Continued)

(Continued)

Fact-Finding—a dispute resolution procedure that relies on a neutral third party who conducts hearings, researches contentious issues, and makes nonbinding recommendations for consideration.

Arbitration—a dispute resolution procedure that relies on a neutral third party who reviews the facts and makes determinations that are binding on both sides.

Arbitration takes many forms:

- **Interest arbitration**—refers to arbitration dealing with the terms of the negotiated contract; it can be voluntary or compulsory.
- **Grievance arbitration**—or rights arbitration, to resolve outstanding disputes regarding employee grievances.
- **Final-offer arbitration**—the arbitrator's decision is restricted to the position taken by one or the other of the parties—this can include selection of a position taken by one side or the other on all issues taken together (by package) or selection on an issue-by-issue basis.
- **Med-arb**—requires an arbitrator to begin with mediation, settle as many disputes as feasible, and move to arbitration only on items that remain contentious.

REPRESENTATION AND COLLECTIVE BARGAINING

National labor laws that govern **collective bargaining** and representation rights for federal and private sector employees do not pertain to state and local government employees. State and local public employees' bargaining and representational rights are enumerated wherever authorized by state law and, less frequently, by local ordinance or executive order. Currently, many states authorize collective bargaining for public employees. Some states restrict coverage to certain occupational groups (e.g., public safety, teachers). Other states lack collective bargaining statutes for their state and local government employees; however, in some instances executive orders or local ordinances confer rights to bargain or have representation (AFL-CIO, 1997).

Collective bargaining is the process whereby labor and management representatives meet to set terms and conditions of employment for employees in a bargaining unit. Certain legal factors help to frame bargaining and union-management relationships. They are also influenced by and help to determine the strength of public unions. Identification of these factors is a necessary prelude to painting a portrait of the bargaining process. These include the nature of the bilateral relationship, the type of union security provisions, the kind of administrative arrangements, the range of **unfair labor practices**, and the existence of dispute resolution or impasse procedures. These legal distinctions are clarified in Exhibit 10.16.

The bargaining process itself is shaped by these factors. It typically unfolds in three phases: organizing to bargain, bargaining, and administering the contract. Each phase is characterized by distinct activities, discussed in turn below.

Organizing to Bargain

Collective bargaining, as traditionally practiced, does not occur until (a) an appropriate bargaining unit is determined, (b) a representation election is held, (c) an exclusive bargaining agent is certified, and (d) a bargaining team is selected. Each step is necessary to determine who will engage in negotiations. **Bargaining unit determination** identifies whom a union or other association in negotiation sessions will represent. An administrative agency, a statute, a union, or an arbitrator makes such determinations. Specifically, the FLRA makes unit determinations at the federal level, and **Public Employee Relations Boards (PERBs)** do so in many states. The criteria used in determining the composition of the bargaining unit varies state by state, but the following NLRB guidelines are typically followed:

- Community of interest—common job factors, for example, similar position classifications, duties, skills, working conditions, kinds of work, or geographic locations
- Bargaining history—prior patterns of negotiation, representation, or labor-management relations
- Unit size—units that are too small can absorb too much bargaining representatives, time, create unwieldy fragmentation, and create a **whipsaw effect** (gains by one union might be used to justify benefits for another); those that are too large may lack cohesion and a community of interest
- Efficiency of operations—bargaining structures may impede efficiency if they are a poor "fit" with existing human resource policies and procedures
- Exclusion of supervisory/confidential employees—this is predicated on the idea that there is a potential conflict of interest in a unit that combines supervisors (management) with employees

Election is the next step in this phase of the process. Identification of who is to represent the union in negotiations need not involve an election; the employer may choose to voluntarily recognize a union for this purpose. More typically, a *representation election* is held. Although either the employer or the union may request such an election, the union usually must "make a showing" that a certain percentage (e.g., 30%) of workers in the unit want representation. As the unfair labor practices (ULPs) in Exhibit 10.16 indicate, certain management tactics (intimidation, force, coercion) are prohibited during a representation election. Unions must receive a majority vote in a secret ballot election to achieve recognition as the exclusive bargaining agent for workers in the unit. State laws vary regarding the definition of "majority vote" in a representation election. It can mean either a majority of votes cast (most common) or an absolute majority of eligible bargaining unit members without regard to the number of votes actually cast.

The actual **certification** as the appropriately constituted exclusive **bargaining agent** for the unit is done by the relevant administrative agency (FLRA, PERB, or equivalent). Certification status may be rescinded if workers become sufficiently dissatisfied, if the agent violates the bargaining law (e.g., decertification of the Professional Air Traffic Controllers by the FLRA in 1981), or if another union "makes sufficient showing" of support to challenge the exclusive bargaining agent. In such cases, a decertification election modeled on the same procedures described above is held to determine who, if anyone, should represent employees in the unit.

Selection of the bargaining team is a crucial task. There is considerable variation in bargaining team composition depending on the level of government in question, the extent of professionalism existing within the labor relations office (if such an office exists), and the preferences of the labor and management leadership groups. Each side designates a chief negotiator. This may be a professional labor negotiator, a labor lawyer, or a savvy manager or union leader. In local government, the management team may include the chief administrative officer (city/county manager), someone from the legal office, or an HR and/or budget professional, among others. Top union leaders often handpick their most rhetorically gifted and politically astute spokespersons as negotiators. Other stakeholders (public, media) may attend or comment on negotiations in some states (e.g., Florida, Minnesota, and North Dakota), but this is more the exception than the rule.

Bargaining

Once the stage has been set and the cast determined, the curtain goes up on bargaining, although the audience is often restricted to the key participants. The great drama is usually reserved for the final scene, when negotiations become most heated. In the beginning, the more mundane preparations occupy center stage. Getting prepared involves studying the lines of the existing contract, collecting and analyzing relevant comparative data (wages, salaries, benefits), and sorting through bargaining priorities. Bargaining strategy needs to be clarified. Opening gambits need to be scripted and choreographed differently from the compelling scenes in the last act. The costs and benefits of alternative bargaining proposals need to be weighed carefully. The logistical details of where, when, how, and how long to conduct bargaining sessions require attention, as does the agenda for each meeting.

Legal and behavioral considerations come into play here. Two legal requirements in particular require attention: Bargaining must be conducted in good faith, and the scope of negotiations is often prescribed. Although the term "good faith" is subject to multiple interpretations, the public sector has relied heavily on NLRB rulings and private sector case law to determine its meaning. *Good faith* is perhaps best understood by considering examples of its opposite. Employer negotiators who reject union proposals but advance no counterproposals, undermine or bypass the union, schedule meetings arbitrarily, or fail to respond to a union request for a bargaining session are not dealing in good faith (Baker, 1996). A bargaining checklist and behavior observation sheet is presented in Appendix B at the end of the chapter. The negative behaviors by bargaining team members shown in section A are contrasted with the positive behaviors listed in section B. Although some of the section A examples may be "bargaining as usual" rather than legal violations of the "good faith" requirement, they are likely to be off-putting to the other side, and the temptation might be for the opposite team to respond in kind, thereby escalating the hostility.

The scope of negotiations is often addressed in the law but contentious in practice. Conflict arises because unions want more "perks" and want to haggle over a broad range of issues. "What does labor want?" When the press asked this question to Samuel Gompers, the first president of the American Federation of Labor, he began by responding "More . . ." and since then, his entire comment has been edited down to that single word. Gompers's unabridged response was, "We want *more schoolhouses* and less jails, *more books* and less arsenals, *more learning* and less vice, *more constant work* and less crime, *more leisure* and less greed, *more justice* and less revenge." If unions want "more," management, intent on preserving its prerogatives, often wants to give "less" and takes a more restrictive, narrow view of what is negotiable. Vague statutory language frequently specifying the scope to include "wages, hours and conditions of employment" fuels the debate over the legitimate array of discussable items. Issues fall (not always neatly) into three categories:

- Mandatory—"must do" matters that fall within the porous language of "wages, hours and terms, or other terms and conditions of employment"; however, wages and hours of federal employees are excluded from bargaining
- Permissive—"may do" subjects about which the negotiating team may bargain if they opt to (i.e., they are neither mandatory nor prohibited), but disagreements are especially heated regarding the phrase "other terms and conditions of employment"
- Prohibited—"can't do" topics that authorizing statutes, administrative agencies (PERBs or FLRA), or the courts have determined are not subject to bargaining or beyond the employer's authority to bargain (e.g., civil service laws, organizational mission)

Mandatory subjects can be pushed to impasse; neither team is required to concede. One novel "permissive" topic from the private sector that Briggs and Siegele (1994) urge on public sector bargainers is a 13-point "ethics standards clause" for inclusion in collective bargaining agreements that would formalize a commitment to ethical behavior and discourage attempts to pursue unethical agendas incompatible with employee or organizational interests.

Principled negotiations, or integrated bargaining, sometimes characterize proceedings at the bargaining table; other times distributive bargaining prevails. In distributive bargaining, hostility is high, relationships are conflictual, bargaining parties are viewed as adversaries, and one side's gain is another side's loss. Integratived bargaining is less prevalent and more consensus oriented. It stresses identification of common ground, focuses on cooperative problem solving, and thrives in an open trusting environment (Walton & McKersie, 1965). Fisher and Ury's (1981) well-known version of integrative bargaining (also known as principled negotiations) lays out a list of suggested guidelines:

- Separate the people from the problem
- Focus on interests, not positions
- Invent options for mutual gain
- Insist on use of objective criteria

Where both parties to negotiations are committed to pursuing partnership strategies, such approaches find fertile ground to take root; where more abrasive and conflictual relations prevail, principled bargaining may lack the nurturance necessary to bear fruit.

Prevailing economic conditions influence bargaining strategy. In recent years, belt tightening, downsizing, and privatizing have led to two related trends: concession bargaining and **productivity bargaining**. Negotiators on the management team are responding to taxpayer concerns that sometimes require "give-backs" from unions or promises to "do more with less" (heightened worker productivity in the future). Unions in such environments have had to switch adroitly from offense to defense, fighting a rear-guard action to preserve past bargaining victories or to protect their flanks from onerous threats (e.g., reductions in force, two-tier wage structures, benefit copayments). Management may demand greater productivity (e.g., incentive-based plans) or changes in performance-impeding work rules (e.g., staffing ratios). Unions may agree with such changes to avoid concessions on less palatable alternatives. Organized labor's productivity-related demands might include worker autonomy, flextime, or gainsharing (Salzman, 1994).

As labor relations have become more formalized, there has been greater reliance on written agreements and less on verbal understandings or symbolic handshakes. Indeed, state bargaining statutes specify that written contracts must be drawn up on the mandatory issues of wages, hours, and working conditions; most agreements go beyond these topics, covering a broad range of additional matters. Verbal agreements are too easy to squeeze out of and are subject to (sometimes intentional) misinterpretation. Legal contracts are written to minimize this problem; however, skillful lawyers are also contortionists who may use legalese to obscure meaning and preserve "wiggle room" or loopholes to slip through when formal contracts contain objectionable provisions.

Written contract provisions may create inflexibility. This may occur with a policy like pattern bargaining, in which every union receives the same percentage raise. Such a policy has been contentious in some cities. For example, in New York City certain unions (e.g., police, teachers) have called for an end to pattern bargaining, arguing for more flexibility in job categories like theirs, where noncompetitive salaries make it difficult to attract enough qualified personnel (Greenhouse, 1998). Scrapping the pattern bargaining approach to union contracts, they argue, would help put salaries on par with those in adjacent communities. In the New York City case, however, eliminating pattern bargaining would likely sour relations between city hall and other municipal unions and among the unions themselves.

Once the parties have reached agreement on key sticking points and contractual language has been approved, both sides must seek ratification of the contract. Members of the union bargaining team must convince their membership that the final product of negotiation deserves their consent; managers seek ratification from the relevant governing body (e.g., city/county council, state legislature). If negotiators have assiduously maintained open lines of communication with their respective constituencies, ratification is likely to be pro forma. Where information sharing has been more sporadic, negotiators could be told that their work product was deficient and to reopen negotiations.

Impasse procedures are triggered when bilateral negotiations come to a standstill. If contract disagreements cannot be resolved in the course of normal bargaining, mechanisms of "first resort" or "last resort" may be necessary. Most states use **mediation** as a first step in dispute resolution. Neutral third-party mediators seek to serve as catalysts to keep the parties talking and suggest alternative proposals to reach voluntary agreement on outstanding issues. If mediation fails, the next step is **fact-finding**. Appointed by the FLRA or the PERB, fact finders hold hearings, sift through arguments, and issue advisory opinions laying out proposed grounds for settlement.

If these "first resort" options do not succeed, "last resort" alternatives include **interest arbitration** (distinct from **grievance** or rights arbitration) or strikes, where available. Because strikes are prohibited in most public sector jurisdictions (and declining where permitted, as noted earlier), binding arbitration (conventional and **final offer**) is the most common means of final resolution. Exhibit 10.16 defines arbitration and lists the various forms it can take. Nearly half of all public sector arbitration cases dealt with discharge, wages, suspensions, and benefits from 1985 to 1992 (Mesch & Shamayeva, 1996). Critics express reservations about binding arbitration, contending that (a) settlements are imposed by outsiders, which runs counter to voluntary two-party contract bargaining; (b) arbitrators lack political accountability (neither directly nor indirectly accountable to the electorate); and (c) parties may drag their feet in negotiations or "first resort" stages of dispute resolution in hopes of succeeding with favorable arbitration decisions (Tomkins, 1995).

Administering the Contract

Contract administration is the third phase of the bargaining process. The principal mechanism here is a grievance procedure, typically provided for in the negotiated agreement. Grievance procedures lay out the available steps or levels to resolve disputes about contract interpretation or implementation. Binding arbitration typically is the last step in this process.

Two key players in contract administration are the union steward and the first line supervisor. Both must be intimately familiar with the provisions in the contract and well trained in interpersonal skills and cooperative problem solving if contract administration is to proceed smoothly. Despite the knowledge, skills, and best intentions of stewards and supervisors, there are bound to be disagreements that lead to the filing of grievances. Grievance mechanisms provide a peaceful and fair way to address these contentious issues with minimal disruption of the workplace. It is important to observe due process and to resolve issues definitively. Binding arbitration of grievances provides finality to the resolution of disputes. Although some writers portray arbitration as a low-cost and impartial alternative to litigation, others, however, contend that arbitration is more costly, tilts in favor of defendants, and yields lower monetary awards to plaintiffs (Vinson, 2002).

HOSTILITY VERSUS HARMONY

Ideas shape institutions. The ideas undergirding public sector collective bargaining are borrowed from models previously designed for the private sector. A critical view of public unionism and collective bargaining was put forward by David Denholm (1997), the publisher of the journal, *Government Union Review*. He contends that key labor-management relations concepts drawn from the private sector are inappropriate when applied in government because of key differences between the two sectors. Concepts such as competition, market economy, and free contracts are defining characteristics in the private sector, whereas government is characterized by monopoly, politics, and sovereignty. The **doctrine of hostility** between parties is fundamental to traditional collective bargaining (adversarial, conflictual, confrontational). Critics argue that the **doctrine of harmony** offers a more appropriate set of ideas and behaviors to guide public sector LMRs (cooperation, service orientation, participation) and advance the public interest, as discussed in the Wye River Conference (see Exhibit 1.11). Denholm posits that the public interest in public employment includes the following:

- Maintaining a peaceful, stable employer-employee relationship
- Protecting the rights of all public employees
- Protecting the right of the citizenry to control government policy and costs through their elected representatives
- Providing services in the most efficient and orderly manner possible

He argues that collective bargaining is ill-suited to government and that the public interest is ill-served by it. His conclusion: "It is time to move beyond the failed nostrums of the past into a better future for public employees and the public they serve" (Denholm, 1997, p. 52).

Key distinctions between these two approaches are outlined in Exhibit 10.17. The most exciting recent developments in LMRs are those guided by the doctrine of harmony. They take

---

✖ EXHIBIT 10.17   Traditional Bargaining Versus Problem-Solving Bargaining

---

Traditional bargaining: Opposing bargaining teams engage in zero-sum posturing and demands.

Problem-solving bargaining: Discussion is resolution oriented, leading to mutually agreeable and beneficial answers to common problems.

Traditional bargaining: Each side has but one goal—to wring the maximum number of concessions from the other side in exchange for the minimum amount of effort, focusing on short-term gains over long-term benefits.

There are several key avenues to reaching that goal:

- Emphasizing form over substance
- Using highly legalistic language
- Obscuring real wants and needs
- Using a hierarchy to limit communication

Although traditional bargaining can be functional, it is rarely efficient, as the process itself necessitates repetition every few years.

Problem-solving bargaining repudiates the antagonistic stance of the traditional model and seeks to forge long-lasting agreements based on the needs of all stakeholders.

There are several courses of action that accomplish this:

- Honestly appraise what needs to be changed.
- Inform other stakeholders of these basic needs.
- Encourage exchange of possible solutions.
- Reach agreements on specific solutions.

Problem-solving bargaining creates real, self-sustaining solutions to problems that benefit all stakeholders.

---

the form of collaborative problem solving, participative decision making, and partnerships (Fretz & Walsh, 1998; Parsons et al., 1998; U.S. Department of Labor [U.S. DOL], 1996). Instructive examples of such creative experiments are found at all levels of government. Those profiled in Exhibit 10.18 are drawn from state and local jurisdictions. Cooperative problem solving is more likely to succeed when there is mutual trust, commitment, and leadership from all participants as well as flexible, adaptive organizational structures (Levine, 1997; Rubin & Rubin, 2001). Among the improvements attributed to partnerships of this kind are better service, lower costs, improved quality of work life, fewer grievances, speedier dispute settlement, increased use of gainsharing, more effective discipline, and more flexible negotiated agreements (Lane, 1996). Although it is important not to oversell win-win bargaining and harmony-based solutions or to undervalue the merits of traditional bargaining (see Lobel, 1994), these examples suggest that public unions and managers should explore diverse paths and think strategically about ways to improve LMRs and citizen services in the future.

This move from unilateral to consensus decision making is still in its infancy, but some experiences with cooperative partnerships have been encouraging. For example, at the federal level the U.S. Department of Commerce's Patent and Trademark Office is partnering with

---

✂ EXHIBIT 10.18 Five Examples of State and Local Governments Engaged With Unions in Cooperative Problem Solving

---

- A labor-management committee in Connecticut's Department of Mental Retardation with District 1199 of the SEIU tackled the issue of how to improve employee safety. In 1 year, the committee's recommendations produced a 40% reduction in injuries and a 23% reduction in what had been an annual $25 million worker's compensation expenditure.
- Health care costs in Peoria, Illinois, were climbing annually at 9–14%, while city revenues were declining. With the cooperation of all city unions, Peoria took health care off the table and placed it in its own joint labor-management committee. The result was a 20% reduction in health care costs and a 100% decline in health care decision arbitration.
- As part of citywide planning in Madison, Wisconsin, labor-management cooperation dramatically improved a contentious relationship between city building inspectors, represented by AFSCME Local 60, and private electrical contractors. Management, employees, and their union worked together with contractors to develop a compliance effort that emphasizes education instead of punishment and a program that enhances safety, savings, and results.
- In Phoenix, Arizona, a long-standing dispute between management and the Firefighters Local 493 was ended by using joint annual plans to address problems and seek improvements. As a result, arbitration has not been used in more than 10 years.
- In Indianapolis, Indiana, the mayor and the AFSCME union initially came to loggerheads over privatization of 25% of the city workers, but when the union was allowed to bid for work projects and share in the cost reductions below the bid, unionized departments frequently won, and not a single union job was lost.

SOURCES: Fretz and Walsh (1998); Osborne and Plastrik (1998); Parsons et al. (1998); U.S. DOL (1996).

---

the National Treasury Employees Union to implement a telecommuting program. A similar partnership between the U.S. Department of Housing and Urban Development and the American Federation of Government Employees supports pilot projects that include telecommuting but go beyond it to cover a wide range of family-friendly workplace initiatives.

One way to think about labor-management relations, proposed by James Flint (2002), is to visualize a relationship continuum. This continuum is depicted in stages that vary based on dimensions of control and effectiveness (most to least). Exhibit 10.19 maps the stages across the relationship continuum with Stage 1 (Healthy Workplace Environment) at one end, with most control and greatest effectiveness, and Stage 5 (Resort to Litigation) at the other end, with least control and least effectiveness. The continuum is both a diagnostic tool to isolate where labor-management relations are in a jurisdiction at a given point in time and a prescriptive device that helps participants see what is necessary to move from where they are (e.g., acrimony) to where they want to be (e.g., cooperation).

SUMMARY AND CONCLUSION

Unions have played an important role in government for the past four decades. As stressed in the subtitle and opening vignette of this chapter, unions function as protectors, partners, and punishers. Reactions to unions are far from uniform. Employees and managers both

---

✖ EXHIBIT 10.19   Effectiveness and Control on the Relationship Continuum

Most Effective   Least Effective

<--->

| Healthy Workplace Stage 1 | Need for Problem Solving Stage 2 | Need for Mediation Stage 3 | Arbitration Required Stage 4 | Resort to Litigation Stage 5 |

Most Control   Least Control

<--->

Stage 1 Healthy Workplace Environment: Commitment to leadership by both management and labor; commitment by both to build a positive, trusting relationship; collaboration; creating an organizational infrastructure to ensure accountability and employee development.

Stage 2 Need for Problem Solving: Training in problem-solving skills; investment in employees and the organization; selection of problem-solving tools; recognition of inevitable conflict and decisions on proactive responses.

Stage 3 Need for Mediation: Incurring moderate expenses; reliance on external problem solving; expending additional time to reach agreement; recognizing that an acceptable result may not occur; damaging labor-management relationship.

Stage 4 Arbitration Required: Absorbing increasing expenses; accepting arbitrator's decision without appeal; relinquishing control for resolution to arbitrator; creating a more confrontational environment; producing a result that may be unsatisfactory to one or both parties; altering labor-management relationship; reducing effective communication.

Stage 5 Resort to Litigation: Requiring the often expensive process of rebuilding the labor-management relationship; heightening of adversarial relations; relying on experts who lack knowledge of in-house relationships; creating win/lose decisions; injuring labor-management relations; blocking effective communication.

SOURCE: Adapted from Flint (2002).

---

have "love-hate" relationships with unions. One fundamental paradox in labor-management relations is that the doctrine of hostility from the private sector was adapted with minor modifications by the public sector, thereby inhibiting emergence of a competing model built on the doctrine of harmony. The legal structures underlying public labor-management relations ensure the continued dominance of the adversarial approach of traditional bargaining. Recent experiments, however, point the way to promising experiences with cooperative problem solving.

Dealing with unions is a way of life for many managers as they struggle to cope with thorny human resource problems. Difficulties are inevitable if administrators fail to understand the (actual or potential) role of organized labor and to heed requirements spelled out in the negotiated contract or mutual agreement. Public managers need to track current and future trends and variations in labor relations. The activities associated with each phase and stage of the collective bargaining process requires careful monitoring if managers are to do their job properly. At the same time, officials should be aware that alternatives to traditional bargaining exist.

Where labor-management relations are extremely adversarial and hostile, both workers and managers are likely to fail former Secretary of Labor Robert Reich's "pronoun test" (1998). He assessed employees' feelings toward their employers by listening carefully to the way they responded to questions about their work. If they use "they" and "them" in referring to the organization instead of "we" and "us," they fail Reich's pronoun test of collective commitment. Similarly, "we-they, us-them" characterizations of labor-management relations suggest an ingrained adversarial environment, making principled negotiations (win-win) and cooperative problem solving less likely. In workplaces predominantly peopled by those who pass the pronoun test, strategies built on the doctrine of harmony and incorporating participative decision making are more likely to succeed.

Heeding the tips and avoiding the traps below can provide a lubricant to reduce unnecessary friction in labor management relations:

Tips

- Be willing to share power to solve problems
- Be patient and acknowledge mistakes
- Invest time and effort in building relationships and in resolving differences
- Cooperate where the interests of both sides converge

Traps

- Unwillingness to fix deteriorating relationships
- Failing to recognize the inevitability of conflict
- Inattention to cultivating a harmonious work atmosphere
- Tardy and unfair response to complaints

Given entrenchment of existing legal structures and behavior patterns built on four decades of experience with traditional union-management relations, movement from institutional patterns built on the doctrine of hostility to those grounded in the doctrine of harmony will be slow and incremental. Government managers must carefully assess the organizational cultures and institutional arrangements in their jurisdiction and decide whether they should press for change in labor-management relations or work through existing human resource/labor-management relations mechanisms to achieve public purposes.

APPENDIX A

Tips for Managers When Dealing With Unions

- Reach out to all employees and let them know that their work is valued.
- Survey employee attitudes on working conditions.
- Provide a healthy and safe work environment.
- Examine pay rates and benefit packages to maintain them at or above "market" levels
- Maintain close contact with first-line supervisors on employee-relations matters.
- Develop a cordial and personalized relationship with union officers.
- Work with union representatives in communicating policies to employees.
- Build trust between unions and management.
- Foster transparency in labor-management relations.
- Avoid arbitrariness in personnel and management decisions.
- Give employees a voice in their own working conditions.
- Respect employees' right to self-organization.
- Involve labor when implementing privatization plans.
- Respond promptly and fairly to grievances.
- Seek to resolve complaints about unfair labor practices informally.
- Consult with lawyers on a case-by-case basis as needed.
- Tailor your approach to unions depending on their ideology, political organization, and leaders' personalities.
- Recognize that it takes time to negotiate separately with every recognized bargaining agent.
- Accept negotiators as equals; do not underestimate them.
- Document each meeting with labor representatives by taking careful notes.
- Keep negotiators focused on giving customers (taxpayers, clients, citizens) what they want.
- Make effective use of third parties in resolving collective bargaining deadlocks.
- Develop a crisis management plan.
- Prepare a media and public relations plan.
- Create labor-management committees to discuss short- and long-term objectives of the organization.
- Agree only to those terms that are likely to be ratified by decision makers on both sides.

APPENDIX B

Bargaining Checklist and Observation Sheet

✖ **APPENDIX 10.B** Bargaining Checklist and Observation Sheet

Observed Behaviors	Management		Union	
	Yes	*No*	*Yes*	*No*
A. Negative Behaviors				
Did the bargaining team . . .				
Underestimate the other party?	Y	N	Y	N
Overestimate the strength of their case?	Y	N	Y	N
Seem unprepared?	Y	N	Y	N
Advance vague proposals?	Y	N	Y	N
Argue among themselves?				
Lose their temper?	Y	N	Y	N
Make assumptions about the other party's priorities?	Y	N	Y	N
Escalate demands unrealistically?	Y	N	Y	N
Oversell?	Y	N	Y	N
Compromise too readily?	Y	N	Y	N
Act defensive?	Y	N	Y	N
Interrupt the other parties?	Y	N	Y	N
Rush the proceedings?	Y	N	Y	N
React prematurely to the other party's proposals?	Y	N	Y	N
End the meeting on a negative note?	Y	N	Y	N
Make promises they could not keep?	Y	N	Y	N
Lie?	Y	N	Y	N
Break confidences?	Y	N	Y	N
B. Positive Behaviors				
Did the bargaining team . . .	Y	N	Y	N
Act calm and cool?	Y	N	Y	N
Show respect to the other party?	Y	N	Y	N
Demonstrate flexibilty?	Y	N	Y	N
Act reasonably?	Y	N	Y	N
Listen carefully?	Y	N	Y	N
Focus on relevant issue?	Y	N	Y	N
Study alternatives and new information?	Y	N	Y	N
Caucus when needed?	Y	N	Y	N
Avoid intimidation?	Y	N	Y	N
Respect confidentiality?	Y	N	Y	N
Negotiate in good faith?	Y	N	Y	N
Exhibit careful planning?	Y	N	Y	N
Heed mutually agreed-upon deadlines?	Y	N	Y	N
Tell the truth?	Y	N	Y	N

SOURCE: Adapted from Colosi (1985).

KEY TERMS

Agency shop
Arbitration
Bargaining unit determination
Certification of the bargaining agent
Collective bargaining
Civil Service Reform Act (CSRA) of 1978
Doctrine of harmony
Doctrine of hostility
Doctrine of sovereignty
Dues check-off
Fact-finding
Federal Labor Relations Authority (FLRA)
Final-offer arbitration
Free rider
Grievance arbitration
Impasse procedures
Interest arbitration

Maintenance of membership
Med-arb
Mediation
Meet-and-confer rights
Open shop
Principled negotiations
Problem-solving bargaining
Productivity bargaining
Public Employee Relations Boards (PERBs)
Representation election
Right-to-work state
Special responsibility theory
Traditional bargaining
Unfair labor practices (ULPs)
Union shop
Whipsaw effect

EXERCISES

Class Discussion

1. What are the key implications of (a) the doctrine of hostility and (b) the doctrine of harmony as they pertain to public sector LMRs?

2. Which is preferable: traditional bargaining or cooperative problem solving? Why?

3. Based on past trends in public and private labor relations, what do you predict that the future will hold?

4. What important obstacles are likely to be encountered in each of the three phases of collective bargaining? How can each be resolved? How is this like a chess game?

5. Invite someone who is involved on a collective bargaining team to visit your class. Ask the visitor to discuss his or her experiences involving some of the negative and positive bargaining behaviors listed in Exhibit 10.19.

Team Activities

6. Divide into four groups: one is an aggrieved employee, one is a mediator, one a fact finder, and one an arbitrator. Group 1 defines the nature of the grievance, and each of the third-party neutrals indicate how they would go about resolving the grievance.

7. Divide into four groups, each group representing a different type of arbitration (see Exhibit 10.16). Within the group, discuss the pros and cons of the type of arbitration. Report back to the class as a whole.

8. Should public employees have the right to strike? Is this preferable to binding arbitration? Why?

9. What is the case against collective bargaining in the public sector?

10. Divide into two groups. One group will develop arguments in favor of Prop. 226 and the other will develop arguments against. Discuss both with the full class.

Individual Assignments

11. Why do some employees join public sector unions? Why do some employees fail to join?

12. What are the special challenges of managing in (a) a union environment and (b) a nonunion environment?

13. Why are there so many paradoxes and contradictions in public sector labor relations? Select five important paradoxes and consider how they can be resolved by using the techniques in Exhibit 0.3.

14. How is collective bargaining similar and different in the public and private sectors?

15. Why have private sector unions lost members, whereas public sector unions have gained members?

NOTES

1. Where an open shop exists, a union can represent workers, but nonunion members have no financial obligations to the union. Workers who join a union under an open-shop arrangement do have a financial obligation to the union.

2. A free rider, in this context, is a worker in a bargaining unit who acquires a benefit from union representation without the effort or costs that accompany union membership.

3. Federal employees do not have the right to strike. In most states, it is illegal for state employees to strike. Some states give employees a limited right to strike.

REFERENCES

AFGE's "fighting spirit": Gage outlines challenges. (2003, December 1). *Federal Times,* p. 8.

AFL-CIO. (1997). Public employees bargain for excellence. Washington, DC: Author.

American Federation of Teachers. (2004, June). *AFT public employee compensation survey.* New York: AFT. (www.aft.org/salary/2004/download/aftpe04survey.pdf)

Americans for Tax Reform. (1998). *The case for paycheck protection.* Retrieved August 21, 2003, from www.atr.org/paycheck/070198pb.html

Aronowitz, S. (1998). *From the ashes of the old.* New York: Houghton Mifflin.

Bacon, D. (1999, January 10). UC buckles under grad student strike. *In These Times,* p. 7.

Bailey, E. (1998, June 8). Labor upset Prop. 226 by focusing on backers. *Los Angeles Times,* p. A1.

Baker, J. G. (1996, April). Negotiating a collective bargaining agreement: Law and strategy. *Labor Law Journal,* 253–266.

Benest, F., & Grijalva, R. (2002, January/February). Enhancing the manager/fire chief relationship. *Public Management.* Retrieved October 25, 2003, from www.icma.org/upload/library/IQ/500632.htm

Berke, R. (1998, June 4). Primaries '98: The unions: Labor defeats threat to its muscle. *New York Times,* p. A24.

Bernstein, A. (1998, December 14). Grad students vs. California. *BusinessWeek,* 6.

Brackey, H. (1999, September 6). Economy passes by younger workers. *Miami Herald,* pp. A1, A17.

Briggs, S., & Siegele, M. H. (1994). The ethical standards clause: A lesson from the private sector for the public sector. *Journal of Collective Negotiations, 23*(3), 181–186.

Bureau of Labor Statistics. (2003). *Union affiliation of employed salary workers by occupation.* Retrieved February 25, 2003, from www.bls.gov/news.release/union2.t03.htm

Bureau of Labor Statistics. (2004). *Union members summary.* Retrieved February 3, 2004, from http://bls.gov/news.release/union2.nr0.htm

Coleman, C. (1990). *Managing labor relations in the public sector.* San Francisco: Jossey-Bass.

Colosi, T. R. (1985). The negotiating process. In R. Helsby, J. Tener, & J. Lefkowitz (Eds.), *The evolving process: Collective negotiations in public employment* (pp. 217–232). Fort Washington, PA: Labor Relations Press.

Council of State Governments. (1998). *Book of the states.* Lexington, KY: Author.

Crampton, S., Hodge, J., Mishra, J. (2002). The use of union dues for political activity: Current status. *Public Personnel Management, 31*(1), 121–129.

Denholm, D. Y. (1997). The case against public sector unionism and collective bargaining. *Government Union Review, 18*(1), 31–52.

Devinatz, V. G. (1997). Testing the Johnston "public sector union strike success" hypothesis: A qualitative analysis. *Journal of Collective Negotiations, 26*(2), 99–112.

Dibble, R. E. (1997). Alternative dispute resolution of employment conflicts: The search for standards. *Journal of Collective Negotiations, 26*(1), 73–84.

Fisher, R., & Ury, W. (1981). *Getting to yes.* New York: Penguin.

Flint, J. (2002, August). Mending labor-management relationships. *Public Management.* Retrieved October 25, 2003, from www.icma.org/upload/library/IQ/500289.htm

Folmar, K. (1999, June 18). UCI teaching assistants vote to unionize. *Los Angeles Times,* p. B10.

Fretz, G. E., & Walsh, D. E. (1998). Aggression, peaceful coexistence, mutual cooperation—it's up to us. *Public Personnel Management, 27*(2), 69–76.

Green, S. (1998, May 17). Union members split over Proposition 226. *Sacramento Bee.* Retrieved January 10, 2005, from www.sacbee.com

Greenhouse, S. (1998, October 12). Friction seen in future talks on city labor. *New York Times,* p. B1.

Greenhouse, S., & Arenson, K. (2004). Labor board says graduate students at private universities have no right to unionize. *New York Times.* Retrieved August 8, 2004, from www.nytimes.com/2004/07/16/education/16union.html

International Brotherhood of Electrical Workers. (2004, June). IBEW, unions fight new defense rules. *IBEW Journal.* Retrieved June 30, 2004, from www.ibew.org/stories/04journal/0406/p9.htm

Kaufman, T. (2004, February 16). Union-busting DOD style. *Federal Times,* pp. 1, 6, 7.

Kearney, R. C. (1998a). Labor law. In J. Shafritz (Ed.), *International encyclopedia of public policy and administration* (pp. 1241–1244). Boulder, CO: Westview Press.

Kearney, R. C. (1998b). Strike. In J. Shafritz (Ed.), *International encyclopedia of public policy and administration* (pp. 2180–2182). Boulder, CO: Westview Press.

Kearney, R. C. (2003). Problems and prospects for public employee unions and public managers. In S. Hays & R. Kearney (Eds.), *Public personnel administration: Problems and prospects.* (4th ed., pp. 310–333). Upper Saddle River, NJ: Prentice Hall.

Lane, C. M. (1996, February). Unions and management are finding common ground, but cultural change is slow and difficult for these former adversaries. *Government Executive,* p. 41.

Levine, M. (1997). The union role in labor-management cooperation. *Journal of Collective Negotiations, 26*(3), 203–222.

Lobel, I. B. (1994, December). Realities of interest-based (win-win) bargaining. *Labor Law Journal,* 71–777.

Losey, S. (2004, April 12). Why weaker unions worry managers. *Federal Times,* pp. 1, 8.

Mesch, D., & Shamayeva, O. (1996). Arbitration in practice: A profile of public sector arbitration cases. *Public Personnel Management, 25*(1), 119–131.

Northrup, H. (1984). The rise and demise of PATCO. *Industrial & Labor Relations Review, 37*(2), 167–184.

Orzechowski, W., & Marlow, M. (1995). Political participation, public sector labor unions and public spending. *Government Union Review, 16*(2), 1–25.

Osborne, D., & Plastrik, P. (1998, March/April). Empowerment in the public sector. *New Democrat,* 21.

Palmaffy, T. (1999, June 7). Class struggle. *New Republic,* 20–24.

Parsons, P. A., Belcher, J., & Jackson, T. (1998). A labor-management approach to health care cost savings: The Peoria experience. *Public Personnel Management, 27*(2), 23–38.

Reich, R. (1998). *Locked in the cabinet.* New York: Vintage.

Rubin, B. & Rubin, R. (2001). Labor-management partnerships: A new approach to collaborative management. Arlington, VA: IBM Endowment for the Business of Government. (www.businessof-government.org)

Salzman, J. D. (1994). Reinventing government: A unionist's perspective on productivity bargaining in the public sector. *Journal of Collective Negotiations, 23*(3), 251–264.

Sanchez, R. (1996, February 4). Graduate teaching assistants press their call for equity in academia. *Washington Post,* p. A3.

Tomkins, J. (1995). *Human resource management in government.* New York: HarperCollins.

Union foes use state as key battleground. (1998, March 22). *Los Angeles Times.* Retrieved January 10, 2005, from http://pqasb.pqarchiver.com/latimes/results.html?num=25&st=basic&QryTxt=Union+foes+use+state+as+key+battleground&sortby=RELEVANCE&datetype=0&x=41&y=18

U.S. Bureau of the Census. (2003). *Labor force, employment, and earnings.* Retrieved June 30, 2004, from www.census.gov/prod/2002pubs/01statab/labor.pdf

U.S. Department of Labor. (1996). *Working together for public service.* Washington, DC: Author.

U.S. labor struggles to regain clout. (1998, September 7). *Miami Herald,* p. 7A.

Vinson, J. (2002, May/June). Report debunks arbitration's low-cost myth. *Public Citizen,* 1, 5.

Walton, R. E., & McKersie, R. B. (1965). *A behavioral theory of labor negotiations.* New York: McGraw-Hill.

What to do when the union knocks. (1966, November). *Nation's Business,* 107.

Young, I. (2001, March 12). Partnership directive bewilders unions, agencies. *Federal Times,* pp. 4, 17.

11

HRM AND PRODUCTIVITY

It is a wretched taste to be gratified with mediocrity when the excellent lies before us.

—Isaac Disraeli

After studying this chapter, you should be able to

- Understand how HRM helps create workplaces receptive to change
- Describe ways in which HRM is involved in specific productivity improvement efforts
- Discuss efforts for improving the HRM function

Rapid change, rising expectations, tides of reform, effective training, new missions, pressure to do more with less—people are searching for ways to increase productivity. To prosper in the 21st century, public agencies must continue to improve their services. **Productivity** is defined as the efficient, as well as the effective, use of resources to achieve outcomes. Both efficiency and effectiveness are key to public service. Efficiency matters because it allows institutions to stretch resources; effectiveness matters because of the importance of attaining outcomes. Efficient provision of training, for example, can lead to more effective service delivery. Productivity depends on the quality of human resources. It will not be fully attained without people.

HRM has important roles to play in improvement efforts. Pertinent policies and practice can contribute to ensuring that agencies are open and receptive to reform, regardless of specific productivity initiatives. Human resource management also supports improvement programs. For example, the applications of information technology have significant implications for HRM: Information technology often reduces the need for some tasks but increases staffing requirements (for example, for people who manage the IT systems) and requires appropriate training.

Productivity initiatives require managers to deal with the inherent tensions between organizational and individual needs (the paradox of needs). If organizations and the personnel who staff them were interested only in productivity, then ways would always be found. But countervailing pressures clearly exist; sometimes ideas are only pursued that are consistent with prevailing ideologies or which have little downside in terms of uncomfortable change (Farson, 1996, p. 142). The status quo often prevails. Productivity also invokes tensions between civil rights and work rights (the paradox of democracy), discussed in earlier chapters.

Productivity initiatives, then, require managers to deal with the inherent tensions. Resolution is far from easy, and creative HRM is essential. The following sections explore how human resource management can foster open organizations, performance improvement strategies, and the effectiveness of human resource management itself.

RECEPTIVITY TO CHANGE

Departments that demonstrate a high **receptivity to change** welcome new ideas and opportunities for improvement. They periodically scan the horizon for new ways of doing business and are not afraid to question basic assumptions about how they operate. They set high goals, measure progress, and change their goals and processes when needed. They search for concepts from many sources, and new employees are especially welcomed for their ideas and infusion of energy. Such organizations value productivity. Employees and managers often pursue their continuing professional development, and young graduates embrace the opportunities that these workplaces provide (Laiken, 2003; Light, 1998).

Other agencies, guided by a "don't-rock-the-boat" philosophy, are much more reluctant to change. People are complacent, attuned to maintaining their positions and ensuring retirement. Those who want to make change are advised to "wait their turn." Looking good is better than doing good. It is not easy in such institutions to reform existing rules and regulations, even when there are good reasons for doing so. And although these departments may adopt changes when forced, they are seldom leaders. Bardwick (1995) has referred to these workplaces as exhibiting an **"entitlement culture."** Another way in which organizations may vary is due to the presence of fear and concern that failure could lead to adverse, personal repercussions. Fear and anxiety stifle ideas and risk taking. Fear-based environments tend to be very unpleasant workplaces for those seeking a supportive environment to make improvements. Indeed, such people often express resentment about the missed opportunities to do better.

Workplaces vary dramatically within agencies; some innovative agents have workplaces that are not especially innovative and vice versa. Most exhibit a mix of cultures; even positive, forward-looking workplaces cannot be oblivious to the possibility that failure could have negative ramifications and that people do value job security. Thus, elements of resistance to change are usually present, to some extent, in most workplaces; to correctly assess the nature of workplaces, and the extent of resistance, takes time and insight.

Human resource policies and practices set the stage for managers and employees by sending powerful messages about incentives, expectations, and rewards. When HRM supplies managers with employee salary increases that recognize superior work, then it is clear that performance matters. The same is true for such issues as training and promotion: Who gets the training? How much and for what purpose? How do workplaces balance performance and seniority in promotion decisions? In short, the alignment of human resource policies and practices helps shape the climate for productivity. A cardinal precaution, however, is in order: Pervasive problems with techniques such as performance pay likely reflect an unhealthy organizational culture more than the failure of management policy.

Strategic HRM is used to match personnel policies to organizational goals. Policies may develop in a piecemeal fashion that, over time, are not necessarily coherent. Then it is useful to periodically assess the totality of HRM policies and strategies against overall goals. Managers might ask: How well do HRM policies support performance and innovation? How might these policies be reshaped and improved in order to provide greater support and incentives for performance and innovation?

Indeed many organizational initiatives have emphasized a strategic approach to **human capital development**. To this end, HRM departments have evaluated their practices to ensure (a) that highly capable persons are recruited, (b) that targets are met for the workforce composition (diversity and quality), (c) that superior performance is rewarded in significant ways, and (d) that a variety of practices (i.e., training, travel, benefits) is used to attract and support productive people—and those who are not are encouraged to separate or retire early. These efforts demonstrate the ability to adopt an integrated, strategic perspective and to ensure future workforce productivity.

One way in which HRM can support open and receptive workplaces is by ensuring that administrators receive basic training in the skills and styles needed. Such training can help avert problems that affect productivity; for example, many employees would gladly require that their supervisors receive training in communication or building positive workplace relations. Although many organizations provide some supervisory management training, it is frequently voluntary and brief and may provide little follow-up and mentoring support. Yet managerial KSA areas include leadership and motivation, communication, dealing with dysfunctional behaviors, improving personal effectiveness, coping with change, managing stress, and team building (Patton & Pratt, 2002, ch. 8). This complexity suggests continuous learning efforts necessary to ensure development. Exhibit 11.1 discusses the use of "psychological contracts," a management tool that promises to enhance productivity.

PRODUCTIVITY IMPROVEMENT STRATEGIES: THE HRM CONNECTION

Workplace productivity strategies are common. Some use advances in information technology, whereas others have their origins in quality philosophies—approaches that emphasize customer orientation, process improvement, and employee empowerment. This philosophy was first introduced in the federal government in the late 1980s and in many other governments during the 1990s, and applications have become ubiquitous. Exhibit 11.2 provides some historic background on these efforts. Other improvement initiatives are more traditional but frequently utilized, such as reorganization.

Reengineering

Reengineering is the redesign of existing delivery processes in ways that make them more efficient, effective, timely, and/or less error prone. In a typical effort, every stage in a delivery service is first identified (for example, the steps required to evaluate a permit application),

---

✄ **EXHIBIT 11.1**   Psychological Contracts

Psychological contracts are a useful tool for managers to increase the productivity of their workplaces. They are agreements between two people about the expectations and contributions of each. As a device to address the paradox of needs, they aim to increase worker commitment and alignment with organizational needs. They are informal understandings that supplement formal understandings found in employment contracts, which include agreements about salary, benefits, grievance procedures, and working hours. Their need arises because workers and their managers require many other areas of understanding as well, such as what resources are available for doing a job, when a job will be done, how feedback regarding quality and timeliness is given, and so on. The range of topics is nearly limitless (Osland, Kolb, & Rubin, 2000; Rousseau, 1995).

Psychological contracts are probably best established at the beginning of employment relations. The process typically starts with the supervisor taking initiative to approach the employee, perhaps asking how their job is going and whether it is meeting expectations. What works? What could be done better? Any suggestions? This gives employees an opportunity to express their thoughts broadly, covering many subject areas. Of course, not every suggestion can be acted upon, and supervisors will need to clarify why something can or cannot be done. Importantly, this dialogue also allows the supervisor to interject his or her expectations, concerns regarding the employee, and what individuals can do to meet these concerns. A psychological contract is effective because it is based on a mutual understanding—a perceived fair balance of what is being asked and what is likely to be obtained. It also allows supervisors and employees to revisit the understanding in weeks or months ahead, perhaps to solidify the understanding or address a perceived "pinch point." In short, psychological contracts powerfully increase alignment and commitment and, hence, productivity.

According to a 2002 study of cities with populations over 50,000, 57.3% of respondents reported that in their jurisdiction most supervisors establish a psychological contract with employees and that in 19.2% of jurisdictions such understandings are required. When asked, however, whether the understanding also included managerial efforts to ensure that employees expectations were balanced with their willingness to give, these numbers were reduced to, respectively, 20.7% and 10.4% (Berman & West, 2003, provides further information on the process and content of such contracts).

---

and then, second, each step, as well as the entire process, is examined for new and better ways to provide the service. Steps are eliminated (e.g., unnecessary approvals), simplified, or combined with others. Third, a new process is then designed from scratch, asking the question: "Ignoring current efforts, what is in fact the best way to produce our services and meet our aims?" Answers to this question often use reduced or simplified steps of the existing delivery process, if appropriate. Also, called a "blank slate" approach to process design, reengineering encourages managers to develop wholly new processes rather than merely tinker with existing ones (Linden, 1998, 2003).

A rather typical application of process reengineering has been the creation of many "one-stop shopping centers" for obtaining permits that may be required in, for instance, construction. It provides users with a single point of contact, which is a significant departure from traditional processes that require approvals from multiple offices. In one-stop shopping, employees are responsible for coordinating stakeholder requests and ensuring customer satisfaction. They, rather than clients, deal with sometimes competing departmental requirements. The result is a shorter process and increased client satisfaction. Procurement of materials and supplies likewise has been reengineered in some jurisdictions to speed interagency

---

✖ EXHIBIT 11.2   Fundamentals of Quality

Historically, the origins of quality can be traced to World War II when production demanded a higher level of performance, reliability, and timeliness: Defective warplanes and radios posed a clear threat. The resulting new production processes were abandoned in the United States after the war but absorbed by Japanese companies who rebuilt and, eventually, gained international recognition. By the late 1970s, U.S. multinational corporations took a renewed interest in quality, then called **total quality management** (TQM). During the 1980s, it was adopted by many large companies and the federal government, and by the 1990s many elements of TQM were first used by state and local governments.

Today, quality is understood as a philosophy encompassing a set of distinct improvement efforts: increasing customer orientation and service, benchmarking, continuous improvement, employee empowerment, and reengineering. The quality mantra is that services should exceed customer expectations in performance, cost, and reliability (Berman, 1998; Swiss, 1992). To this end, agencies survey customers and research other organizations to identify best practices. Such benchmarking leads to continuous improvement through performance measurement. Quality managers also believe that productivity is increased when employees are empowered to achieve results (like satisfied customers) rather than merely follow rules and regulations. Many organizations now recognize the importance of quality, and it is quite common to learn in small steps, sometimes through pilot projects that are later expanded throughout the organization. Alternatively, service delivery is sometimes totally redesigned to meet changing citizen needs.

---

coordination and approval processes. Other applications involve the elimination of red tape (superfluous decision clearances), the use of information technology, and running processes in parallel rather than sequential fashion to expedite requests or delivery (Berman, 1998; Linden, 1998).

HRM can enhance such efforts. First, as old tasks are eliminated, a need exists to reassign or retrain workers for new responsibilities, especially when reengineering leads to the partial or complete dissolution of departments or tasks. Workers may be fearful that such changes will adversely affect their jobs; the task of human resource management is to address this anxiety and explain how employees will be helped to find comparable jobs within the organization. Second, reengineering strongly depends on employee cooperation and input; it thrives in workplaces open to change because employees have firsthand knowledge of existing processes and likely have suggestions for improvements. Again, HRM can help by laying the groundwork: assessing the receptivity for change and ensuring that managers are trained to implement reengineering efforts. Human resource management, in addition, may be involved in the transfer or recruitment of employees required to fulfill new tasks.

Information Technology

Like reengineering, information technology (IT) is common in modern organizations. IT improves organizational performance by increasing the speed of transactions; enhancing electronic access for agency stakeholders and increasing interdepartmental communications; reducing the cost of data storage, access, and utilization; and facilitating linkage among databases within and between agencies (Edmiston, 2003; Haines, 2003; Holden, Norris, & Fletcher, 2003; West, 2004).

The ubiquitous nature of IT today raises critical HRM issues (West & Berman, 2001). Continuous upgrading of technical capabilities requires employees with adequate skills. Existing workers must be provided training in new IT systems and programs. Much of this is outsourced and needs to be budgeted for. When new applications are introduced, the costs of training can be as much as 15–20% of the total purchase price of IT applications. The development of the application and its assets is of strategic significance, and training is therefore of considerable significance.

Another HRM implication is the need to retain IT professionals. Organizations recognize the key role of these personnel, not only as technicians but also as those who shape agency technology strategies. Important decisions concern standards, compatibility, interactions among users and departments, and future IT initiatives. These professionals must be knowledgeable in state-of-the-art applications and be able to move their agencies toward new applications. Accordingly, selected jurisdictions have upgraded these positions so that they better shape agency strategic endeavors. Salary surveys, in addition, are used to ensure that compensation is competitive, thereby enabling effective recruiting. Some organizations have found in recent years that they must offer IT staff significantly higher salaries than other workers with comparable levels of education in different fields. Also, high-skilled technicians could have weak human relations and may benefit from training. In short, like reengineering, IT is a management tool that depends on human resources for its use.

Reorganization

Reorganization is the realigning of the organization with the strategic purpose or business model of the agency. Frequently it is a dreaded word for many employees, synonymous with getting used to new bosses, job descriptions, colleagues, and work arrangements—or job loss. Often highly invasive, reorganizations can take on many forms and purposes. A common objective is to trim back or make sense of departments that have grown in a piecemeal fashion into unwieldy organizations. This is an opportunity to eliminate outdated units and encourage unproductive staff to consider early retirement as an option. A different goal of reorganization, typical of many state governments, is to decentralize operations to district and county offices, thereby encouraging greater responsiveness to local populations (Devine, Reay, Stainton, & Collins-Nakai, 2003).

Human resource management is involved in reorganization in many ways. Typically senior managers will work with HRM staff long before the actual reorganization to develop an organization and staffing plan. The creation of new jobs requires new positions, job descriptions, salary surveys, and recruitment and selection processes. Decisions are made about who is eligible for the new jobs; affected workers often are given priority for new positions, but they may not have a guarantee. HR managers must also assist line administrators with the task of developing separation strategies for those who will not find employment in the new structure. **Outplacement services** are sometimes available and provide job search resources.

During the last decade, many agencies have also engaged in **downsizing** their staff, as more and more operational functions have been transferred to private firms. Light (2003) notes that although the number of federal employees decreased, the total number of jobs associated with government funding, in fact, increased. When the city of Indianapolis privatized many of its functions, it reduced the adverse impacts on most personnel by helping them secure work with the contractors, shifting them to other city jobs, finding related business

---

✕ EXHIBIT 11.3   Downsizing

The Decision to Downsize

Making the Decision to Downsize

Stage 1

- Use downsizing as a last resort.
- Craft a credible vision.

Planning the Downsizing

Stage 2

- Form a cross-functional team.
- Identify all constituents.
- Use experts to smooth the transition.
- Provide training to managers.
- Supply information on the state of the agency.

Making the Announcement

Stage 3

- Explain agency rationale.
- Announce the decision.
- Notify in advance.
- Be specific and time the announcement appropriately.
- Offer employees the day off.

Implementing the Downsizing

Stage 4

- Tell the truth and overcommunicate.
- Help departing employees find other jobs.
- Announce subsequent separations as planned.
- Be fair in implementing separation and generous to laid-off workers.
- Allow for voluntary separations.
- Involve employees in downsizing implementation.
- Provide career counseling.
- Train survivors.

---

positions, and/or offering early retirement—thereby minimizing layoffs. Such services simultaneously avoid negative effects on internal employee relations and external community relations. Exhibit 11.3 shows the steps for downsizing.

Empowerment

Reengineering, IT, and reorganization often provide opportunities for **empowerment,** the process of increasing responsibilities while holding employees accountable for outcomes.

The goal is to get personnel to take responsibility for producing results or outcomes rather than just following rules and regulations without necessarily producing tangible results. For example, one-stop shopping involves the empowerment of frontline employees with more authority so that they can produce satisfied citizens.

Empowerment, too, has significant HRM ramifications. Executives must persuade managers who may be reluctant to give up control and supervision of its virtues. Managers and employees must be trained in empowerment processes in which what counts are "consequences" and "outcomes" rather than "commands." Administrators also work with personnel, perhaps in partnership with unions (Chapter 10), to help them accept new standards of accountability (Glendinning, 2002; Harel & Tzafrir, 2002; Shim, 2001). Typically, part of the empowerment training involves getting employees to ask certain questions in advance, such as whether the proposed course of action is consistent with their department's mission, is legal and ethical, is in the public interest, and is a change for which they are willing to be held accountable. They are then provided with cases and venues for addressing such questions. Employees may resist empowerment when they fear arbitrary evaluation and appraisal standards. Administrators must detail criteria by which employees will be held accountable—with ramifications for training, evaluation, and pay.

Performance Measurement

Performance measurement is increasingly used to guide program development by ensuring that programs meet important goals such as citizen satisfaction and organizational efficiency. It is the measurement of goal attainment, including processes and inputs that can be used to construct efficiency measures. The federal government has mandated the use of such metrics in all departments, and many other jurisdictions have followed suit. For example, measures for a public works department may record the percentage of roads meeting certain conditions, percentage of sidewalk repairs made within 2 weeks, percentage of preventive maintenance completed as scheduled, and so forth. Performance measurement embodies the expression, "What gets measured, gets done" (Behn, 2002; Frederickson, 2002).

Not surprisingly, data collection, performance measurement, and analysis require considerable training. Small departments may lack adequate skills and need additional staff or support. Performance measures can also be used to hold individuals, as well as their departments, accountable. On an annual or semiannual basis, employees meet with supervisors to focus on activities that contribute to departmental objectives and then work with their supervisors to design performance measures by which staff will be held accountable. Managers must ensure that performance measures comply with collective bargaining agreements, as well as respect employee rights and responsibilities (Chapter 2). Often administrators suggest specific measures that have been used in the past, and discussions about performance measures can be used to revisit existing performance appraisal processes and make changes in them.

Overall then, reengineering, IT, reorganizations, empowerment, and performance measurement all have HRM implications. HRM supports the implementation of these efforts through new staffing plans, employee reassignment, training, recruitment, outplacement, and related personnel actions.

IMPROVING THE HRM FUNCTION

Suggestions have been made throughout this book to assist managers in their human resource management functions. The above productivity improvement efforts also apply to human resource management itself, as the following discussion of strategic purpose, reengineering, and performance measurement illustrates. Indeed, HRM activities have seen significant changes, and these forces are likely to continue. Much of this activity implies the expansion of management flexibilities, restriction of unions, and increase the use of contractors, not merely to perform daily duties but also to design new agency personnel policies.

Strategic Purpose

In recent years, there has been considerable discussion about the strategic goals of HRM itself (Hays & Kearney, 2001; Gowing & Lindholm, 2002). Perhaps one of the enduring challenges is to view employees as something more than a legal and economic problem—resources to acquire and maintain at the lowest possible cost with an eye to avoiding lawsuits. An alternative approach is to view humans as an asset to achieve high levels of citizen and client satisfaction and increase organizational effectiveness. Indeed, they are a fountain of new ideas for service delivery and as such are solutions to many problems.

These two views have implications for how human resource management tools are utilized. When human resources are seen as costs, then position descriptions and job evaluations are used to classify employees at the lowest possible pay grades. When people are regarded as strategic assets, however, position descriptions and job evaluations are done to retain and reward staff who contribute high value to organizations. If seen as costs, then training resources are minimal and usually slashed under budget stress. When viewed as adding value, training facilitates cost saving and productivity improvement. If personnel are considered problems to be managed, then appraisal is used for punitive purposes. When perceived as a competitive resource, appraisal is used for developmental purposes.

Efforts to see human resources as a source of competitiveness are likely to prevail where programs such as service improvement are adopted that are consistent with exemplary management and high performance. Even forward-looking managers must be concerned with matters of economy, however; value-added perspectives of human resources can prevail only when they make good economic sense. Supervisors must show that higher employee costs (resulting, for instance, from increased training) result in better service at lower costs (when used in more efficient or reengineered ways). Paradoxically, it may be more economical to pay fewer employees competitive salaries than to pay more employees poor, below-market salaries.

Agencies must decide which view of human resources will prevail. Either by design or by default, HRM policies send a powerful message to employees about their role in the department. One way in which these views will be articulated is through their application in service of organizational strategic goals such as workplace productivity discussed earlier. Another way is to create coherent HRM policies that reflect views of employees as competitive resources under the umbrella term of human capital development. This approach aims to increase workforce effectiveness by evaluating and adopting HRM practices to ensure that highly capable persons are recruited, that targets are met for the workforce quality and composition (diversity), that superior performance is rewarded, that personnel practices (for example, training, travel, benefits) are used to attract and support productive people—and that policies also are adopted to deal effectively and rapidly with unproductive workers (including retraining, transfer, voluntary separation, early retirement, and termination).

Such efforts demonstrate the ability to adopt an integrated perspective and to ensure workforce productivity in future years. Part of this objective may be accomplished through reengineering.

Reengineering HRM Activities

Human resource functions have been reengineered in recent years, reflecting the aim to reduce red tape and take advantage of information technology. Many agencies have revisited their rules and regulations that promote due process and equity over speed and effectiveness. Traditionally, for example, selection has aimed to ensure that candidates met minimum qualifications and that processes were fair, competitive, and open. Though these are valid aims, the ways in which such processes were implemented led to considerable delays, which in turn caused leading candidates to be recruited by other employers. Then, paradoxically, the very rules and regulations that promoted excellence sometimes defeated that purpose. Today, reengineering is used to achieve these aims in more timely and less burdensome ways.

Information technology has also reengineered HRM, and often produced cost savings, too. IT is used in hiring and selection processes whereby applicants submit their applications electronically and specialized software analyzes the materials. Information technology has also assisted HRM departments to communicate faster and more frequently with staff about new opportunities, rules, and policies. It also gives employees greater control over their benefit selection, allowing them to make such changes electronically and with reduced intervention by human resource staff. Payroll functions are also increasingly paperless electronic files.

IT and reengineering have led to the **decentralization** of many human resource activities. To illustrate, in some organizations supervisors and employees develop performance appraisal measures by which employees are held accountable. This brings authority closer to where it is needed and thus increases the relevance of the appraisal process. Likewise, rethinking leave programs has led some agencies to give line managers greater authority to meet employee requirements. Thus, by providing line managers with guidelines and resources, administrators can better deal with the paradoxes of freedom and needs that affect employee motivation and productivity.

Taking this approach has also encouraged the **privatization** of routine activities such as benefits administration, payroll, employee assistance programs, temporary staffing, pension record keeping, and computer and communications training. The rationale for outsourcing is that third parties may perform these functions at lower cost and because of their higher volume and specialization, bring expertise to bear. This trend affects both the public and private sectors. The benefits of outsourcing also include the possibility of developing a more strategic approach to human resources. Thus, privatizing some HR functions may permit the improvement of key recruitment and selection processes or the cultivation of a culture of revitalization.

Performance Measurement in HRM

Strategic perspectives on human resources also shape how they are assessed, and performance measurement has emerged in recent years to evaluate progress and provide

---

✕ EXHIBIT 11.4   Human Resource Performance Indicators

Area Descriptors

   Key functions performed by human resources department
   Number of unions and percentage of employees covered by unions
   Benefits as a percentage of total salaries and wages

Indicators

   Percentage of nonmanagement employees reporting satisfaction with human resources services
   Percentage of management employees reporting satisfaction with human resources activities
   Employee turnover rate
   Number of grievances per 100 FTEs
   Percentage of grievances resolved before passing from management control
   Average number of calendar days to complete an external competitive recruitment and selection process
   Average number of calendar days to complete an internal competitive recruitment and selection process
   Sick leave utilization rate
   Ratio of employees in human resources department to total workforce of jurisdiction

---

SOURCE: International City/County Management Association (2004).

---

accountability (Berman, West, & Wang, 1999; Schay, Beach, Caldwell, & LaPolice, 2002). Yet many existing measures reflect traditional views of human resources (e.g., the number of employees hired, terminated, or transferred; analyses of compensation packages and salary surveys conducted, court cases settled, and the amount of training provided). Such metrics can be stated as efficiency ratios (e.g., the per-employee recruitment cost or the number of court cases per terminated employee) or efforts to "optimize" these activities (such as the time or expense to fill vacancies or the number of highly qualified candidates per job). Likewise, to assess safety and health issues, indicators might include the number of lost days, volume and cost of lost days per employee, number and cost of serious accidents per person, and trends in workforce illness. The International City/County Management Association has identified human resources performance measures (Exhibit 11.4), but the range of possible measures is large indeed (e.g., Berman et al., 1999).

In contrast, performance measures can adopt the view of people as assets. Agencies that emphasize customer orientation, for example, might include measures that encompass the number of employees who received citizen service training, evaluations that include assessments of customer responsiveness or indicators of client satisfaction.

The Government Performance Project issued a report card on each of the 50 states (Maxwell School, 2002). The rating criteria included the following:

- Conducting strategic analysis of present and future human resource needs
- Obtaining a skilled workforce
- Maintaining appropriately skilled personnel

- Motivating the staff to perform effectively in support of government's goals
- Having an HRM structure that supports the government's workforce goals, including a coherent classification system and flexible personnel policies in terms of promotion and compensation.

Exhibit 11.5 provides the state-by-state report card. South Carolina received the highest grade (A) because of substantial recent reforms on consolidating job classifications, decentralizing activities, and reducing paperwork requirements for pay increases. It also introduced various fee-based training initiatives, train-the-trainer programs, and strategies to introduce training in workforce analysis. Whereas South Carolina is a vanguard state, receiving the only "A" grade, some states received a "C" grade. This reflected problems such as job classes tied to dated central examinations, excessive numbers of provisional hires, rigid policies and procedures, union blockage to pay for performance, seniority-based promotions, and deficient performance appraisal training and practices. At both the state and federal levels, from specific practices such as broadbanding and performance pay to systemic changes like those at the Department of Homeland Security and the Defense Department, the scope of change is wide, dramatic—and often problematic.

SUMMARY AND CONCLUSION

Human resource management can be applied in the service of many organizational goals, including workplace productivity. As organizations are asked to do more with less and prioritize their objectives, HRM is called on to support these goals. One way in which this is done is by taking a strategic perspective of ways in which the many different human resource policies and practices support or detract from the organization's goals. The purpose of this is, of course, to increase the alignment between HRM policies and organizational goals. This chapter assessed how policies in such areas as hiring, selection, compensation, and can be aligned with creating organizations that are receptive to change and productivity. One of the ways in which HRM has adopted a strategic perspective has been with regard to human capital. The purpose is to ensure that organizations acquire the right mix of skilled people—that human resources are adequately motivated to perform, that talented employees remain with the organization.

The role of HRM in implementing workplace productivity improvement efforts has also been examined. Improvement efforts such as reengineering, information technology, reorganization, and empowerment all have HRM implications for training, selection, and dismissal, for example. Managers who seek to implement productivity improvement cannot ignore these implications. The chapter concluded with a brief examination of how these strategies have been used to make HRM more productive. Human resource processes have benefited from the use of information technology and reengineering in an attempt to align the needs of employees and their organizations. This process, as all the chapters have shown, involves a continuous collision of opposites. Managing with these contending forces is the challenge that all those interested in public service must confront.

⊠ EXHIBIT 11.5   State-by-State Report Card on Human Resources

State	Grade	State	Grade
Alabama	D+	Montana	C+
Alaska	C	Nebraska	C
Arizona	C	Nevada	D+
Arkansas	C	New Hampshire	C+
California	C	New Jersey	C–
Colorado	B–	New Mexico	B–
Connecticut	C	New York	C+
Delaware	B	North Carolina	B+
Florida	B–	North Dakota	B
Georgia	B–	Ohio	B
Hawaii	B	Oklahoma	C–
Idaho	B	Oregon	C
Illinois	B	Pennsylvania	B+
Indiana	B	Rhode Island	C–
Iowa	B+	South Carolina	A
Kansas	B+	South Dakota	B–
Kentucky	B+	Tennessee	B–
Louisiana	B	Texas	B
Maine	B–	Utah	B–
Maryland	B	Vermont	C
Massachusetts	B–	Virginia	B+
Michigan	B+	Washington	A–
Minnesota	C+	West Virginia	C+
Mississippi	B–	Wisconsin	A–
Missouri	B+	Wyoming	C+

SOURCE: Maxwell School (2002).

KEY TERMS

Decentralization
Downsizing
Entitlement culture
Human capital development
Outplacement services
Performance measurement
Privatization

Productivity
Psychological contract
Receptivity to change
Reengineering
Reorganization
Strategic HRM
Total quality management

EXERCISES

Class Discussion

1. Identify some characteristics of productive workplaces that are innovative and receptive to change. How do HRM policies and practices support such workplaces? What additional policies might be developed? Then identify some important barriers to agencies being receptive to change and discuss the role of HRM with regard to these barriers.

2. Discuss HRM performance measures, focusing first on traditional areas of HRM activity and then on more recent interests relating to human capital development and productivity.

3. Do you feel that managers in your organization are adequately trained to increase productivity and quality in their units? If not, what type of training might help?

4. Discuss recent efforts to increase productivity through information technology in organizations. What are the implications for human resource management?

5. How can government recapture its reputation as a model employer?

Team Activities

6. As a role-playing effort, develop a psychological contract between two members of your team, one member playing the role of supervisor and the other an employee. Team members observe and assist these two actors in formulating questions and reflect on the adequacy of the proposed understanding.

7. Develop a strategy for downsizing a department. How will you deal with reassignments and terminations?

8. Discuss the hiring process in agencies with which you are familiar. What recommendations do you have for improving some of these processes? Do you have any suggestions for adding additional steps?

Individual Assignment

9. Discuss your experiences with reorganization. What went right and what went wrong? Were either the paradox of democracy or the paradox of human needs present? What is the role of human resource management in ensuring positive outcomes?

10. Name five rewards that are attainable and that motivate you. What can you and your supervisor or professor do to increase your eligibility for them?

11. Do you prefer to control or empower your subordinates? What do you see as the benefits and liabilities of each approach? How will you improve your management style in the future?

12. If you were the HR director of your agency, which five strategic priorities would you adopt to increase workforce effectiveness?

REFERENCES

Bardwick, J. (1995). Danger in the comfort zone. New York: AMACOM.

Barrett, K., & Greene, R. (1999, February). Grading the states. *Governing,* 17–90.

Behn, R. (2002, September). The psychological barriers to performance management: Or why isn't everyone jumping on the performance-management bandwagon? *Public Performance and Management Review, 26,* 5–25.

Berman, E. (1998). *Productivity in public and nonprofit organizations.* Thousand Oaks, CA: Sage.

Berman, E., & West, J. (2003). Psychological contracts in local government: A preliminary survey. *Review of Public Personnel Administration, 23*(4), 267–285.

Berman, E., West, J., & Wang, X. (1999). Using performance measurement in human resource management: A survey of U.S. counties. *Review of Public Personnel Administration, 19*(2), 5–17.

Devine, K., Reay, T., Stainton, L., & Collins-Nakai, R. (2003). Downsizing outcomes: Better a victim than a survivor? *Human Resource Management, 42*(2), 109–124.

Edmiston, K. (2003). State and local e-government: Prospects and challenges. *American Review of Public Administration, 33*(1), 20–46.

Farson, R. (1996). *Management of the absurd.* New York: Simon & Schuster.

Frederickson, G. (2002, July). Getting to green. *PATimes,* p. 11.

Glendinning, P. (2002). Performance management: Pariah or Messiah. *Public Personnel Management, 31*(2), 161–179.

Gowing, M., & Lindholm, M. (2002). Human resources management in the public sector. *Human Resource Management, 41*(3), 283–295.

Haines, D. (2003). Better tools, better workers: Toward a lateral alignment of technology, policy, labor, and management. *American Review of Public Administration, 33*(4), 449–478.

Harel, G., & Tzafrir, S. (2002). HRM practices in the public and private sectors: Differences and similarities. *Public Administration Quarterly, 25*(3/4), 316–356.

Hays, S., & Kearney, R. (2001). Anticipated changes in human resource management: Views from the field. *Public Administration Review, 61*(5), 585–598.

Holden, S., Norris, D., & Fletcher, P. (2003). Electronic government at the local level: Progress to date and future issues. *Public Performance & Management Review, 26*(4), 325–344.

International City/County Management Association. (2004). *Center for performance measurement.* Retrieved January 6, 2005, from www.icma.org/performance/PI-support.cfm

Laiken, M. (2003). Models of organizational learning: Paradoxes and best practices in the post industrial workplace. *Organization Development Journal, 21*(1), 8ff.

Light, P. (1998). *Sustaining innovation: Creating nonprofit and government organizations that innovate naturally.* San Francisco: Jossey-Bass.

Light, P. (2003). Fact sheet on the new true size of government. Washington, DC: Brookings Institute, Center for Public Service. Retrieved January 6, 2005, from www.brookings.org/dybdocroot/gs/cps/light20030905.pdf

Linden, R. (1998). *Workbook for seamless government.* San Francisco: Jossey-Bass.

Linden, R. (2003). Learning to manage horizontally: The promise and challenge of collaboration. *Public Management, 85*(7), 8–11.

Maxwell School. (2002). *Paths to performance in local and state government: A final assessment from the Maxwell School of Citizenship and Public Affairs.* Syracuse, NY: Author.

Osland, J., Kolb, D., & Rubin, I. (2000). *Organizational behavior.* New York: Prentice Hall.

Patton, D., & Pratt, C. (2002). Assessing the training needs of high-potential managers. *Public Personnel Management, 31*(4), 465–485.

Rousseau, D. (1995). *Psychological contracts in organizations: Understanding written and unwritten agreements.* Thousand Oaks, CA: Sage.

Schay, B., Beach, M., Caldwell, J., & LaPolice, C. (2002). Using standardized outcome measures in the federal government. *Human Resource Management, 41*(3), 283–295.

Schein, E. (1985). *Organizational culture and leadership.* San Francisco: Jossey-Bass.

Shim, D. (2001). Recent human resources developments in OECD member countries. *Public Personnel Management, 30*(3), 323–348.

Swiss, B. (1992). Adapting total quality management to government. *Public Administration Review, 52*(4), 356–362.

West, D. (2004). E-government and the transformation of service delivery and citizen attitudes. *Public Administration Review, 64*(1), 15–27.

West, J., & Berman, E. (2001). From traditional to virtual HR: Is the transition occurring in local government? *Review of Public Personnel Administration, 21*(4), 63–89.

CONCLUSION

The Future as Opportunity, Not Destiny

There are costs and risks to a program of action, but they are far less than the long-range risks and costs of comfortable action.

—John F. Kennedy

Peering into the 21st century, it is clear that the future is already here. At the beginning of the 20th century, the public service was dramatically transformed by the merit system (Chapter 1) undergirded by bureaucratic structures and the scientific management principles of the Machine Age. In the context of spending cuts and demands for better service delivery, contemporary times have witnessed fundamental challenges to these ideas—privatization (provision of public services by business), devolution (transfer of federal functions to subnational jurisdictions), and reinvention (reform of agencies) in the name of better, smaller, more flexible, and efficient government. What is needed is a systemic approach to such initiatives that deals with the overall role of government, the place of civil and military servants in that role, and the root causes of workforce problems. Strategies that focus on citizen needs, process improvement, and employee involvement likely will generate appropriate approaches, thereby enhancing the quality and productivity of government.

One hundred years ago, the public sector in all its size and diversity was an ideal laboratory for merit system innovations; in developing best practices, it became a model employer for the nation. Although remnants of such practices remain, notably in areas such as equal employment opportunity and employee-friendly policies, it has largely ceded its leadership position in the last several generations (Doeringer, Watson, Kaboolian, & Watkins, 1996). How or whether that proud heritage is restored depends on its response to at least two major societal changes now under way: rapidly expanding technologies and the demand for human competency.

NEW TECHNOLOGIES AND HUMAN COMPETENCIES

Most obvious is the explosion of office technology. What was once seen as merely a productivity measure is now affecting the definition of work and how it is organized: Tasks once done by a room full of personnel can now be handled by one person—anytime, anywhere. These technologies have only begun to be tapped, but the "death" of time and distance in a virtual work environment has already substantially altered the flexiblity and speed of policy making—and who may be involved in decisions. These developments have affected a wide range of human resource functions with the advent of virtual recruitment centers, online job analysis systems, just-in-time computer-based training, and personnel appraisal software. Although information technologies may advance faster than human capacities to use them responsibly, they can foster broad participation on the part of the workforce. To the extent that this occurs, pathways through the paradoxes of competing needs and democracy may be discovered.

As technologies become widely accessible, requirements for human competency will expand. These range from technical know-how such as client server technologies, virtual teaming, and Web-based videoconferencing to personal qualities such as genuine trust and sincere service. Indeed, in a high-tech atmosphere, the only way that public agencies may be able to distinguish themselves from competing private providers is by the performance of their employees. Downsizing and disrespect have made it clear that individuals must antici-pate change and add value and be responsive to change, yet unless or until they are seen as an asset worthy of investment, beginning with their selection, it is difficult to see how the public interest will be served effectively. When labor is regarded as a cost to be reduced rather than a value to be enhanced, quality, productivity, and citizen service usually are sacrificed.

TAKING INDIVIDUAL RESPONSIBILITY FOR PARADOXES

The scope and diversity of these technological and human capacity changes mandate that there is no one best way to manage people. Management is a highly individualized art, as one must discover what works in difficult circumstances. Any number of techniques can succeed when aligned with the needs and goals of an agency, its employees, the populace they serve, and the manager's own natural style. Readers having come this far have ideas about what to do and why, but only those who have a strong desire to influence the performance of others and get genuine satisfaction in doing so will learn how to manage effectively.

Turning this page marks the end of the beginning for the keen student of the management of human resources. As an introduction to the subject, the book represents an invitation to be both an informed participant and a critical observer of the field. Common and surprising, con-fusing and understandable, the paradoxes, processes, and problems pondered here will con-tinue to animate theory and practice throughout your career. It is only fitting that the book stops where it started, with the paradoxes of democracy and needs.

Striving for excellence means dealing with conflicting organizational and individual needs, and that may be done by emphasizing democratic values at work. The workplace is in trans-formation as agencies are doing everything to maximize use of technology and human capac-ities by revamping hiring strategies, refiguring job designs, broadening employee skill bases, and redesigning reward systems. An example of this is the federal departments of Homeland Security and Defense, which other agencies and jurisdictions may emulate before this decade is out. These changes can be used to review and build on the key recruitment, compensation, and evaluation functions discussed in this book. For instance, consider the extent to which these agencies' pay-for-performance plans (http://www.dhs.gov/dhspublic/index.jsp;http://www.defenselink.mil/) are likely to be successful.

Investments in new technologies and human capital are what drives the future (Ingraham, Selden, & Moynihan, 2000). When people are treated as ends for which government exists rather than as means to be manipulated, the quality and productivity of public service can only improve in the years ahead.

ENVOI

The challenge is not to "tell it like it is," but instead to "tell it as it may become"—to eliminate hypocrisy and live up to cherished values. Unless the disconnect between autocratic organizational values and societal democratic values is bridged, human resource problems will only intensify. The entire range of an agency's human resource management functions— selection, recruitment, position management, compensation, workplace adaptation, training, appraisal, and labor-management relations—must be aligned with the values of democratic culture if the dilemmas and contradictions discussed in this volume are to be resolved. The alternatives are either to accept the status quo as fate or to abandon ideals for the security of authoritarian institutions. Either way, life will surely be a series of collisions with the future.

Dr. Jonas Salk, discoverer of the first vaccine against polio half a century ago, reflected on his achievement:

> Ideas came to me as they do to all of us. The difference is I took them seriously. I didn't get discouraged that others didn't see what I saw. I had trust and confidence in my perceptions, rather than listening to dogma and what other people thought, I didn't allow anyone to discourage me—and everyone tried. But life is not a popularity contest. (1998, p.11)

This book, too, has sought to provoke new ideas and to encourage readers to create their own futures. In so doing, few coin-in-the-slot solutions have been offered, for to do so would defeat the purpose. Instead, general principles and specific propositions have been suggested, leaving the discerning individual to align, adapt, and apply them to make the public service, in the words of John F. Kennedy, "a proud and lively career."

REFERENCES

Doeringer, P., Watson, A., Kaboolian, L., & Watkins, M. (1996). Beyond the merit model: New directions at the federal workplace? In D. Belman, M. Gunderson, & D. Hyatt (Eds.), *Public sector employment in a time of transition* (pp. 163–200). Madison, WI: Industrial Labor Relations Research Association.

Ingraham, P.W., Selden, S.C., & Moynihan, D.P. (2000). People and performance: Challenges for the future of the public service—the report from the Wye River Conference. *Public Administration Review*, 60(Jan./Feb.): 54–60.

Salk, J. (1998, December 3), *Bits and Pieces*, p.11.

GLOSSARY

Actor/observer bias. An actor sees his behavior as blameless but when observing the same behavior by another, sees it as blameworthy.

Adoption assistance. Includes benefits ranging from time off to reimbursement of expenses following adoption of a child.

Adult learning. A theory of employee training that integrates employee experience, active participation, motivation for self-improvement, problem solving, and control over the learning material.

Adverse action. Employer's sanction against an employee for unsatisfactory performance or misconduct.

Adverse impact discrimination. Discrimination in which plaintiffs claim adverse impact on a class of employees characterized by race, gender, or other protected conditions. Adverse impact is generally defined as a selection rate of less than 80% of the group with the highest selection rate. See also *Disparate treatment discrimination.*

Affirmative action. A strategy which aims to overcome barriers to equal employment opportunities or remedy the effects of past discrimination. See also *Quotas.*

Age Discrimination in Employment Act. Prohibits discrimination in employment decisions based on age. Applies to workers 40 years and older.

Agency shop. Employee is not required to join the union but must contribute a service charge to cover collective bargaining, grievance process, and arbitration costs.

Alternative work schedules. The arrangement of hours of the day, days of the week, and place of work that differs from the traditional 8-to-5 hours, Monday-through-Friday days, and the in-office work site.

Americans With Disabilities Act. Prohibits discrimination in employment decisions based on disability and requires employers to provide reasonable accommodations.

Arbitration. A dispute resolution procedure that relies on a neutral third party who conducts hearings, researches contentious issues, and makes nonbinding recommendations for consideration.

Assembled tests. When the selection process requires one or more tests in addition to experience and education such as a typing exam, psychological test, or work sample.

At-will employment. A doctrine by which both employers and employees can sever their relations at a moment's notice. The bulk of the public sector provides tenure rights that require a demonstration of appropriate cause, due process proceedings, and internal and external appeals processes.

Authorized salary range. The range of pay stipulated in the pay plan of the jurisdiction. The range is generally provided in a series of step increments. In the past, new employees were required to start at the first step of the range and generally moved along it according to time in position. Today there is more willingness to grant exceptions to experienced employees or where employee shortages exist. Broadbanding essentially increases the authorized salary range to include several positions.

Bargaining unit determination. Identifies whom a union or other association in negotiation sessions will represent.

Behavior-based evaluation systems. The evaluation of performance based on specific behaviors.

Behaviorally anchored rating system (BARS). Behavioral approach to appraisal, consisting of a series of scales based on key dimensions of performance.

Benchmark jobs. In a comprehensive pay study, a portion of the total number of positions is compared with jobs outside the organization to ensure external equity. That is, these positions become pay benchmarks for the entire compensation system. These positions are anchored to general market salary ranges as indicated by reliable compensation information gathered directly either by those conducting the pay study or organizations that periodically provide compensation survey information.

Benefits. All indirect payments provided to employees as part of their membership in the organization.

Bonus. A one-time payment made as a supplement or replacement for a raise that is added to base pay.

Broadbanding. When several grades are combined, creating a broader salary range for a position. Formal promotions are not required for substantial pay movement (as is the case with more traditional—and narrow—classification series that limit pay movement. Broadbanding has the effect of allowing greater discretion at the agency level, provides more organizational flexibility, and provides incentives for long-term development. It also seems to increase total employee costs to the organization over time.

Certification of the bargaining agent. Action by the appropriate administrative agency (FLRA, PERB, or equivalent) recognizing that an exclusive bargaining agent for a unit is appropriately constituted.

Certified lists. Lists of technically qualified applicants provided by an authorized selection body, originally a civil service commission but more recently human resource departments. With the devolution of selection responsibilities to line departments, the use of certified lists is waning.

Civil Rights Act of 1964. A broad law which prohibits employers from discriminating against employees in hiring, promotion, and termination decisions, based on their race, color, religion, national origin, or gender.

Civil service. Refers to the branches of public service excluding legislative, judicial, or military and in which positions are typically filled based on competitive examinations and a professional career public service exists with protections against political influence and patronage.

Civil service commission. The governing body authorized to oversee the civil service employment system. Originally, civil service commissions administered all competitive examinations, reviewed qualifications for technical merits, provided certified lists, and acted as a judicial review board for hiring abuses. Today most selection functions have been moved to human resource departments in the executive branch or to the line agencies themselves. Where they continue to exist, civil service commissions tend to be policy and review boards.

Civil service reform. Efforts to modify the structures, process, and functions of the civil service system, such as the Pendleton Act of 1883 and the Civil Service Reform Act of 1978.

Civil Service Reform Act of 1978. Federal law replacing the U.S. Civil Service Commission with two agencies: the Office of Personnel Management as the staff arm of the chief executive and the Merit Systems Protection Board to adjudicate employee appeals. It also created the Federal Labor Relations Authority to oversee federal labor-management policies.

Class series. Refers to job classifications that are linked developmentally such as Secretary I, II, III, and IV.

Closed personnel system. Typical in rank-in-person system in which few opportunities exist for lateral entry for those outside the organization. Ideally such systems encourage employee development through job rotation and foster employee loyalty. See also *Open personnel system.*

Coaching. The training practice of assigning an experienced employee to help other employees master various job situations.

Collective bargaining. A process whereby labor and management representatives meet to set terms and conditions of employment for employees in a bargaining unit.

Comparable worth. The theory that different jobs, equal in value to the organization, should be paid the same.

Compressed work week. A flex option where the number of hours worked per week is condensed into fewer days.

Constitutional torts. Lawsuits against public employees for violation of the constitutional rights of others. See also *Right to disobey.*

Contamination. Occurs when evaluations include factors unrelated to actual performance.

Contingent hiring. A preliminary hiring status that can be procedurally overturned if certain contingencies intervene. Appropriate contingencies include a postselection physical examination or drug test, funding availability, job freezes, and completion of specialized training programs. Where important contingencies such as these exist, it is important to inform the selected candidate in the letter of intent.

Contrast error. Tendency to rate people relative to others instead of to performance criteria.

Cost of living adjustment (COLA). Across-the-board pay change based on economic conditions, not performance.

Critical incident technique. Records key acts assumed to make the difference between effective and ineffective performance.

Cross-training. The practice of training employees to fill multiple job functions.

CSRA of 1978. Civil Service Reform Act, which abolished the U.S. Civil Service Commission and replaced it with the Office of Personnel Management, created the Senior Executive Service, the Merit System Protection Board, the Federal Labor Relations Authority, and expanded the use of merit pay for midlevel managers.

Decentralization of training. The shifting of responsibilities for training from the central HR department to operating departments and line managers.

Deficiency. Occurs when evaluations fail to include all essential elements of performance.

Development. Preparing employees for assuming future responsibilities. See also *Training*.

Devolution. Delegation responsibility to lower governments or departments.

Dialectic. Systematic reasoning that juxtaposes contradictory, competing ideas (theses, antitheses) and seeks to resolve them by creating a new synthesis.

Disparate treatment discrimination. Discrimination in which plaintiffs claim that adverse personnel actions are based on race, gender, or other protected conditions. See also *Adverse impact discrimination.*

Diversity policies. Employers' policies which promote an environment that allows all employees to contribute to organizational goals and experience personal growth, regardless of individual ethnic or other differences.

Doctrine of harmony. Relationship between labor and management in which both sides emphasize cooperation, service orientation, participation, and the public interest.

Doctrine of hostility. Relationship between labor and management under traditional collective bargaining (adversarial, conflictual, confrontational).

Doctrine of sovereignty. Maintains that government has a responsibility to protect all societal interests; therefore, it is inappropriate to require it to share power with interest groups (e.g., unions in negotiations) or dilute managerial rights.

Domestic partnership coverage. Refers to benefits such as health insurance and sick/bereavement leave that may be made available to a person designated as a domestic partner of an employee.

Downshifting. Process of scaling back career ambitions and giving more time/attention to family and personal needs.

Downsizing. Reducing the number of employees, often caused by government reductions in force, outsourcing, base closure, and so forth.

Dress codes. Employer standards for employee appearance concerning clothing and grooming.

Due process rights. Pertains to public employees' right to a hearing when faced with adverse action.

Dues check-off. Employee may select payroll deduction option to pay union dues to representing union.

EAPs. Employee assistance programs designed to improve employees' health and help them cope with personal problems such as the difficulties resulting from work/family conflict.

Education and experience evaluations. Includes application forms as well as requests for information about specific job competencies, which can be addressed in skill inventories (such as checklists), cover letters, and/or resumes.

Effectiveness. The level of outputs or outcomes achieved.

Efficiency. The ratio of outputs to inputs (O/I).

Eighty percent rule. A standard for determining discrimination. Any selection process that results in qualification rates of protected groups that are less than 80% of the highest group.

Electoral popularity selection. The basis for representative democracy. As a selection method, it is good for the selection of major policy makers but ineffective as a method for selecting those who primarily fill administrative functions.

Empowerment. The delegation of decision making to employees, usually accompanied by increased employee accountability.

Entitlement culture. Organizational culture typified by lethargy and complacency.

Equal Employment Opportunity Commission. Federal agency that processes complaints of discrimination and reviews affirmative action plans.

Equal Pay Act of 1963. Prohibits sex discrimination in compensating people doing substantially the same jobs.

Error of central tendency. All staff receive average ratings or all dimensions of performance are rated average.

Essential function. The contemporary term for the major job duties of a position. The term was ushered in by the ADA, which prohibits discrimination of "an individual with a disability who, with or without reasonable accommodation, can perform the essential functions of the employment position."

Ethics Reform Act (1989). Federal law establishing uniform financial disclosure requirements, prohibiting lobbying of former departments, and raising pay for executive, legislative, and judicial officials.

External equity. The comparison of what employees are paid with the pay of those performing similar jobs in other organizations. Generally implemented in pay plans through occasional pay studies that compare a sample of positions (benchmark positions) to anchor the entire wage scale.

Fact finding. A dispute resolution procedure that relies on a neutral third party who conducts hearings, researches contentious issues, and makes nonbinding recommendations for consideration.

Fair Labor Standards Act of 1938. Basic federal statute that established the minimum wage and hours of work.

Family and Medical Leave Act. Provides eligible workers with up to 12 weeks of unpaid leave during any 12-month period for childbirth or adoption; for care-giving to a child, elderly parent, or spouse with a serious health problem; or for a personal illness.

Fear-based culture. Organizational cultures that are typified by anxiety and a concern for protecting jobs rather than seeking improvement.

Federal Labor Relations Authority (FLRA). The federal administrative unit charged with overseeing, investigating, and enforcing rules pertaining to labor-management relations.

Federal Pay Reform Act of 1990. Sought to make compensation of federal employees comparable to those in the private sector.

Fifth Amendment. Provides for due process, among other stipulations.

Final-offer arbitration. The arbitrator's decision is restricted to the position taken by one or the other of the parties. This can include selection of a position taken by one side or the other on all issues taken together (by package) or selection on an issue-by-issue basis.

First Amendment. Protects freedom of speech and exercise of religion, among other stipulations.

Flextime. Work schedules that allow flexible starting and quitting times but specify a required number of hours within a particular time period.

FLRA. Federal Labor Relations Authority.

Fourteenth Amendment. Requires that no state shall make or enforce any law that shall abridge the privileges or immunities of citizens of the United States thereby, in effect, ensuring constitutional protections to state citizens and its employees, among other stipulations.

Fourth Amendment. Protects persons against unreasonable searches and seizures by the government, among other stipulations.

Free rider. In the context of labor-management relations, one who is a worker in a bargaining unit who acquires a benefit from union representation without the effort or costs that accompany union membership.

Free speech rights. The rights that public employees have to speak out as citizens in matters of public debate. These rights, however, do not protect them from adverse action when speaking out disrupts the efficiency of their workplace.

Gainsharing. Financial gains as a result of organizationwide performance are shared with employees.

General skills test. Provides information about abilities or aptitudes in areas such as reading, math, abstract thinking, spelling, language usage, general problem solving, judgment, proofreading, and memory.

Generation X. People under 35 years of age.

Grievance arbitration. Or rights arbitration. Used to resolve outstanding disputes regarding employee grievances.

Hatch Act. Law prohibiting political activities by public employees. Some restrictions of this 1939 law were relaxed under the Federal Employees Political Activities Act of 1993.

Herzberg theory of motivation. Determinants of job satisfaction, such as recognition, relate to job content; determinants of job dissatisfaction are associated with job context, such as physical facilities.

Hidden workforce. Temporary employees or outside workers (consultants, contractors) whose numbers and costs are increasing.

Human capital. Productive human capabilities (knowledge, skills, abilities, attributes) that can be acquired and used to yield income and improved performance in the workplace.

Human resource management. A perspective that recognizes that human resources are important assets that must be managed strategically and proactively to improve organizational performance; development of processes for the effective utilization of people in an organization.

Impasse procedures. Procedures, typically involving third parties, established to reconcile differences between labor and management.

Individual equity. Perceived fairness of individual pay decisions.

Individual vs. "pool" hiring. Broad, entry-level classifications in moderately large organizations generally are filled using pool hiring in which many positions are advertised simultaneously or advertising for a job classification is continuous. All other positions generally hire on an individual basis.

Inside (internal) vs. outside (external) recruitment. Refers to whether recruitment and hiring is limited to organizational members or not. Generally, this decision is a matter of organizational tradition. Those organizations that are rank based hire internally, whereas those that are position based hire from outside as well.

Institutional recruitment. Similar to hiring from a "pool" (see above).

Interest arbitration. Refers to arbitration dealing with the terms of the negotiated contract; it can be voluntary or compulsory.

Internal equity. Comparison of what employees are paid doing similar jobs in an organization.

Internship recruitment. The practice of using internship programs as a source of recruitment. Often used to attract high-quality management and professional candidates.

Job analysis. A systematic process of collecting data for determining the knowledge, skills, abilities, and other characteristics required to successfully perform a job and to make numerous judgments about the job.

Job (position) announcements. Generally tailored to the specific purpose to which they are being addressed. A full job announcement generally includes the job title and agency/organization affiliation, salary range, description of the job duties and responsibilities, minimum qualifications, special conditions, application procedures, and notice of EOE and AA. May also include classification, career potential, and special benefits.

Job classification. Clusters of individual positions with similar characteristics that are organized in groups for classification purposes. Other terms often used as synonyms are *job, classification, job class,* or simply *class.*

Job description. Written statements that describe or list the typical or average duties (sometimes by using work examples), levels of responsibility, and general competencies and requirements of a job classification.

Job duties. The term most commonly used in the past to refer to the major functional responsibilities of a position. The more common term today, because of ADA, is *essential function.* Job duties can be further divided into job tasks in job analysis.

Job evaluation. Systematic determination of the value of each job in relation to others in an organization.

Job factor system. Breaks jobs down into their component parts (for either analysis or evaluation) by categories such as job requirements, responsibilities, working conditions, physical demands, difficulty of work, and personal relationships.

Job posting. Posting was originally placing a job announcement on walls in prominent places. Many civil service systems require posting in a minimum number of public places. Today it also refers to listing jobs with in-house job bulletins, newspapers, or communications such as intranet or e-mail.

Job sharing. Enables two employees to split the responsibilities, hours, salary, and (usually) the benefits of a full-time position.

Job task. Elements of job duties. See also *Job duties* and *Essential function.*

Labor market. A geographical area or occupational field within which the forces of supply and demand, often constrained by political factors, interact to affect the size of the workforce and its pay level.

Labor market survey. A critical source of information about long-term staffing trends.

Lateral entry. When non-entry-level positions can be filled from outside the organization. Lateral entry is more common in rank-in-job systems, which tend to encourage competition based on technical qualifications.

Learning plateau. A period during which employees must first fully absorb and assimilate the training material before they learn more.

Leave sharing. A type of employee-to-employee job benefit whereby healthy workers donate sick time or other benefits to coworkers in crisis.

Leniency error. All individuals or all performance dimensions are rated favorably.

Letter of intent. A letter that confirms the offer of a specific position and may stipulate major work conditions such as starting date, salary, and/or hiring contingencies (if any).

Liberation management. A reform tide with the goal of higher performance characterized by implementation strategies such as standards, evaluations, and outcomes and typified by laws such as the Government Performance and Results Act of 1993.

Mail recruitment. A highly personalized approach in which individuals are encouraged by letter to apply for positions. Today it may include e-mail recruitment as well.

Maintenance of membership. Employee is obligated to maintain union membership in the representative union once affiliated during the life of the contract.

Management by objectives (MBO). Results-oriented rating system based on how well managers achieve predetermined goals.

Med-arb. Requires an arbitrator to begin with mediation, settle as many disputes as feasible, and move to arbitration only on items that remain contentious.

Mediation. A dispute resolution procedure that relies on a neutral third party who attempts to facilitate communication and bring the parties together to reach an agreement.

Medical testing. Tests that may be required as part of selection processes when employees are suspected of substance abuse, or after workplace accidents.

Meet-and-confer rights. Laws requiring agency heads to discuss, but not to settle, grievances.

Mentoring. A development approach through which employees develop their career potential through ongoing, periodic dialogue with more experienced employees.

Merit pay. System under which permanent increases in base pay based on performance are received.

Merit-based selection. Emphasizes technical qualifications using processes that analyze job competencies and require open application procedures.

Merit system. A fair and orderly process for recruitment, promotion, rewards, and punishments on the basis of qualifications, performance, and competitive selection as judged by experts.

Merit Systems Protection Board (MSPB). Established by CSRA of 1978 with responsibility to hear appeals from employees who allege that their rights under the civil service system laws and regulations have been violated.

Misconduct. Prohibited employment practices that are cause for adverse action. Includes using a public position for private gain, acceptance of favors or bribes, working within conflicts of interest, abuse of authority, release of confidential information, favoritism, or nepotism.

National Partnership for Reinventing Government. Initiative by the Clinton administration that sought to cut red tape, improve government performance, and hold public employees responsible for program results.

Needs assessment. A strategy related to training that involves surveying employees and managers about their training needs.

Negligent hiring. When employers are deemed not to have used satisfactory screening through reference checks, background investigations, and thorough selection processes for positions that have a public safety dimension. Examples include driving, law enforcement, corrections, elder care, and those working with children.

Neutral competence. A standard or value that civil service reformers thought should be applied in selecting and retaining civil servants, as opposed to patronage.

Noncompetitive recruitment. A single official completes the hiring process with a formal comparison of candidates. Sometimes immediate hiring is allowed if candidates meet certain standards; at other times *noncompetitive recruitment* means that the decision maker has the authority to select those people deemed appropriate, for whatever reason.

Nontraditional families. Includes gay and lesbian couples, unmarried couples in committed relationships, single-parent families, and reconstituted families.

Occupational families: The grouping of class series (or positions that are not in a class series) into large clusters. Examples include firefighters, administrative support staff, corrections personnel, and human service personnel. Occupational families are sometimes based primarily on job function (law enforcement regardless of agency affiliation) and sometimes on job mission (law enforcement related to drug enforcement).

On-the-job training. Learning that employees do as they master the unique requirements of their specific jobs.

Open personnel system. Typical in rank-in-job systems in which opportunities exist for lateral entry for those outside the organization. Ideally such systems foster high technical qualifications, healthy competition, and prevent organization "inbreeding" and "groupthink." See also *Closed personnel system.*

Open shop. Where this exists, a union can represent workers, but the nonunion workers have no financial obligations to the union.

Organization-centered evaluation. Organizational processes are monitored and evaluated on the premise that employees will work effectively within the system if it is well designed by management.

Organizational culture. Norms, values, and practices that tell employees and managers which objectives should be pursued and how they should be pursued.

Overlearning. The assimilation of material so that it becomes second nature.

Paradox. Seemingly incompatible ideas; clashes between apparent truths.

Paradox of democracy. People as citizens have many civil rights, but as employees of organizations they surrender them.

Paradox of needs. Individuals and organizations need one another, but their respective needs are as likely to conflict as they are to coincide because people are dynamic and organic, whereas many organizations are static and mechanical.

Parental leave. Provides leave from work for the employee to care for needy family members.

Patronage. Applies to a broad class of selection decisions in which a single person is responsible for designating officials or employees without a requirement for a formalized application process. Generally, it is expected that those deciding patronage appointments will balance party loyalty, personal acquaintance, and technical competence. Such appointments may or may not be subject to a confirmation process. Although *patronage* and *spoils* are frequently used interchangeably, they are not identical terms. *Spoils* refers to the use of patronage appointments primarily as a means of reward and where technical qualifications are noticeably lacking. *Spoils* also refers to handling positions in the career service as patronage appointments. See also *Spoils system.*

Pay (broad) banding. Base pay method that reduces many pay levels into several broad bands.

Pay compression. The narrowing of differentials between pay grades in an agency.

Pay equity. The perception that the compensation received is equal in value to the work performed.

Pay plan. A pay schedule in which the grades, steps, and related pay is determined. In reality, most jurisdictions have numerous schedules as a part of their pay plan for different occupational clusters, often based on union representation of different occupational groups.

Peer evaluation. Method of appraisal in which employees at the same level in the organization rate each other.

Pendleton Act (1883). Law passed in 1883 establishing a system of open competition for government jobs via examinations, prohibiting firing of civil servants for partisan reasons, authorizing creation of a Civil Service Commission, and empowering the president to alter the extent of civil service coverage.

PERBs (Public Employment Relations Boards). State administrative agencies typically charged with determining appropriate bargaining units, overseeing certification elections, and resolving unfair labor practices.

Performance measurement. Efforts to measure and monitor an agency's performance, sometimes with numerical goals.

Performance tests in selection. Directly assesses the skills necessary for specific jobs. Can apply to physical skills, knowledge tests of job aspects, or work samples (or assessment centers). In all performance tests, the connection between the test and some aspect of the job should be direct, unlike aptitude and skill tests in which the connection may be indirect.

Personal contact recruitment. Occurs when recruiters, managers, or search panel members attend job fairs, conduct on-campus recruiting, or personally contact top candidates for positions.

Personnel administration. A series of activities—recruitment, compensation, discipline—directed at enhancing productivity of the people who work within an organization. Synonymous with human resource management.

Piecemeal personnel system. One that lacks grades or ranks and assigns salaries on an ad hoc basis. Only common in very small jurisdictions.

Point factor analysis. Job evaluation method that assigns points to compensable factors, which are summed to determine pay.

Point factor method. Starts with the assumption that factors should be broad enough to apply consistently to all jobs in an organization or schedule. Differs from job factor systems that may only use those factors directly related to specific positions.

POSDCORB. Acronym for *planning, organizing, staffing, directing, coordinating, reporting,* and *budgeting.* Originated by Frederick Taylor during the scientific management "tide" in an effort to provide the "one best way" to administer government programs.

Position. The job of a single individual, as well as the specific duties and responsibilities.

Position classification system. Provides grades or ranks for all merit positions as well as for nonmerit positions. Position classification systems can provide both the basis for position evaluation and management, on one hand, and job support and design on the other.

Position description. Written statement that defines the exact duties, level of responsibility, and organizational placement of a single position.

Position management system. Generally refers to the allocation of positions for budgetary purposes.

Positive discipline. A step-by-step participatory procedure that encourages employees to take responsibility for correcting problems.

Positive reinforcement. Feedback that helps employees reduce errors and meet standards and enhances their motivation to excel.

Pre-employment background checks. Various procedures used to validate applicant-provided information and to otherwise determine the suitability of candidates.

Principled negotiations. Negotiation process that stresses identification of common ground between labor and management, focuses on cooperative problem solving, and thrives in an open trusting environment.

Principles of learning. Key pointers for the effectiveness of training that involve increasing employee motivation, relevance, transference, attention to general principles, repetition, feedback, and positive reinforcement.

Privacy expectation. Public employees are protected against unreasonable searches and seizures at the workplace, including spaces that they regard as private.

Privatization. Contracting out public services to private sector providers.

Problem-solving bargaining. Resolution-oriented discussion leading to mutually agreeable and beneficial answers to common problems.

Proceduralism. Connotes processes that have become excessively detailed, complicated, protracted, and/or impersonal.

Productivity. The efficient and effective use of resources to achieve outcomes.

Productivity bargaining. Labor-management negotiations on matters affecting the efficiency and effectiveness of government operations.

Progressive punishment. An adverse-action approach that uses penalties with increasing severity and provides opportunities to correct problems prior to termination (also known as *progressive discipline*).

Psychological tests in selection. Examines the personality traits of the individual and compares them to the job requirements. Although psychological tests can include general intelligence tests and motivation tests, these have generally not met the rigorous validity standards expected in the public sector. Tests, however, that measure the ability to handle stress, the inclination toward aggressiveness, and the disposition toward high standards of moral integrity have been used with frequency in the public sector.

Public Employee Relations Boards. State administrative agencies typically charged with determining appropriate bargaining units, overseeing certification elections, and resolving unfair labor practices.

Qualified immunity. The doctrine that public employees are sheltered from the threat of subsequent lawsuits only if they act in good faith.

Quotas. Court imposed targets for increased hiring of underrepresented groups of employees.

Race-norming. The practice of adjusting test scores of minority groups to ensure that a sufficient number of candidates can be hired. Race-norming is disallowed by the Civil Rights Act of 1991.

Rank-in-job. A personnel strategy in which rank and salary is determined by the job one holds. Substantial salary increases and higher status is attained only through a better job (promotion or reclassification), but multiple promotions within an organization are uncommon beyond predetermined job series.

Rank-in-person. A personnel strategy that emphasizes the development of incumbents over time within the organization through the use of closed systems and movement through ranks. No matter what the assignment of the individual, they are generally paid according to their rank. Tends to encourage the development of generalists (except in academic settings). Often has an "up-or-out" philosophy in which those passed over for promotion are encouraged or required to leave the organization.

Recency effect. Gives undue weight to recent occurrences when evaluations are done.

Recruitment process. Generally includes three major steps: planning and approval of the position, preparation of the position announcement, and selection and use of specific recruitment strategies.

Recruitment strategies. There are at least nine of them. They are posting, newspapers, trade journals, mail, other mass communications, personal contacts, internships, external recruitment (use of a third party), and noncompetitive.

Reengineering. The effort to reconfigure delivery processes to make them more efficient, effective, and timely.

Relevance of training. The extent that training is relevant to specific work situations. See also *Transference*.

Reorganization. Realignment of organizational resources.

Representation election. An election to determine whether a union will be recognized as the exclusive bargaining agent for workers in the unit.

Representativeness in selection. Can be interpreted in numerous ways such as by geography, social class, gender, racial/ethnic groups, prior military service, and disability.

Results-based systems. Rating format that emphasizes what employees produce.

Reverse discrimination. Occurs when a person of a protected class is hired or promoted over an equally or better qualified candidate who is not a member of this class.

Revitalization culture. An organizational culture in which managers and employees feel empowered and energized by challenging and rewarding assignments.

Right to disobey. Public employees have the right to refuse orders that they, in good faith, believe to be unconstitutional. See also *Constitutional torts.*

Right-to-work state. A state where mandatory union membership is outlawed.

Rule of seven. States that people must practice something seven times in order to master it.

Rule of three (hiring). Originally promulgated by civil service commissions. Restricted hiring to the top three candidates on the certified list. Recent trends have been to allow the hiring authority as much latitude as possible among those technically qualified.

Rule of three (training). States that people only hear things that have been said three times.

Sandwich generation. Workers who are sandwiched between responsibilities for young children and for elderly parents.

Scientific management. A reform tide with the goal of efficiency, characterized by the use of implementation strategies such as structure, rules, and experts and typified by laws such as the Reorganization Act of 1939.

Self appraisal. A rating completed by the employee him- or herself.

Seminars and presentations. Common training strategies for conveying information.

Senior Executive Service. Top-level administrators; mostly career civil servants and a lesser number of political appointees.

Seniority-based selection. Uses time in the hiring organization as a primary or exclusive factor for promotion. Philosophically, it asserts that those already employed in the organization have been through the merit process once, have been screened in probationary and evaluation processes, and have superior organizational insight and loyalty because of their employment.

Seniority pay. Pay determined by length of service.

Severity error. All individuals or performance dimensions are given an unfavorable rating.

Sexual harassment. Any sexual submission that is a quid pro quo affecting employment condition, or any unwelcome verbal comments or physical contacts of a sexual nature that create a hostile or offensive work environment.

Simulation. A training strategy whereby job conditions and situations are simulated, such as responses to natural disasters and the like.

Skill pay. Compensation for skills that employees have, develop, and use in a multiple-task environment.

Social class selection. Generally illegal as an explicit selection philosophy in the United States. It does indirectly operate at times, however, through proxies such as educational institutions and the subtle imposition of dominant-culture values on minorities in the selection process.

Special responsibility theory. Maintains that public employees hold critical positions in society and therefore should not be permitted to strike.

Spillover (halo or horns) effect. An unusually good or poor trait or performance affects the entire rating.

Spoils system. A special type of patronage in which appointment of jobs is viewed as spoils of office (similar to spoils of war) to those active in the victorious campaign. Can also refer to political nepotism (appointment of the family members and personal friends to salaried positions) and assignment of contracts based on personal contacts rather than technical qualifications. See also *Patronage*.

Staffing. A term that incorporates both the recruitment and selection processes.

Telecommuters. People who work away from the traditional work locale (e.g., at home, at satellite locations, or on the road) by means of an electronic linkup with the workplace.

Temporary employees. Those without tenure rights and usually without benefits. A recent IRS ruling has enhanced the benefits rights of many formally considered temporary employees, creating a new class of term employees. See also *Term employees*.

Term employees. Those without tenure rights but usually with full benefits. Term employees generally have contracts for set periods of time. This is a rapidly increasing category in the public sector in which governments seem to be seeking more flexibility for long-term position management. Increasingly used by the federal government for multiple-year contracts (2–4 years) and state governments, reducing the civil service protections for job classes such as managers in Maryland (see Exhibit 4.1) or whole systems of employees such as in Georgia (see Exhibit 5.3).

Test validity. A psychometric concept that addresses the question of whether the test or selection instrument measures what it is intended to measure. The three types of validity allowed by the *Uniform Guidelines to Employee Selection Procedures* are content, criterion, and construct. *Content validity* requires demonstrating a direct relationship of the test to actual job duties or responsibilities. *Criterion validity* involves correlating high test scores (the predictor) with good job performance (the criterion) by those taking the test. It generally examines aptitudes or cognitive skills for learning and performing well in a given environment (e.g., the aptitude to learn a language, remember key data, or use logical reasoning). *Construct validity* documents the relationship of select abstract personal traits and characteristics (e.g., intelligence, integrity, creativity, and aggressiveness) to job performance.

Three hundred sixty–degree (360) evaluation. Superiors, peers, subordinates, and sometimes people outside the organization rate one another.

Three o'clock (3:00) syndrome. Attention to work-related tasks wanes as employees begin to think about children ready to leave school and return home.

Tides of reform. Four reform philosophies identified by Light (1997)—*scientific management, war on waste, watchful eye, and liberation management*—each of which has its own goals, implementation efforts, and outcomes.

Total quality management. A management philosophy that encompasses empowerment, customer service, reengineering, and performance measurement.

Traditional bargaining. Two bargaining teams opposing each other across the table, each side engaging in zero-sum posturing and demands.

Training. Efforts to increase knowledge, skills, and abilities to better meet the requirements of present jobs. See also *Development*.

Training evaluation. Assessments of the effectiveness-of-training efforts that usually focus on both behavioral changes and results.

Trait-based systems. Systems to examine employees for selected personal characteristics believed to be important in working effectively.

Transference. The extent that training material is relevant in actual job situations.

U.S. Office of Personnel Management (OPM). The federal agency charged with the "doing" side of public HRM—coordinating the federal government's personnel program. OPM's director is appointed/removed by the president and functions as his principal advisor on personnel matters.

Unassembled tests. The selection processes when the initial selection is primarily based on education and experience evaluation.

Unfair labor practices (UFLPs). Practices by unions or employers that are unfair and legally prohibited.

Union shop. New employees must join the representative union after a certain number of days (e.g., 30–90 days) specified in the collective bargaining agreement.

Up-or-out philosophy. Those who are not promoted in rank-in-person systems may eventually be forced to leave the organization. For example, assistant professors who are not promoted to associate after 6 years are generally given terminal contracts.

Veterans' points. Typically veterans serving during wars are eligible for 5 points and wounded veterans are eligible for 10 points, which increases their ratings as job candidates, although practice varies among the states and federal government.

Voluntary affirmative action plans. Affirmative action plans that are voluntarily adopted by organizations. Such plans must be temporary, identify an existing pattern of discrimination, and not trammel on the interest of employees who are not covered by the plan.

V-time. Voluntary reduced time; enables parents to meet their care-giving responsibilities, provides an alternative to layoffs or the use of part-time replacements, and helps phase workers into retirement.

War on waste. A reform tide with the goal of economy, characterized by use of implementation strategies such as generally accepted practices, audits, and investigations and typified by laws such as the Inspector General Act of 1978.

Watchful eye. A reform tide with the goal of fairness, characterized by use of implementation strategies such as whistleblowers, interest groups, and media and typified by laws such as the Administrative Procedure Act of 1946.

Wellness programs. Programs with a goal of altering unhealthy personal habits and lifestyles and promoting behaviors more conducive to health and well being.

Whipsaw effect. In the context of labor-management relations, gains by one union might be used to justify benefits for another.

Whistleblower Protection Act (1989). Law protecting federal employee whistleblowers from unfair retaliation, specifying burden-of-proof requirements regarding retaliation and outlining appeal channels.

Whistle-blowing. Exposing wrongdoing in an organization by informing the media or another organization. Various laws protect whistleblowers from retaliation, but whistle-blowers may nonetheless experience adverse career consequences.

Whole job analysis. Does not systematically break down a job into its constituent parts for purposes of grade and classification but instead relies on past experience and intuition.

Whole job evaluation. Does not systematically break a job down into its constituent parts for purposes of compensation but instead relies on past experience and intuition.

Work samples. When performance tests simulate actual aspects of the job, they are called work samples. For example, having a trainer provide a demonstration is a work sample, as is having a lawyer provide examples of former legal briefs. When a variety of work samples is constructed to test the range of abilities of an applicant over an extended period of time (such as a full day), it is generally called an *assessment center.*

Work stoppages. Strikes.

Name Index

SUBJECT INDEX

Patronage, 60, 87, 90, 93–94, 125, 338
Pay. *See* Compensation
Pay (broad) banding, 338
Pay compression, 171, 339
Pay equity, 167, 339
Pay for performance, 14, 157–158, 169–170
Pay plan, 129, 339
Paycheck protection laws, 276
Peer evaluation, 255, 339
Pendleton Act, 13–16, 40, 94,
    95, 126, 158, 339
Peoria, Illinois, 299
PERBs, 291, 293, 339
Performance:
    adverse action, 43–44
    job analysis applications, 133
    liberation management, 13
    monitoring, 262
    pay for performance, 14, 157–158, 169–170
    state HRM report card, 319–321
    training and excellence, 223
Performance measurement and
        evaluation, 11, 316, 318–320, 339.
        See also Appraisal
Performance tests, 103, 339
Personal contact recruitment, 72, 339
Personality inventory tests, 48
Personnel administration, 6, 339
Phoenix, Arizona:
    labor relations, 299
    management internship program, 73
Physical ability tests, 103
Pickering v. Board of Education, 39–40
Piecemeal personnel systems, 127–128, 339
Planning, 65–66
Pledge statement, 23–24
Point factor methods, 140–141, 339
Political affiliation, 42
Political appointment, 90, 93–94,
        122–123. *See also* Patronage
Political neutrality, 9, 40–41, 93
Polygraph testing, 48, 111
Pool recruitment, 67
POSD-CORB, 11, 339
Position Analysis Questionnaire, 149
Position announcements, 68–70
Position classification systems, 128–129,
        152, 339. *See also* Job classification;
        Position management
Position, defined, 339

Position description, 138–143, 340
    sample, 147–148
Position management, 121–144, 340
    descriptions, 138–143
    equal opportunity and, 126
    job analysis applications, 133
    origins of, 125–127
    piecemeal personnel systems, 127–128
    position classification, 128–129, 152
    sample job description, 145–146
    sample position description, 147–148
    trends, 143–144
    types of personnel strategies, 122–125
        See also Job analysis
Positive discipline, 263–264, 340
Positive reinforcement, 226, 340
Pre-employment background checks,
        46, 48, 340
Presidential Management Fellowship, 72
Principled negotiations, 340
Principles of learning, 224–226, 340
Privacy expectation, 340
Privacy issues, 44–49
    alcohol and drug testing, 45–46
    expectations, 45
    grooming and dress codes, 46, 47
    search and seizure, 44–45
Privatization, 4, 7, 318, 340
    Bush administration and, 20
    constitutional constraints on, 43
    war on waste heritage, 12
Probationary period, 111, 112
Problem-solving bargaining, 298, 340
Proceduralism, 64–65, 340
Productivity, 309–316
    definition, 309, 340
    demand for, 7
    empowerment, 315–316
    information technology, 309,
        313–314, 318, 325–326
    paradox of needs, 310
    performance measurement,
        11, 316, 318–320
    psychological contracts, 311, 312
    receptivity to change, 310–311
    reengineering, 311–313, 318
    reorganization, 314–315
    salary progression, 176
    training and excellence, 311
Productivity bargaining, 295, 340

ABOUT THE AUTHORS

Evan M. Berman is professor of public administration at Louisiana State University. He is active in the American Society for Public Administration and is past Chair of the Section of Personnel and Labor Relations. He has over 100 publications and 7 books in human resource management, productivity, ethics, and local government. He has served on numerous editorial boards such as the *Public Administration Review* and the *Review of Public Personnel Administration.* He is Managing Editor of *Public Performance & Management Review.* His recent books include *The Professional Edge* (ME Sharpe, 2004, with the coauthors of this book), *Essential Statistics for Public Managers and Policy Analysts* (Congressional Quarterly Press, 2002), and *Third Sector Management: The Art of Managing Nonprofit Organizations* (Georgetown University Press, 2001, with Bill Werther). He has been a policy analyst with the National Science Foundation and has assisted local jurisdictions on matters of team building, strategic planning, and citizen participation.

James S. Bowman is professor of public administration at Florida State University. His primary area is human resource management, complemented by work in ethics and quality management. He is author of nearly 100 journal articles and book chapters as well as editor of five anthologies. He collaborated with the other coauthors of this book to write *The Professional Edge* (M. E. Sharpe) in 2004. He is Editor in Chief of *Public Integrity,* a journal of the American Society for Public Administration and serves on the editorial boards of three other professional journals. A Kellogg Foundation Fellow and a past Fellow of the National Association of Schools of Public Affairs and Administration, he has a background in business as well as experience in both the military and civil service.

Montgomery Van Wart is professor and Chair of the Public Administration Department at the University of Central Florida. He has served as the Director of the Center for Public Service at Texas Tech University, the MPA Director at Iowa State University, and the Director of the Advanced Public Executive Program at Arizona State University. As a scholar, he has over 35 publications including five books and a substantial number of articles in the leading journal in his field. His upcoming book is *Dynamics of Leadership in Public Service: Theory and Practice* (ME Sharpe, 2005). His research areas are administrative leadership, human resource management, training and development, administrative values and ethics, organization behavior, and general management. He also serves on eight editorial boards. As an instructor, he has spent as much time teaching and facilitating programs for executives and managers in public agencies as he has teaching graduate students. His training programs have been for individuals in all levels of government in the United States and executives and elected officials from foreign countries.

Jonathan P. West is professor of political science and Director of the Graduate Public Administration Program at the University of Miami. His research interests include human resource management, productivity, local government, and ethics. He has published seven books and nearly 100 articles and book chapters. *Quality Management Today: What Local Government Managers Need to Know* (1995) and *The Ethics Edge* (1998) were published by the International City/County Management Association. His coauthored book titled *American Politics and the Environment* was published by Addison Wesley/Longman in 2002. He is Managing Editor of *Public Integrity* and a member of the editorial board of two other professional journals. He has experience as a management analyst working for the Office of the Surgeon General, Department of the Army.